Kare **First Love**
Vol. 7
Shôjo Edition
Story and Art by KAHO MIYASAKA

English Adaptation/Kelly Sue DeConnick
Translation/Akira Watanabe
Touch-Up Art & Lettering/Steve Dutro
Cover and Interior Design/Hidemi Sahara
Editor/Michelle Pangilinan

Managing Editor/Annette Roman
Director of Production/Noboru Watanabe
VP of Publishing/Alvin Lu
Sr. Director of Acquisitions/Rika Inouye
VP of Sales & Marketing/Liza Coppola
Publisher/Hyoe Narita

Published by VIZ Media, LLC
P.O. Box 77010
San Francisco, CA 94107

Shôjo Edition
10 9 8 7 6 5 4 3 2 1
First printing, February 2006

www.viz.com
store.viz.com

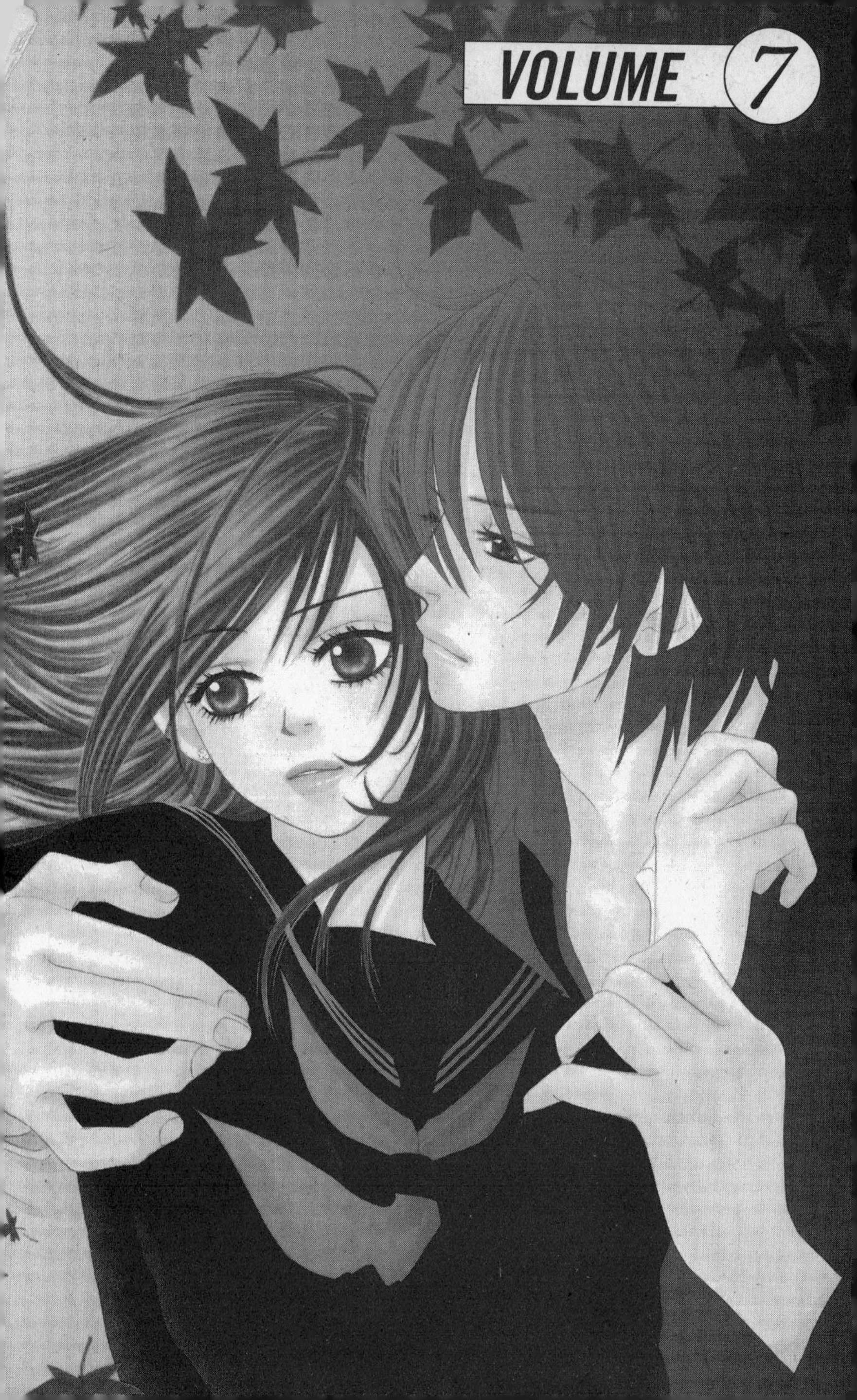
VOLUME 7

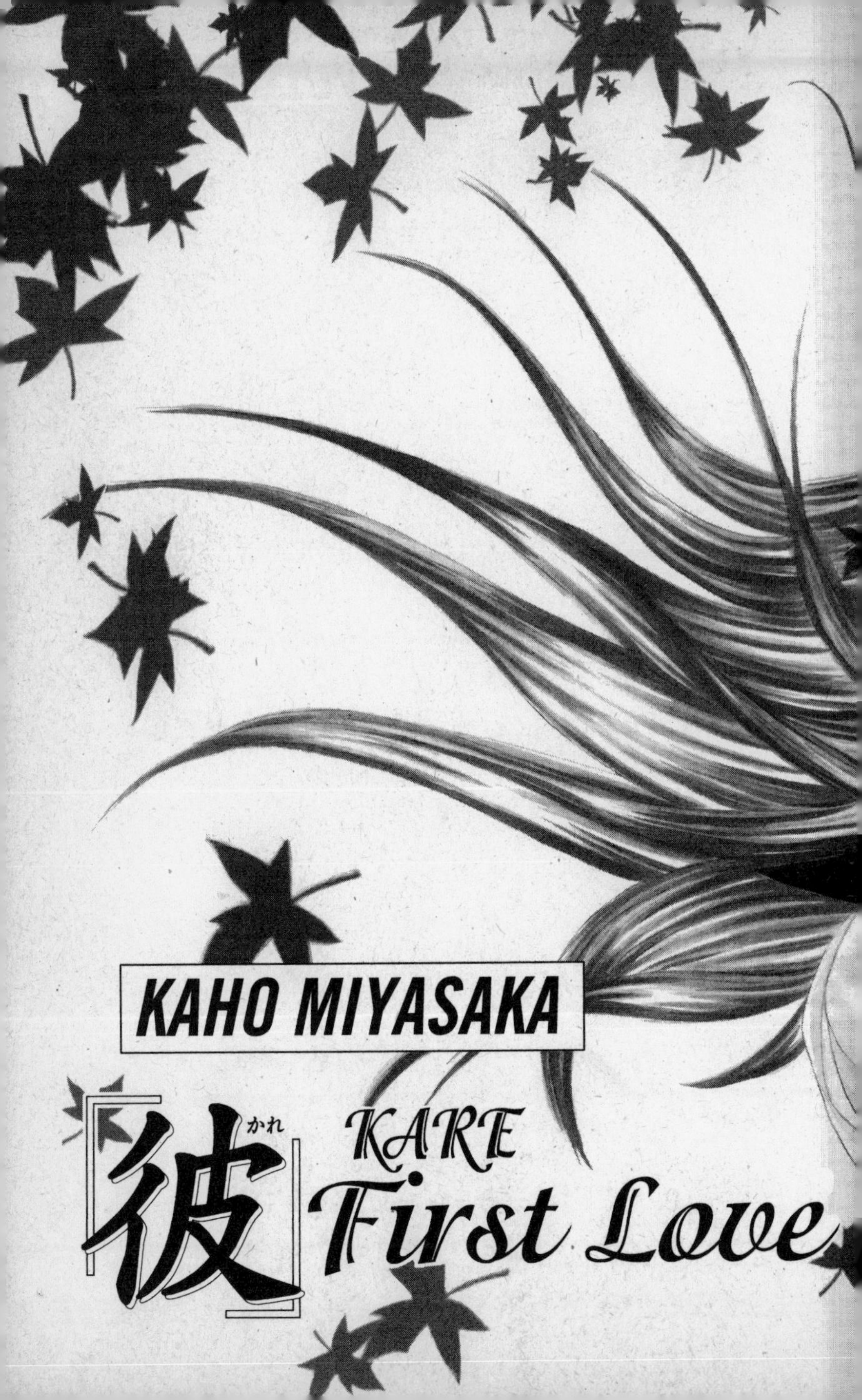

KAHO MIYASAKA

『彼（かれ）』 KARE First Love

Characters and Story Digest

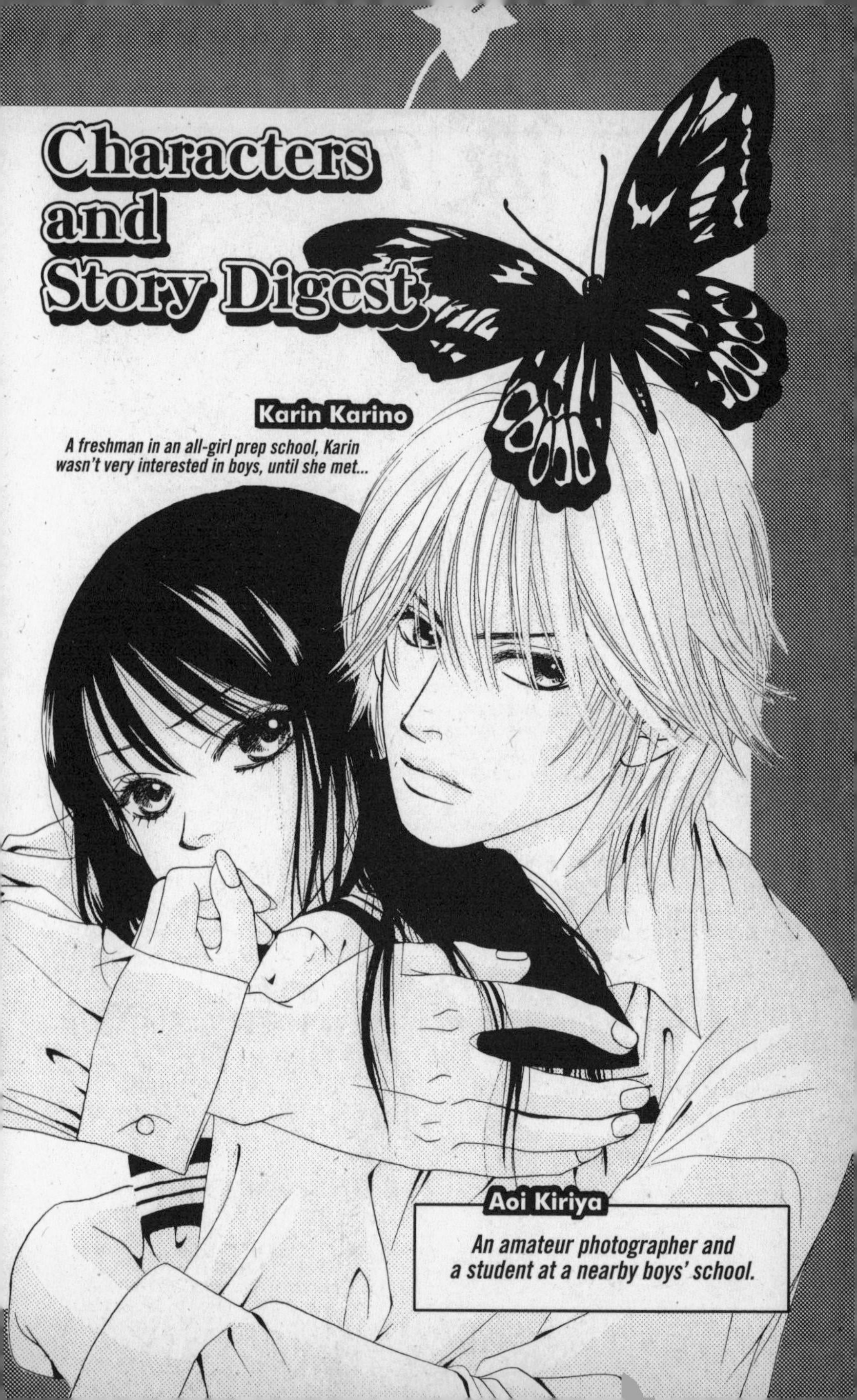

Karin Karino

A freshman in an all-girl prep school, Karin wasn't very interested in boys, until she met...

Aoi Kiriya

An amateur photographer and a student at a nearby boys' school.

KARE First Love

7

Karin chose an all-girls' school because she was never really comfortable around boys. It might not have been bliss, but she managed.

Everything changed when she met Kiriya on the morning bus. Her classmate, Yuka, tried to sabotage them, but with Nanri's support, Karin and Kiriya started going out.

For their first summer vacation together, the two went to Okinawa with their friends. They stayed on the beach near the spot where Kiriya's older brother died a few years before. It was an emotional trip, but it brought Karin and Kiriya closer. They spent the night together, but Karin was so nervous that she drank too much … and the vacation ended with Karin's virginity intact.

When Karin accompanies Kiriya to visit the video shoot of a photographer/cameraman that he idolizes named Shinji Takagi, some video footage of her is used in a TV commercial without her consent. This causes a fight between Kiriya and Karin. Valentine's Day passes without the two reconciling. As Karin roams the town after playing hooky from school not knowing what to do, she is reunited with Kiriya. He tells her, "I don't want to let you go tonight …"

Nanri Ayase

Karin's classmate. She recently broke up with her married boyfriend.

Shoko Akiba

The widow of Kiriya's older brother, the famous photographer Yuji.

Shinji Takagi

A professional photographer who works in many genres. He was Yuji's colleague.

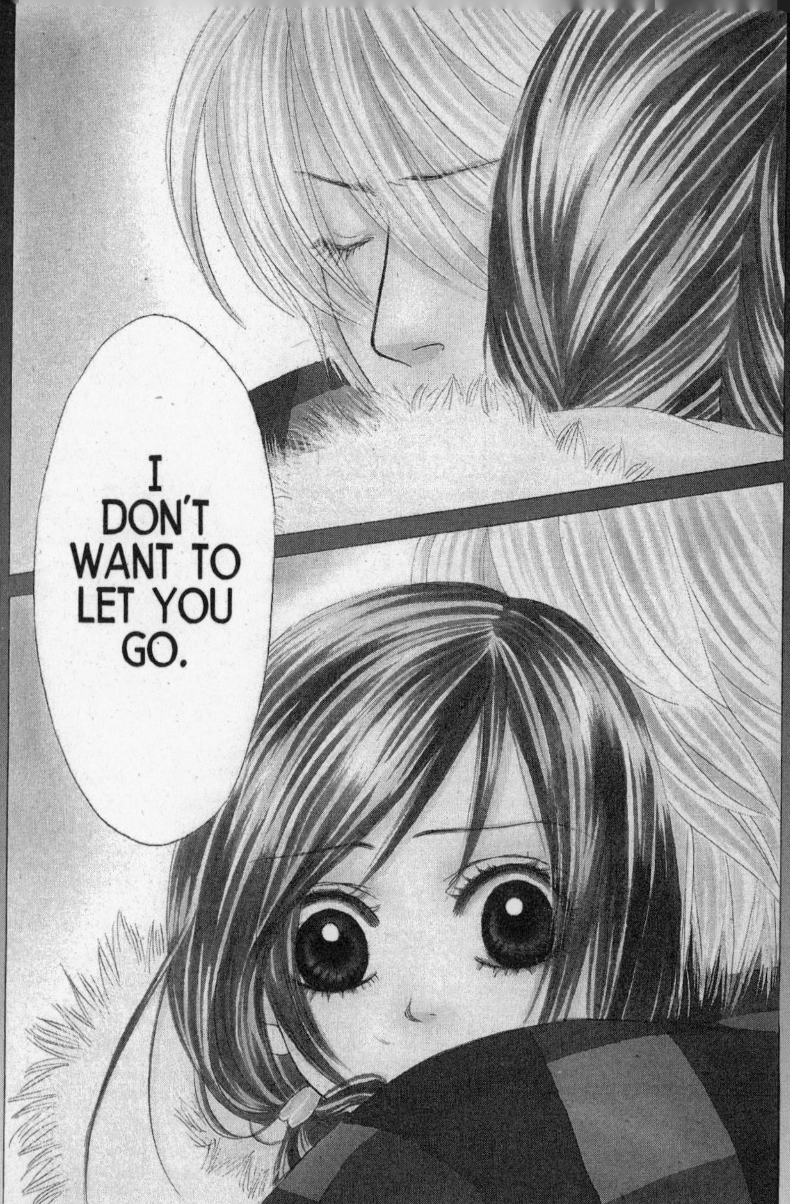
I DON'T WANT TO LET YOU GO.

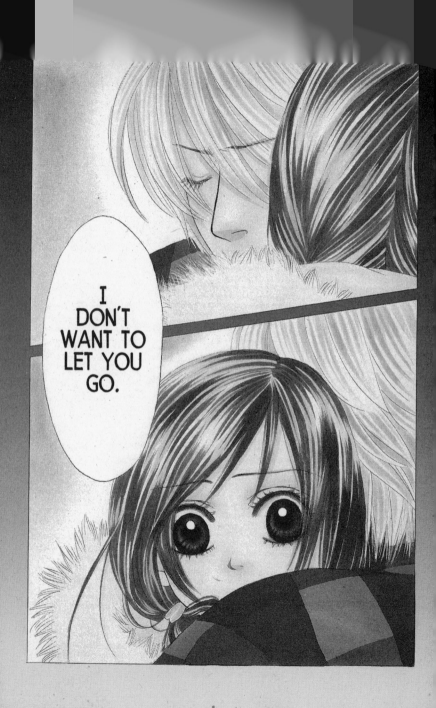

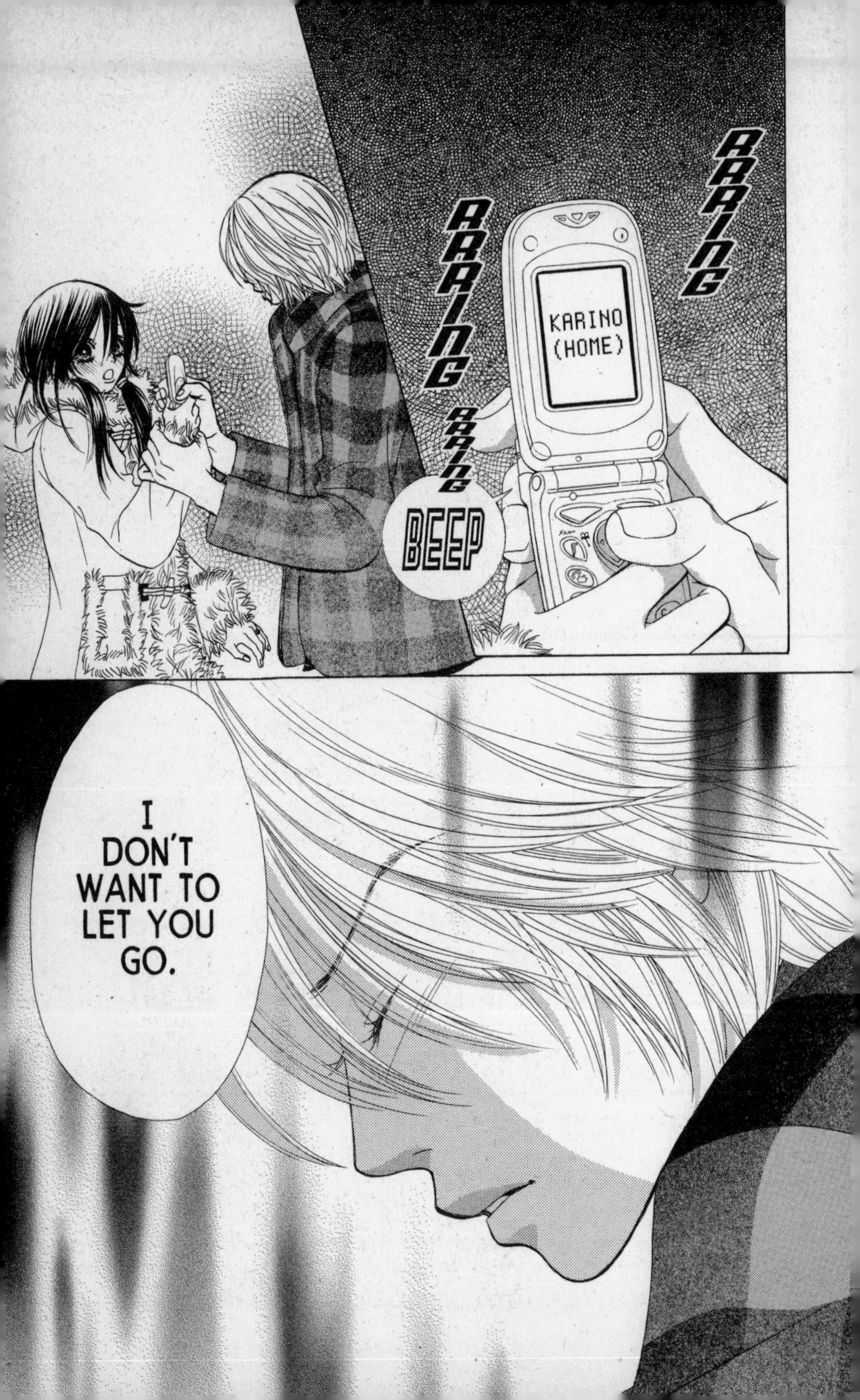
RRRING
KARINO (HOME)
RRRING
RRRING
BEEP
I DON'T WANT TO LET YOU GO.

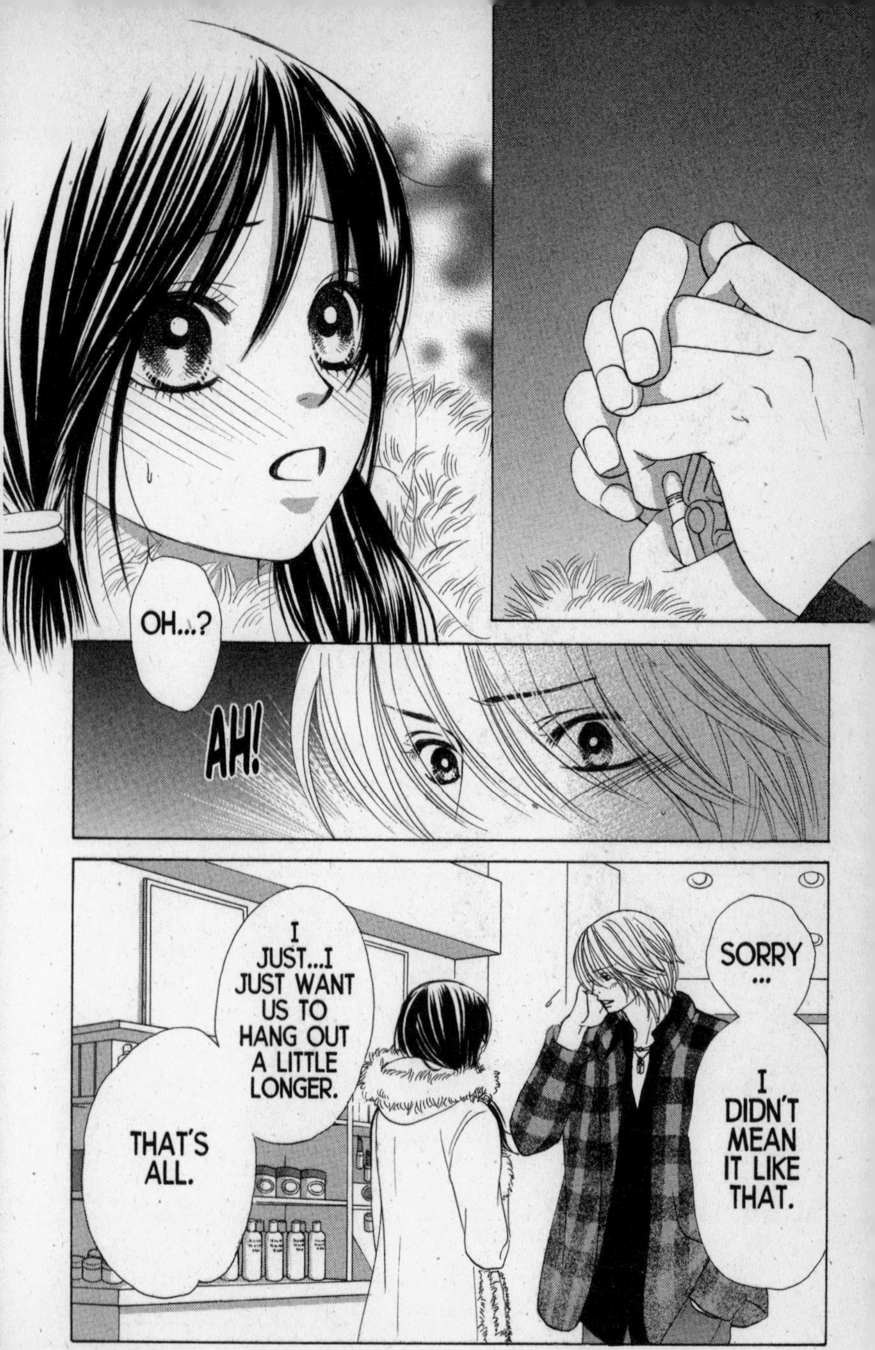
OH...?
AH!
SORRY ...
I DIDN'T MEAN IT LIKE THAT.
I JUST...I JUST WANT US TO HANG OUT A LITTLE LONGER.
THAT'S ALL.

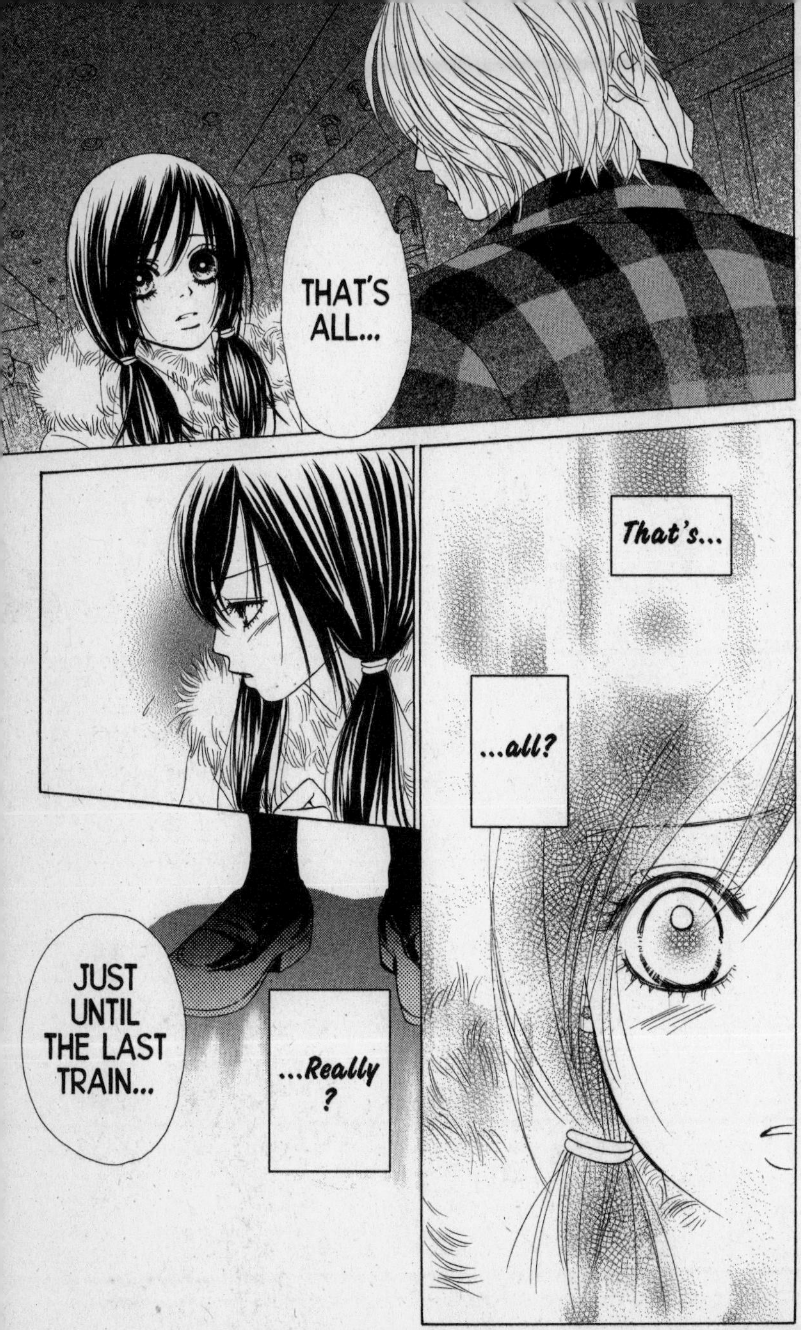
THAT'S ALL...
That's...
...all?
JUST UNTIL THE LAST TRAIN...
...Really?

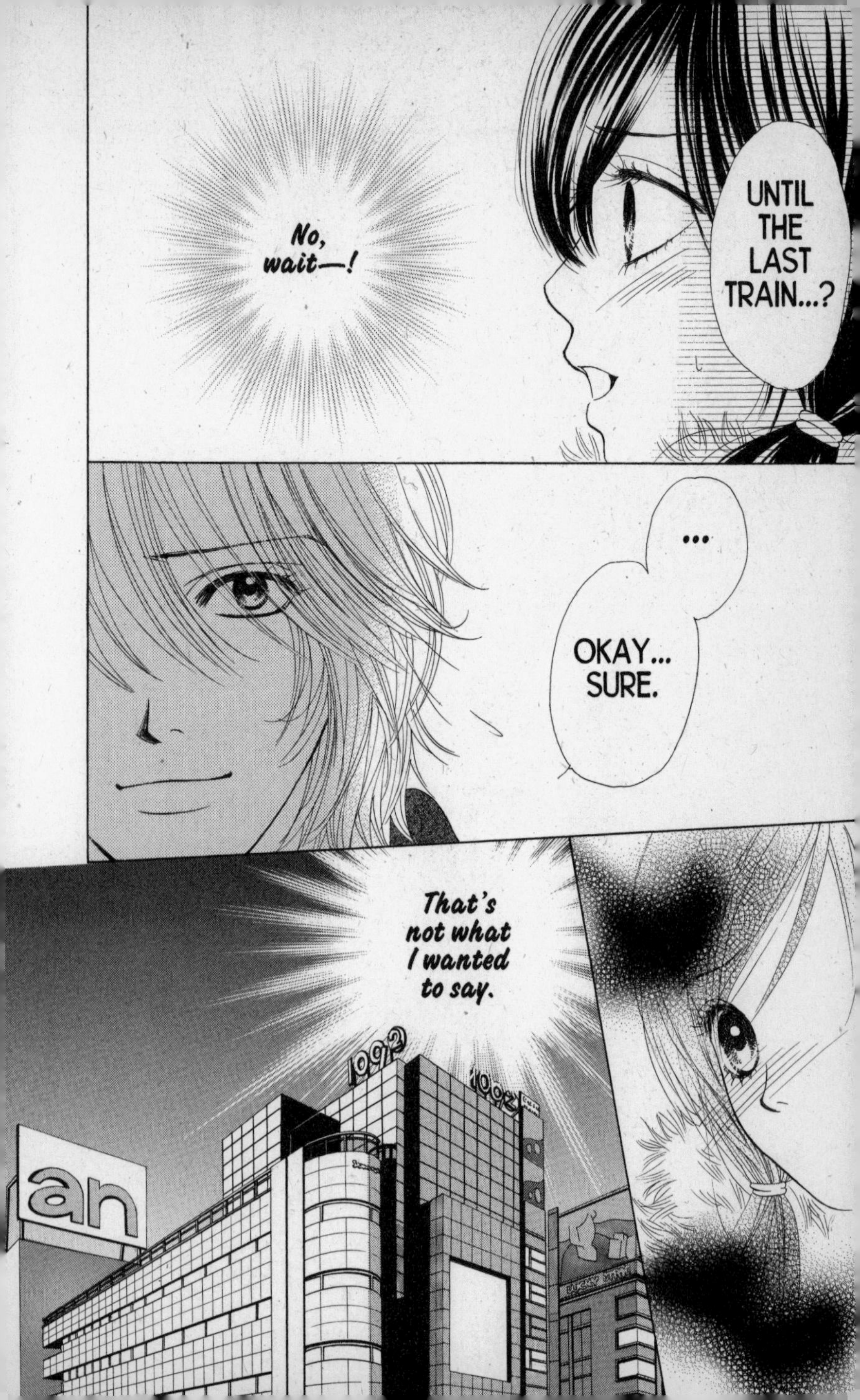
UNTIL THE LAST TRAIN...?
No, wait—!
...
OKAY... SURE.
That's not what I wanted to say.
an

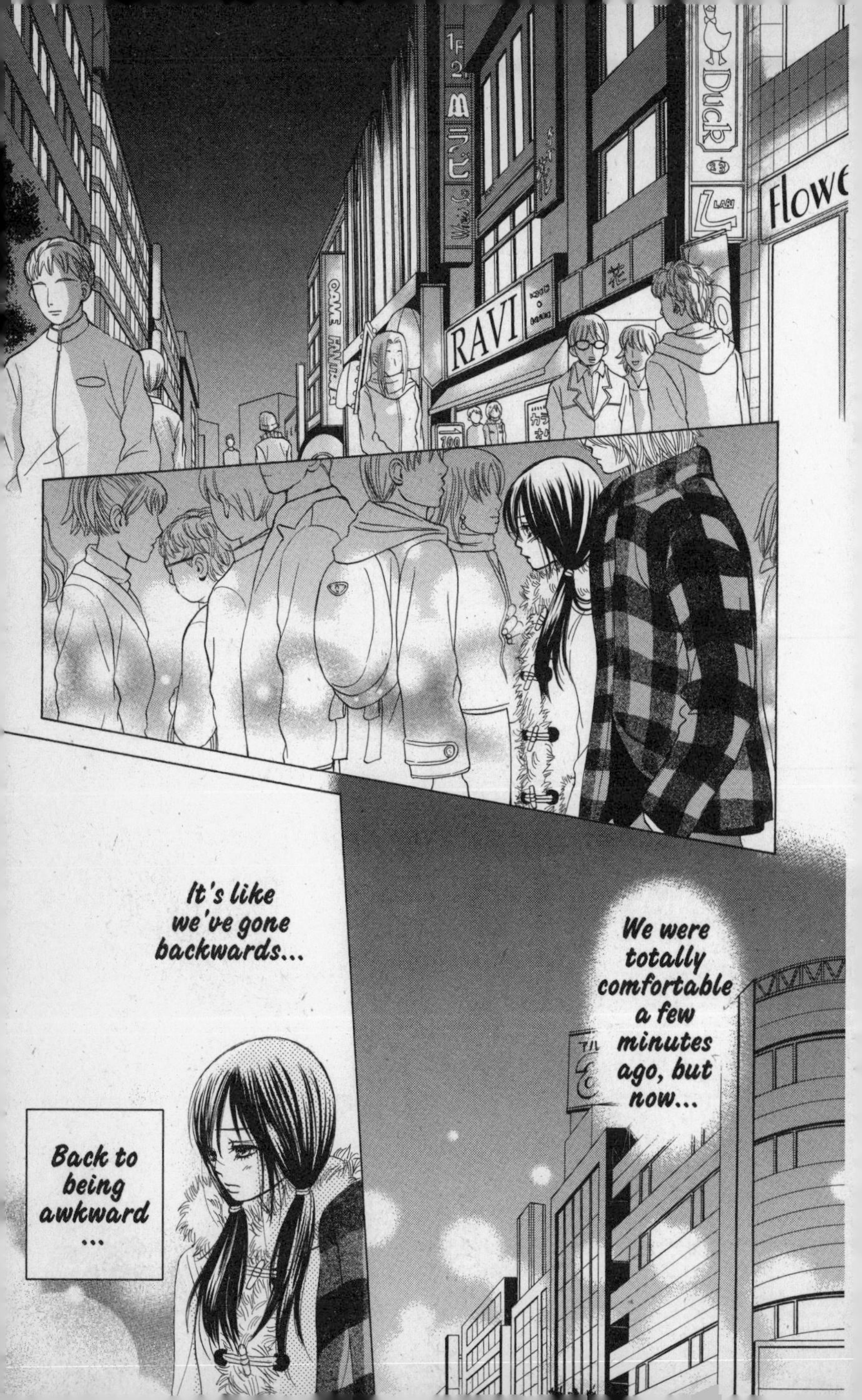
RAVI
Duck
We were totally comfortable a few minutes ago, but now...
It's like we've gone backwards...
Back to being awkward ...

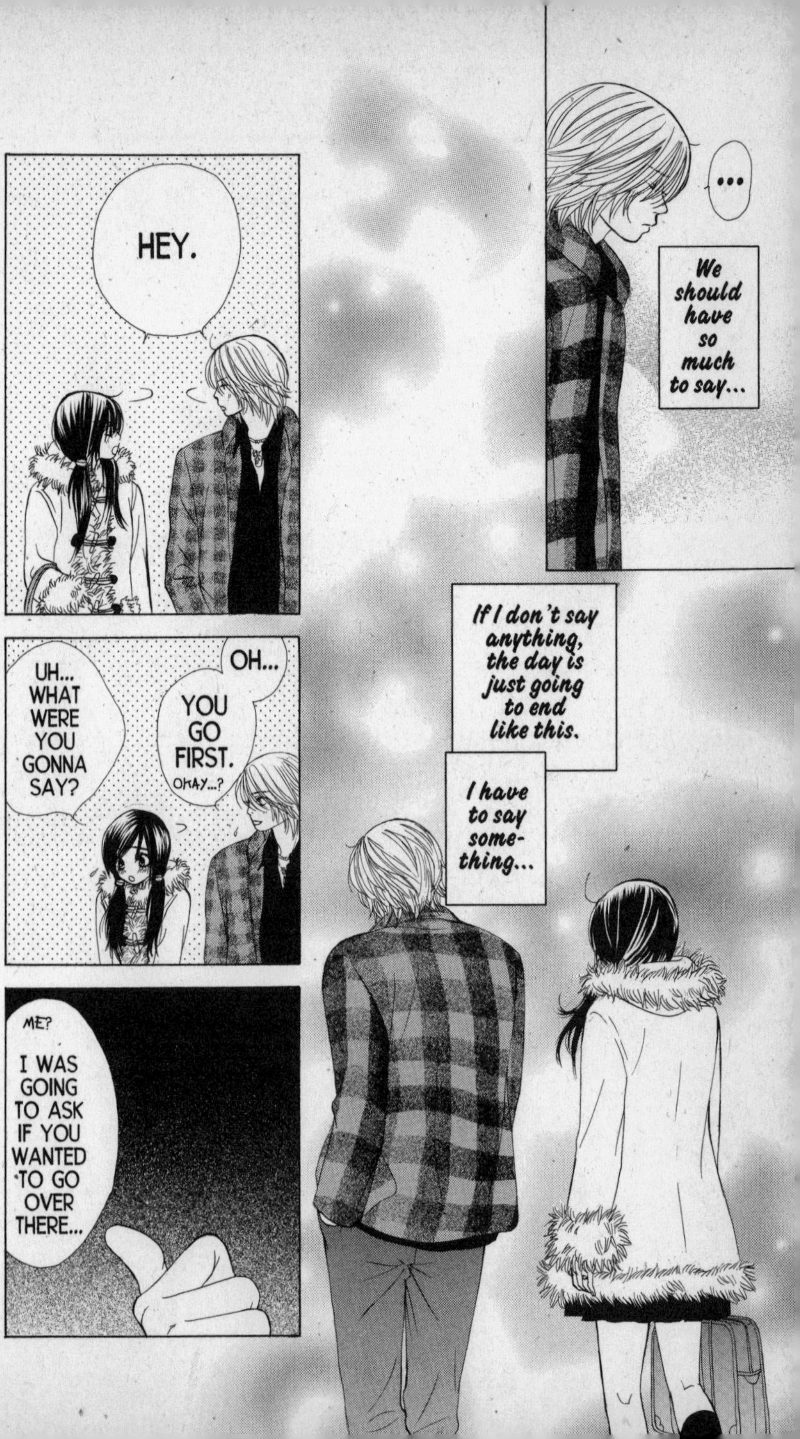
...
We should have so much to say...
If I don't say anything, the day is just going to end like this.
I have to say something...
HEY.
OH...
UH... WHAT WERE YOU GONNA SAY?
YOU GO FIRST.
OKAY...?
ME?
I WAS GOING TO ASK IF YOU WANTED TO GO OVER THERE...

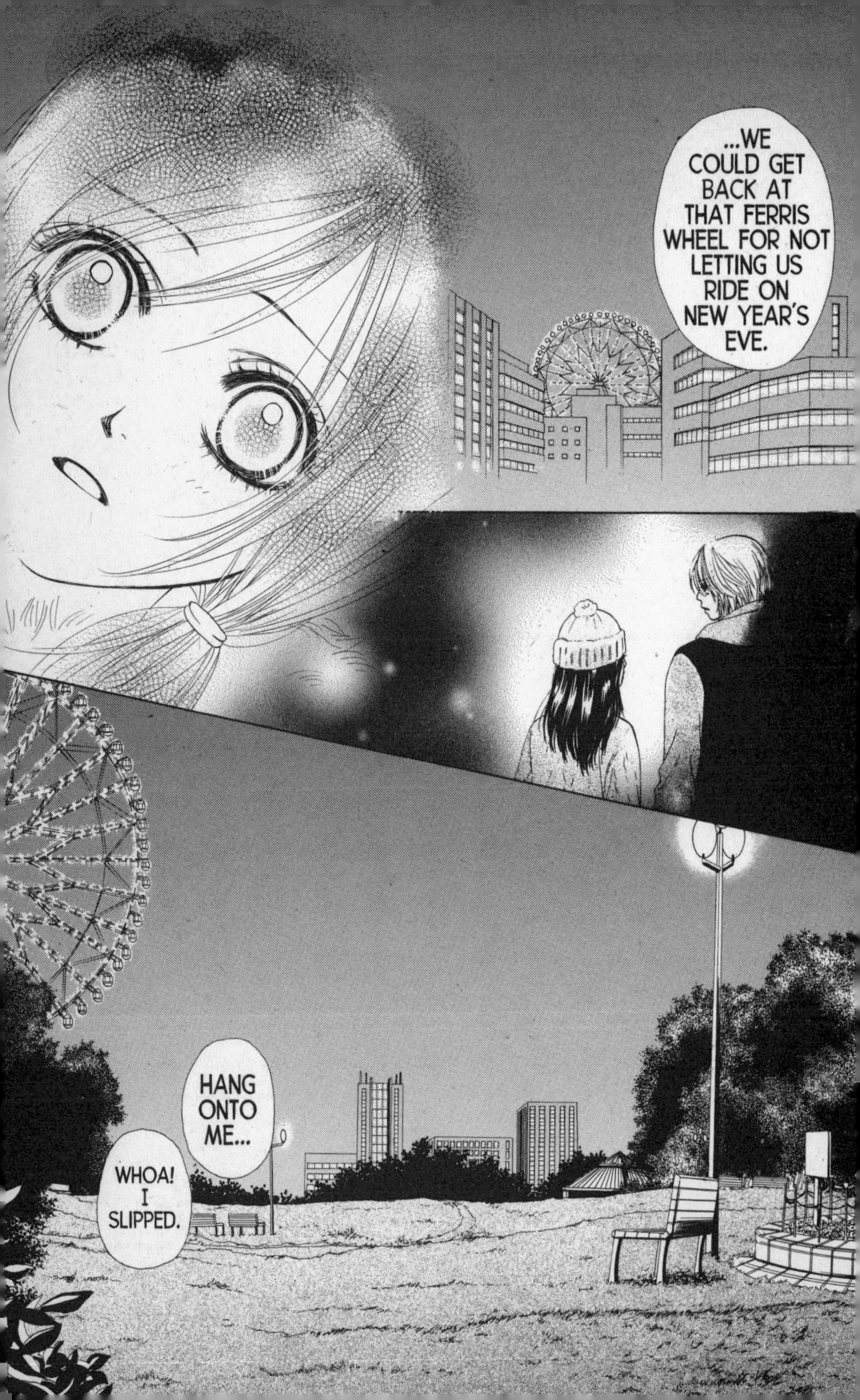
...WE COULD GET BACK AT THAT FERRIS WHEEL FOR NOT LETTING US RIDE ON NEW YEAR'S EVE.
HANG ONTO ME...
WHOA! I SLIPPED.

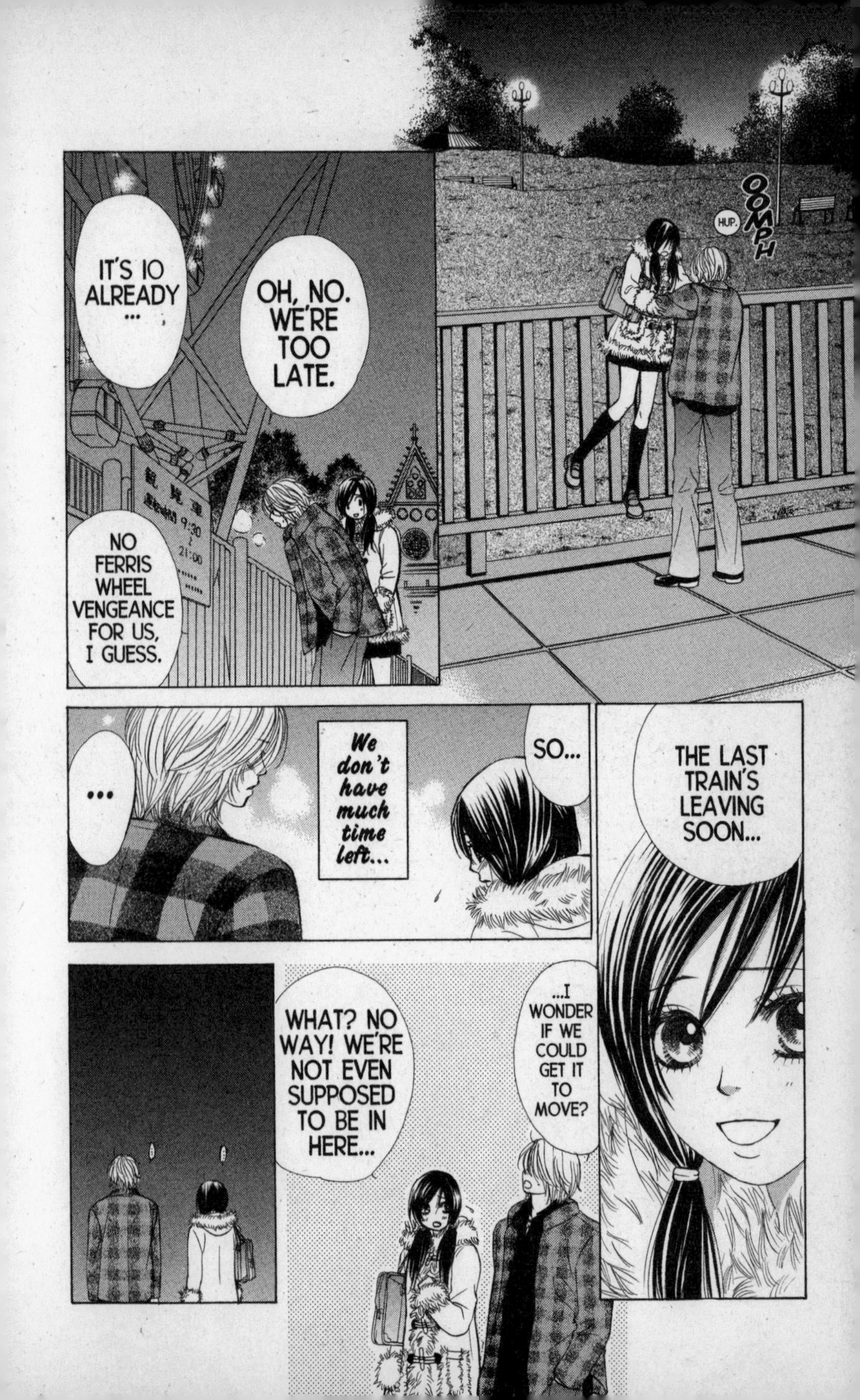
HUP.
OOMPH
OH, NO. WE'RE TOO LATE.
IT'S 10 ALREADY...
9:30
21:00
NO FERRIS WHEEL VENGEANCE FOR US, I GUESS.
THE LAST TRAIN'S LEAVING SOON...
...I WONDER IF WE COULD GET IT TO MOVE?
SO...
We don't have much time left...
...
WHAT? NO WAY! WE'RE NOT EVEN SUPPOSED TO BE IN HERE...

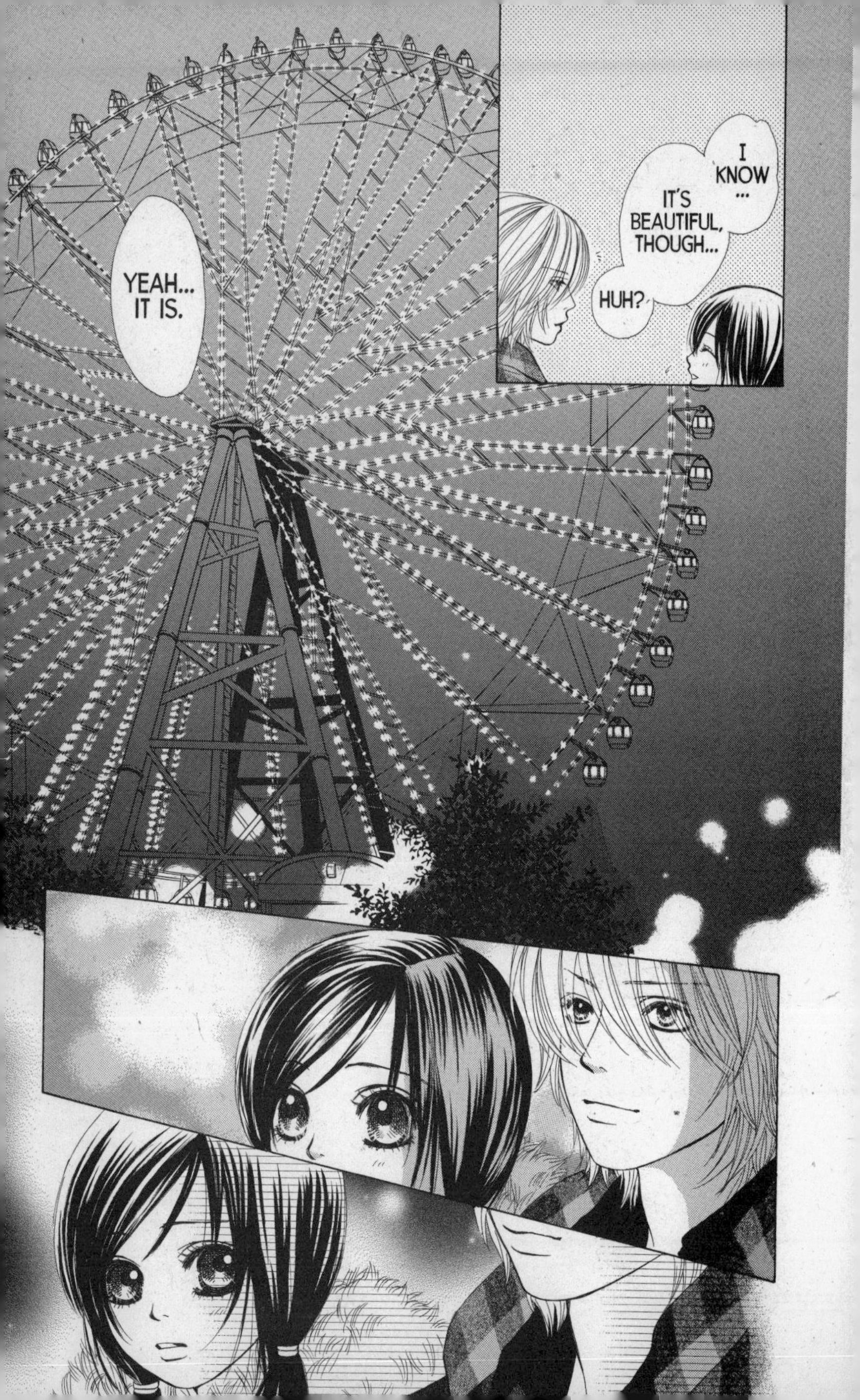
I KNOW ...
IT'S BEAUTIFUL, THOUGH...
HUH?
YEAH... IT IS.

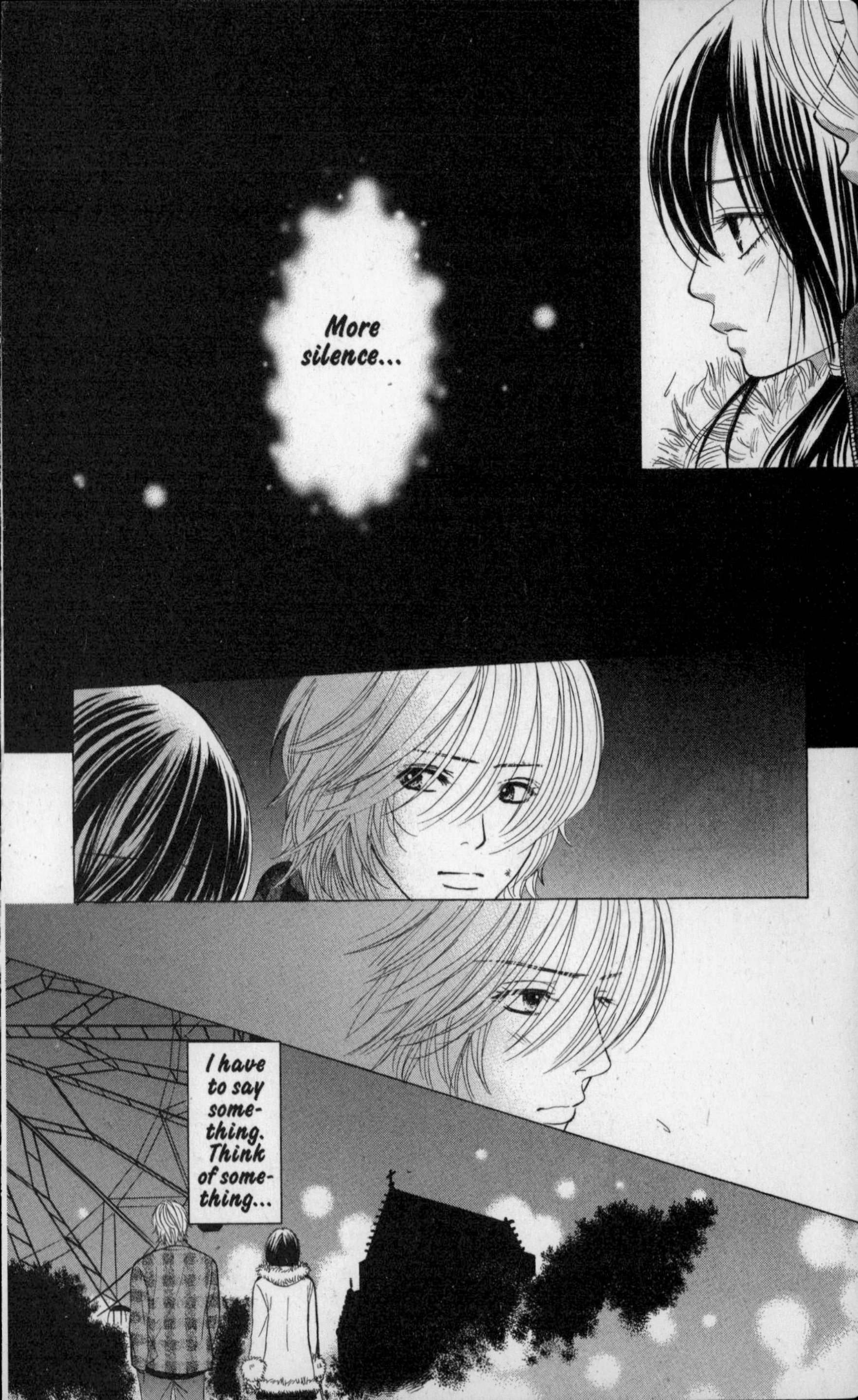
More silence...
I have to say some-thing. Think of some-thing...

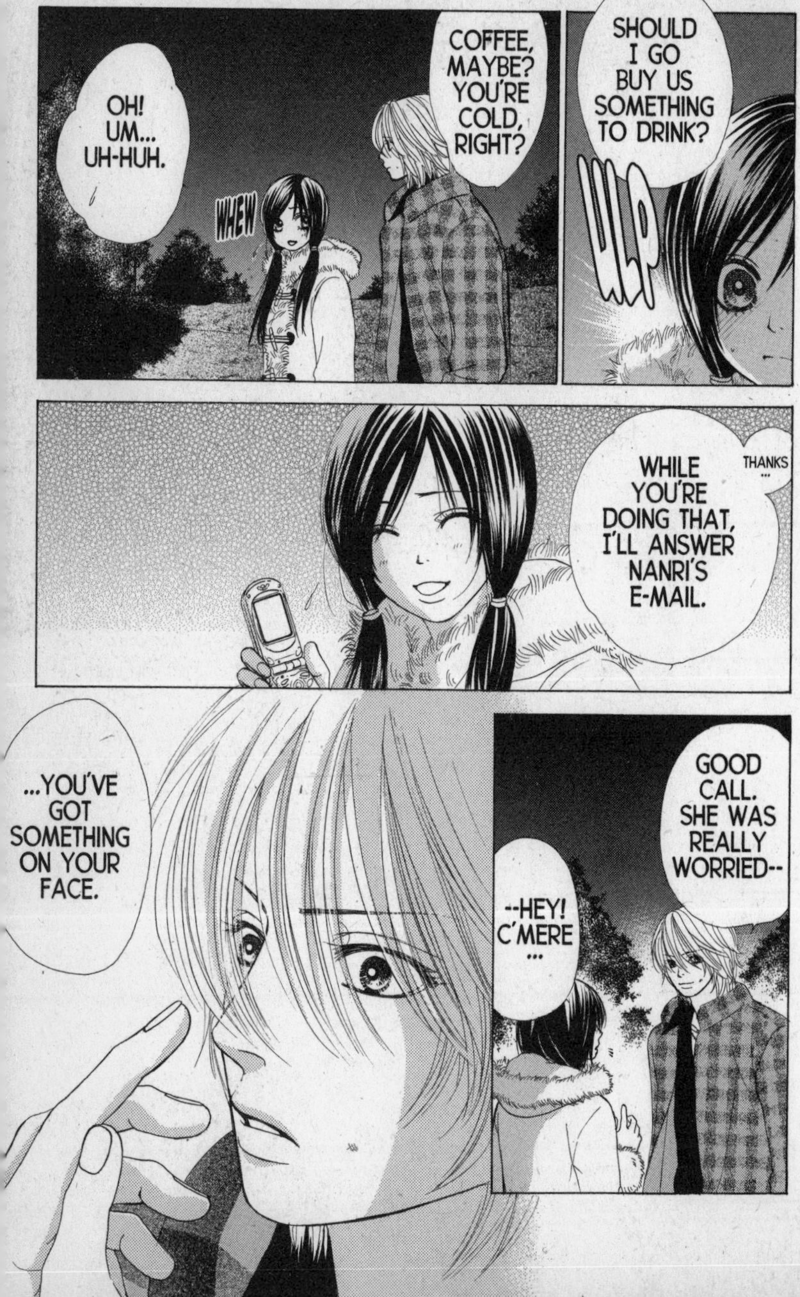
SHOULD I GO BUY US SOMETHING TO DRINK?
ULP
COFFEE, MAYBE? YOU'RE COLD, RIGHT?
OH! UM... UH-HUH.
WHEW
THANKS...
WHILE YOU'RE DOING THAT, I'LL ANSWER NANRI'S E-MAIL.
GOOD CALL. SHE WAS REALLY WORRIED--
--HEY! C'MERE...
...YOU'VE GOT SOMETHING ON YOUR FACE.

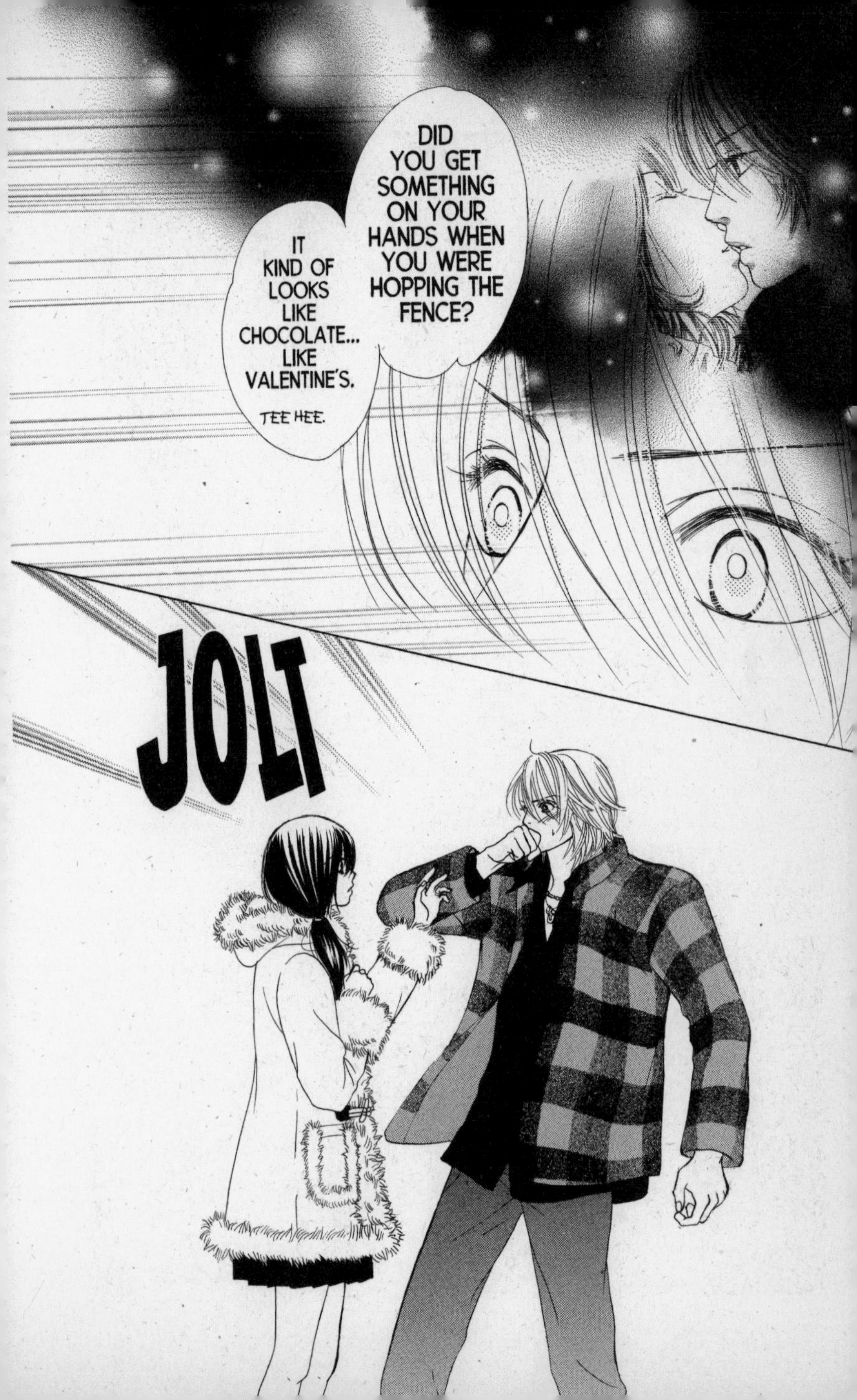
DID YOU GET SOMETHING ON YOUR HANDS WHEN YOU WERE HOPPING THE FENCE?
IT KIND OF LOOKS LIKE CHOCOLATE... LIKE VALENTINE'S.
TEE HEE.
JOLT

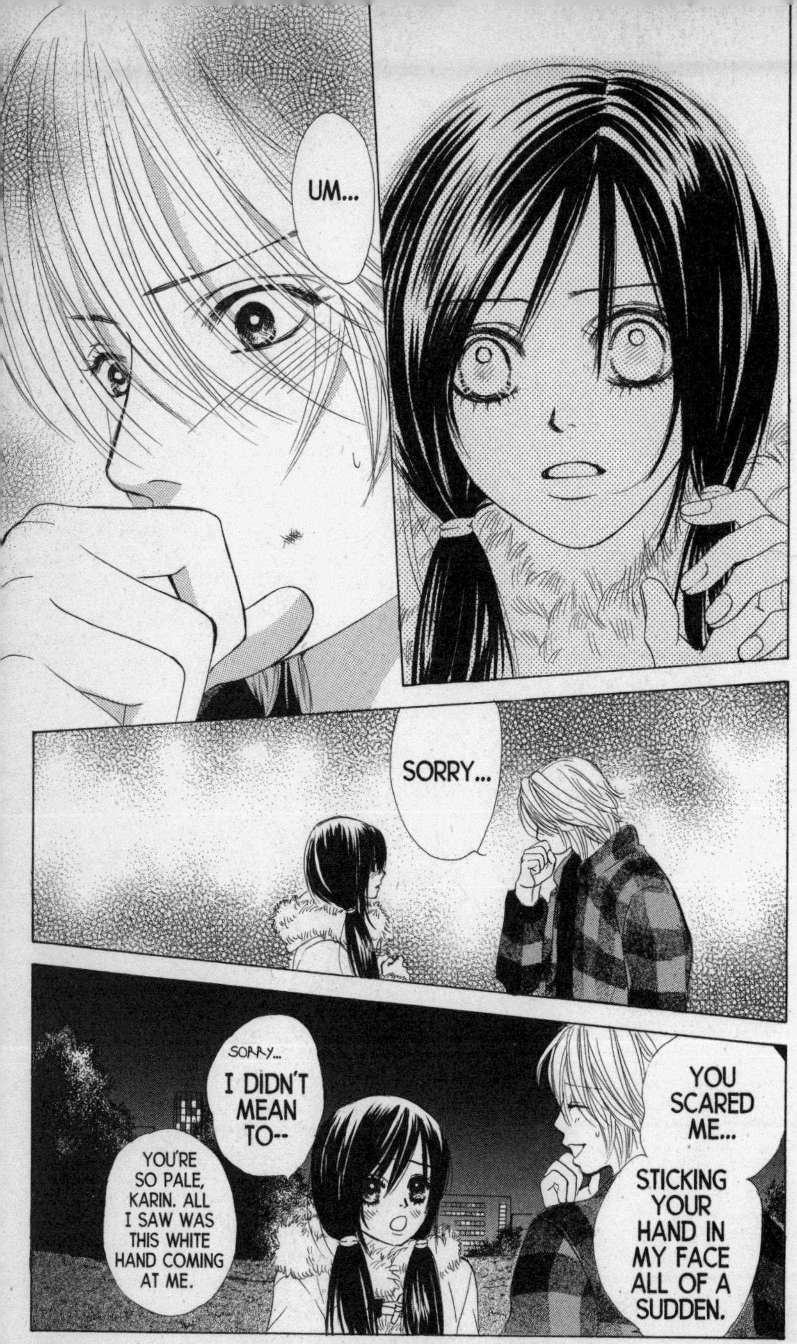
UM...
SORRY...
YOU SCARED ME...
STICKING YOUR HAND IN MY FACE ALL OF A SUDDEN.
SORRY... I DIDN'T MEAN TO--
YOU'RE SO PALE, KARIN. ALL I SAW WAS THIS WHITE HAND COMING AT ME.

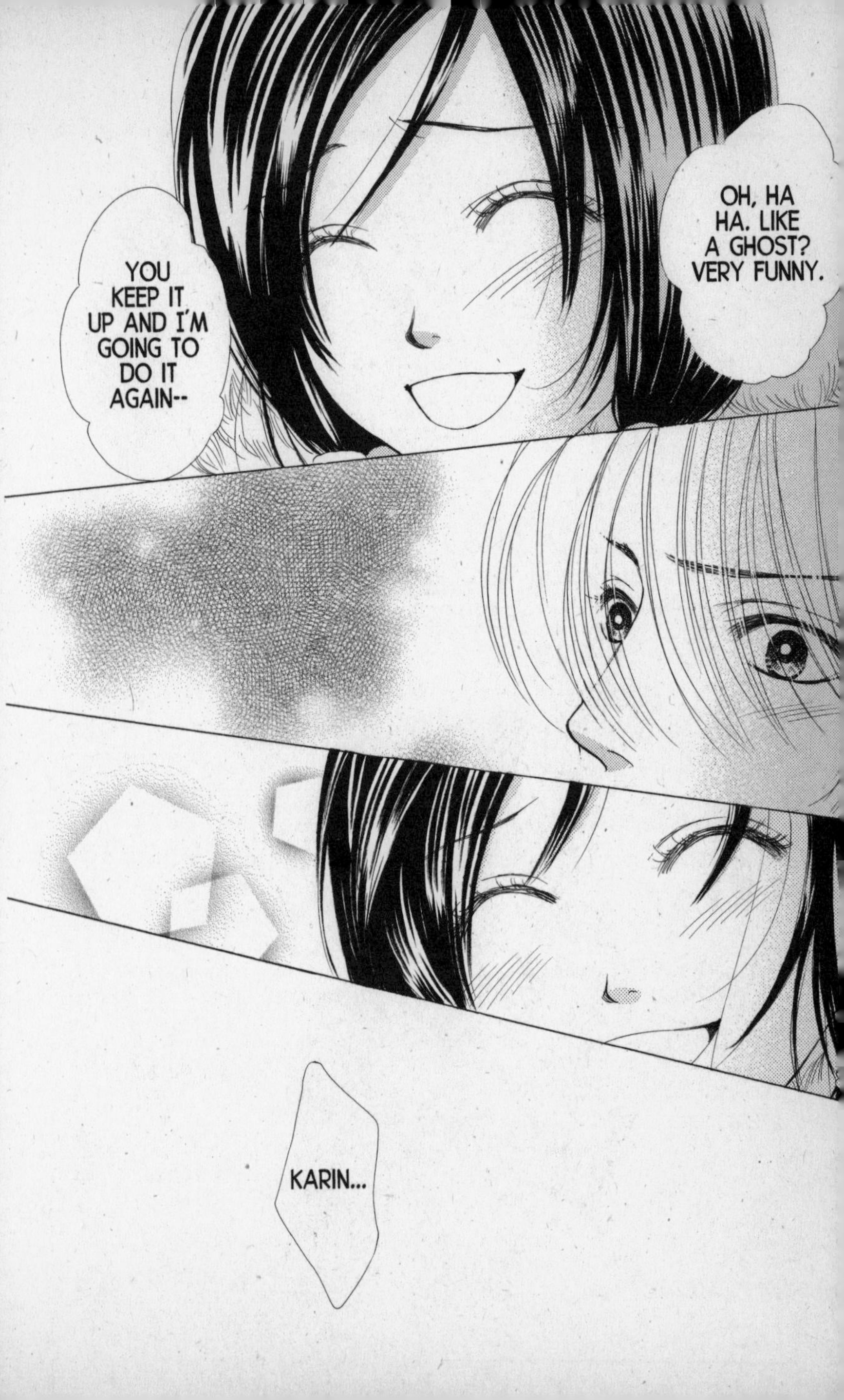
OH, HA HA. LIKE A GHOST? VERY FUNNY.
YOU KEEP IT UP AND I'M GOING TO DO IT AGAIN--
KARIN...

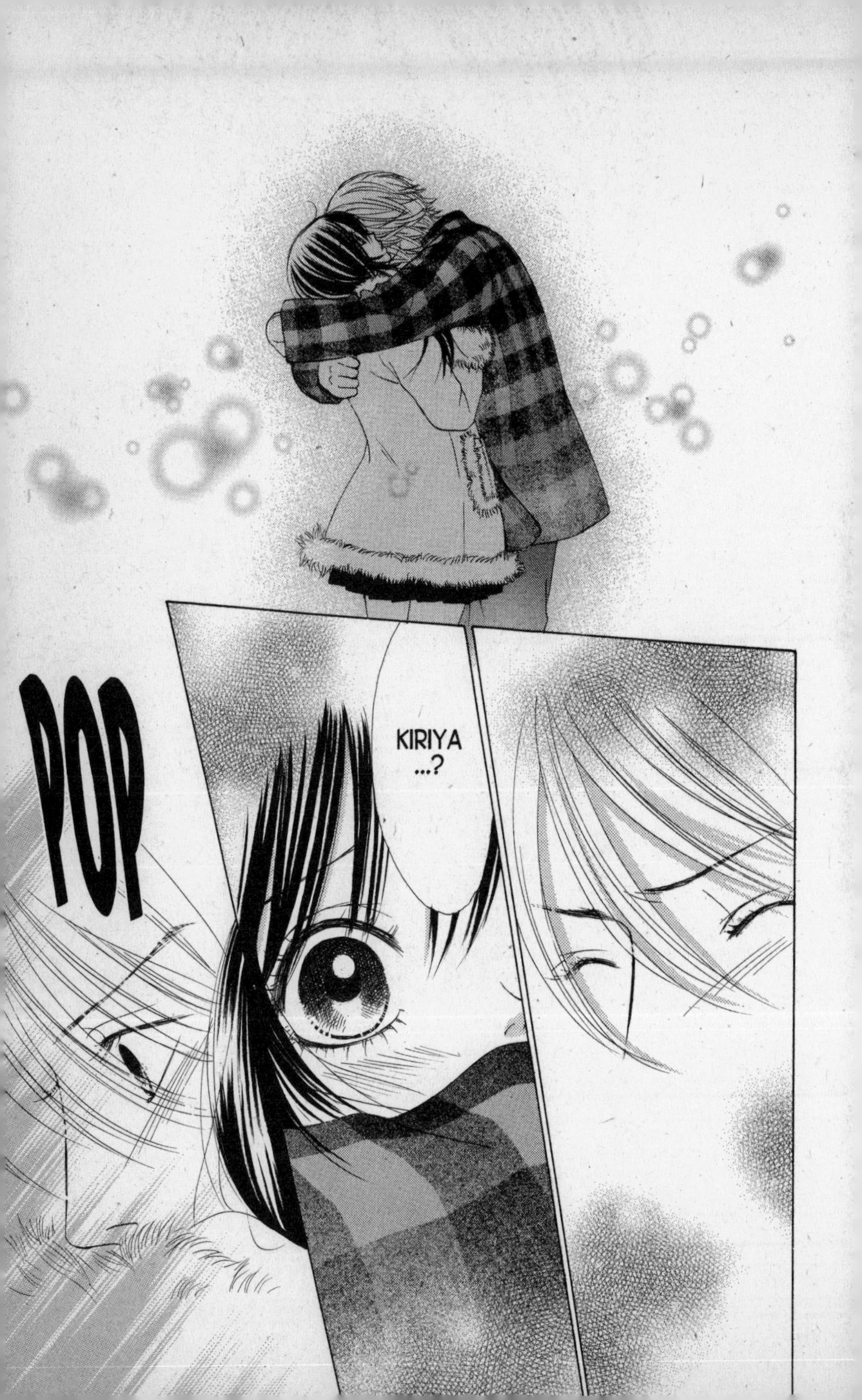
KIRIYA ...?
POP

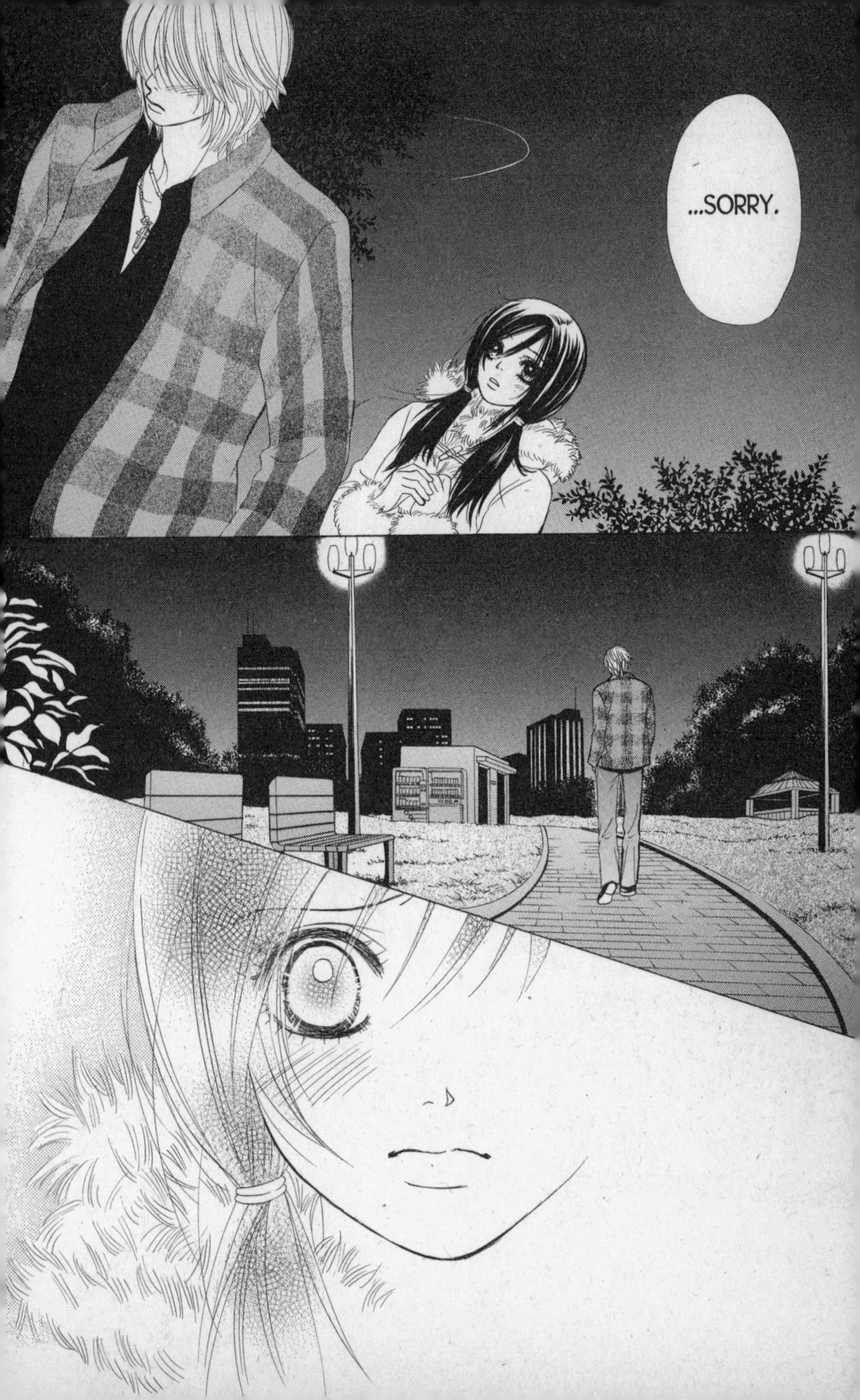
...SORRY.

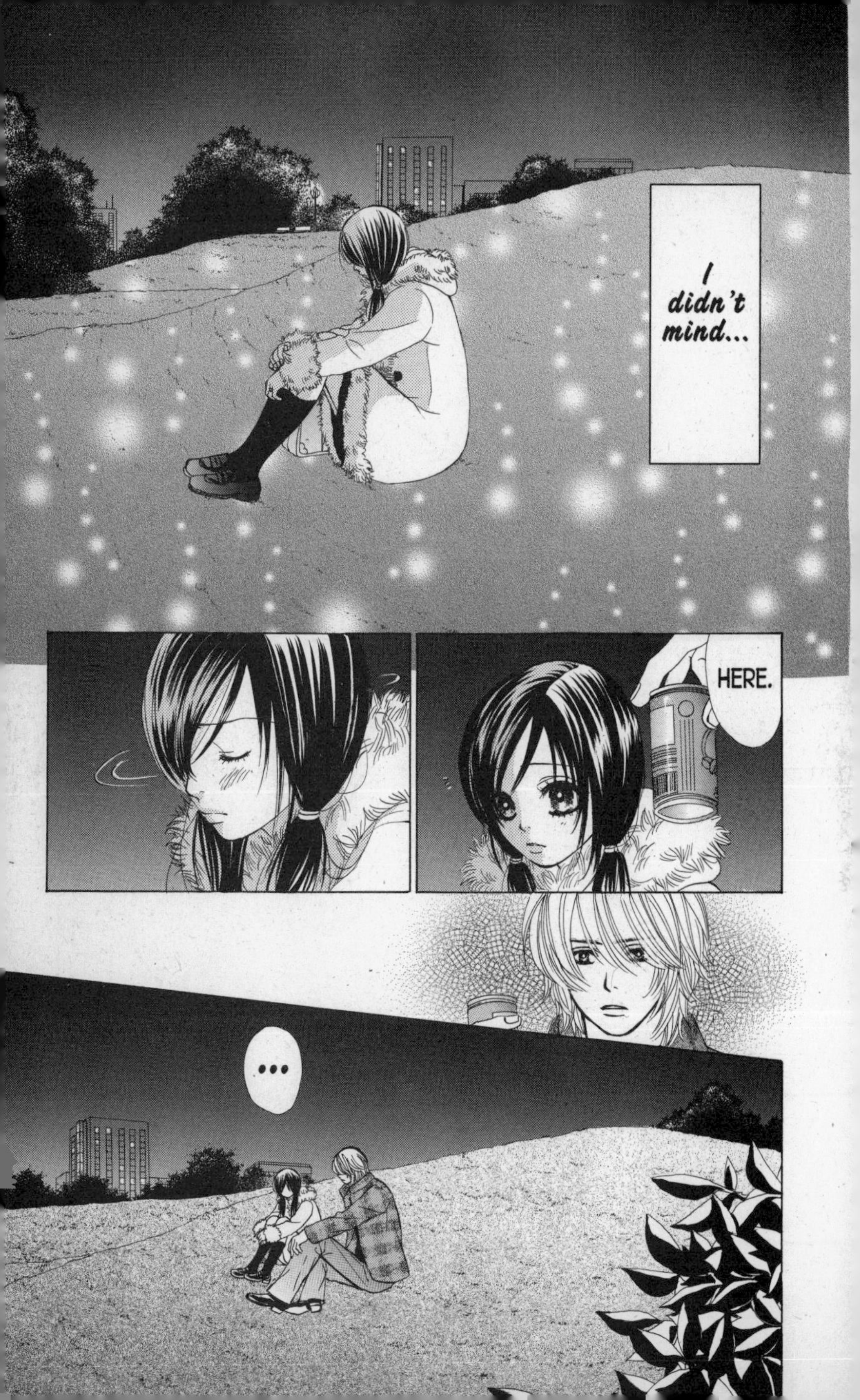
I didn't mind...
HERE.
...

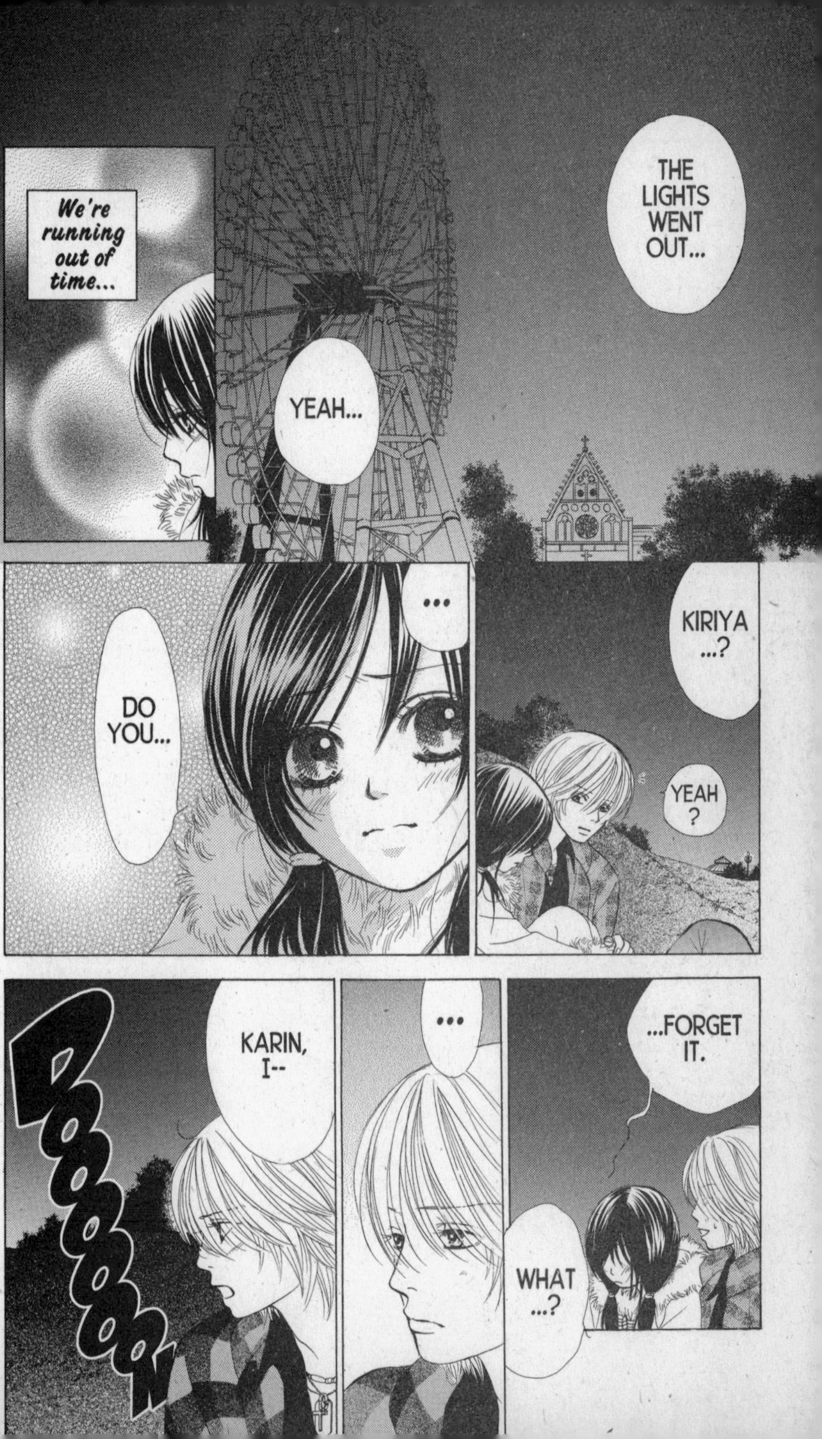
THE LIGHTS WENT OUT...
YEAH...
We're running out of time...
KIRIYA ...?
YEAH ?
...
DO YOU...
...FORGET IT.
WHAT ...?
...
KARIN, I--
DOOOOOON

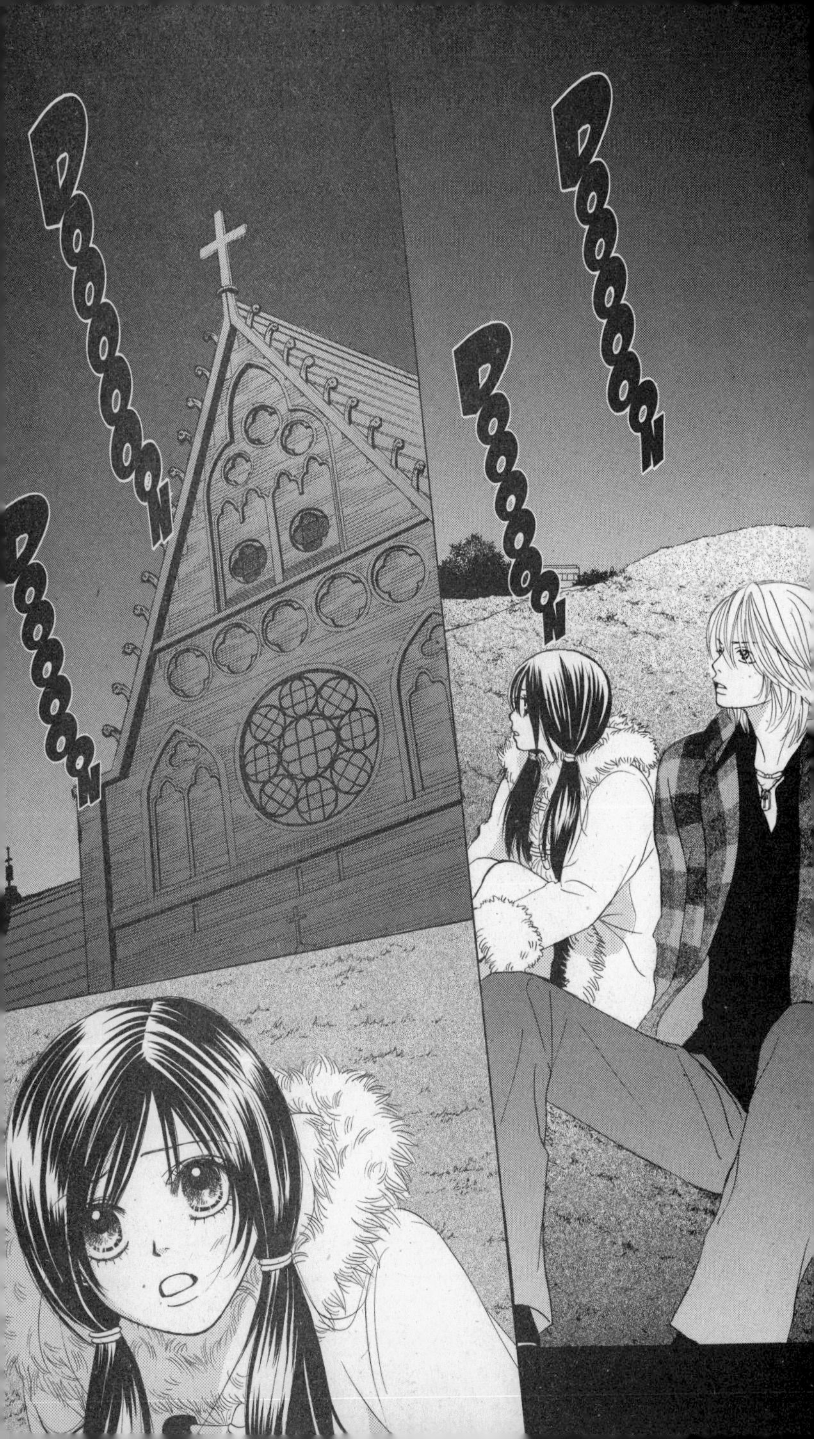
DOOOOOOOOON
DOOOOOOOOON
DOOOOOOOOON
DOOOOOOOOON

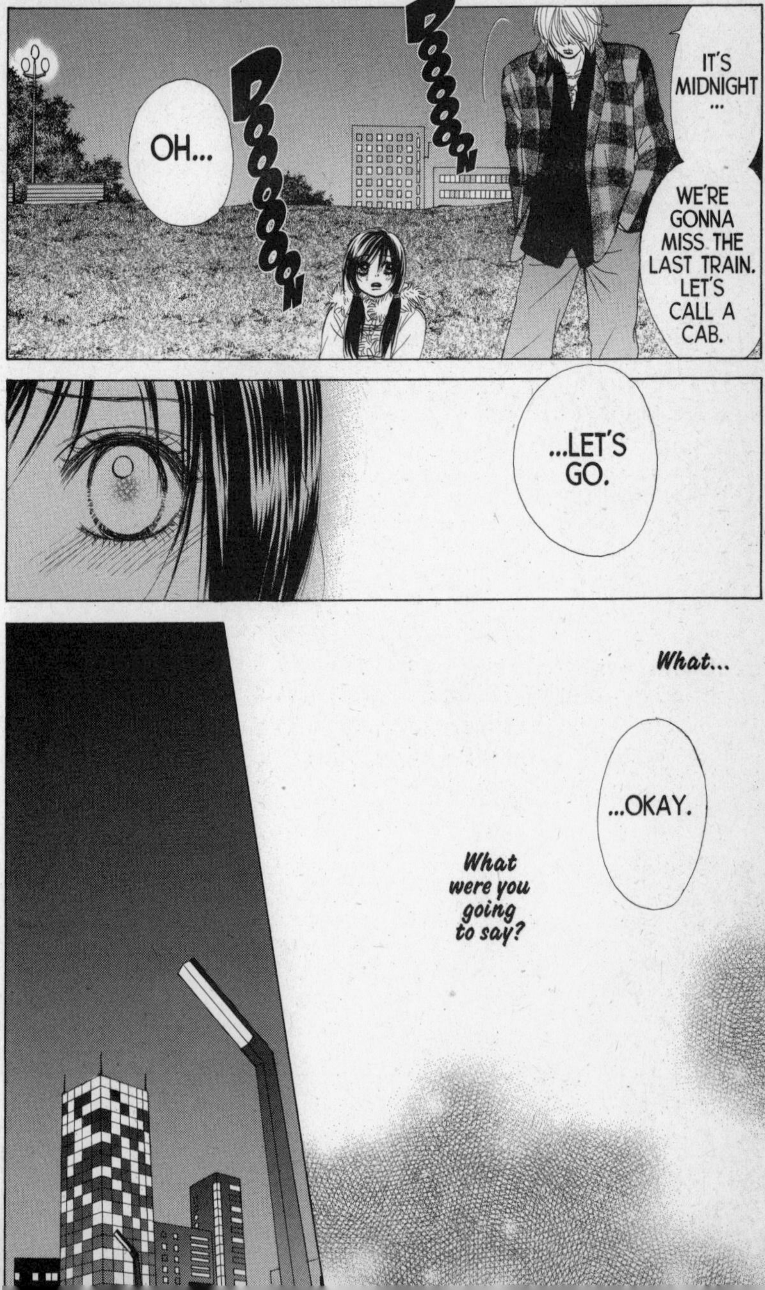
IT'S MIDNIGHT ...
WE'RE GONNA MISS THE LAST TRAIN. LET'S CALL A CAB.
DOOOOOOON
DOOOOOOON
OH...
...LET'S GO.
What...
...OKAY.
What were you going to say?

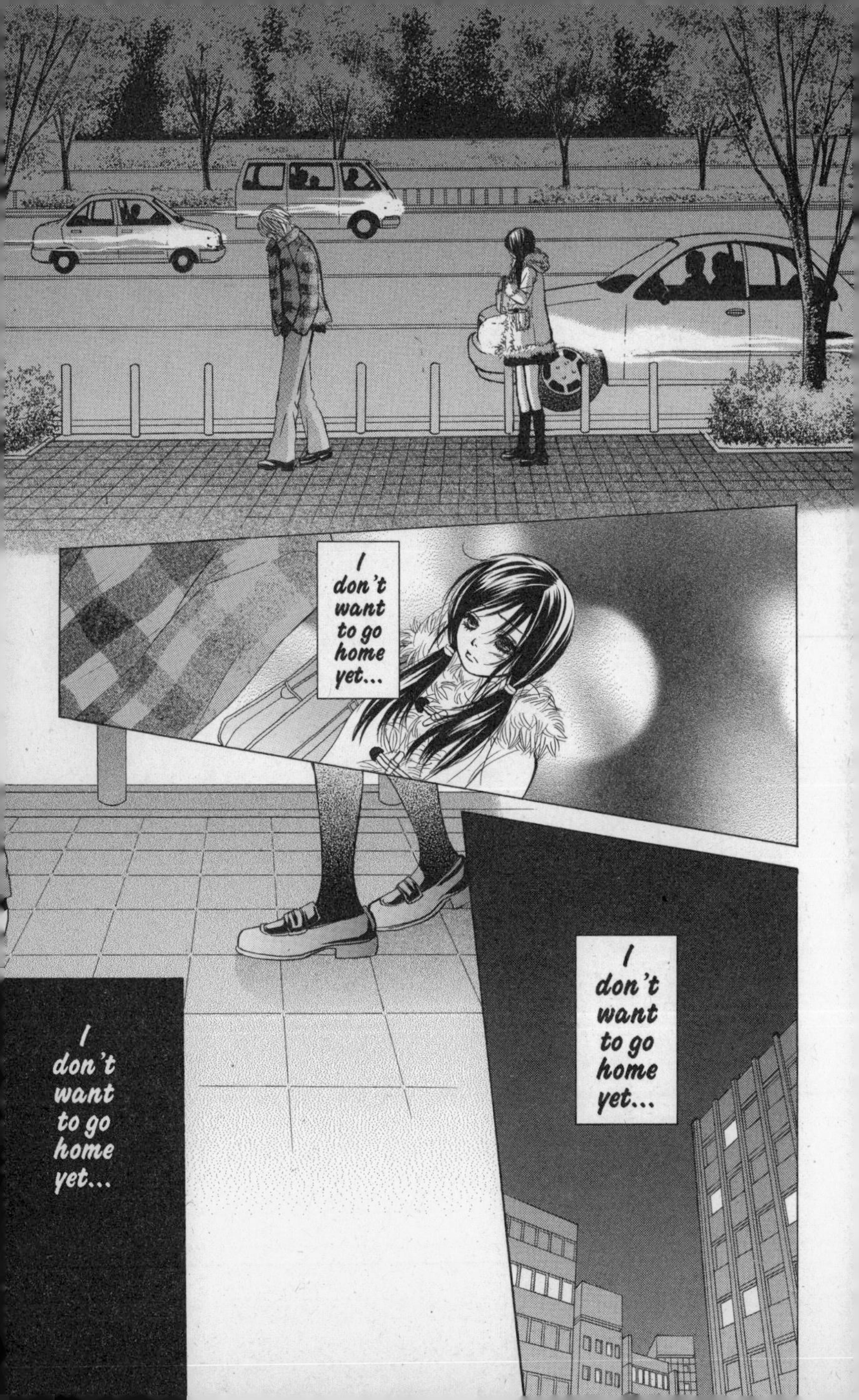
I don't want to go home yet...
I don't want to go home yet...
I don't want to go home yet...

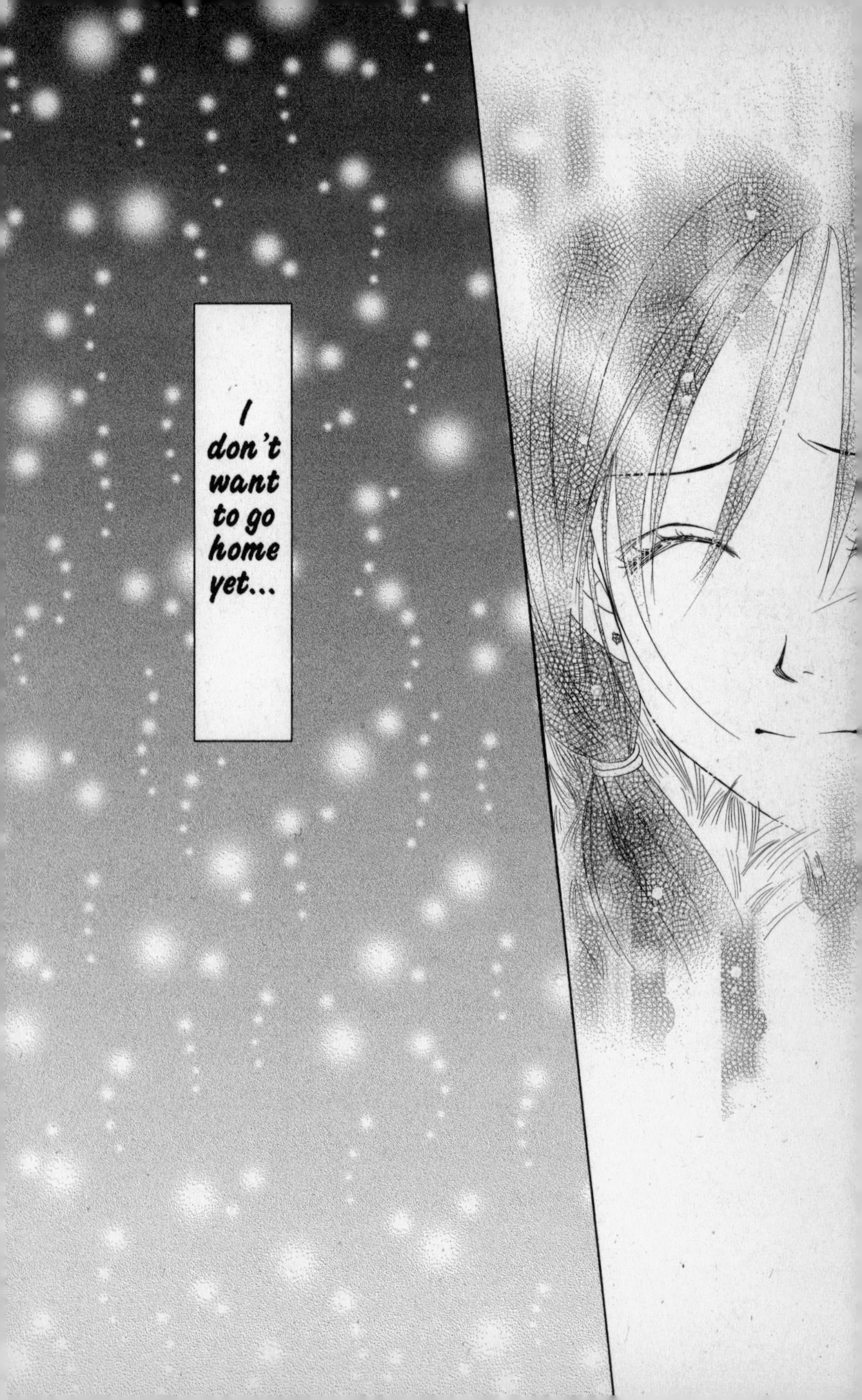
I don't want to go home yet...

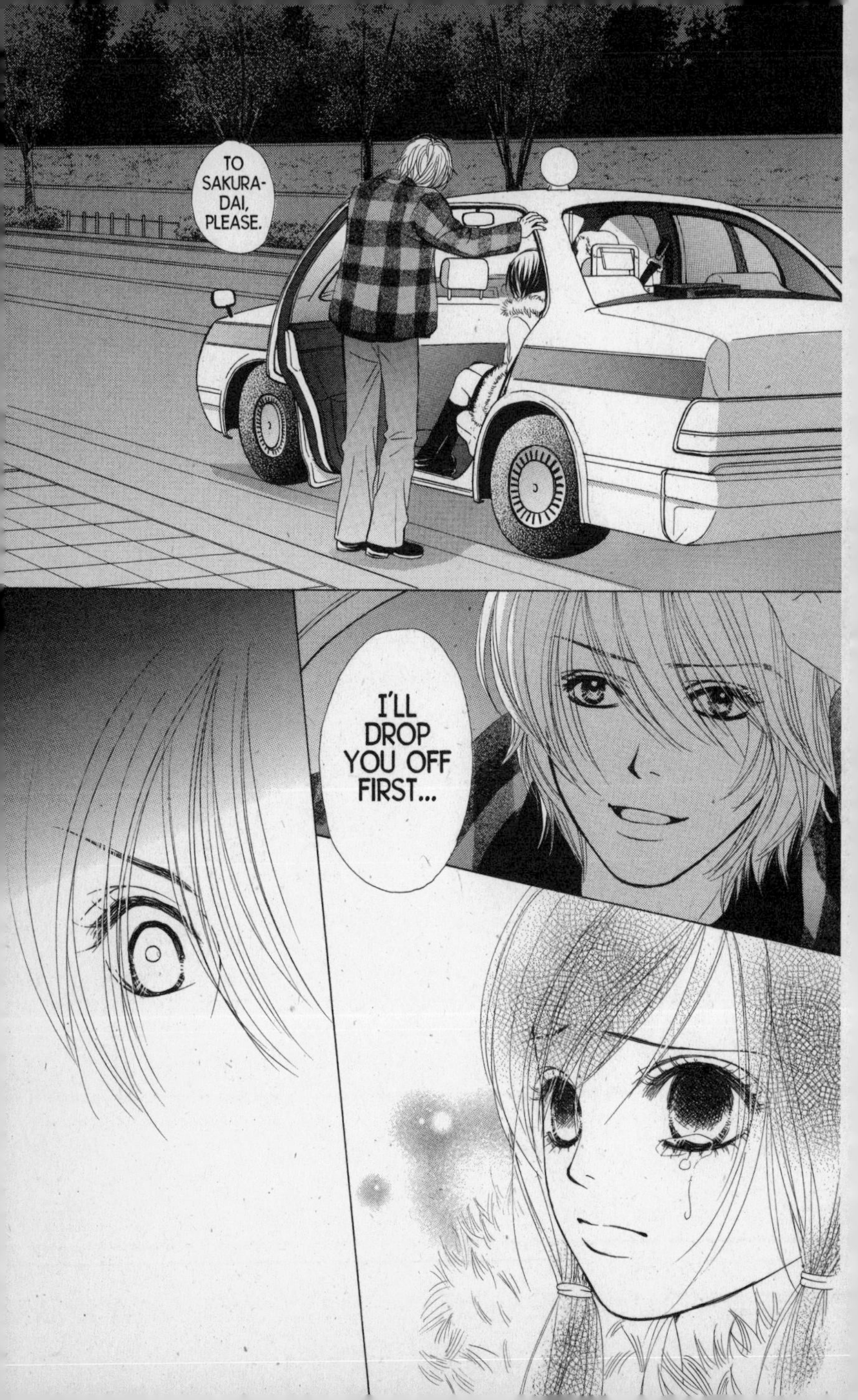
TO SAKURA-DAI, PLEASE.
I'LL DROP YOU OFF FIRST...

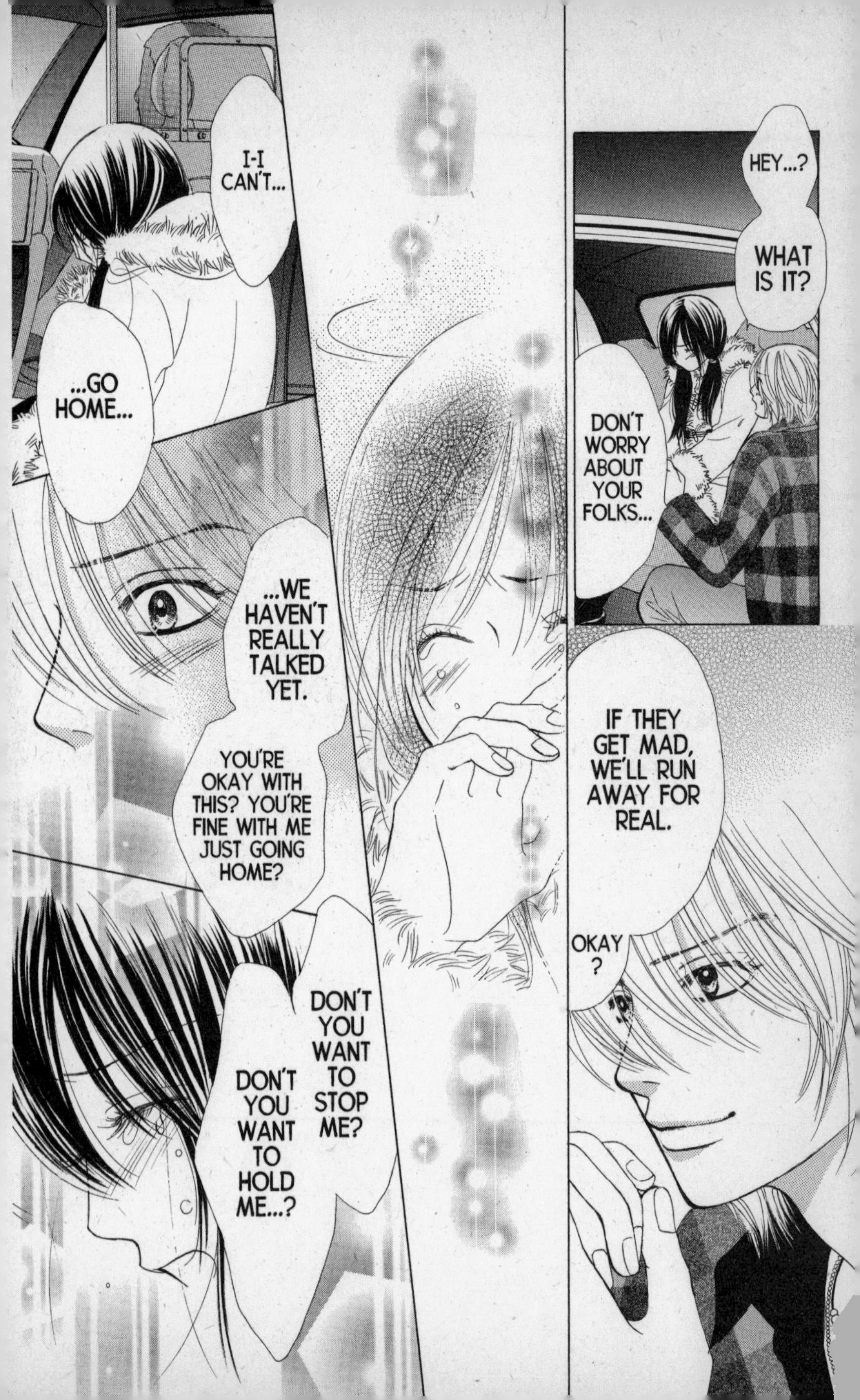
HEY...?
WHAT IS IT?
DON'T WORRY ABOUT YOUR FOLKS...
IF THEY GET MAD, WE'LL RUN AWAY FOR REAL.
OKAY?
I-I CAN'T...
...GO HOME...
...WE HAVEN'T REALLY TALKED YET.
YOU'RE OKAY WITH THIS? YOU'RE FINE WITH ME JUST GOING HOME?
DON'T YOU WANT TO STOP ME?
DON'T YOU WANT TO HOLD ME...?

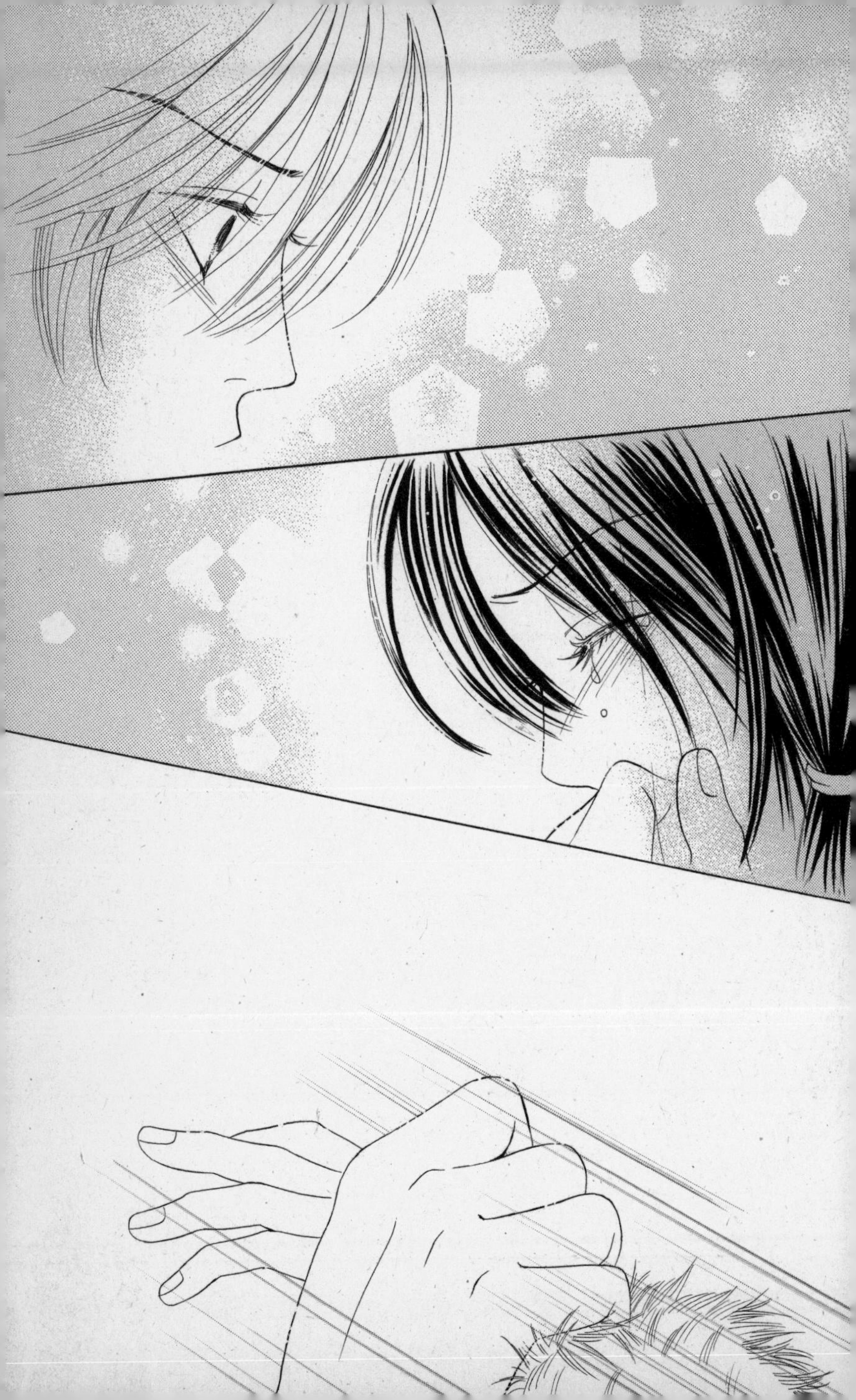

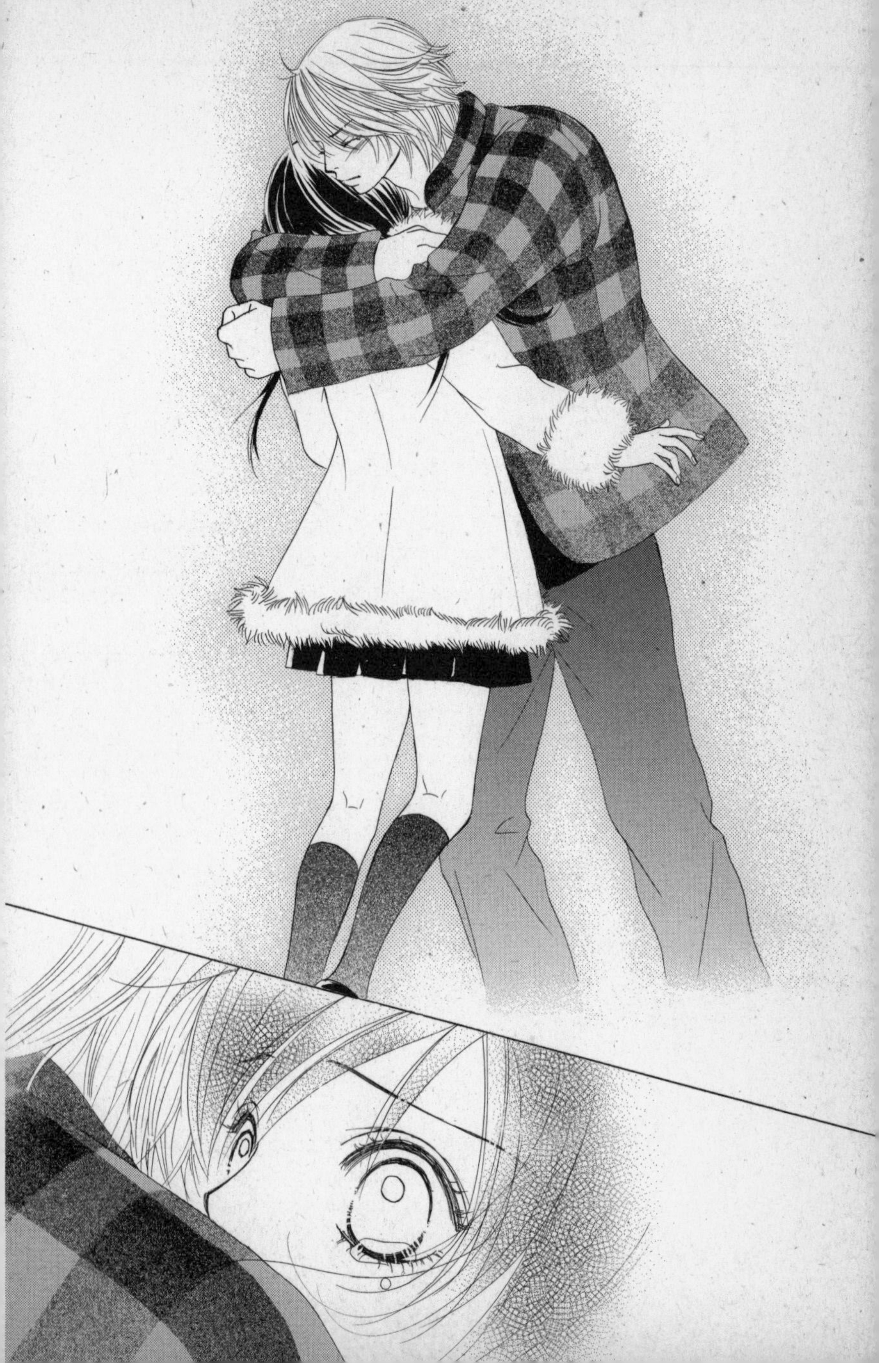

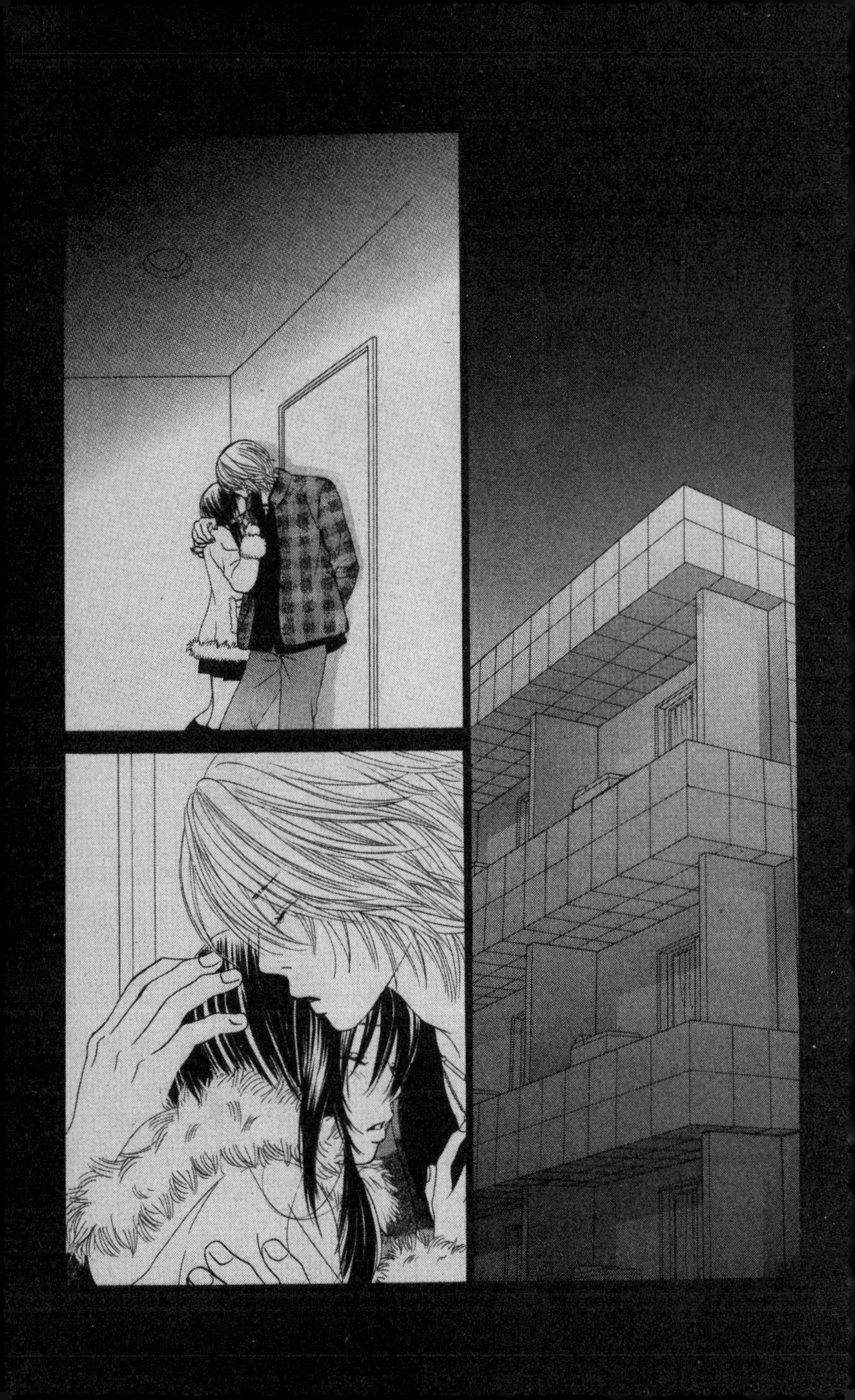

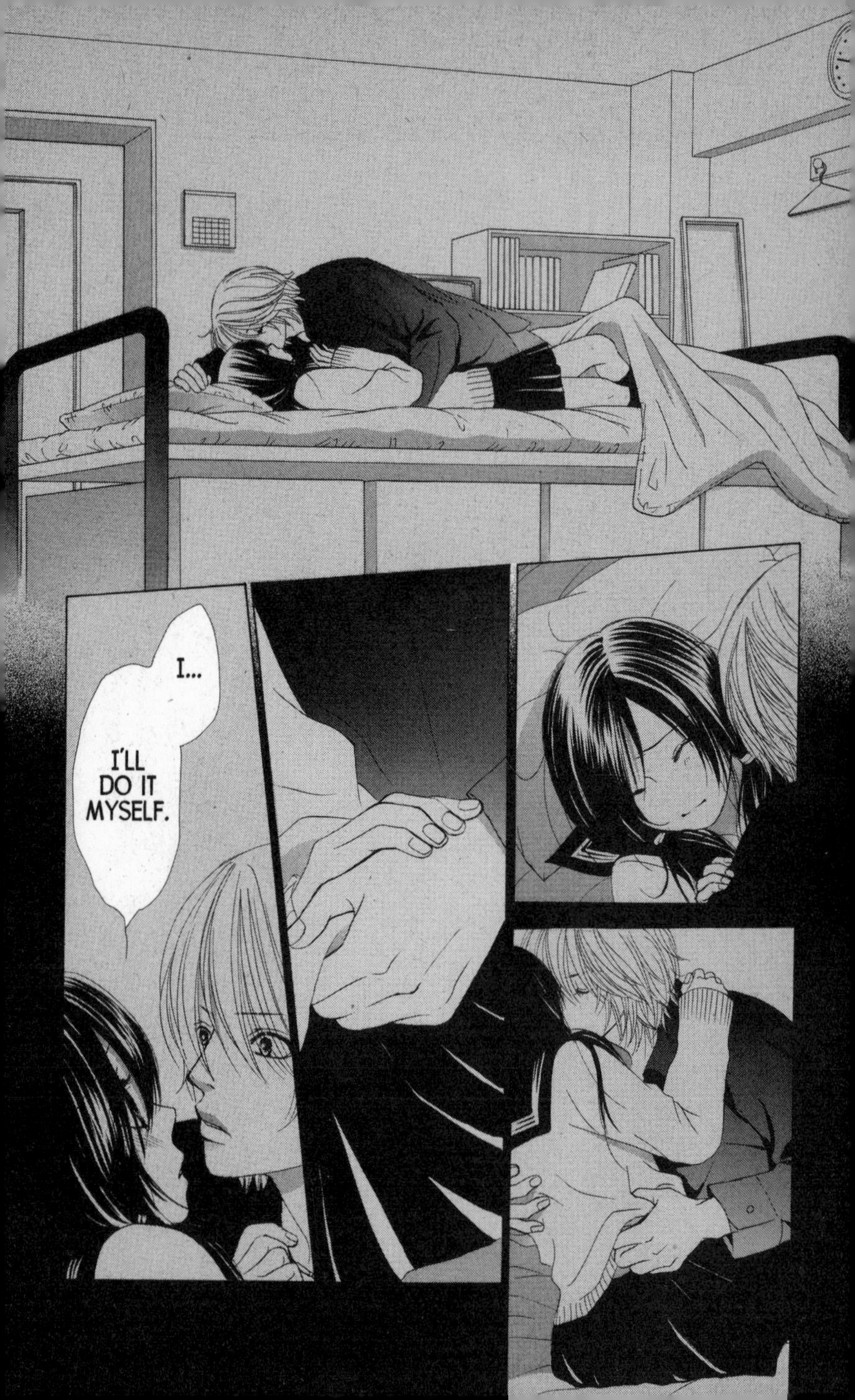
I...
I'LL DO IT MYSELF.

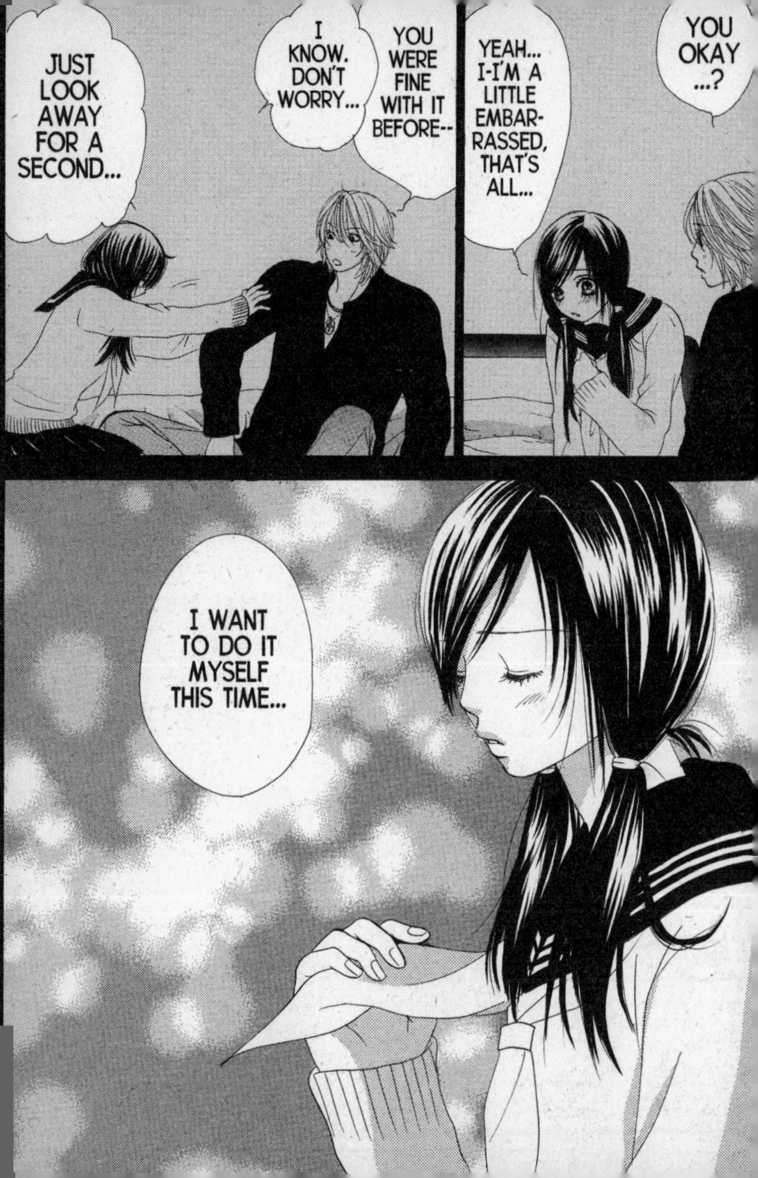
YOU OKAY ...?
YEAH... I-I'M A LITTLE EMBARRASSED, THAT'S ALL...
YOU WERE FINE WITH IT BEFORE--
I KNOW. DON'T WORRY...
JUST LOOK AWAY FOR A SECOND...
I WANT TO DO IT MYSELF THIS TIME...

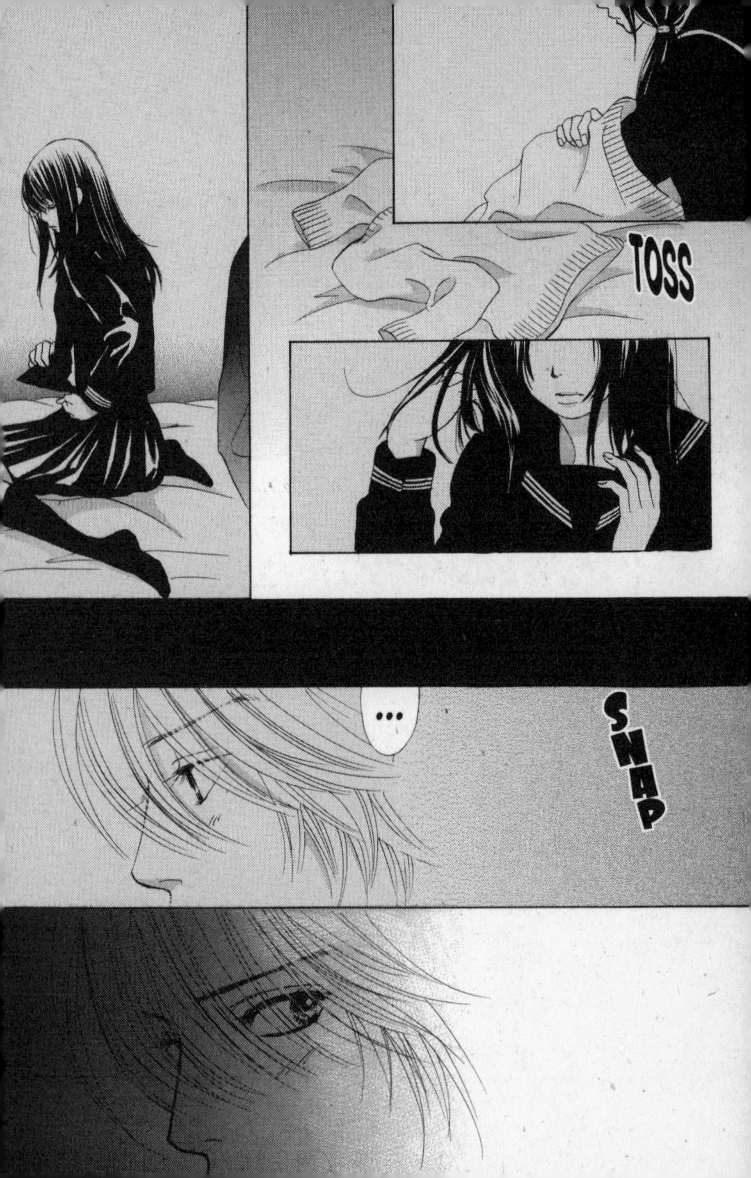
TOSS
SNAP
...

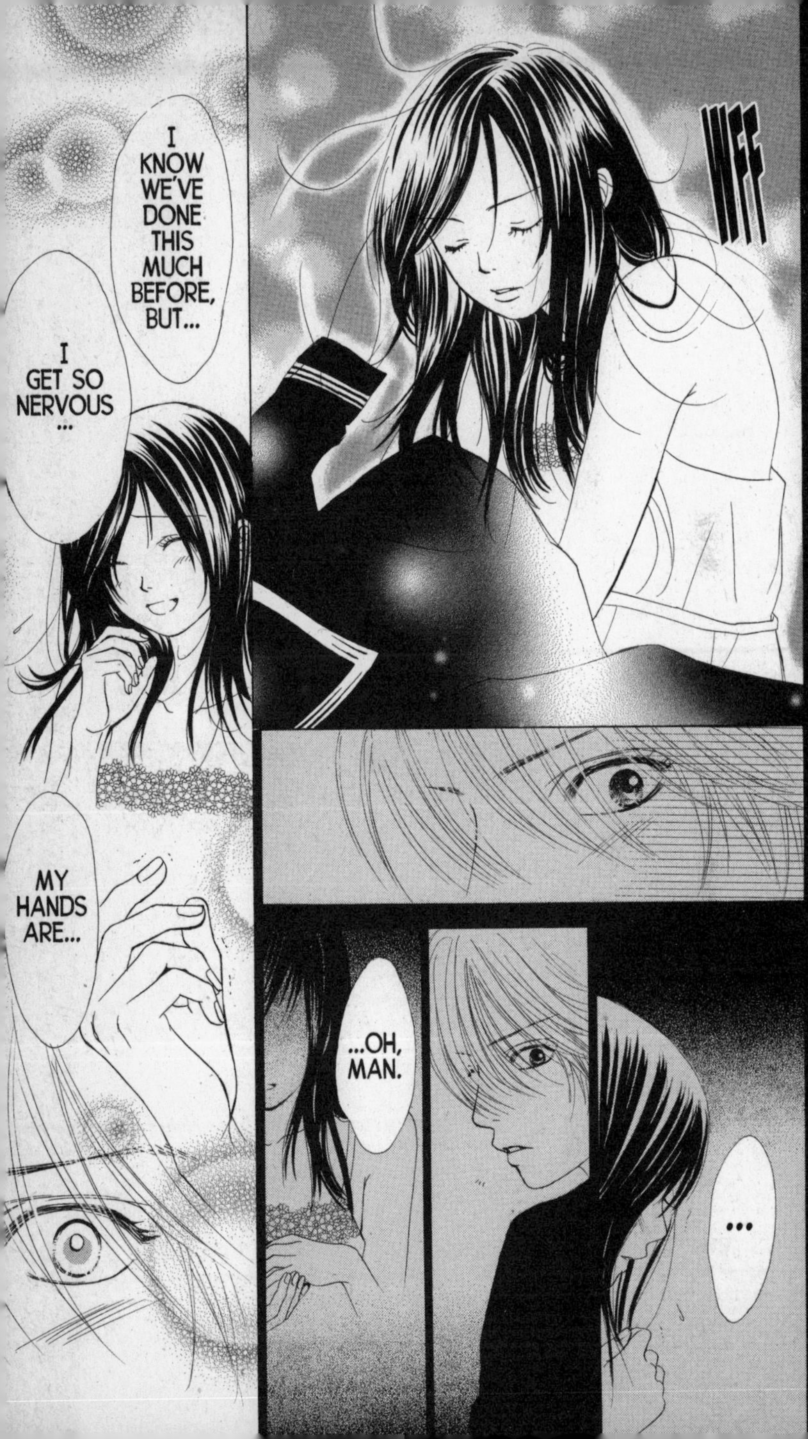
WFF
...
...OH, MAN.
I KNOW WE'VE DONE THIS MUCH BEFORE, BUT...
I GET SO NERVOUS...
MY HANDS ARE...

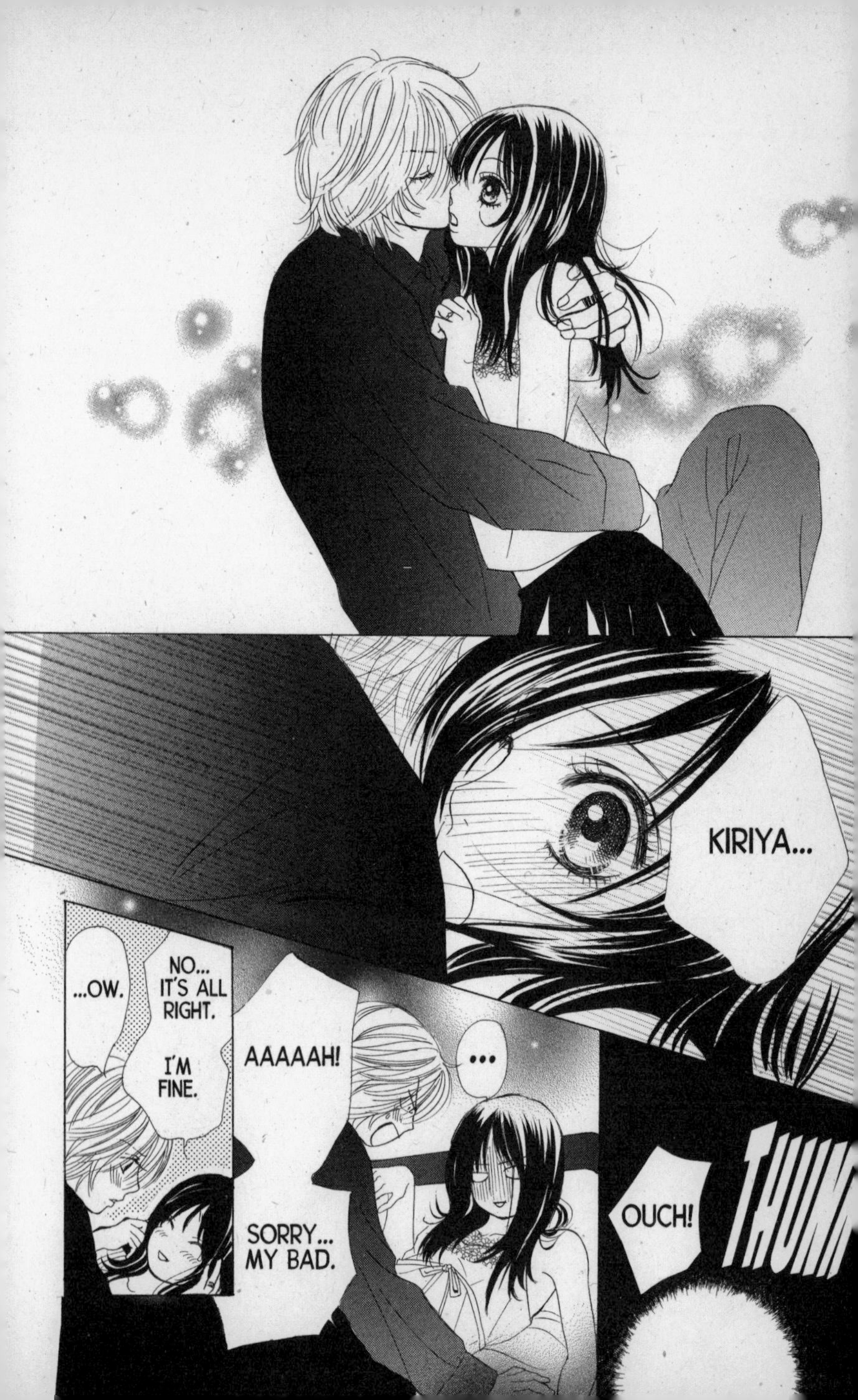
KIRIYA...
OUCH!
THUN
...
AAAAAH!
SORRY... MY BAD.
NO... IT'S ALL RIGHT.
I'M FINE.
...OW.

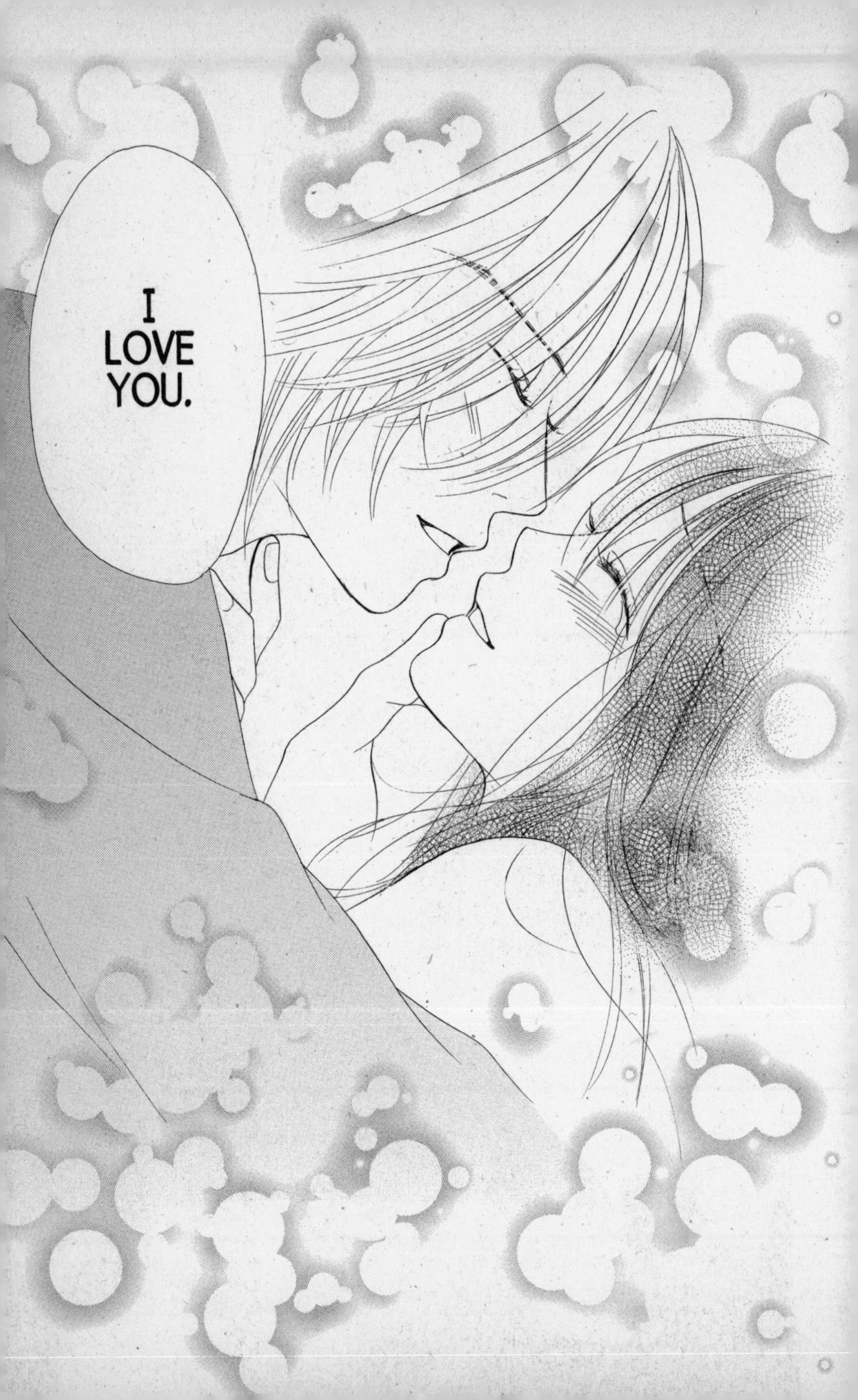
I LOVE YOU.

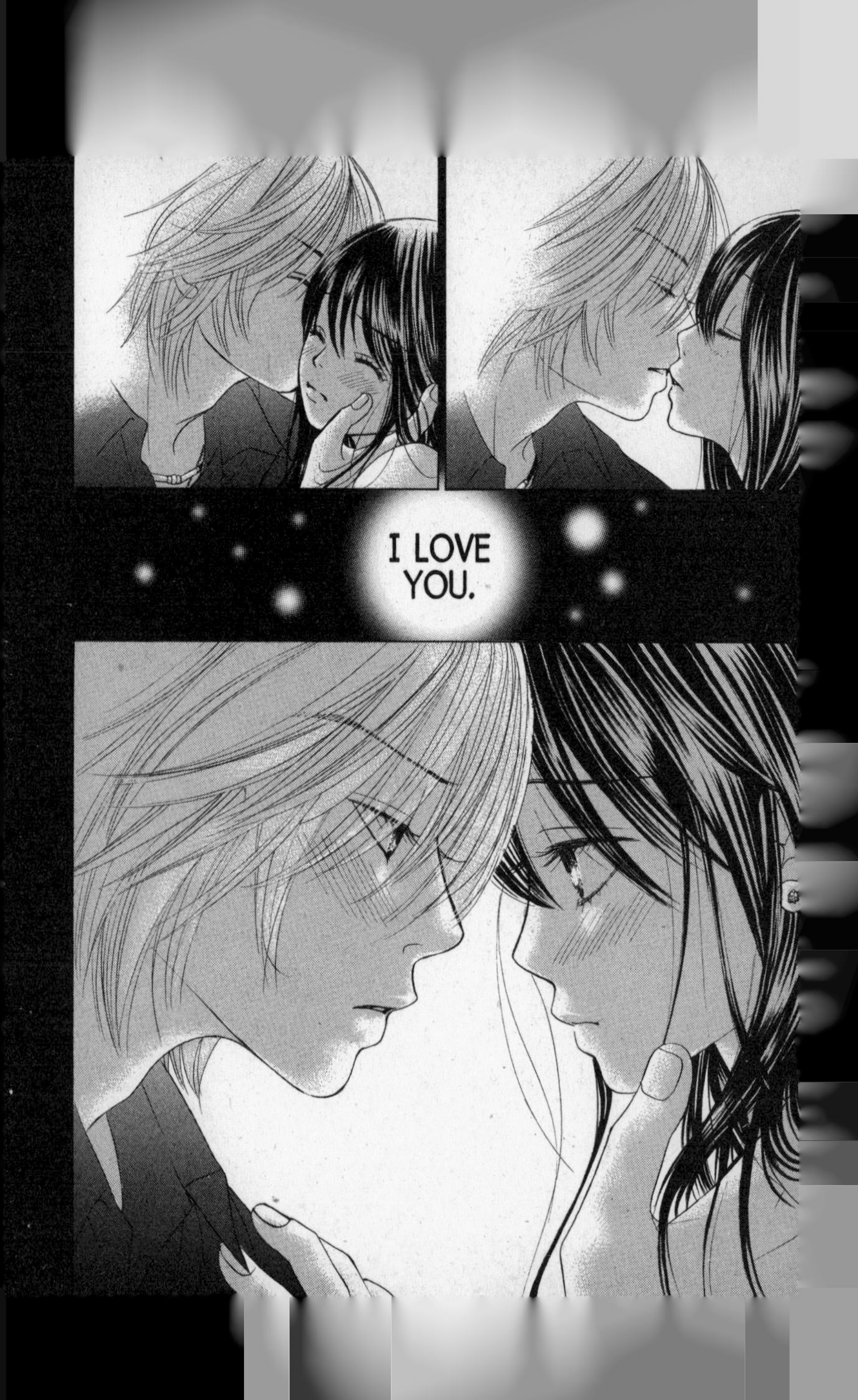
I LOVE YOU.

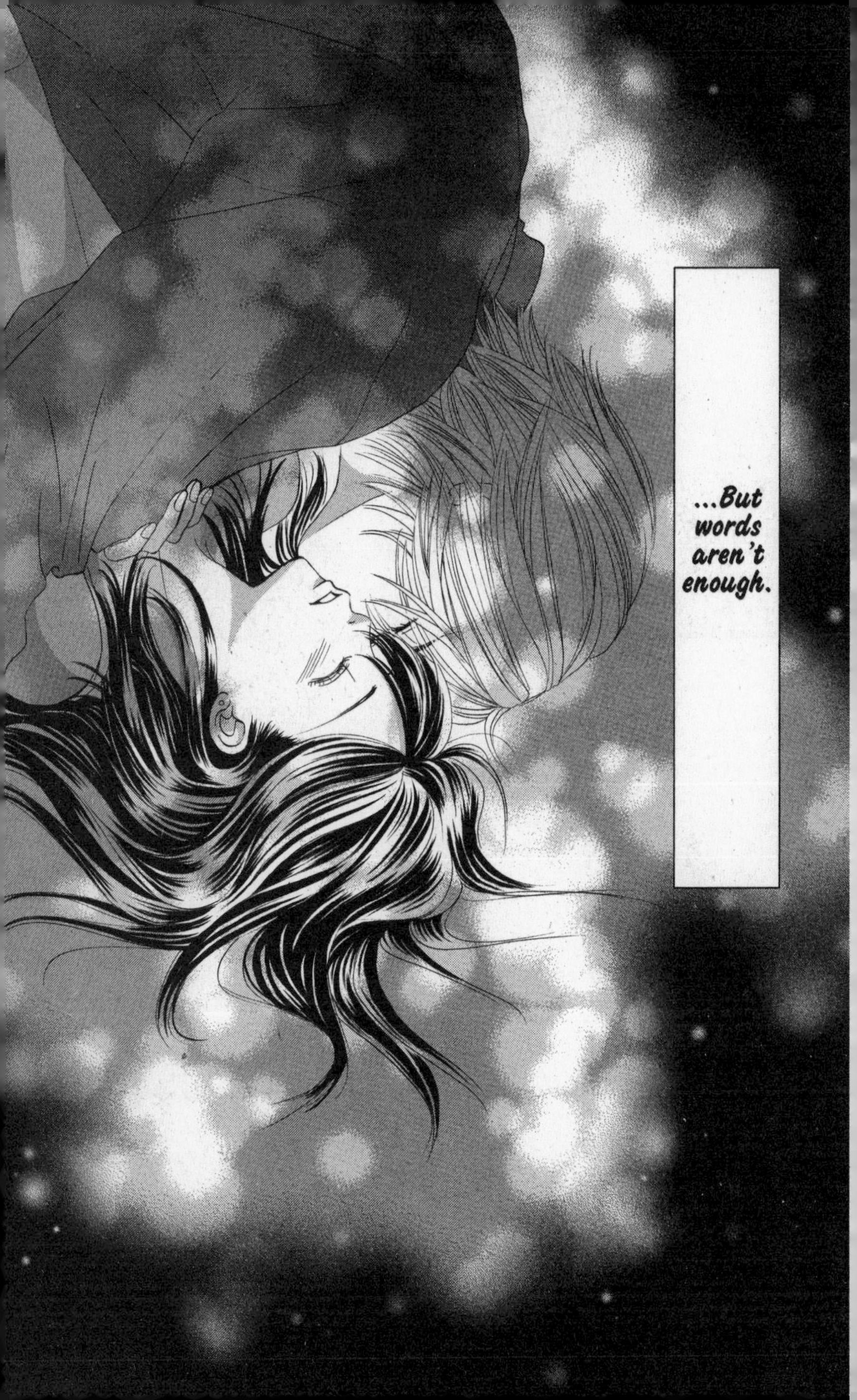
...But words aren't enough.

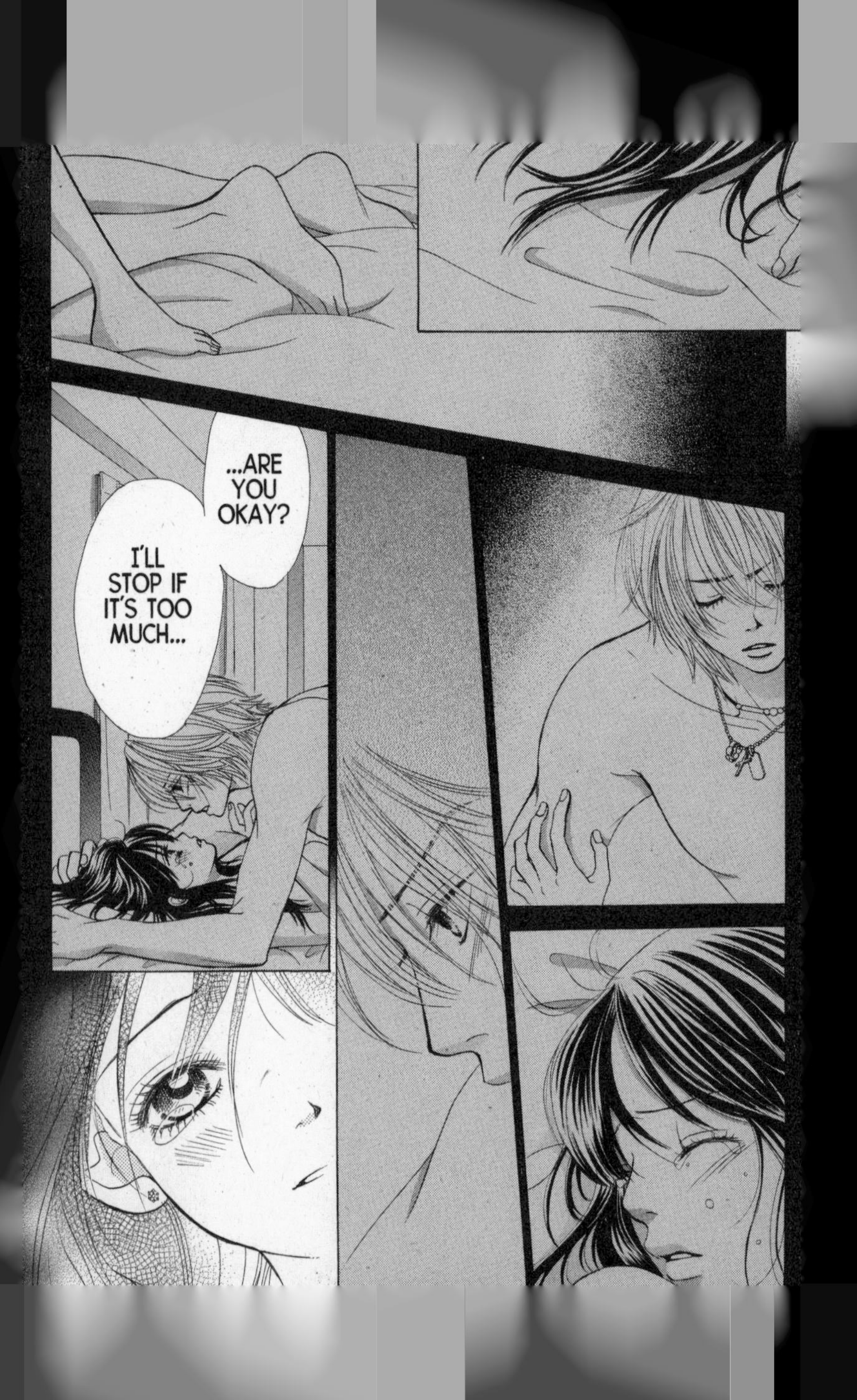
...ARE YOU OKAY?
I'LL STOP IF IT'S TOO MUCH...

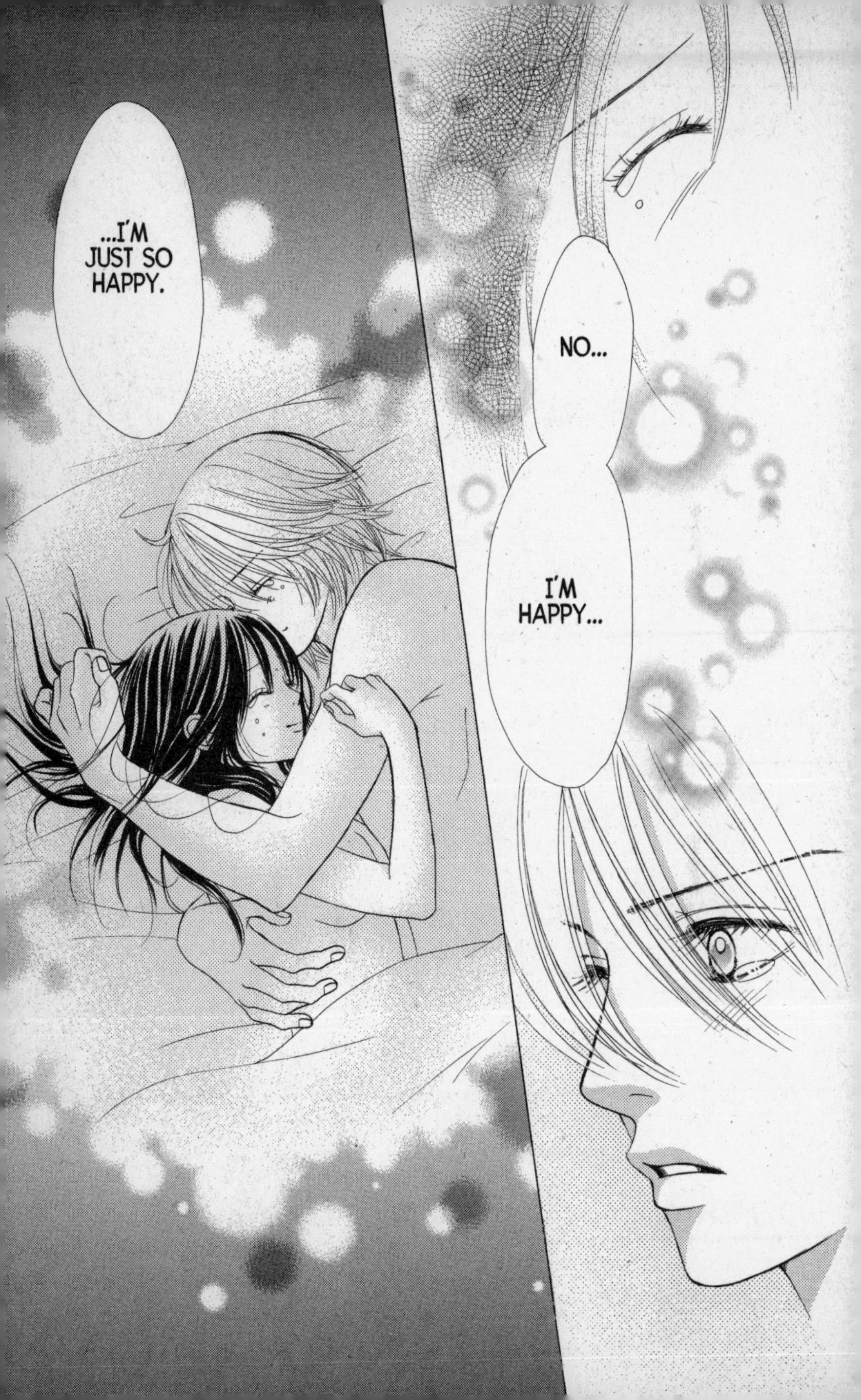
NO...
I'M HAPPY...
...I'M JUST SO HAPPY.

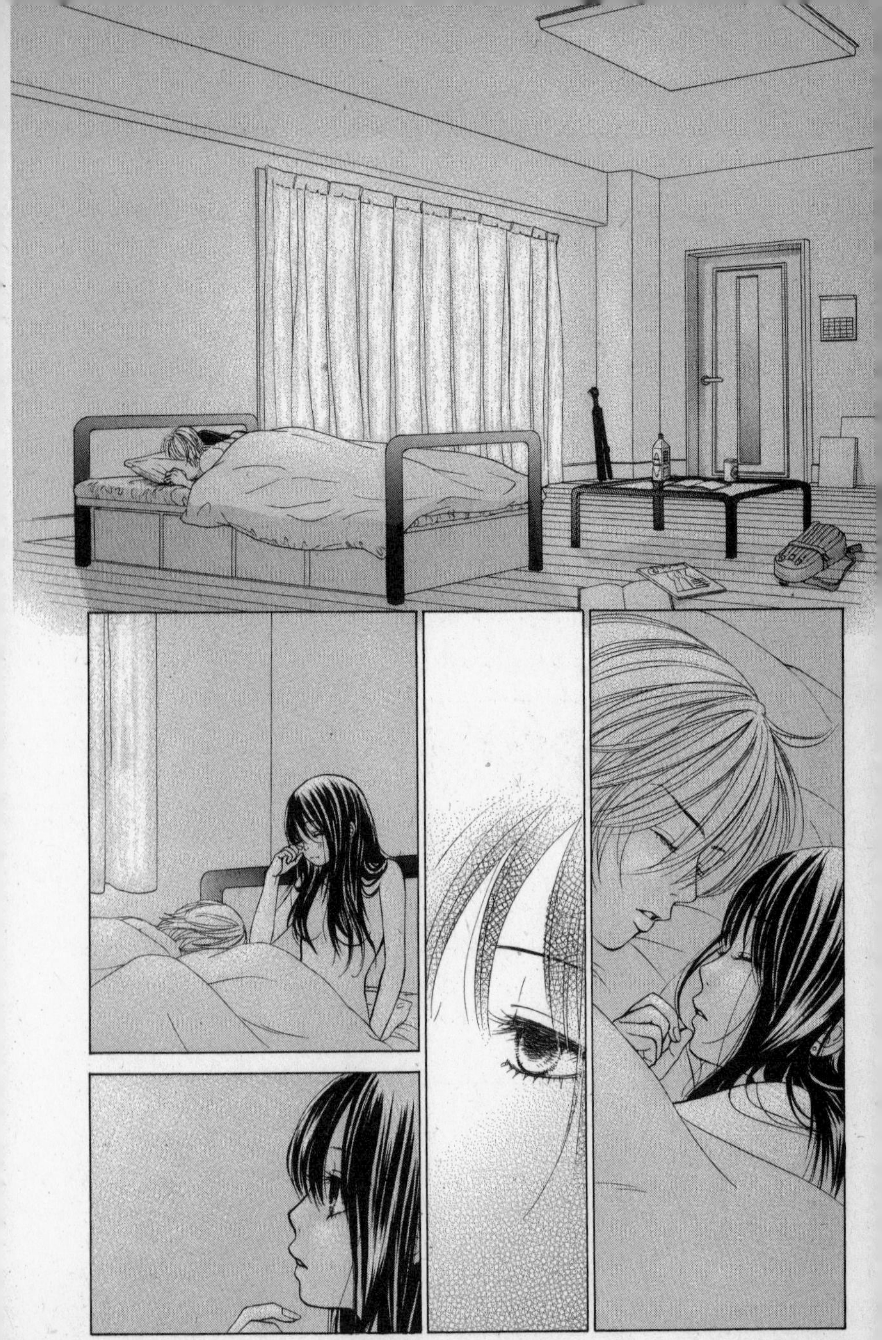

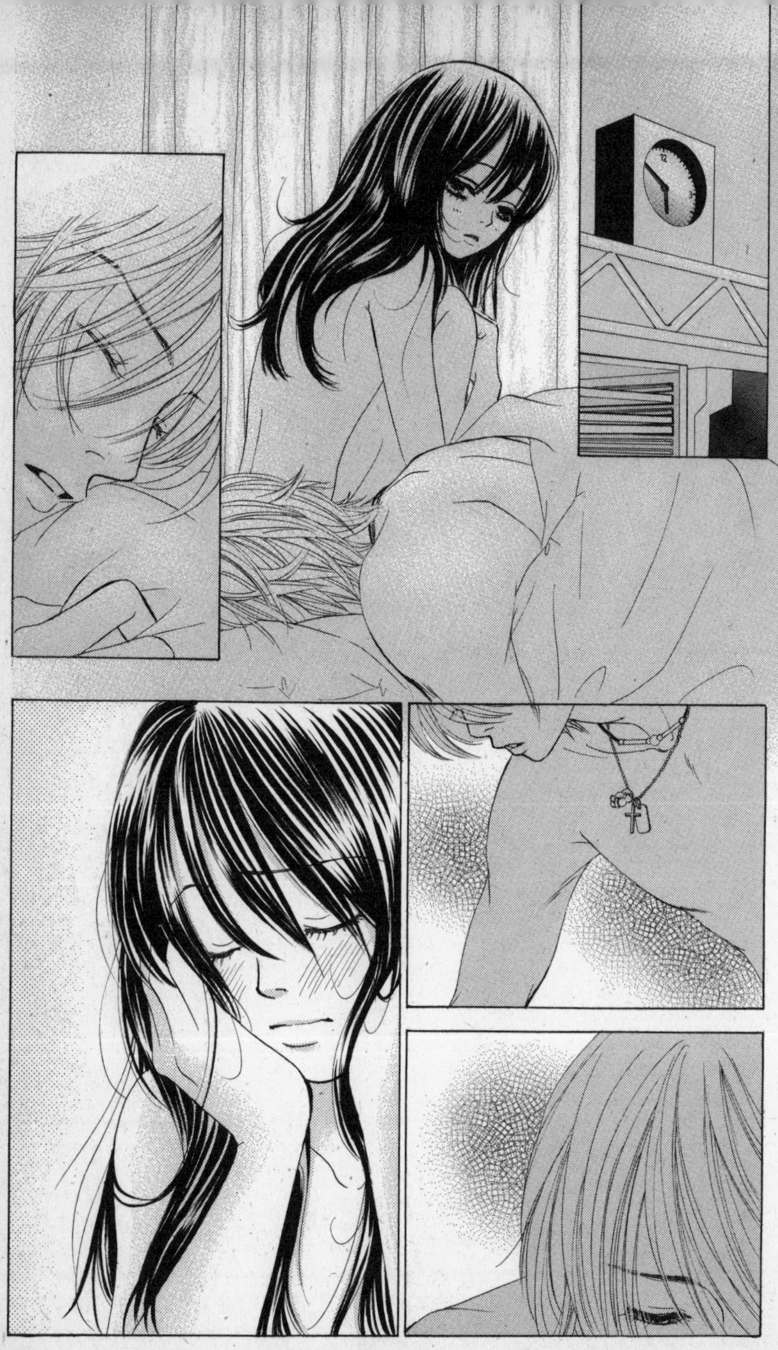

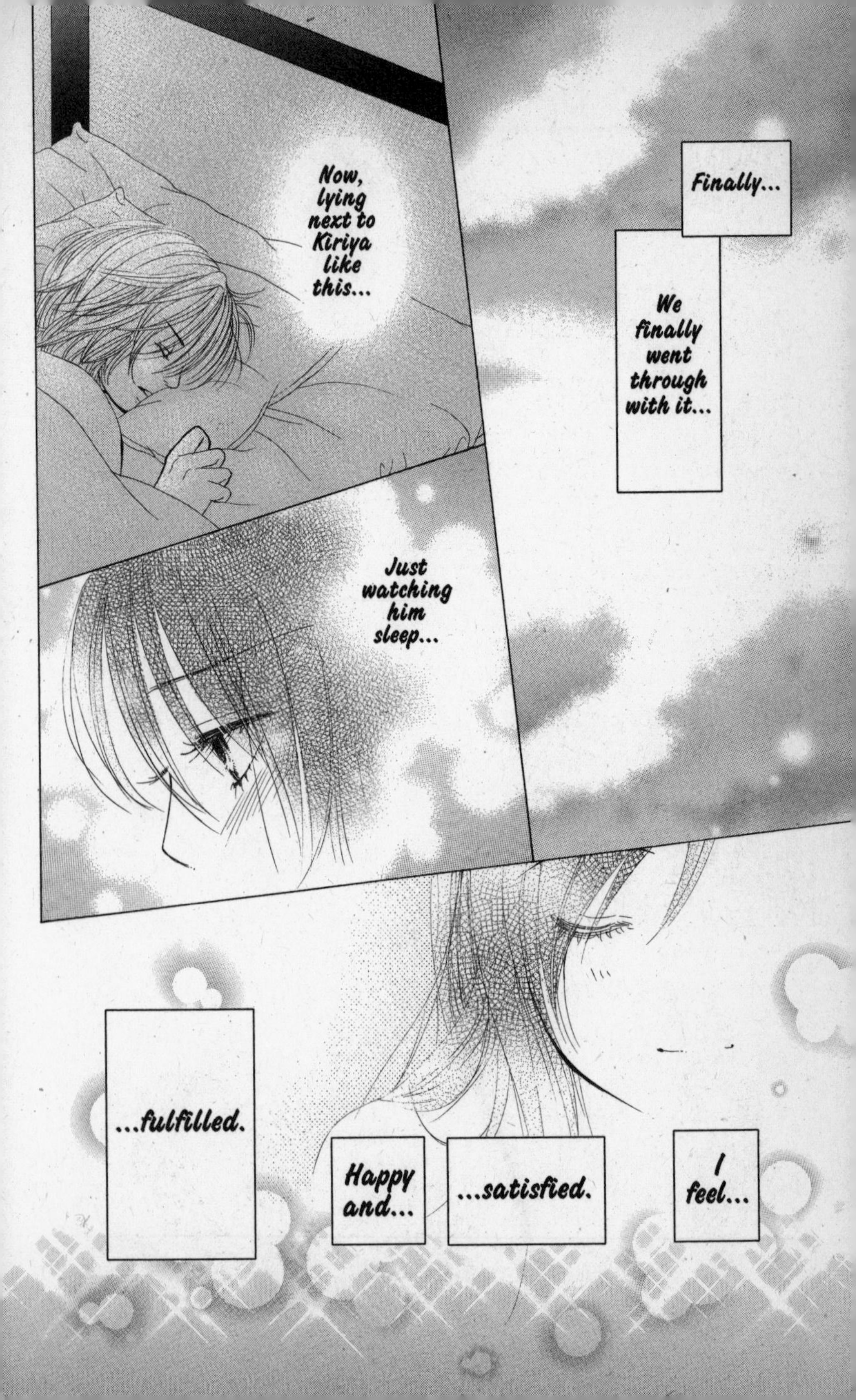
Finally...
We finally went through with it...
Now, lying next to Kiriya like this...
Just watching him sleep...
I feel...
...satisfied.
Happy and...
...fulfilled.

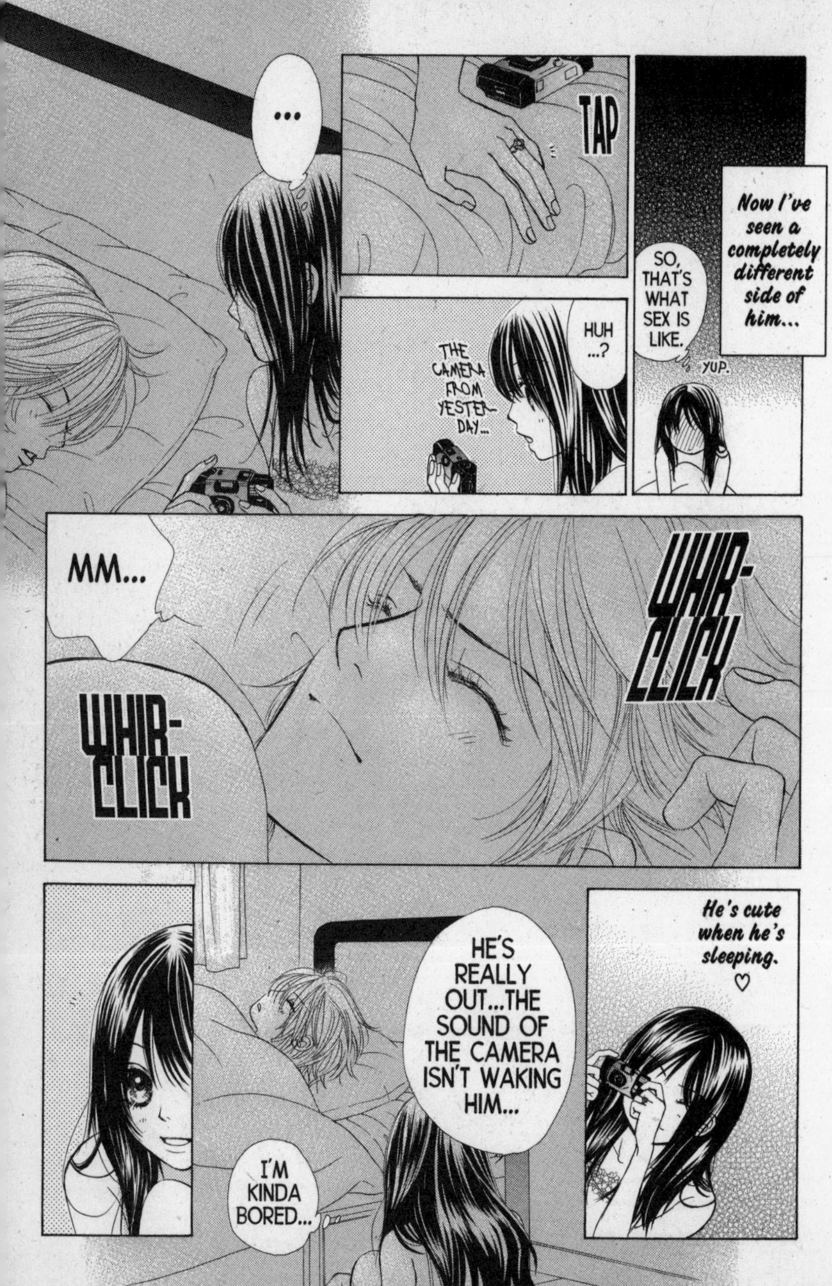

Now I've seen a completely different side of him...
SO, THAT'S WHAT SEX IS LIKE.
YUP.
TAP
HUH ...?
THE CAMERA FROM YESTERDAY...
...
WHIR-CLICK
MM...
WHIR-CLICK
He's cute when he's sleeping. ♡
HE'S REALLY OUT...THE SOUND OF THE CAMERA ISN'T WAKING HIM...
I'M KINDA BORED...

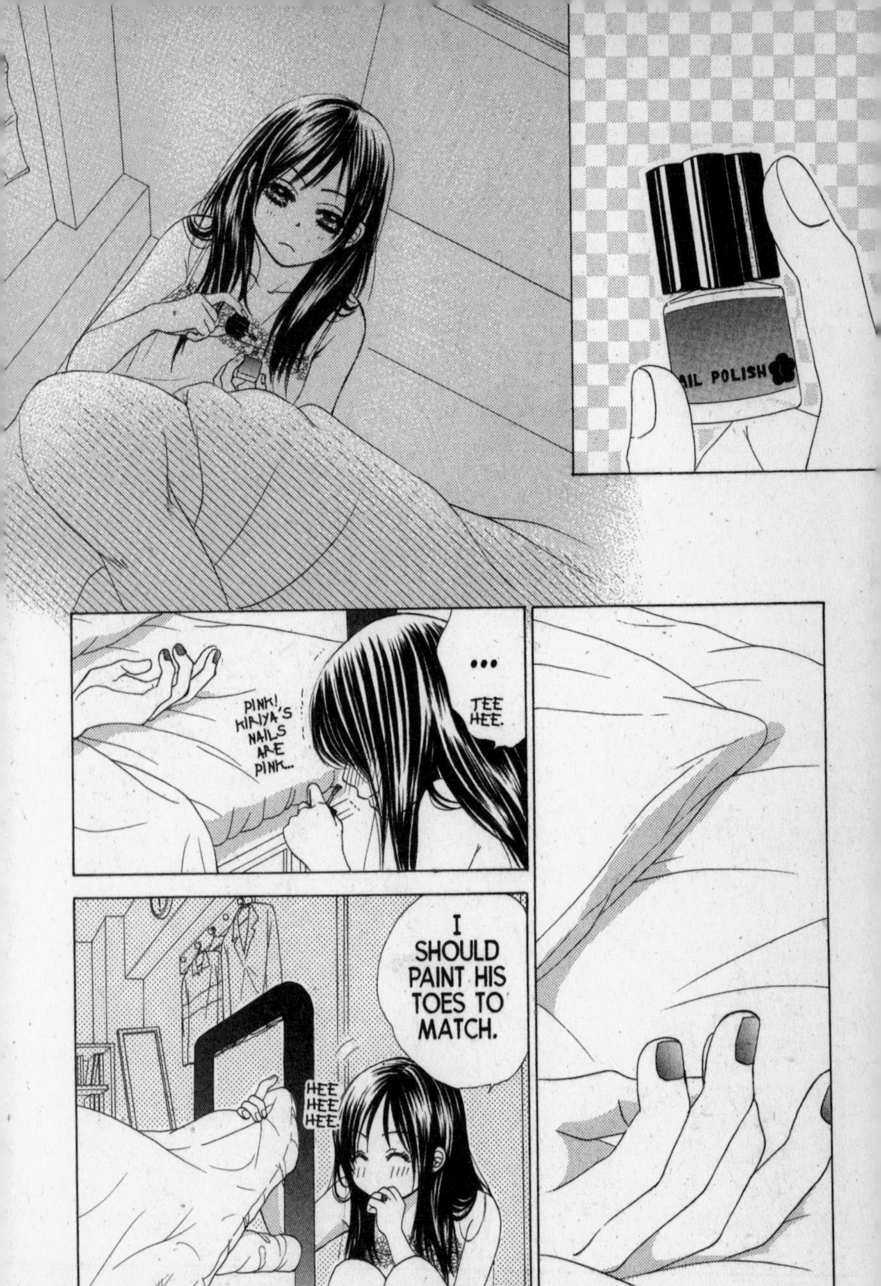
AIL POLISH
...
TEE HEE.
PINK! KIRIYA'S NAILS ARE PINK...
I SHOULD PAINT HIS TOES TO MATCH.
HEE HEE HEE.

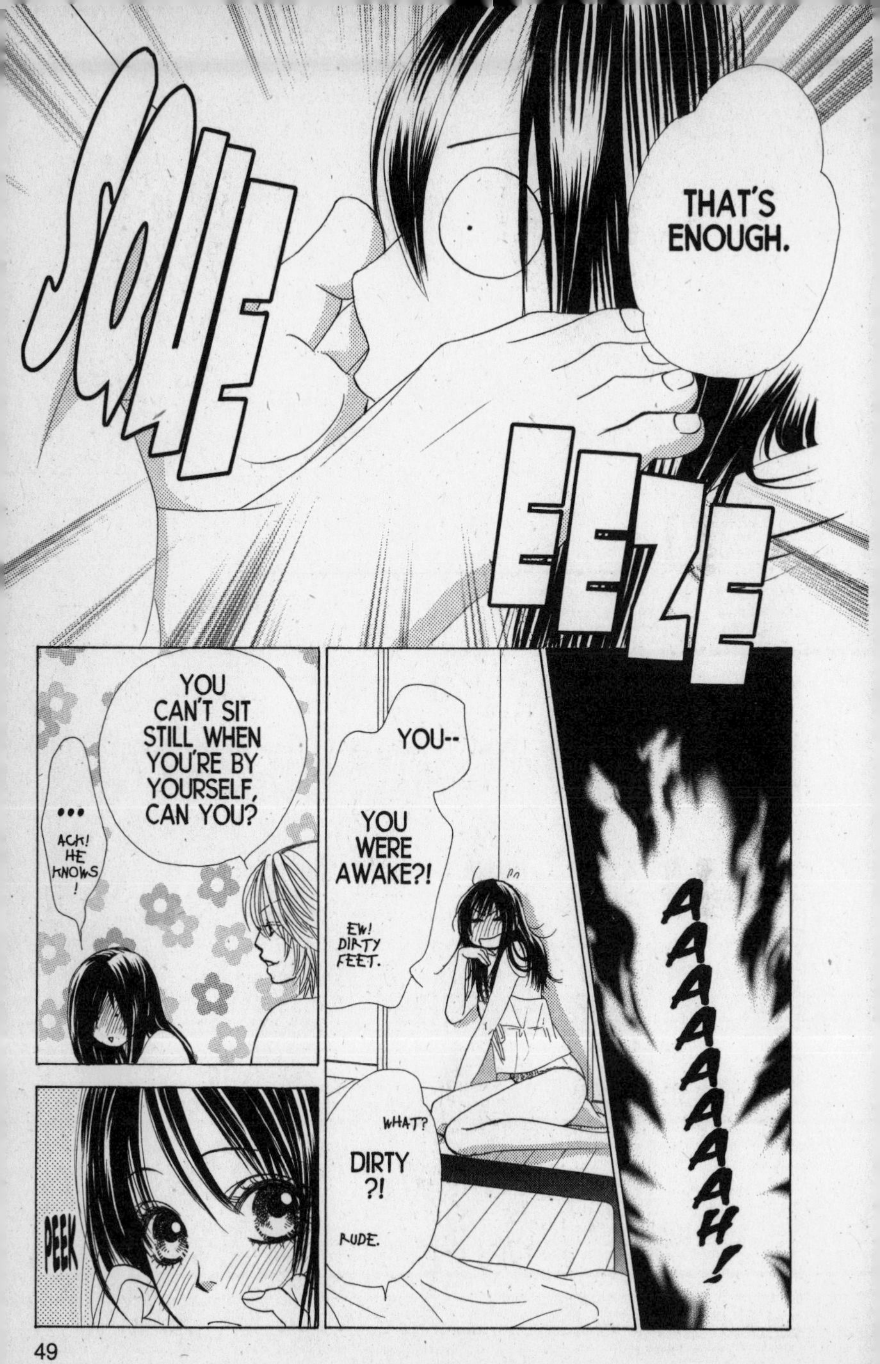
THAT'S ENOUGH.
SQUE
EEZE
AAAAAAAAAH!
YOU--
YOU WERE AWAKE?!
EW! DIRTY FEET.
WHAT?
DIRTY ?!
RUDE.
YOU CAN'T SIT STILL WHEN YOU'RE BY YOURSELF, CAN YOU?
...
ACK! HE KNOWS!
PEEK

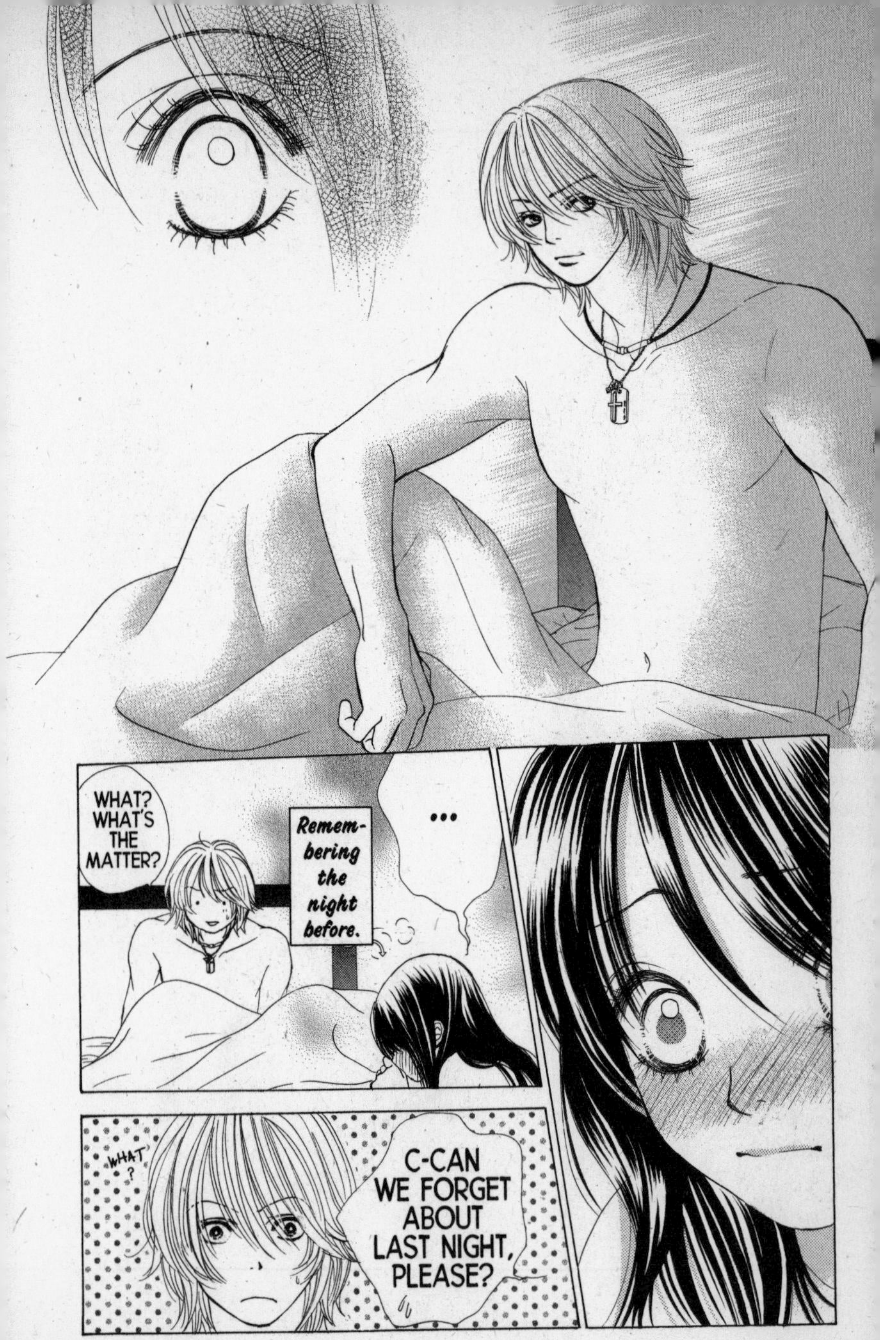
...
Remembering the night before.
WHAT? WHAT'S THE MATTER?
C-CAN WE FORGET ABOUT LAST NIGHT, PLEASE?
WHAT?

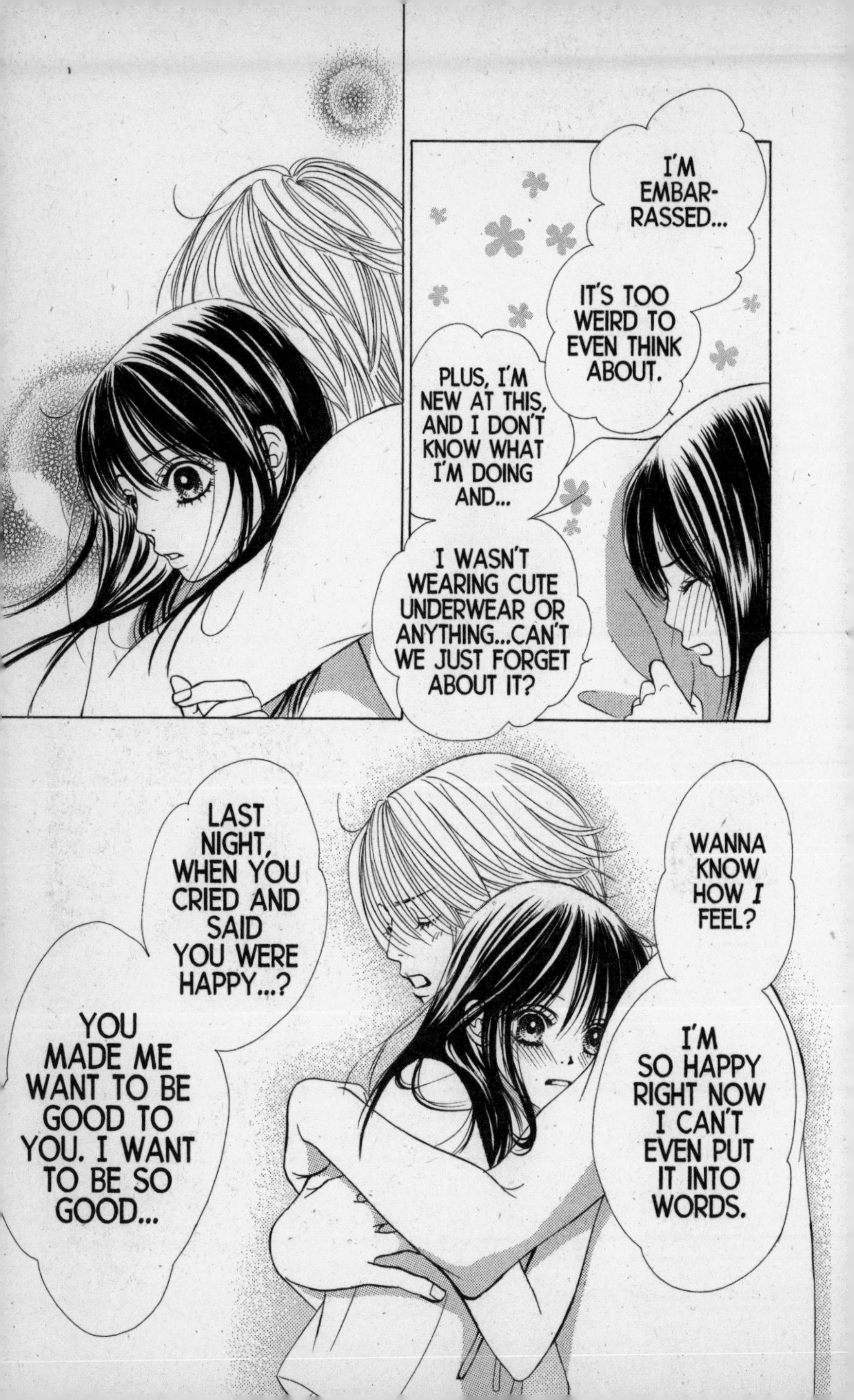
I'M EMBARRASSED...
IT'S TOO WEIRD TO EVEN THINK ABOUT.
PLUS, I'M NEW AT THIS, AND I DON'T KNOW WHAT I'M DOING AND...
I WASN'T WEARING CUTE UNDERWEAR OR ANYTHING...CAN'T WE JUST FORGET ABOUT IT?
WANNA KNOW HOW *I* FEEL?
I'M SO HAPPY RIGHT NOW I CAN'T EVEN PUT IT INTO WORDS.
LAST NIGHT, WHEN YOU CRIED AND SAID YOU WERE HAPPY...?
YOU MADE ME WANT TO BE GOOD TO YOU. I WANT TO BE SO GOOD...

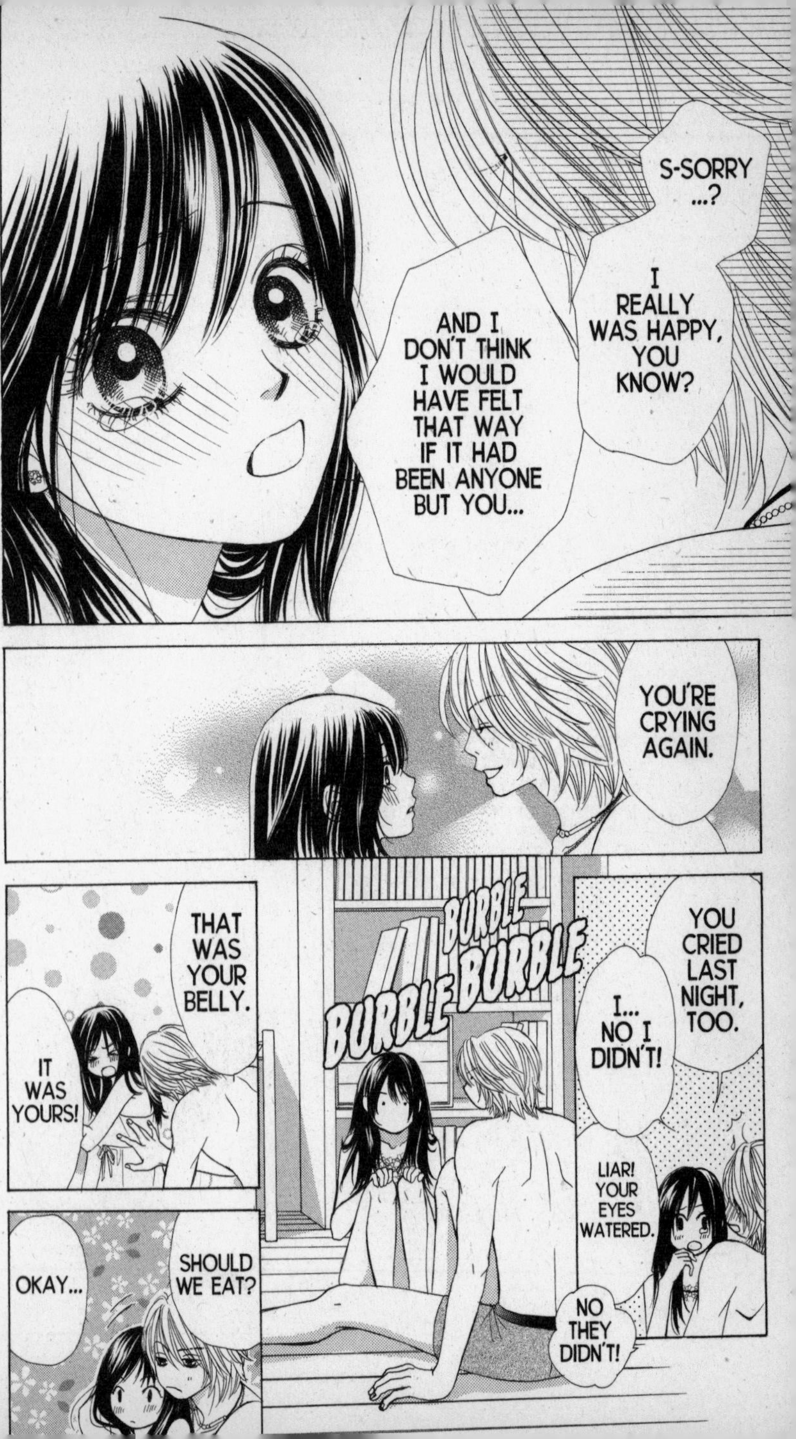
S-SORRY ...?
I REALLY WAS HAPPY, YOU KNOW?
AND I DON'T THINK I WOULD HAVE FELT THAT WAY IF IT HAD BEEN ANYONE BUT YOU...
YOU'RE CRYING AGAIN.
YOU CRIED LAST NIGHT, TOO.
I... NO I DIDN'T!
LIAR! YOUR EYES WATERED.
NO THEY DIDN'T!
BURBLE BURBLE BURBLE
THAT WAS YOUR BELLY.
IT WAS YOURS!
SHOULD WE EAT?
OKAY...

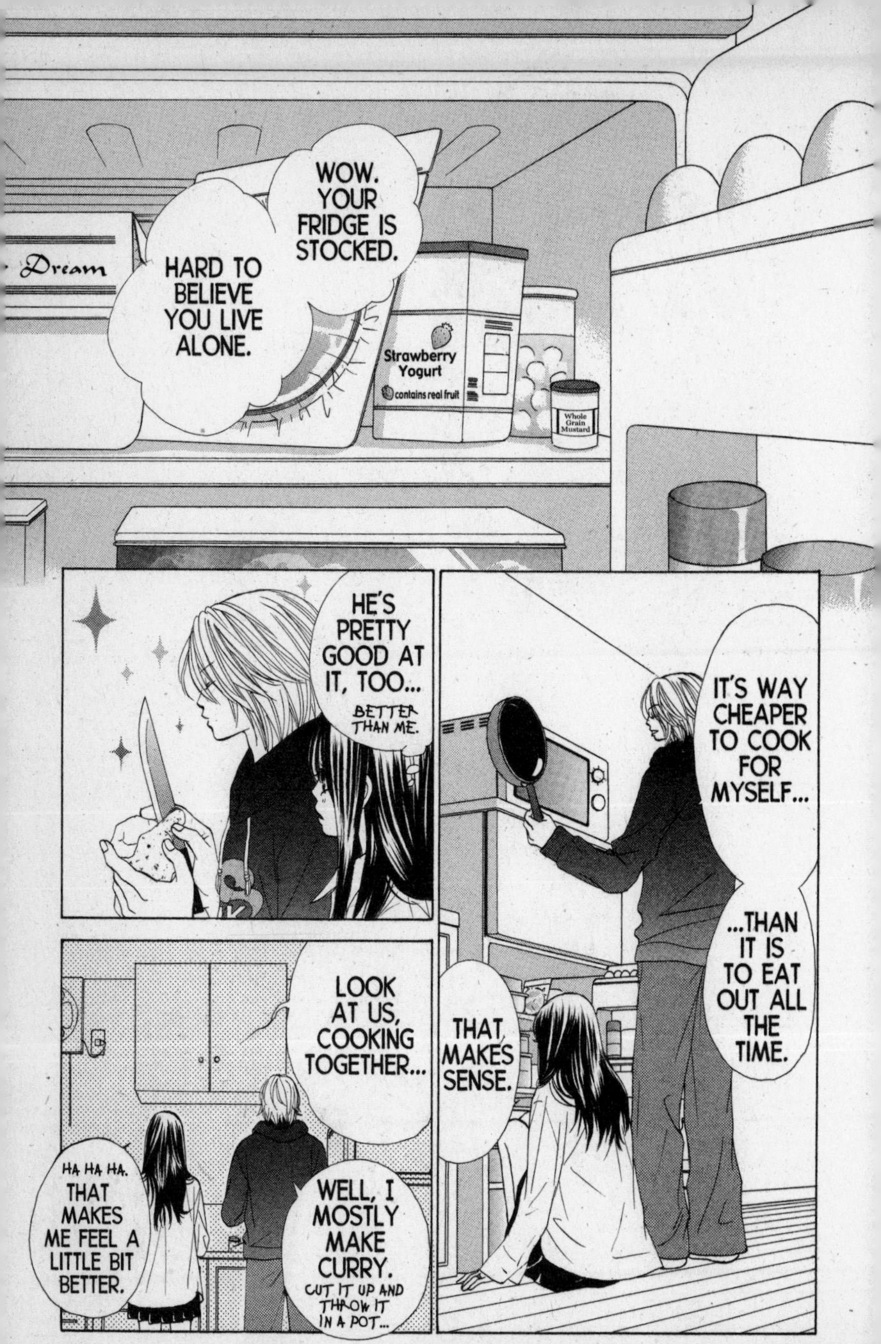
Dream
WOW. YOUR FRIDGE IS STOCKED.
HARD TO BELIEVE YOU LIVE ALONE.
Strawberry Yogurt
contains real fruit
Whole Grain Mustard
IT'S WAY CHEAPER TO COOK FOR MYSELF...
...THAN IT IS TO EAT OUT ALL THE TIME.
THAT MAKES SENSE.
HE'S PRETTY GOOD AT IT, TOO...
BETTER THAN ME.
LOOK AT US, COOKING TOGETHER...
WELL, I MOSTLY MAKE CURRY.
CUT IT UP AND THROW IT IN A POT...
HA HA HA.
THAT MAKES ME FEEL A LITTLE BIT BETTER.

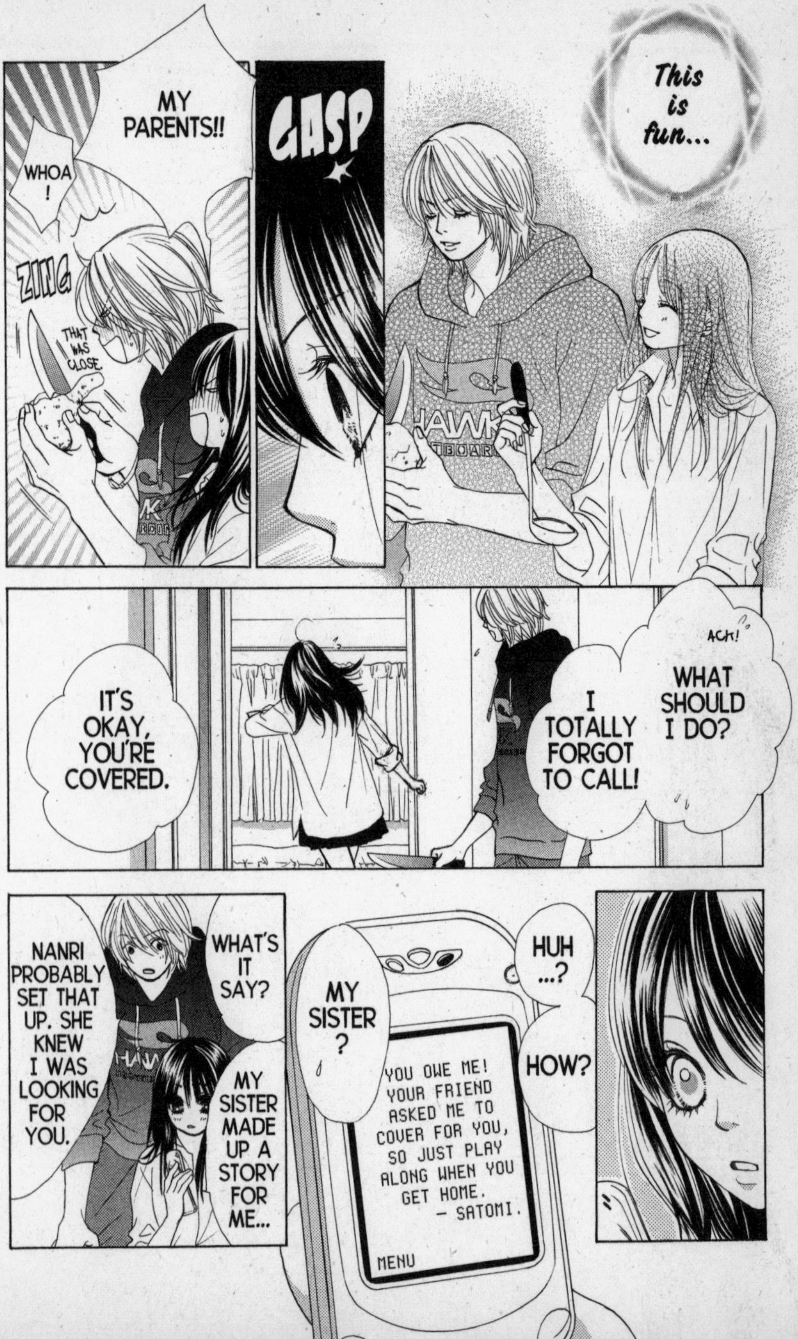
This is fun...
GASP
MY PARENTS!!
WHOA!
ZING
THAT WAS CLOSE.
ACK!
WHAT SHOULD I DO?
I TOTALLY FORGOT TO CALL!
IT'S OKAY, YOU'RE COVERED.
HUH...?
HOW?
MY SISTER?
YOU OWE ME! YOUR FRIEND ASKED ME TO COVER FOR YOU, SO JUST PLAY ALONG WHEN YOU GET HOME. — SATOMI.
MENU
WHAT'S IT SAY?
MY SISTER MADE UP A STORY FOR ME...
NANRI PROBABLY SET THAT UP. SHE KNEW I WAS LOOKING FOR YOU.

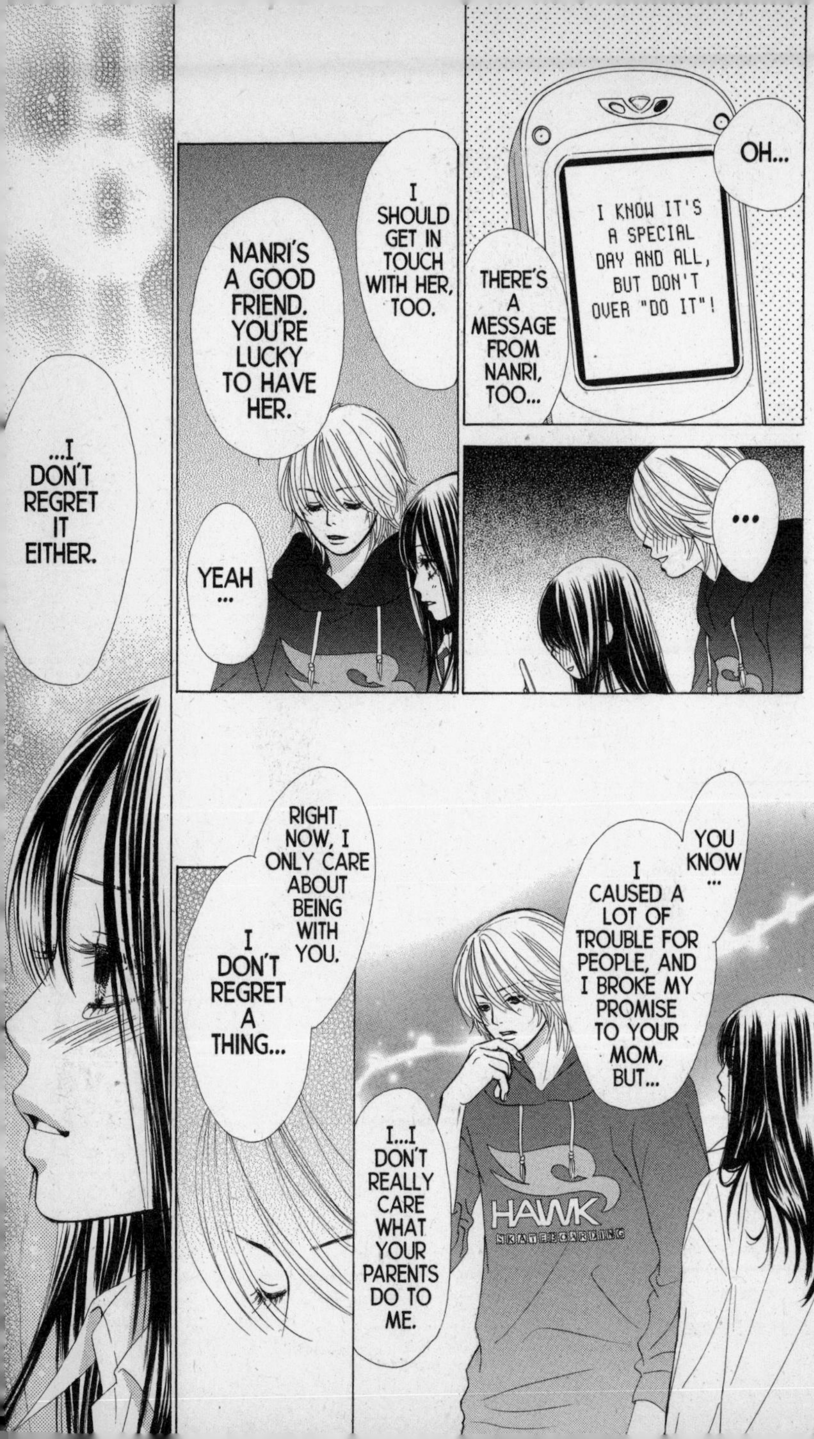
OH...
I KNOW IT'S A SPECIAL DAY AND ALL, BUT DON'T OVER "DO IT"!
THERE'S A MESSAGE FROM NANRI, TOO...
...
I SHOULD GET IN TOUCH WITH HER, TOO.
NANRI'S A GOOD FRIEND. YOU'RE LUCKY TO HAVE HER.
YEAH...
YOU KNOW...
I CAUSED A LOT OF TROUBLE FOR PEOPLE, AND I BROKE MY PROMISE TO YOUR MOM, BUT...
I...I DON'T REALLY CARE WHAT YOUR PARENTS DO TO ME.
RIGHT NOW, I ONLY CARE ABOUT BEING WITH YOU.
I DON'T REGRET A THING...
...I DON'T REGRET IT EITHER.

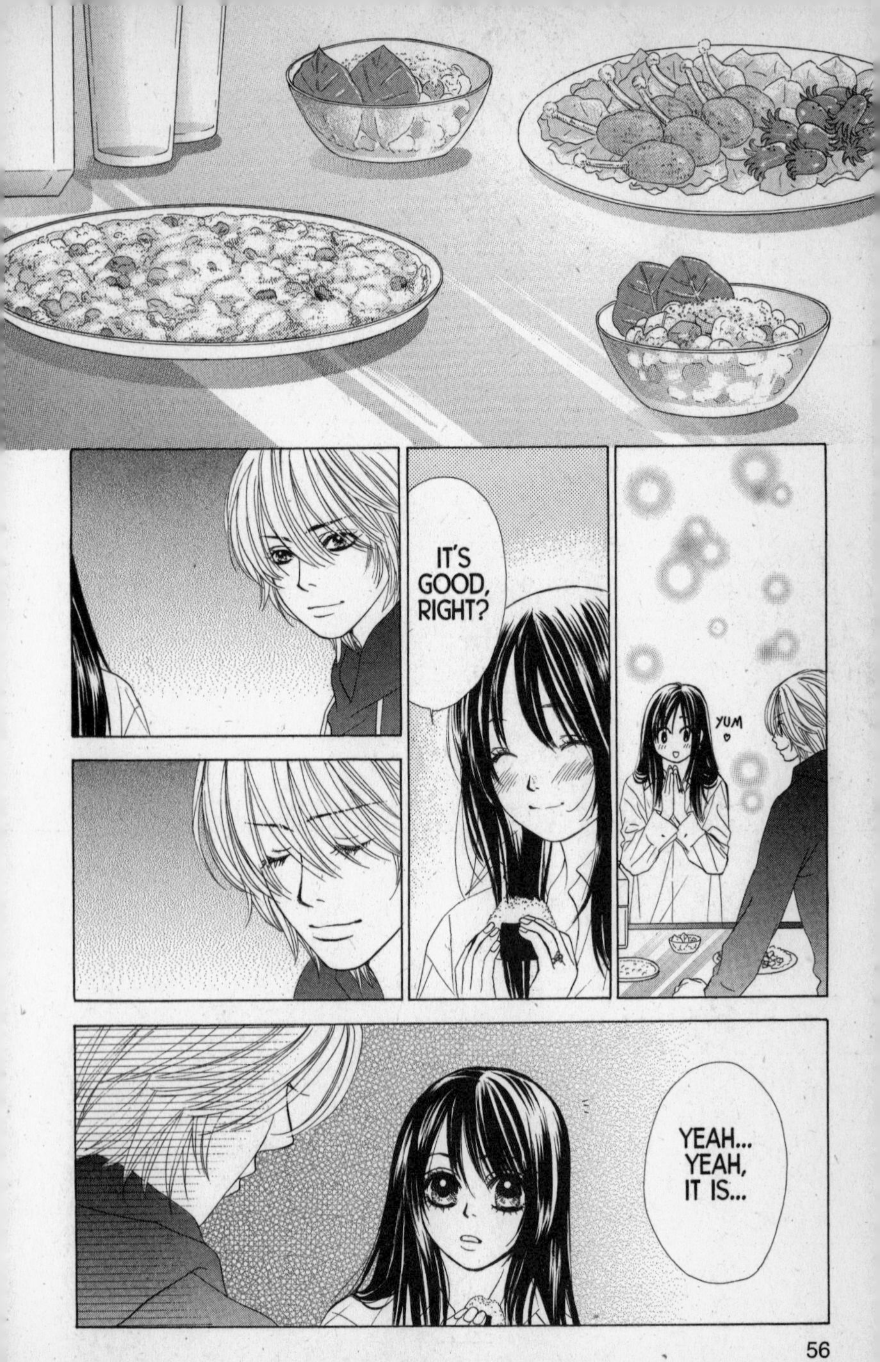
YUM
IT'S GOOD, RIGHT?
YEAH... YEAH, IT IS...

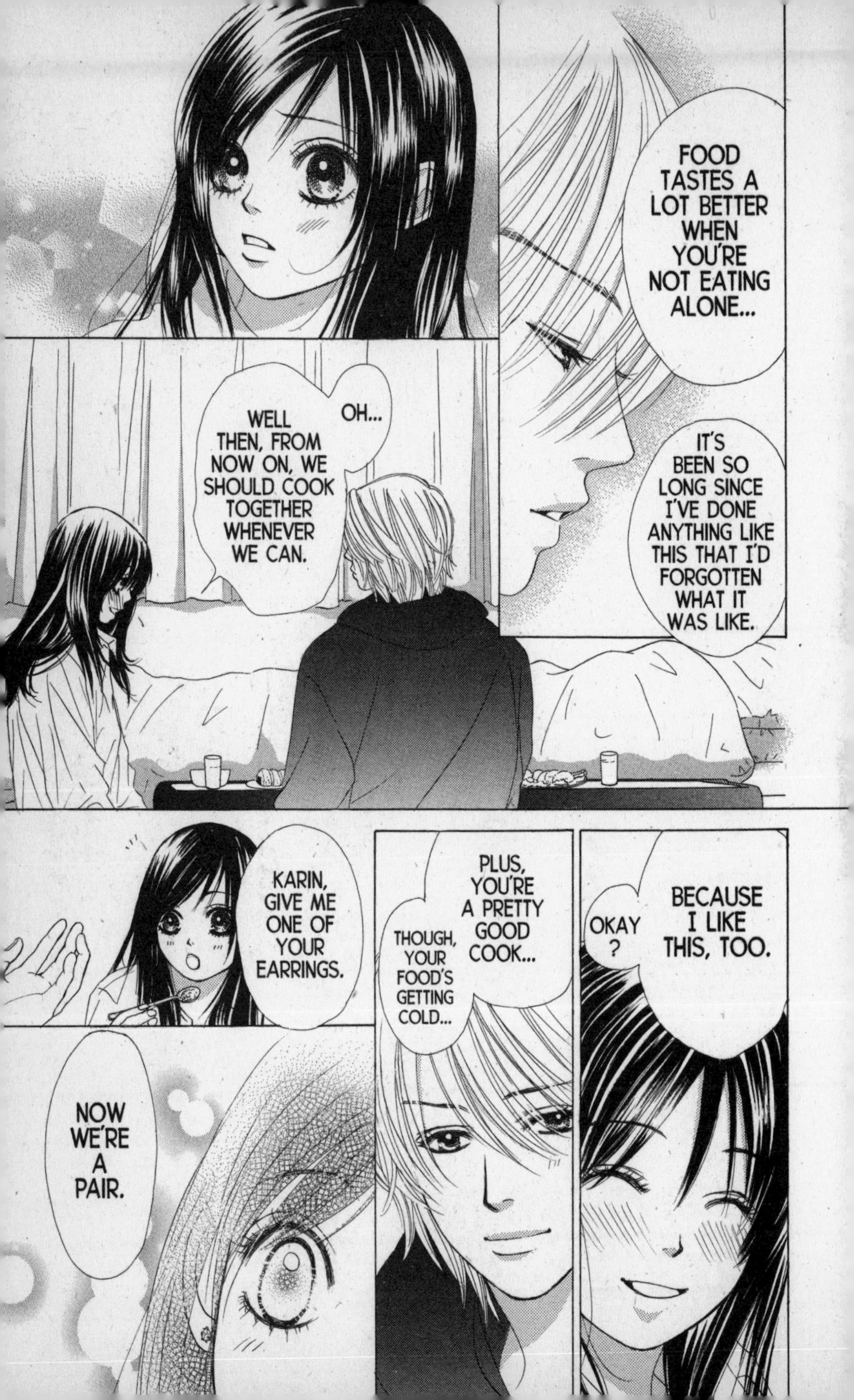
FOOD TASTES A LOT BETTER WHEN YOU'RE NOT EATING ALONE...
IT'S BEEN SO LONG SINCE I'VE DONE ANYTHING LIKE THIS THAT I'D FORGOTTEN WHAT IT WAS LIKE.
OH...
WELL THEN, FROM NOW ON, WE SHOULD COOK TOGETHER WHENEVER WE CAN.
BECAUSE I LIKE THIS, TOO.
OKAY?
PLUS, YOU'RE A PRETTY GOOD COOK...
THOUGH, YOUR FOOD'S GETTING COLD...
KARIN, GIVE ME ONE OF YOUR EARRINGS.
NOW WE'RE A PAIR.

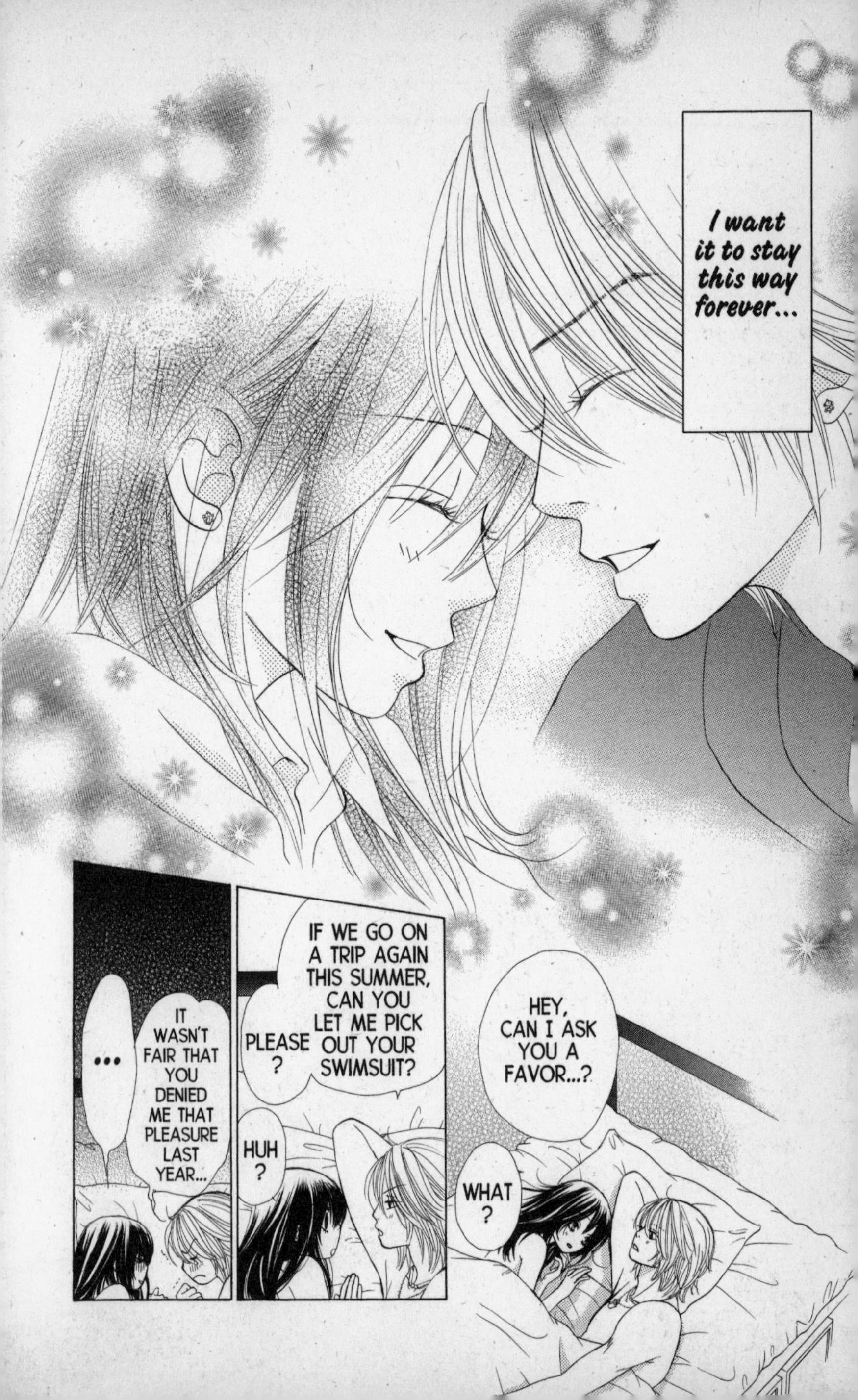

I want it to stay this way forever...
HEY, CAN I ASK YOU A FAVOR...?
WHAT?
IF WE GO ON A TRIP AGAIN THIS SUMMER, CAN YOU LET ME PICK OUT YOUR SWIMSUIT?
PLEASE?
HUH?
IT WASN'T FAIR THAT YOU DENIED ME THAT PLEASURE LAST YEAR...
...

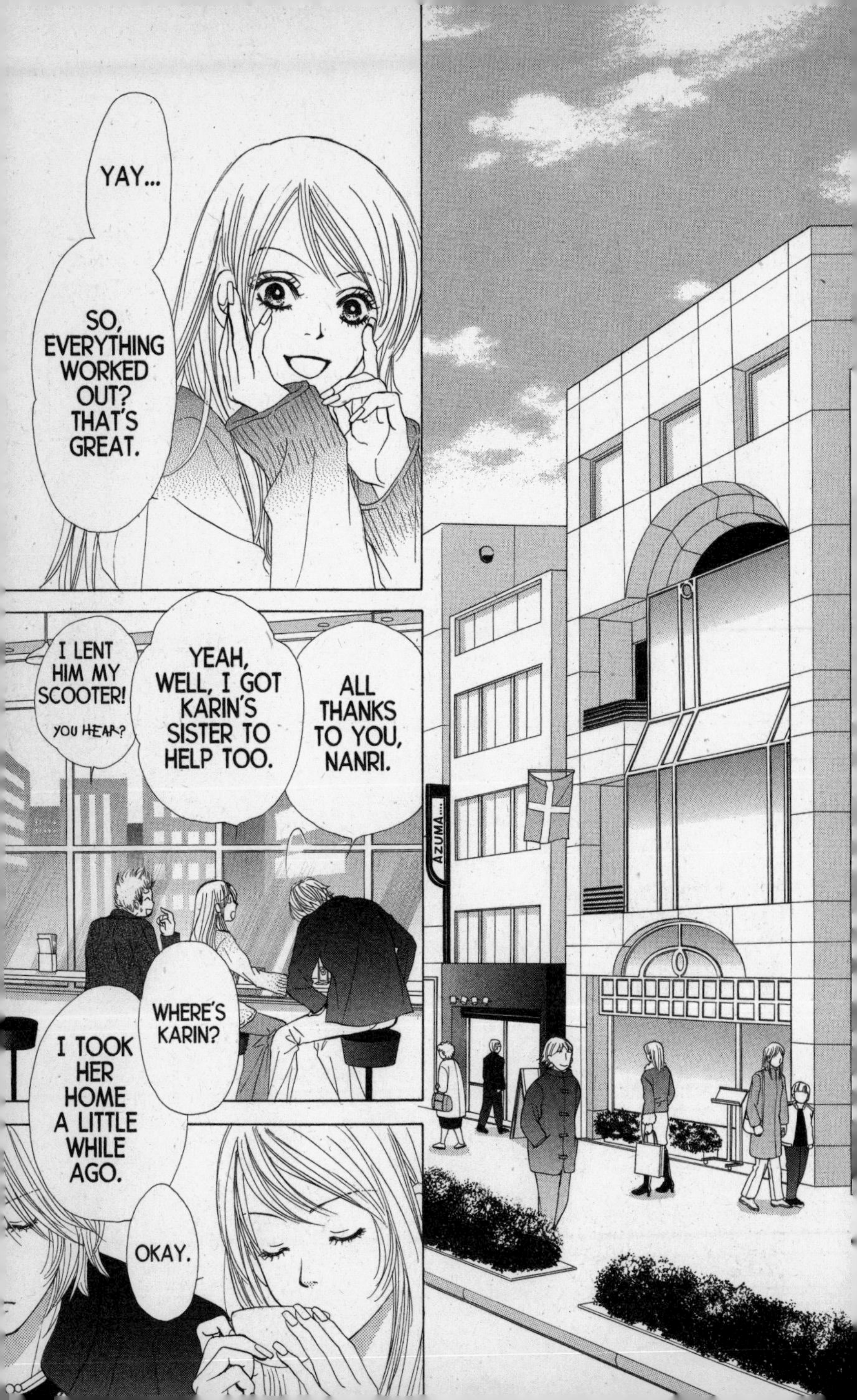
AZUMA...
YAY...
SO, EVERYTHING WORKED OUT? THAT'S GREAT.
ALL THANKS TO YOU, NANRI.
YEAH, WELL, I GOT KARIN'S SISTER TO HELP TOO.
I LENT HIM MY SCOOTER!
YOU HEAR?
WHERE'S KARIN?
I TOOK HER HOME A LITTLE WHILE AGO.
OKAY.

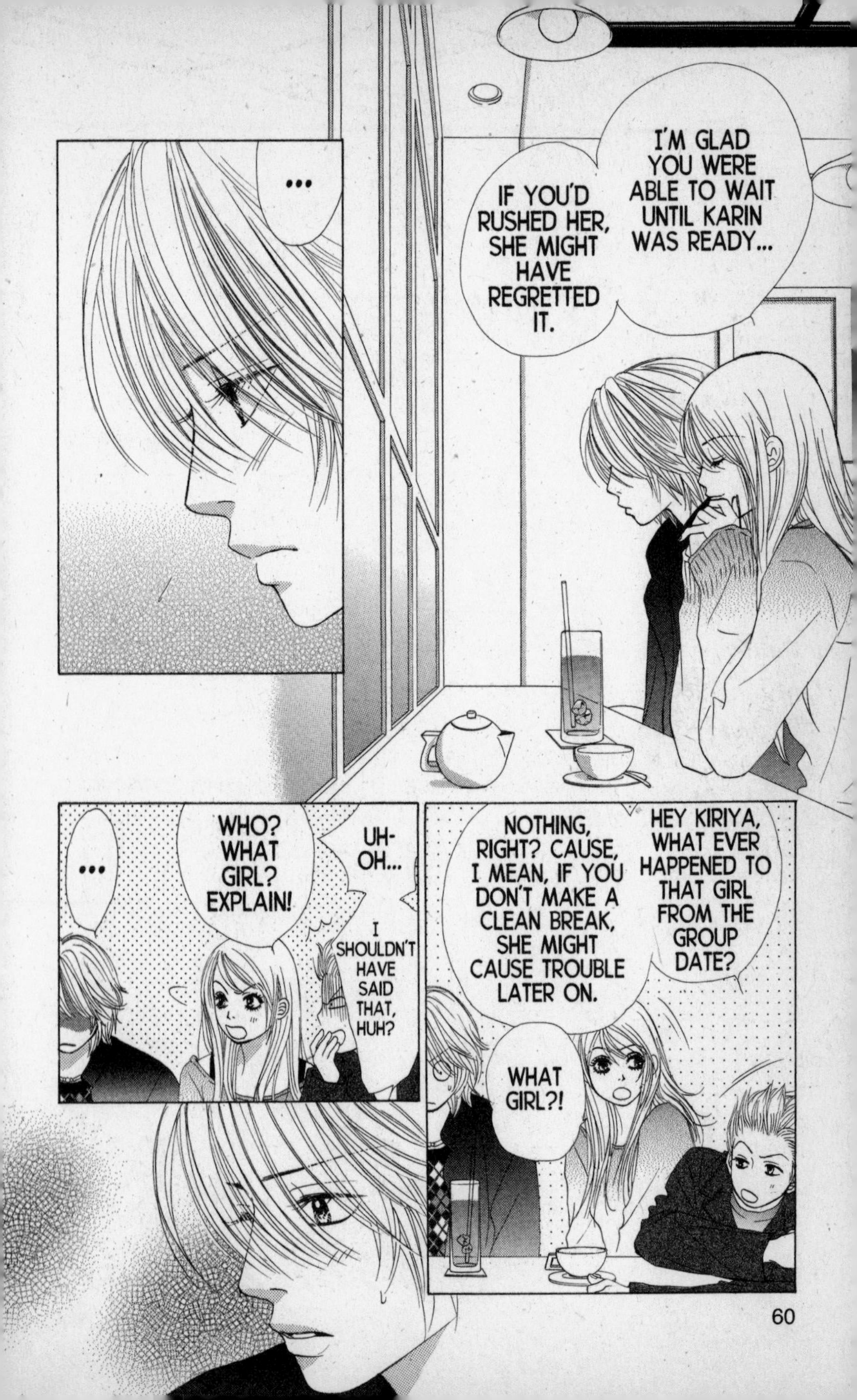
I'M GLAD YOU WERE ABLE TO WAIT UNTIL KARIN WAS READY...
IF YOU'D RUSHED HER, SHE MIGHT HAVE REGRETTED IT.
...
HEY KIRIYA, WHAT EVER HAPPENED TO THAT GIRL FROM THE GROUP DATE?
NOTHING, RIGHT? CAUSE, I MEAN, IF YOU DON'T MAKE A CLEAN BREAK, SHE MIGHT CAUSE TROUBLE LATER ON.
WHAT GIRL?!
UH-OH...
I SHOULDN'T HAVE SAID THAT, HUH?
WHO? WHAT GIRL? EXPLAIN!
...

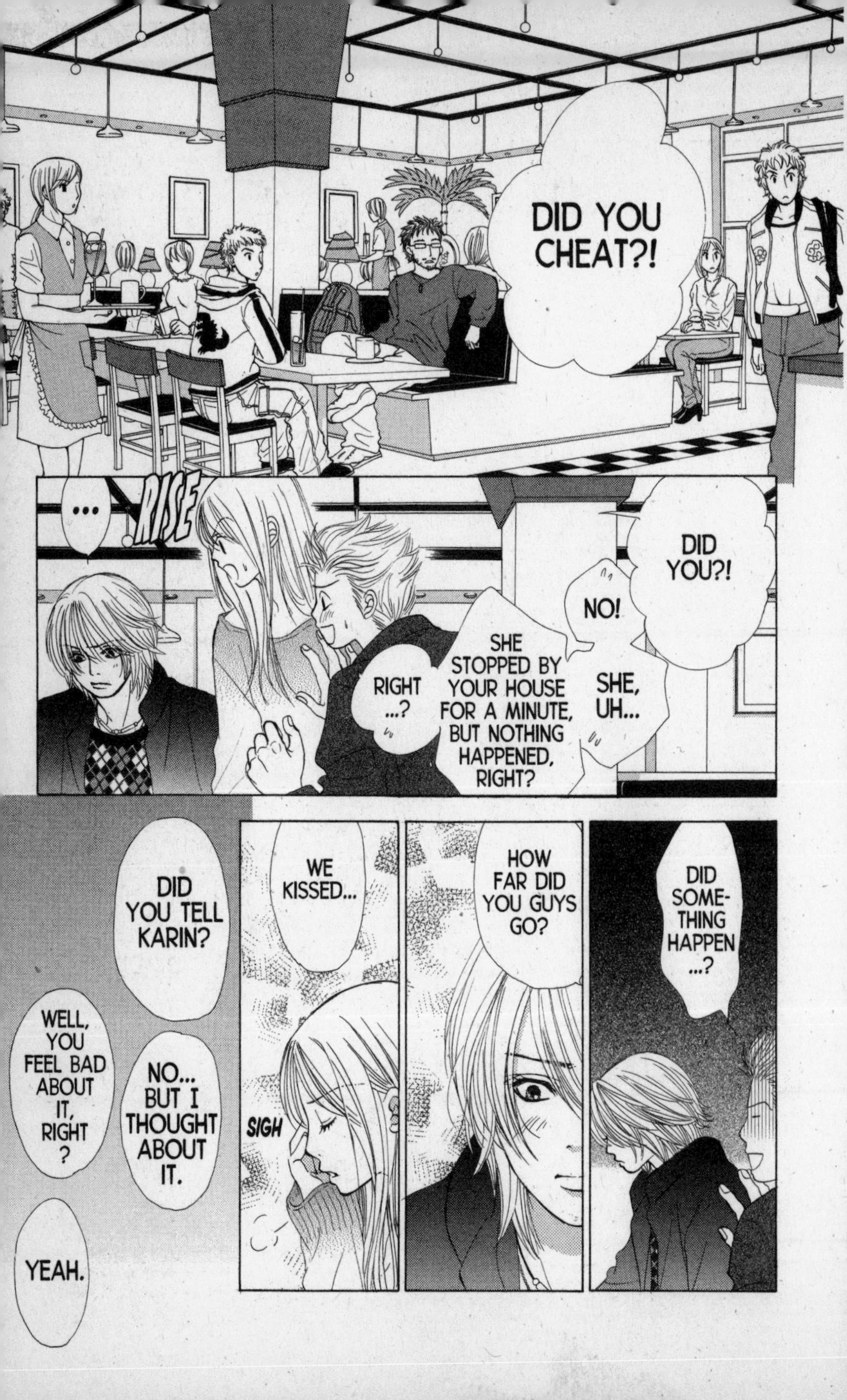
DID YOU CHEAT?!
DID YOU?!
NO!
SHE, UH...
SHE STOPPED BY YOUR HOUSE FOR A MINUTE, BUT NOTHING HAPPENED, RIGHT?
RIGHT ...?
RISE
...
DID SOME-THING HAPPEN ...?
HOW FAR DID YOU GUYS GO?
WE KISSED...
SIGH
DID YOU TELL KARIN?
NO... BUT I THOUGHT ABOUT IT.
WELL, YOU FEEL BAD ABOUT IT, RIGHT ?
YEAH.

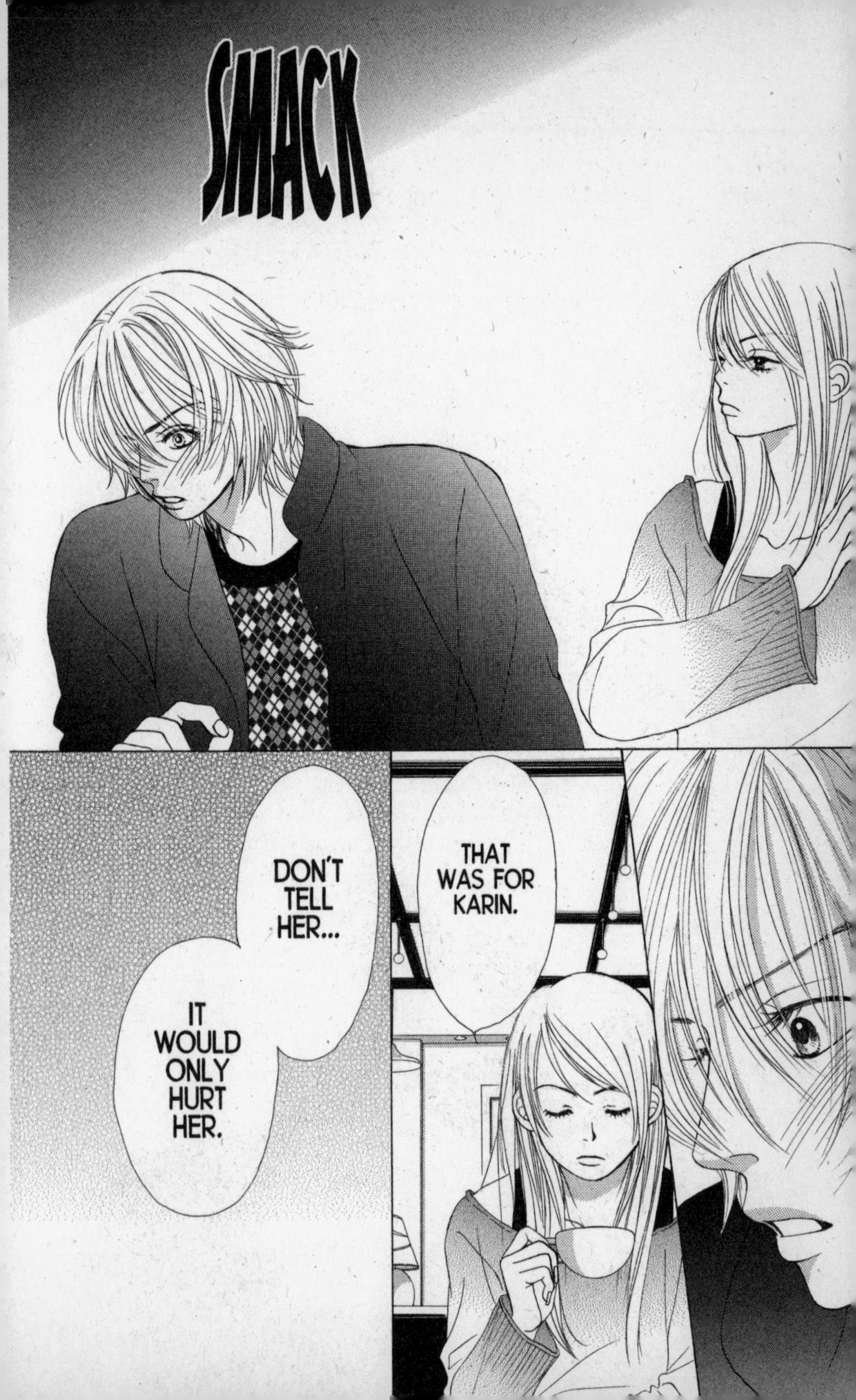
SMACK
THAT WAS FOR KARIN.
DON'T TELL HER...
IT WOULD ONLY HURT HER.

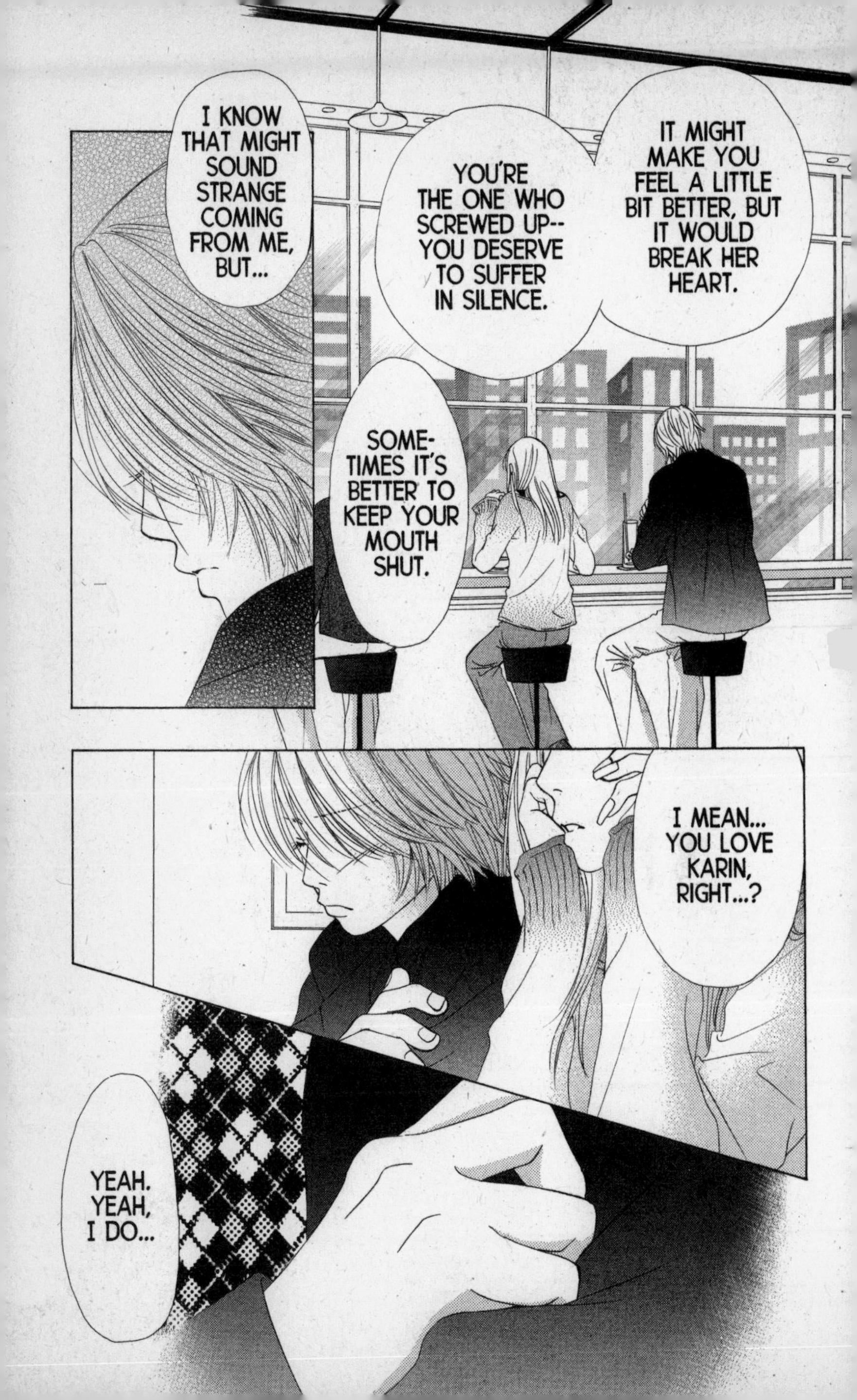
IT MIGHT MAKE YOU FEEL A LITTLE BIT BETTER, BUT IT WOULD BREAK HER HEART.
YOU'RE THE ONE WHO SCREWED UP-- YOU DESERVE TO SUFFER IN SILENCE.
SOME-TIMES IT'S BETTER TO KEEP YOUR MOUTH SHUT.
I KNOW THAT MIGHT SOUND STRANGE COMING FROM ME, BUT...
I MEAN... YOU LOVE KARIN, RIGHT...?
YEAH. YEAH, I DO...

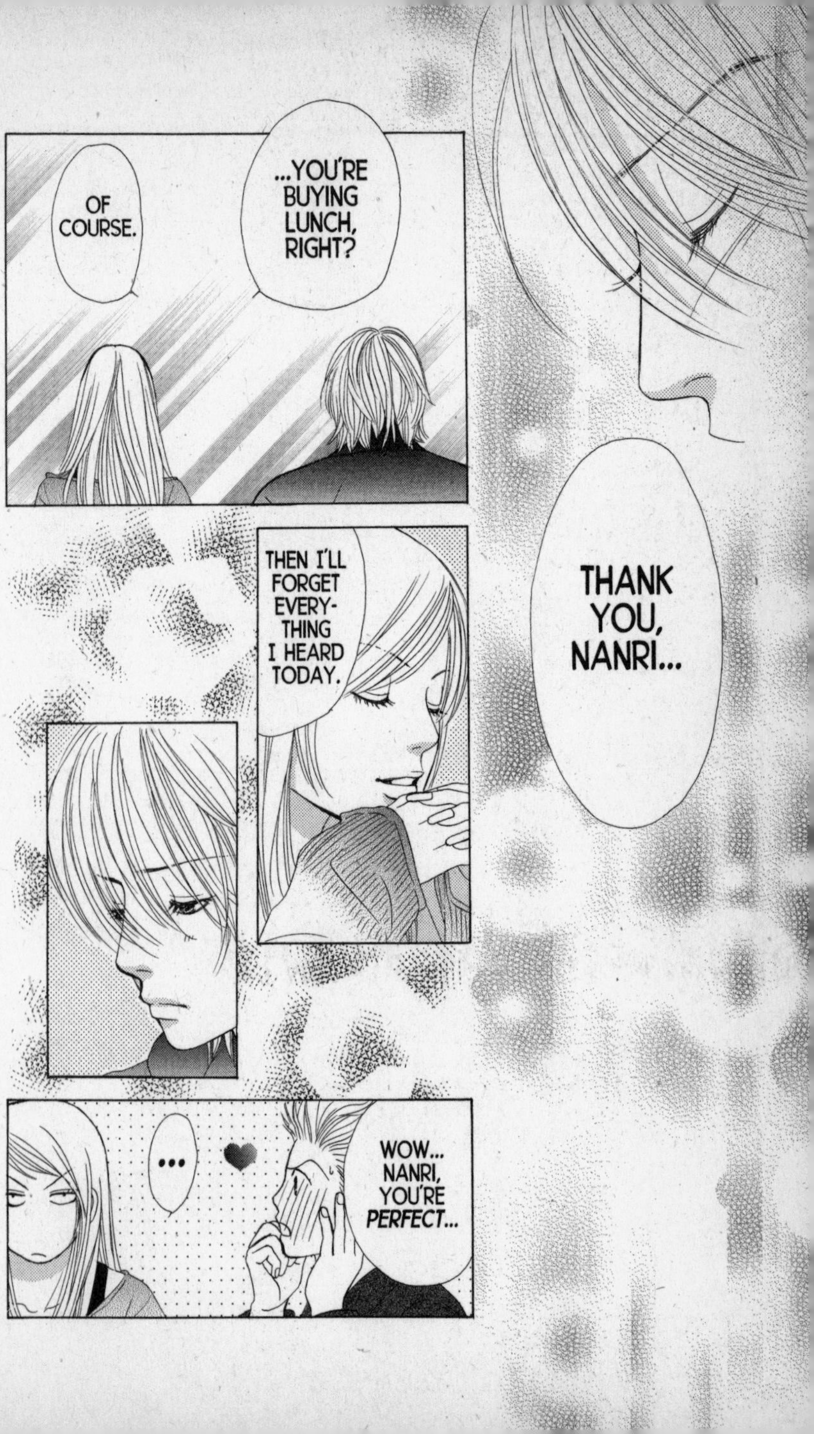
THANK YOU, NANRI...
...YOU'RE BUYING LUNCH, RIGHT?
OF COURSE.
THEN I'LL FORGET EVERY-THING I HEARD TODAY.
WOW... NANRI, YOU'RE *PERFECT*...
...

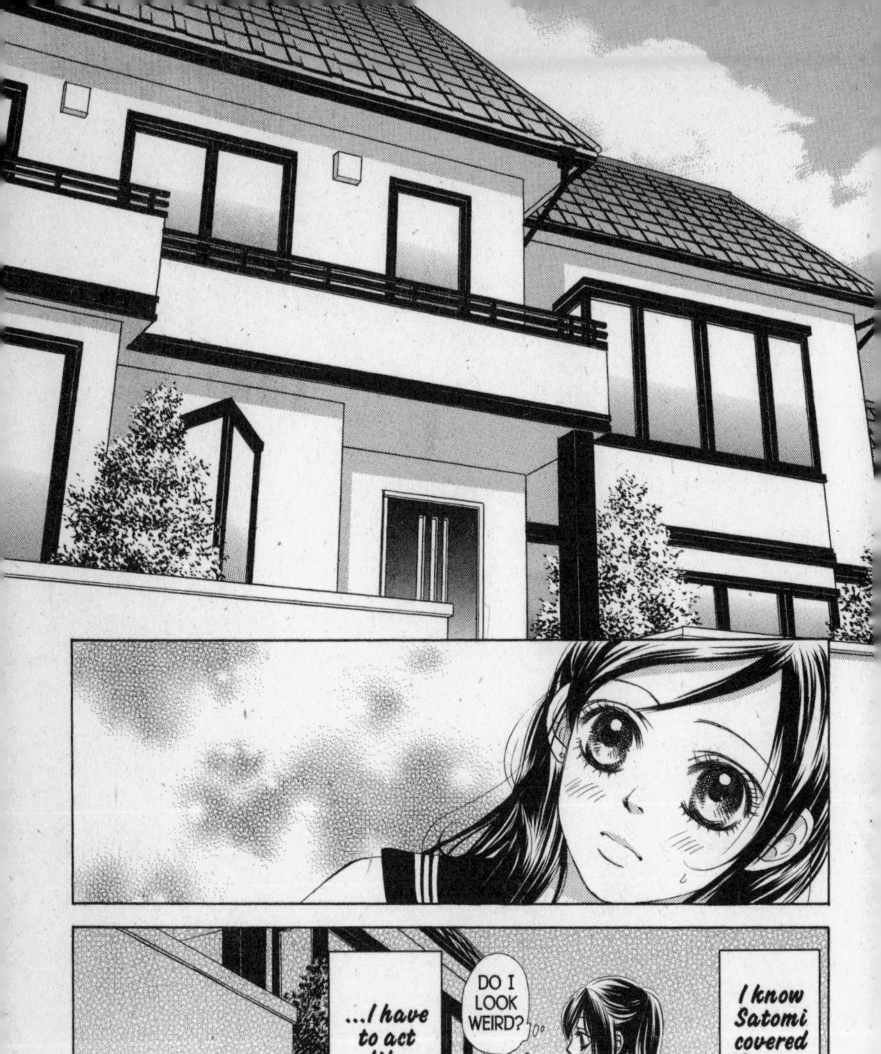
I know Satomi covered for me, but it's still scary going in...
DO I LOOK WEIRD?
...I have to act like nothing happened.
狩野

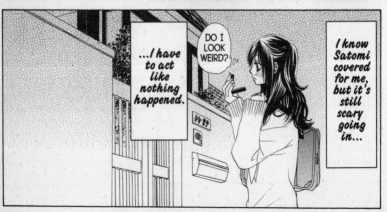

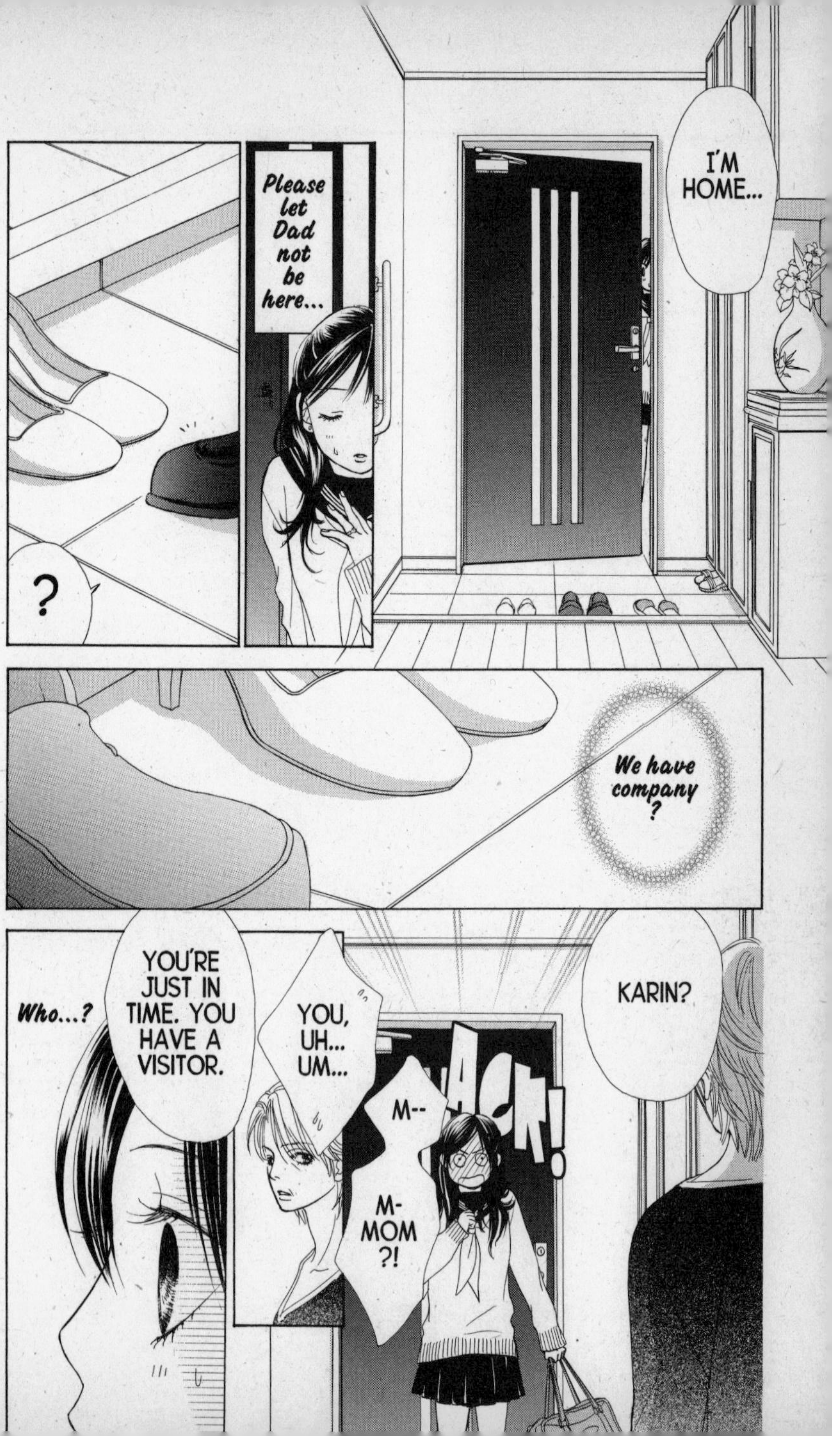
I'M HOME...
Please let Dad not be here...
?
We have company?
KARIN?
M--
M-MOM?!
YOU, UH... UM...
YOU'RE JUST IN TIME. YOU HAVE A VISITOR.
Who...?

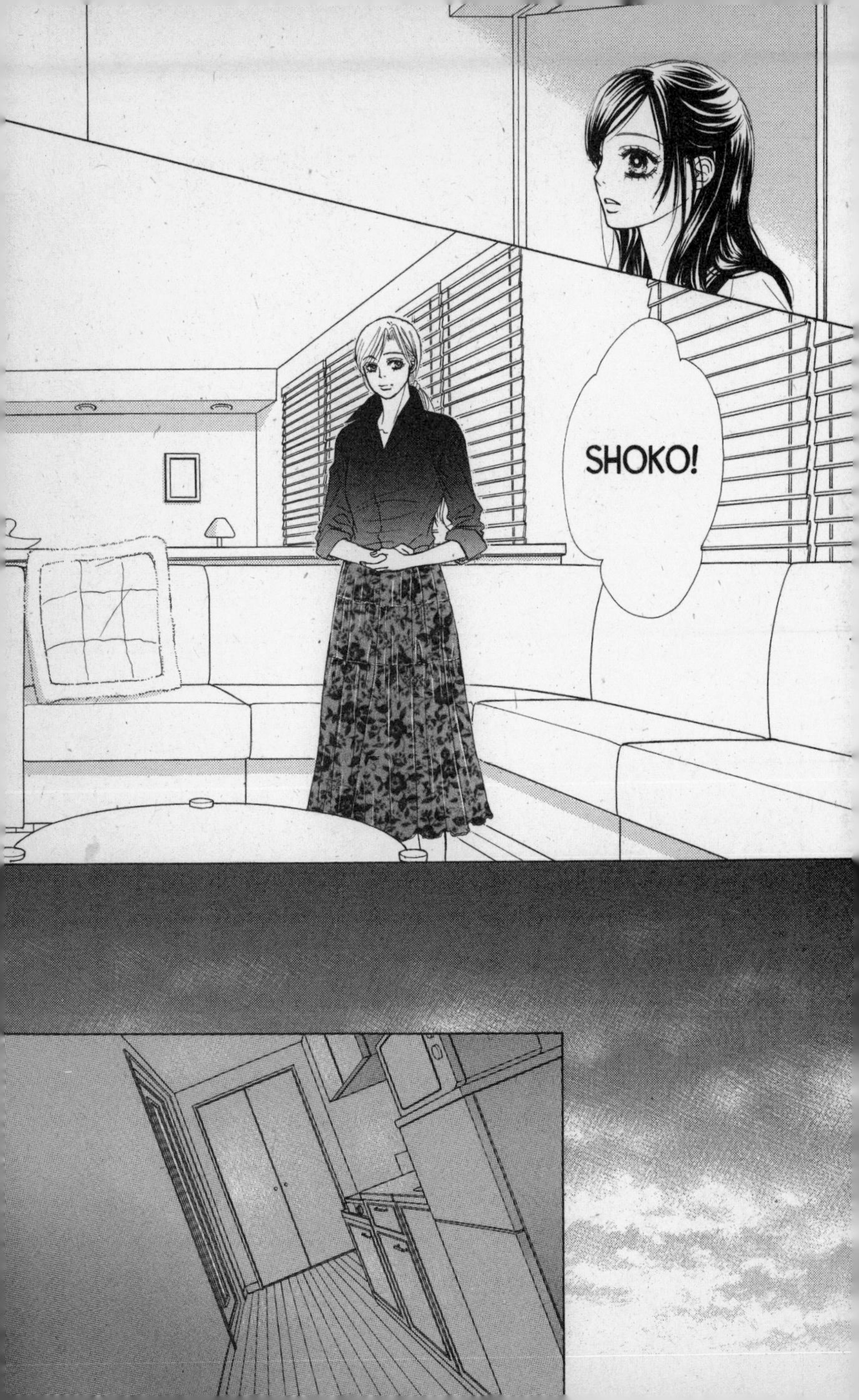
SHOKO!

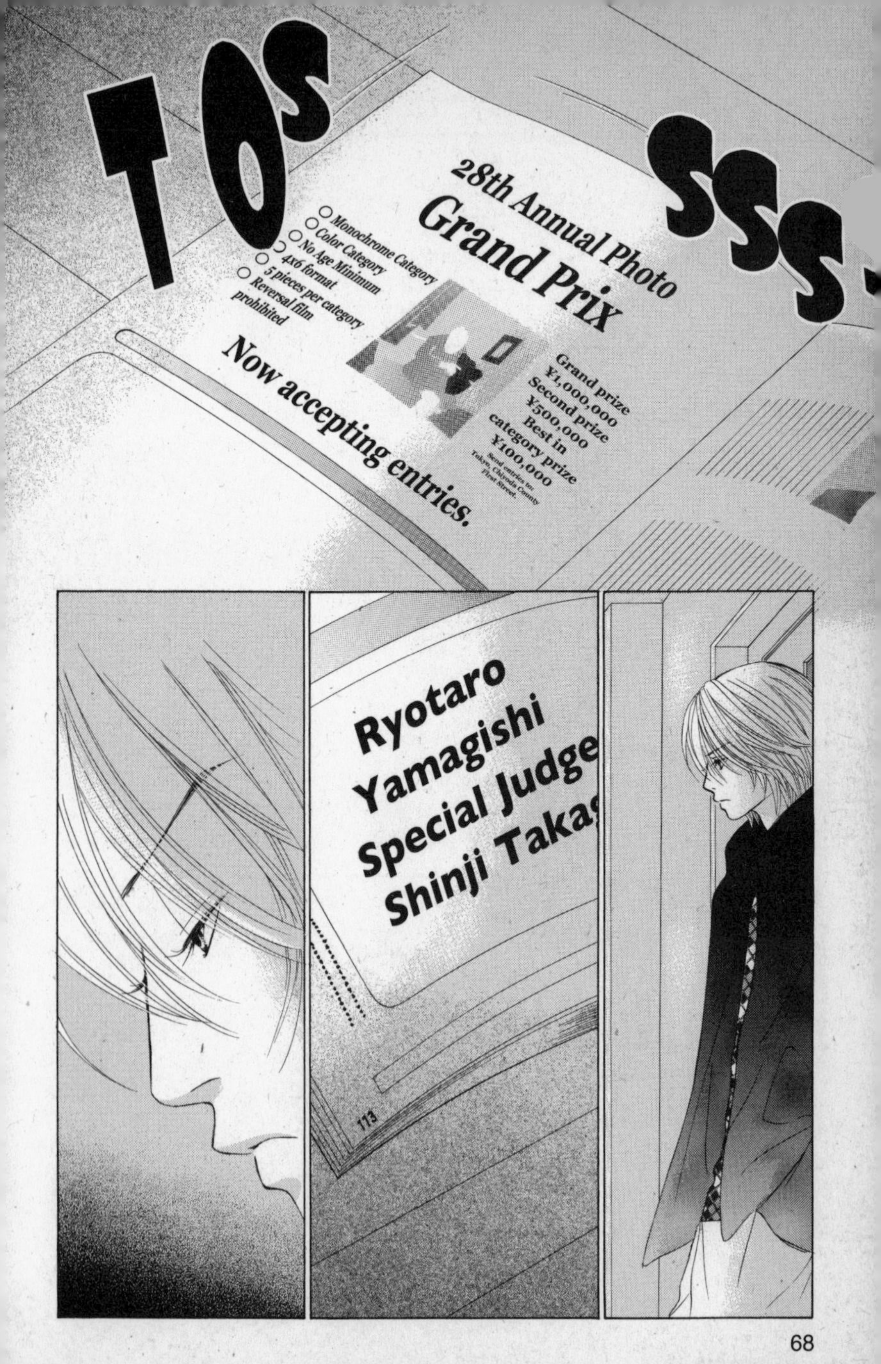
TOS
SSS-
28th Annual Photo
Grand Prix
Monochrome Category
Color Category
No Age Minimum
4x6 format
5 pieces per category
Reversal film prohibited
Grand prize ¥1,000,000
Second prize ¥500,000
Best in category prize ¥100,000
Send entries to: Tokyo, Chiyoda County First Street.
Now accepting entries.
Ryotaro Yamagishi
Special Judge
Shinji Takas
113

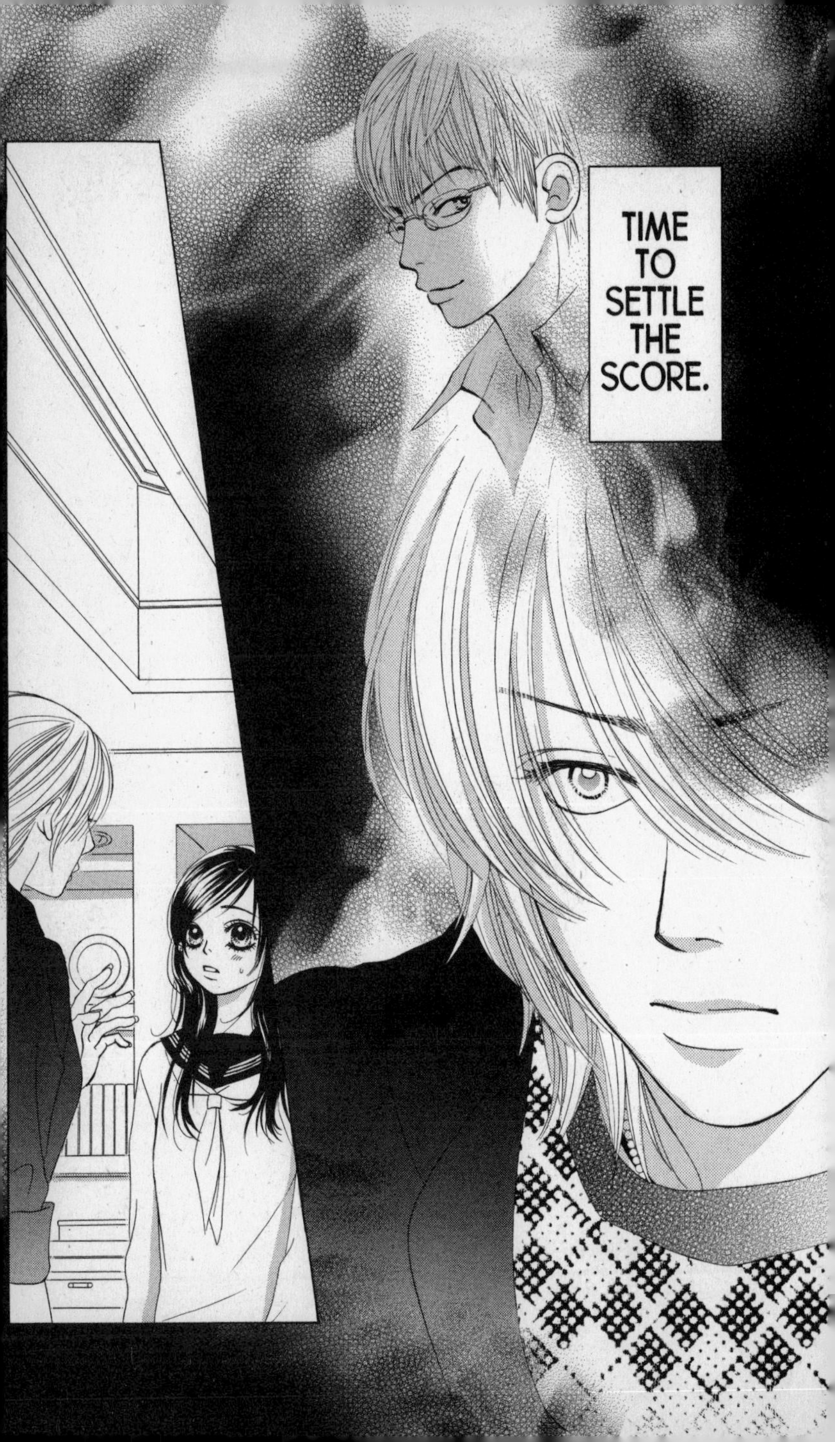
TIME TO SETTLE THE SCORE.

healing CD float
PLAN

SE Planning
Shoko Akiba
(03) 3745-8▒
994-8745-▒
shoko-a@▒

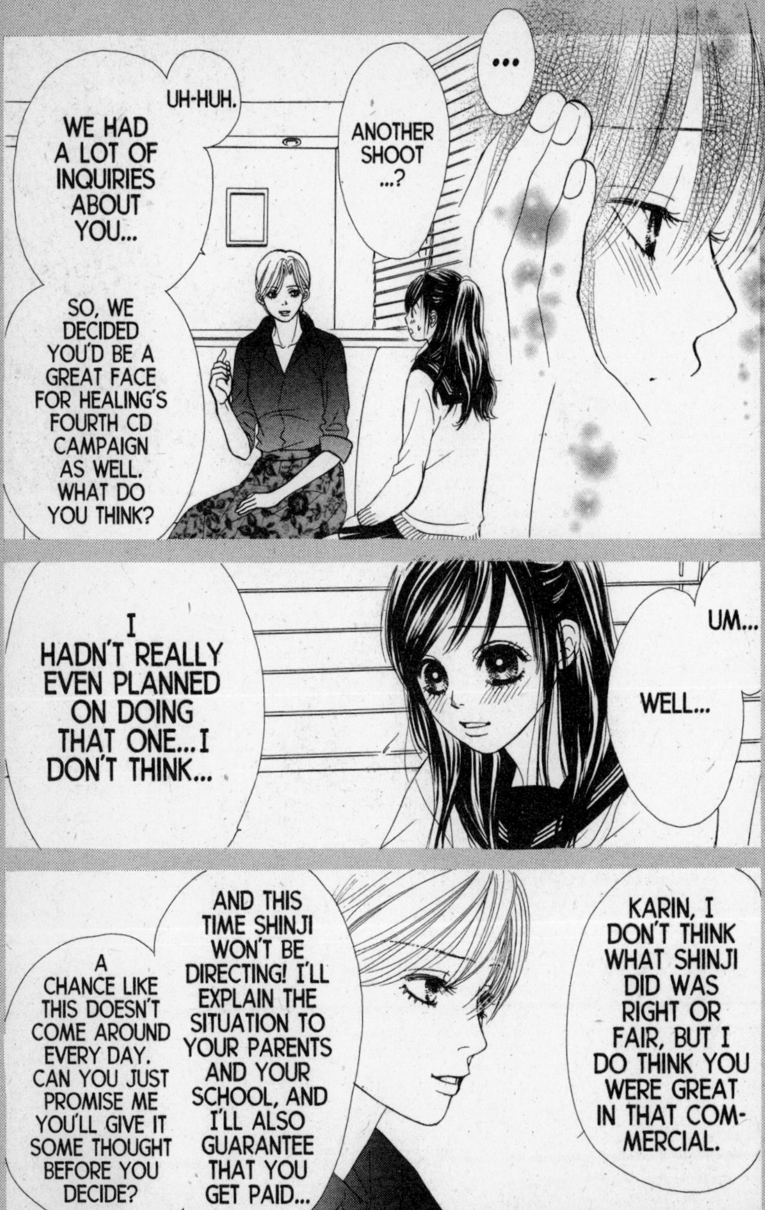
...
ANOTHER SHOOT ...?
UH-HUH.
WE HAD A LOT OF INQUIRIES ABOUT YOU...
SO, WE DECIDED YOU'D BE A GREAT FACE FOR HEALING'S FOURTH CD CAMPAIGN AS WELL. WHAT DO YOU THINK?
UM...
WELL...
I HADN'T REALLY EVEN PLANNED ON DOING THAT ONE...I DON'T THINK...
KARIN, I DON'T THINK WHAT SHINJI DID WAS RIGHT OR FAIR, BUT I DO THINK YOU WERE GREAT IN THAT COM-MERCIAL.
AND THIS TIME SHINJI WON'T BE DIRECTING! I'LL EXPLAIN THE SITUATION TO YOUR PARENTS AND YOUR SCHOOL, AND I'LL ALSO GUARANTEE THAT YOU GET PAID...
A CHANCE LIKE THIS DOESN'T COME AROUND EVERY DAY. CAN YOU JUST PROMISE ME YOU'LL GIVE IT SOME THOUGHT BEFORE YOU DECIDE?

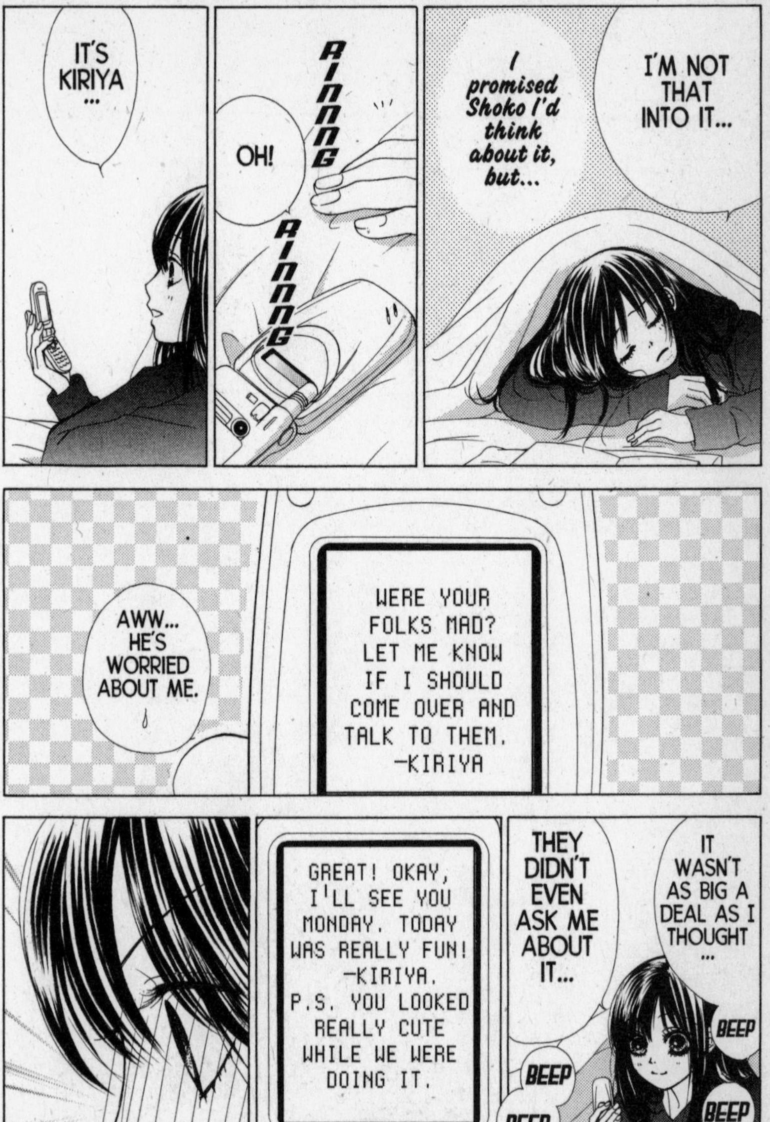
I'M NOT THAT INTO IT...
I promised Shoko I'd think about it, but...
RINNNG
OH!
RINNNG
IT'S KIRIYA...
WERE YOUR FOLKS MAD? LET ME KNOW IF I SHOULD COME OVER AND TALK TO THEM. —KIRIYA
AWW... HE'S WORRIED ABOUT ME.
IT WASN'T AS BIG A DEAL AS I THOUGHT...
THEY DIDN'T EVEN ASK ME ABOUT IT...
BEEP
BEEP
BEEP
BEEP
BEEP
GREAT! OKAY, I'LL SEE YOU MONDAY. TODAY WAS REALLY FUN! —KIRIYA. P.S. YOU LOOKED REALLY CUTE WHILE WE WERE DOING IT.

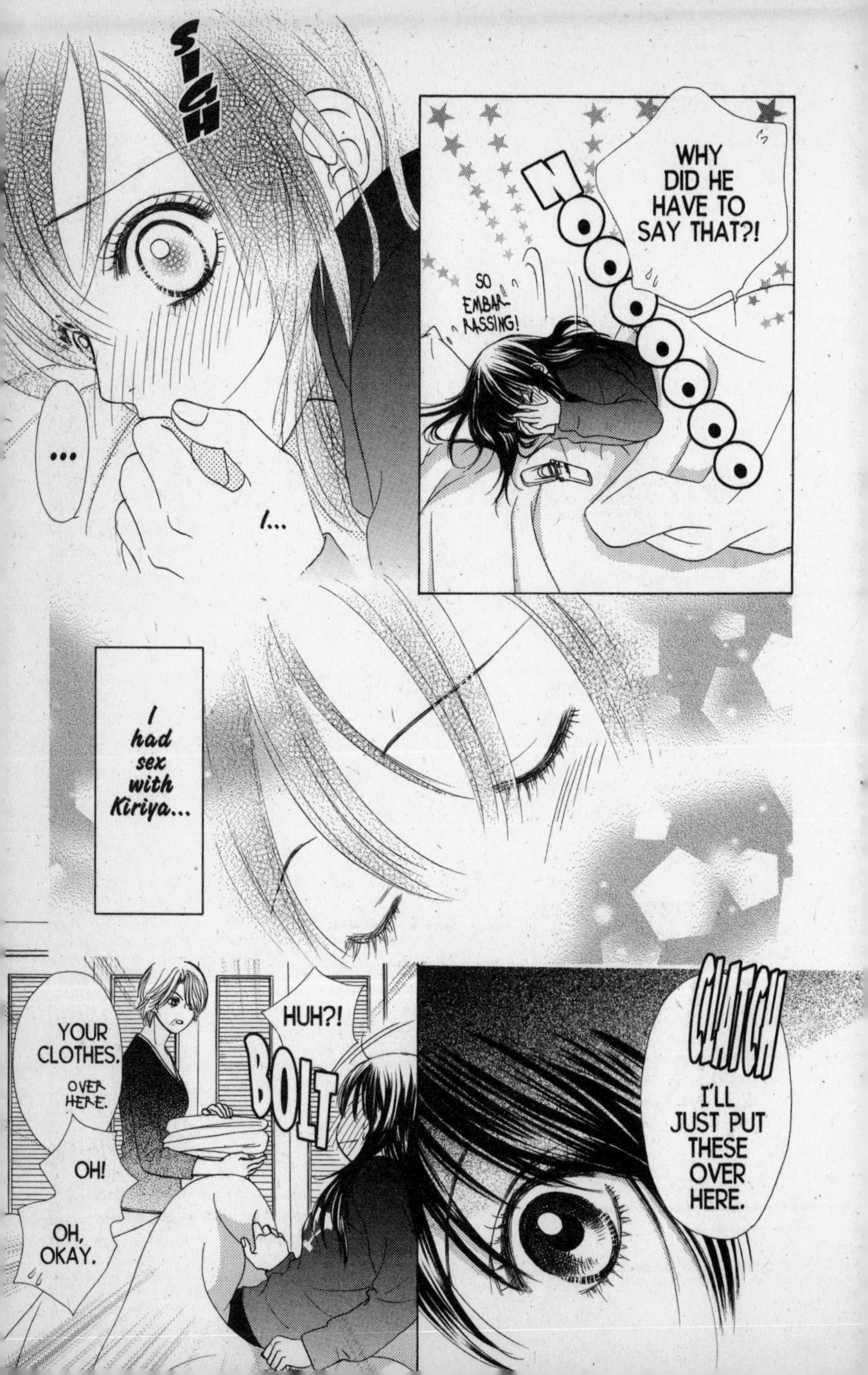
WHY DID HE HAVE TO SAY THAT?!
NOOOOOOOO
SO EMBARRASSING!
SIGH
...
I...
I had sex with Kiriya...
CLATCH
I'LL JUST PUT THESE OVER HERE.
HUH?!
BOLT
YOUR CLOTHES.
OVER HERE.
OH!
OH, OKAY.

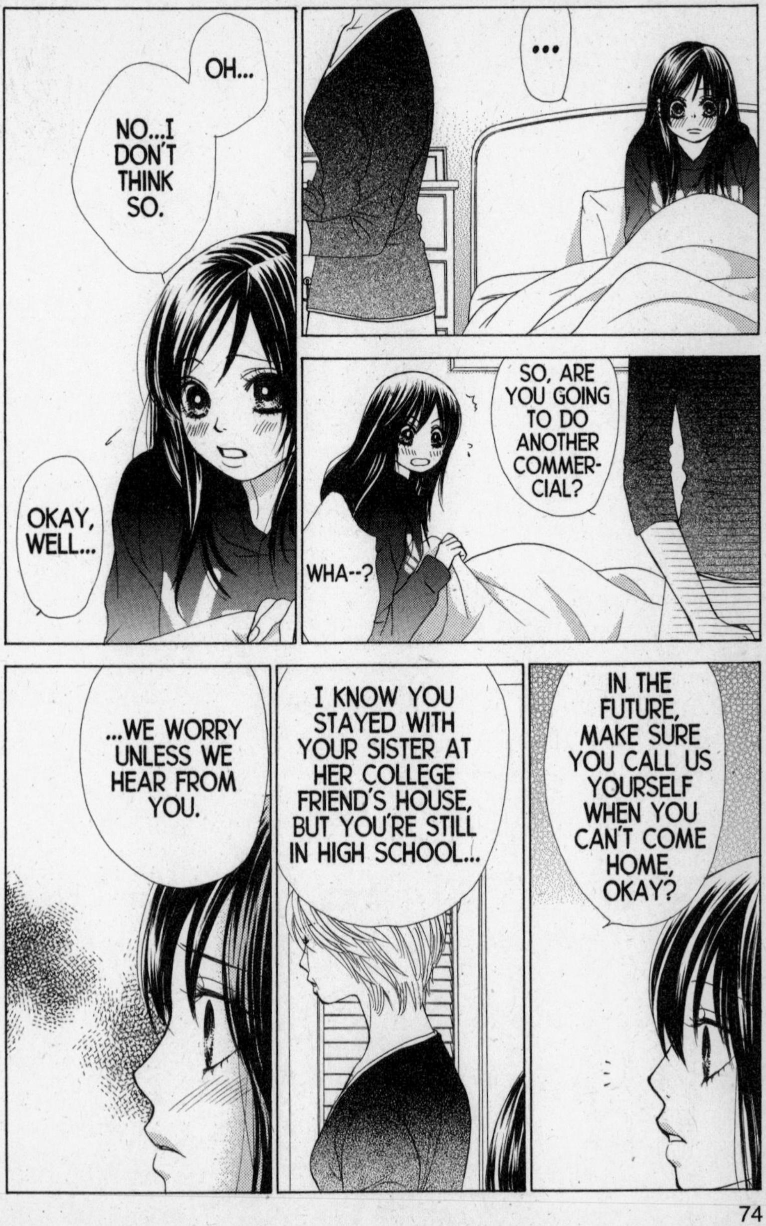
...
SO, ARE YOU GOING TO DO ANOTHER COMMERCIAL?
WHA--?
OH...
NO...I DON'T THINK SO.
OKAY, WELL...
IN THE FUTURE, MAKE SURE YOU CALL US YOURSELF WHEN YOU CAN'T COME HOME, OKAY?
I KNOW YOU STAYED WITH YOUR SISTER AT HER COLLEGE FRIEND'S HOUSE, BUT YOU'RE STILL IN HIGH SCHOOL...
...WE WORRY UNLESS WE HEAR FROM YOU.

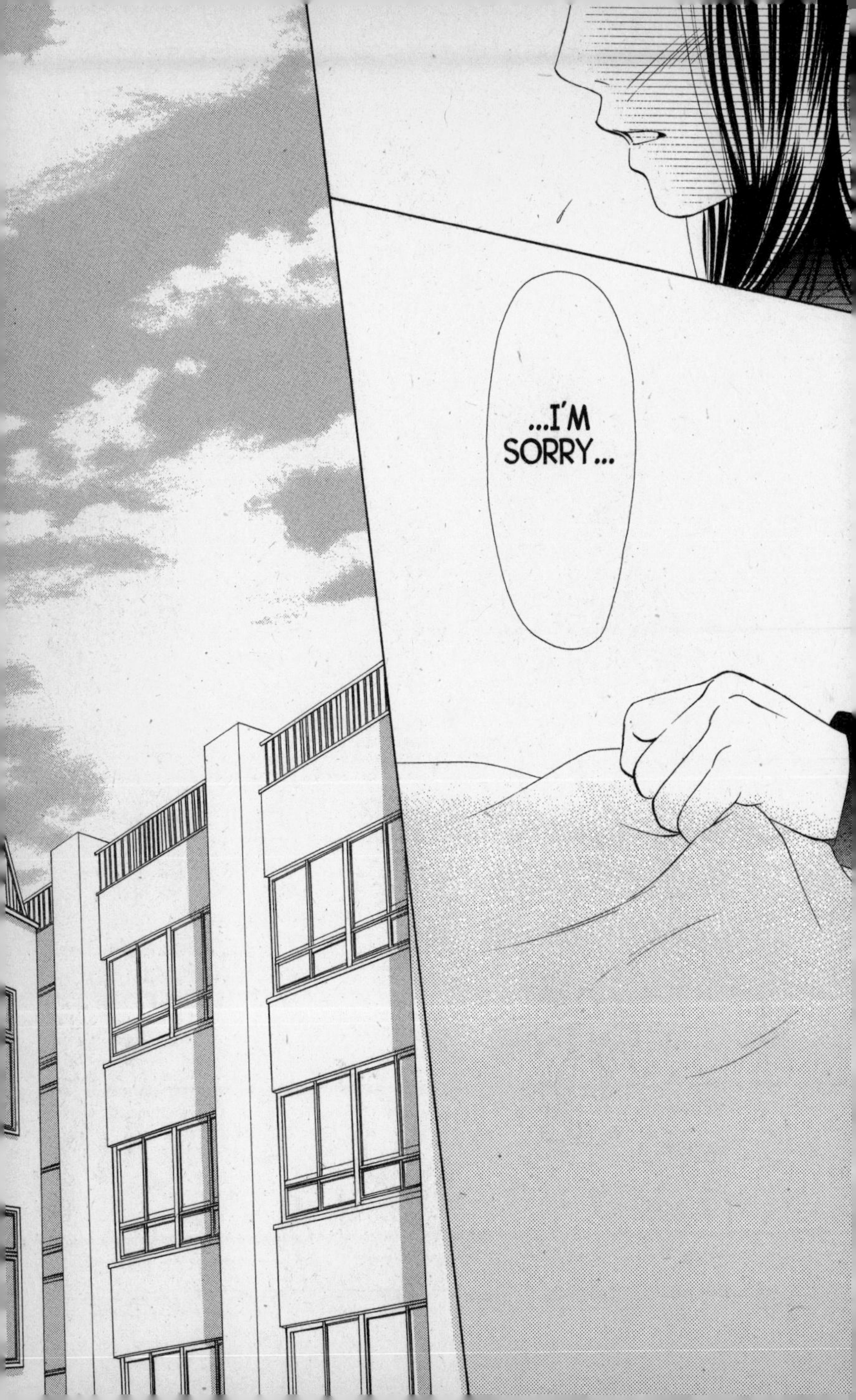
...I'M SORRY...

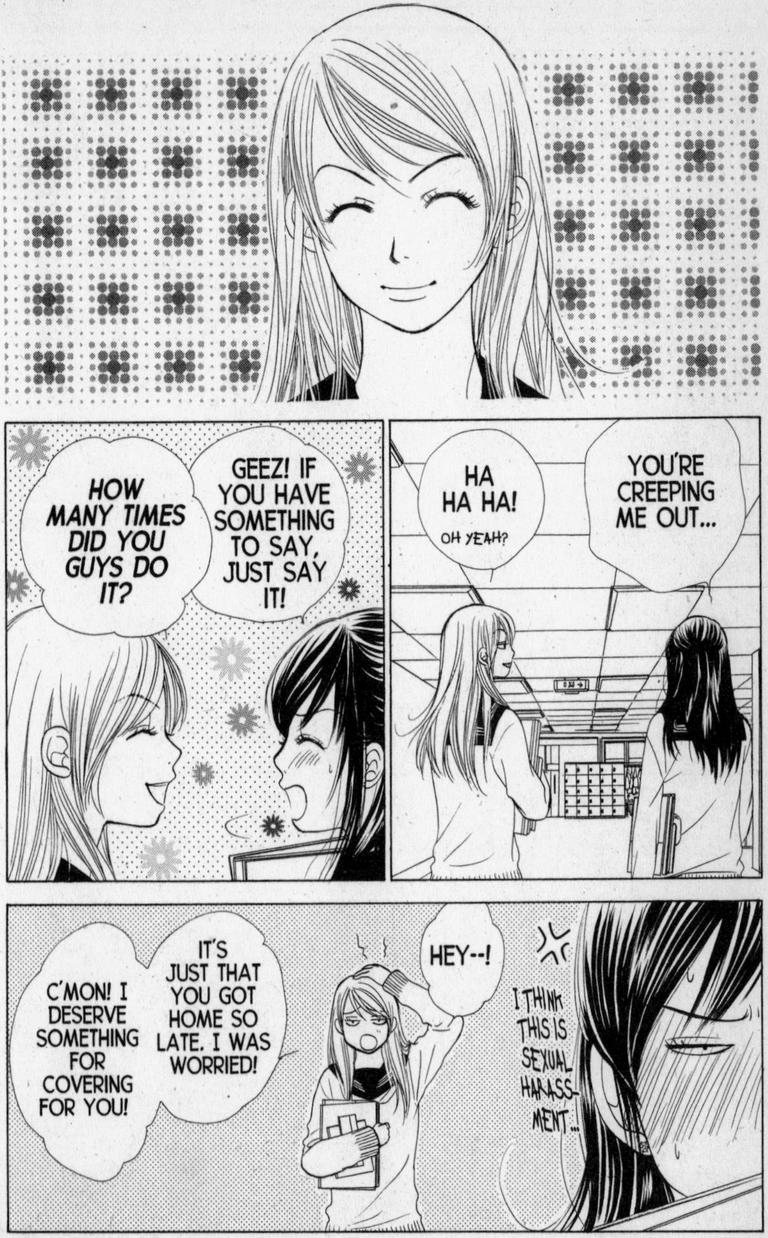
YOU'RE CREEPING ME OUT...
HA HA HA!
OH YEAH?
GEEZ! IF YOU HAVE SOMETHING TO SAY, JUST SAY IT!
HOW MANY TIMES DID YOU GUYS DO IT?
I THINK THIS IS SEXUAL HARASSMENT...
HEY--!
IT'S JUST THAT YOU GOT HOME SO LATE. I WAS WORRIED!
C'MON! I DESERVE SOMETHING FOR COVERING FOR YOU!

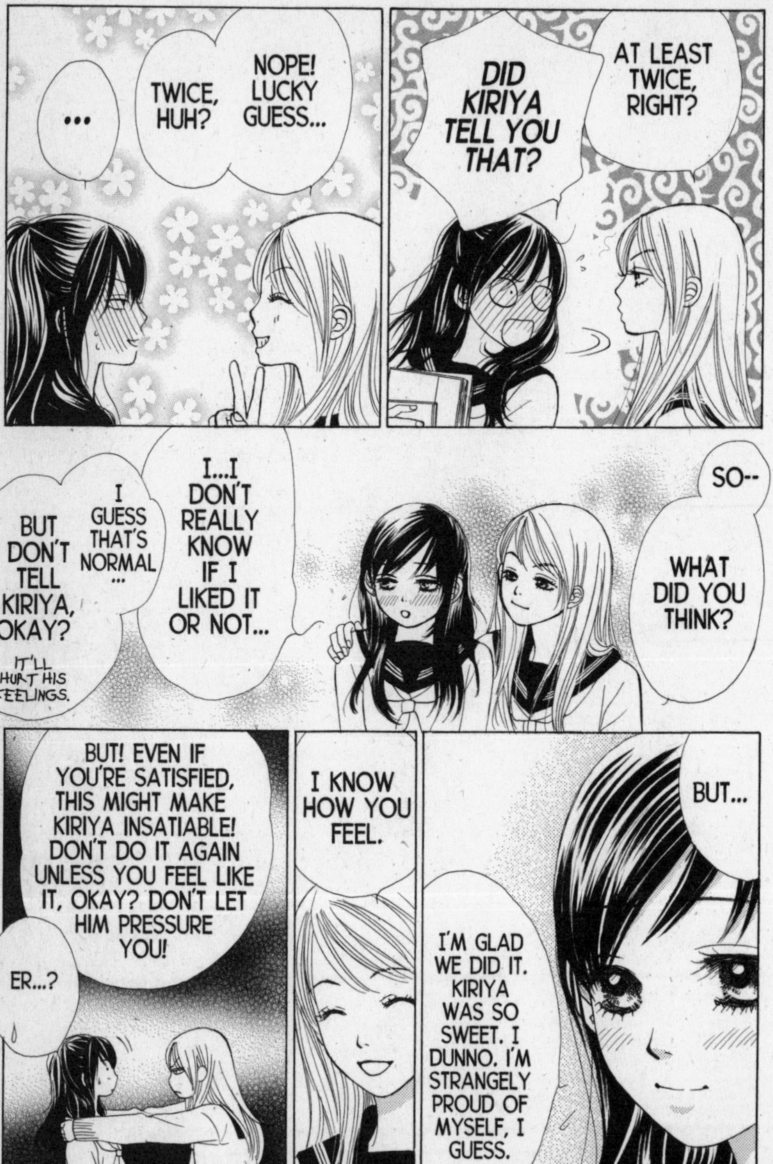
AT LEAST TWICE, RIGHT?
DID KIRIYA TELL YOU THAT?
NOPE! LUCKY GUESS...
TWICE, HUH?
...
SO--
WHAT DID YOU THINK?
I...I DON'T REALLY KNOW IF I LIKED IT OR NOT...
I GUESS THAT'S NORMAL...
BUT DON'T TELL KIRIYA, OKAY?
IT'LL HURT HIS FEELINGS.
BUT...
I'M GLAD WE DID IT. KIRIYA WAS SO SWEET. I DUNNO. I'M STRANGELY PROUD OF MYSELF, I GUESS.
I KNOW HOW YOU FEEL.
BUT! EVEN IF YOU'RE SATISFIED, THIS MIGHT MAKE KIRIYA INSATIABLE! DON'T DO IT AGAIN UNLESS YOU FEEL LIKE IT, OKAY? DON'T LET HIM PRESSURE YOU!
ER...?

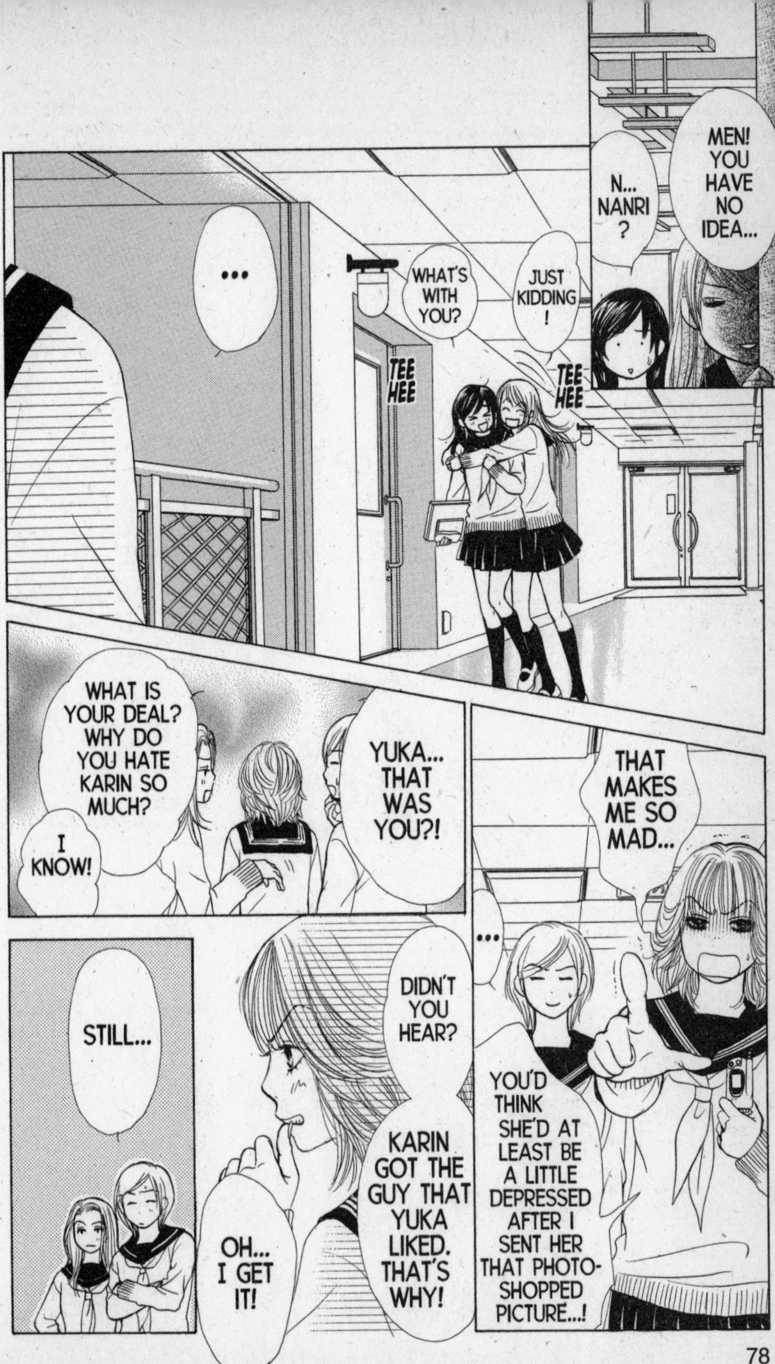
MEN! YOU HAVE NO IDEA...
N... NANRI?
JUST KIDDING!
TEE HEE
WHAT'S WITH YOU?
TEE HEE
...
THAT MAKES ME SO MAD...
YOU'D THINK SHE'D AT LEAST BE A LITTLE DEPRESSED AFTER I SENT HER THAT PHOTO-SHOPPED PICTURE...!
...
YUKA... THAT WAS YOU?!
WHAT IS YOUR DEAL? WHY DO YOU HATE KARIN SO MUCH?
I KNOW!
DIDN'T YOU HEAR?
KARIN GOT THE GUY THAT YUKA LIKED. THAT'S WHY!
OH... I GET IT!
STILL...

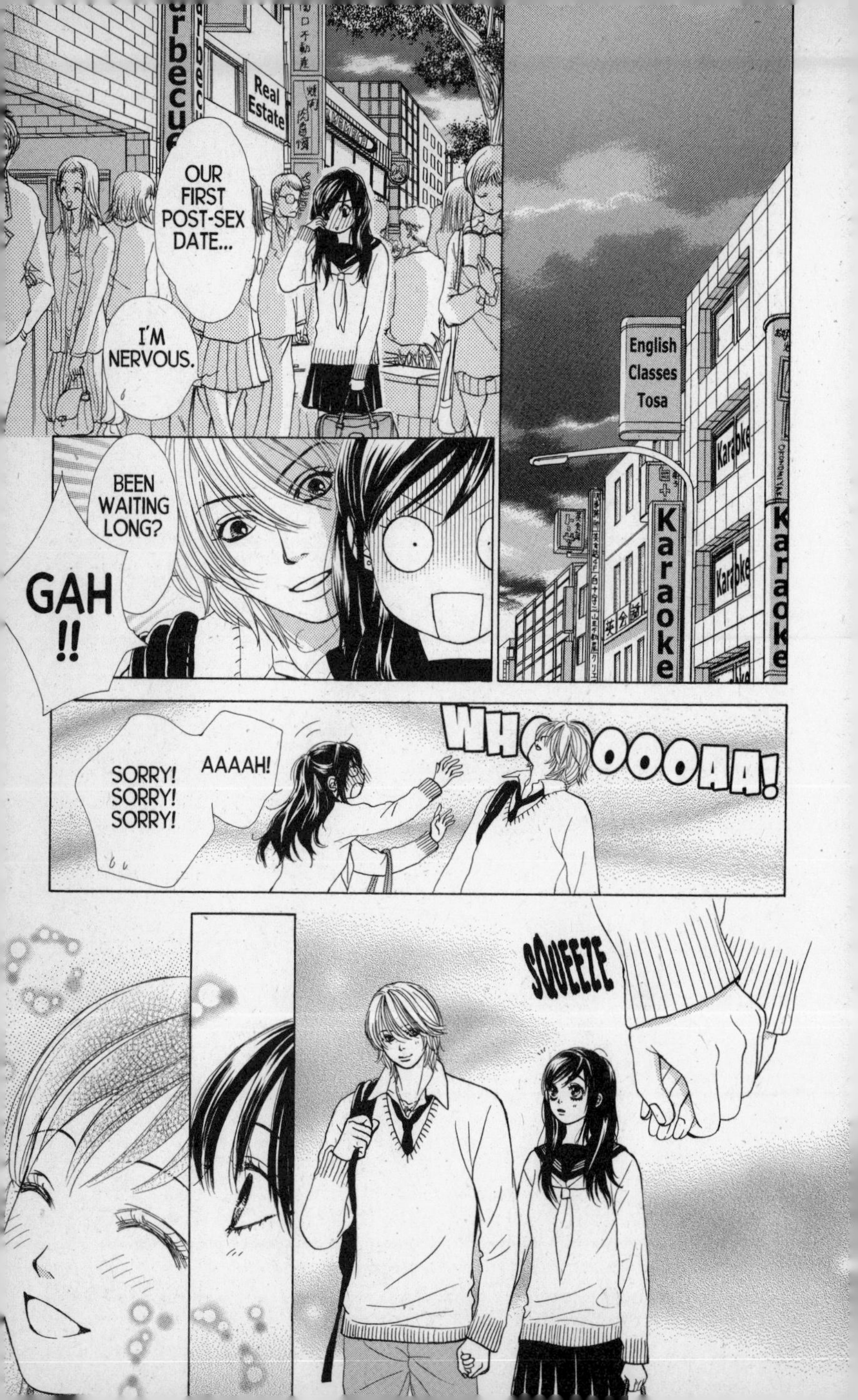
English Classes Tosa
Karaoke
Karaoke
Karaoke
Karaoke
Real Estate
OUR FIRST POST-SEX DATE...
I'M NERVOUS.
BEEN WAITING LONG?
GAH!!
WHOOOOOAA!
AAAAH!
SORRY! SORRY! SORRY!
SQUEEZE

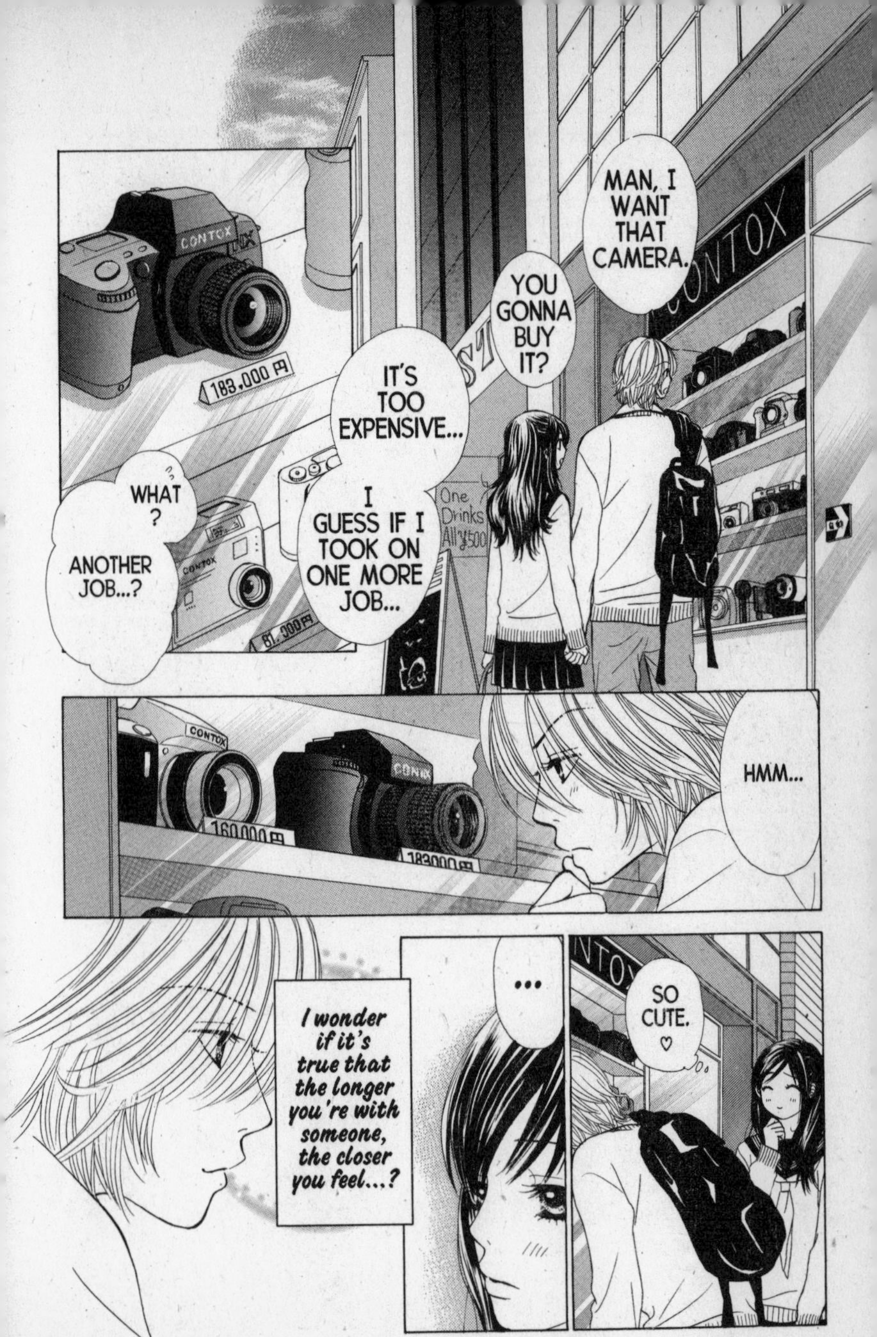
MAN, I WANT THAT CAMERA.
YOU GONNA BUY IT?
IT'S TOO EXPENSIVE...
I GUESS IF I TOOK ON ONE MORE JOB...
WHAT?
ANOTHER JOB...?
HMM...
SO CUTE. ♡
...
I wonder if it's true that the longer you're with someone, the closer you feel...?

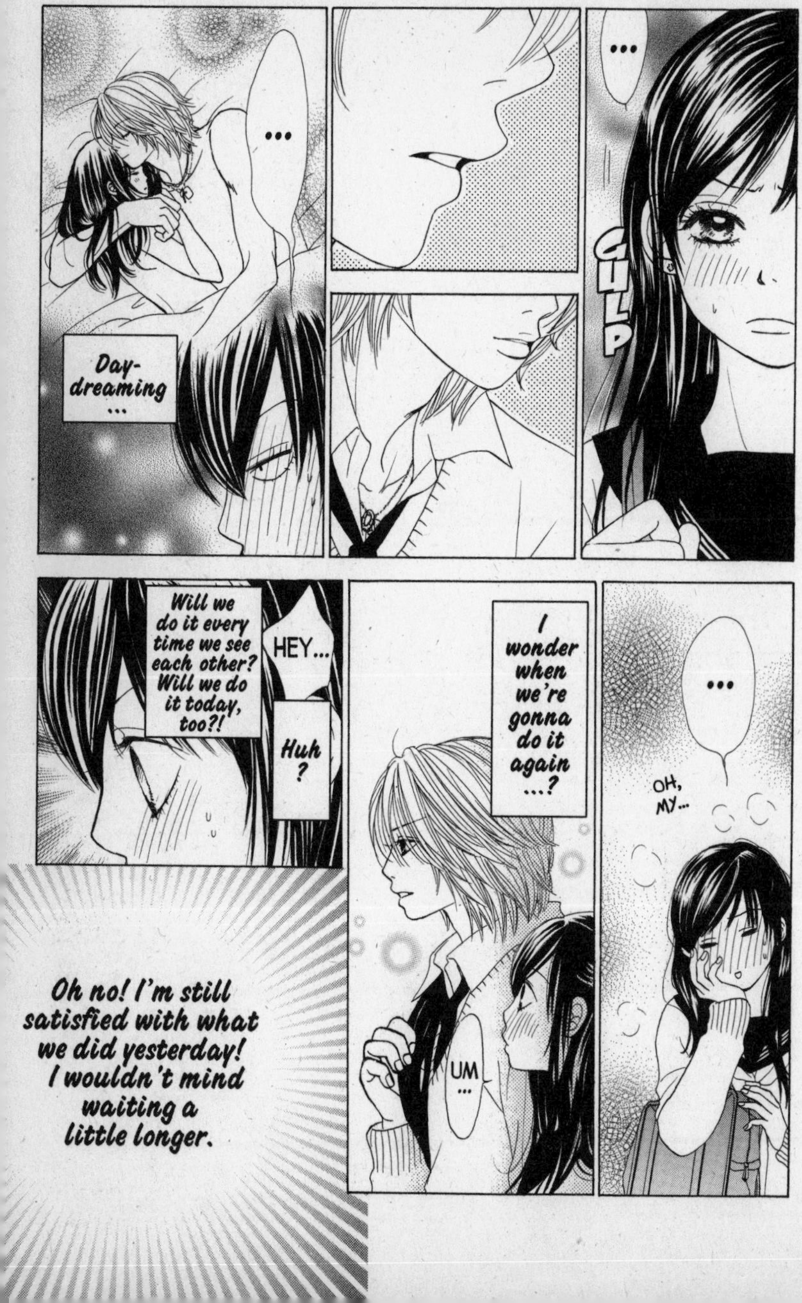
...
GULP
...
Day-dreaming...
...
OH, MY...
I wonder when we're gonna do it again...?
UM...
HEY...
Will we do it every time we see each other? Will we do it today, too?!
Huh?
Oh no! I'm still satisfied with what we did yesterday! I wouldn't mind waiting a little longer.

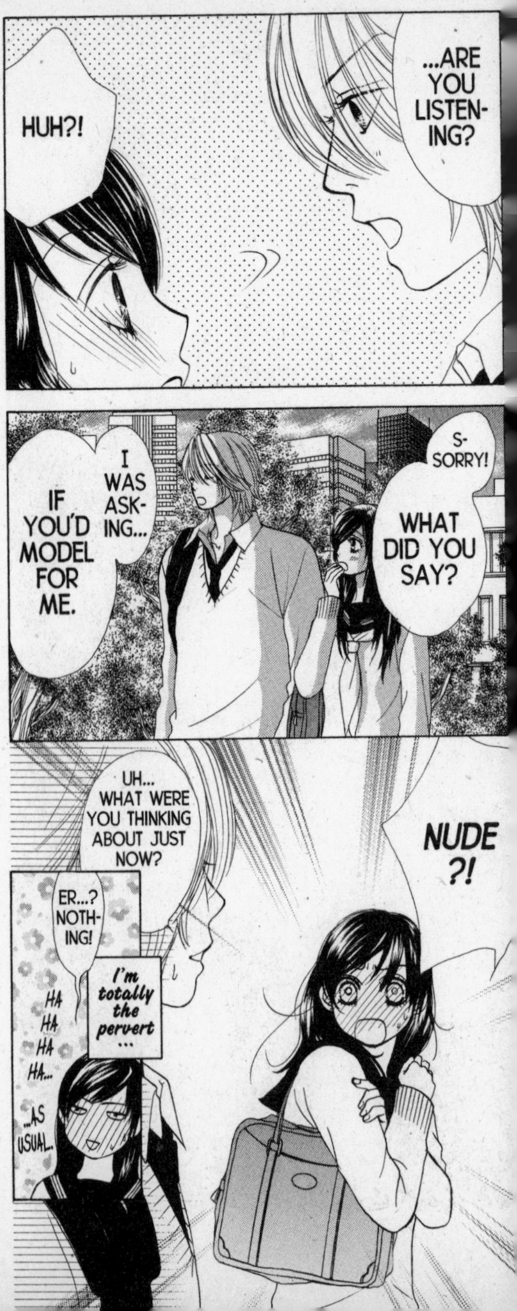
...ARE YOU LISTENING?
HUH?!
S-SORRY!
WHAT DID YOU SAY?
I WAS ASKING...
IF YOU'D MODEL FOR ME.
NUDE?!
UH... WHAT WERE YOU THINKING ABOUT JUST NOW?
ER...? NOTHING!
HA HA HA HA...
I'm totally the pervert...
...AS USUAL.

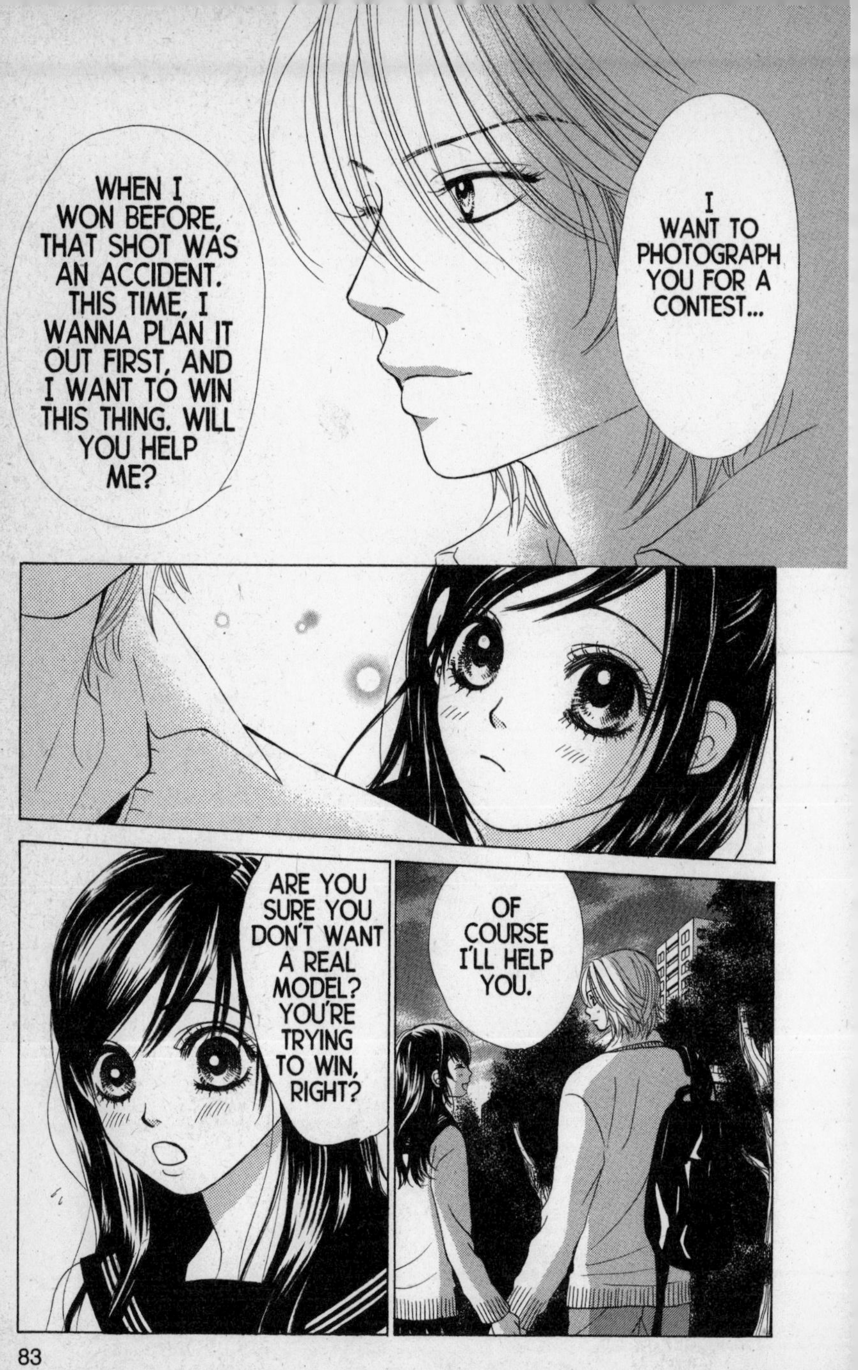
I WANT TO PHOTOGRAPH YOU FOR A CONTEST...
WHEN I WON BEFORE, THAT SHOT WAS AN ACCIDENT. THIS TIME, I WANNA PLAN IT OUT FIRST, AND I WANT TO WIN THIS THING. WILL YOU HELP ME?
OF COURSE I'LL HELP YOU.
ARE YOU SURE YOU DON'T WANT A REAL MODEL? YOU'RE TRYING TO WIN, RIGHT?

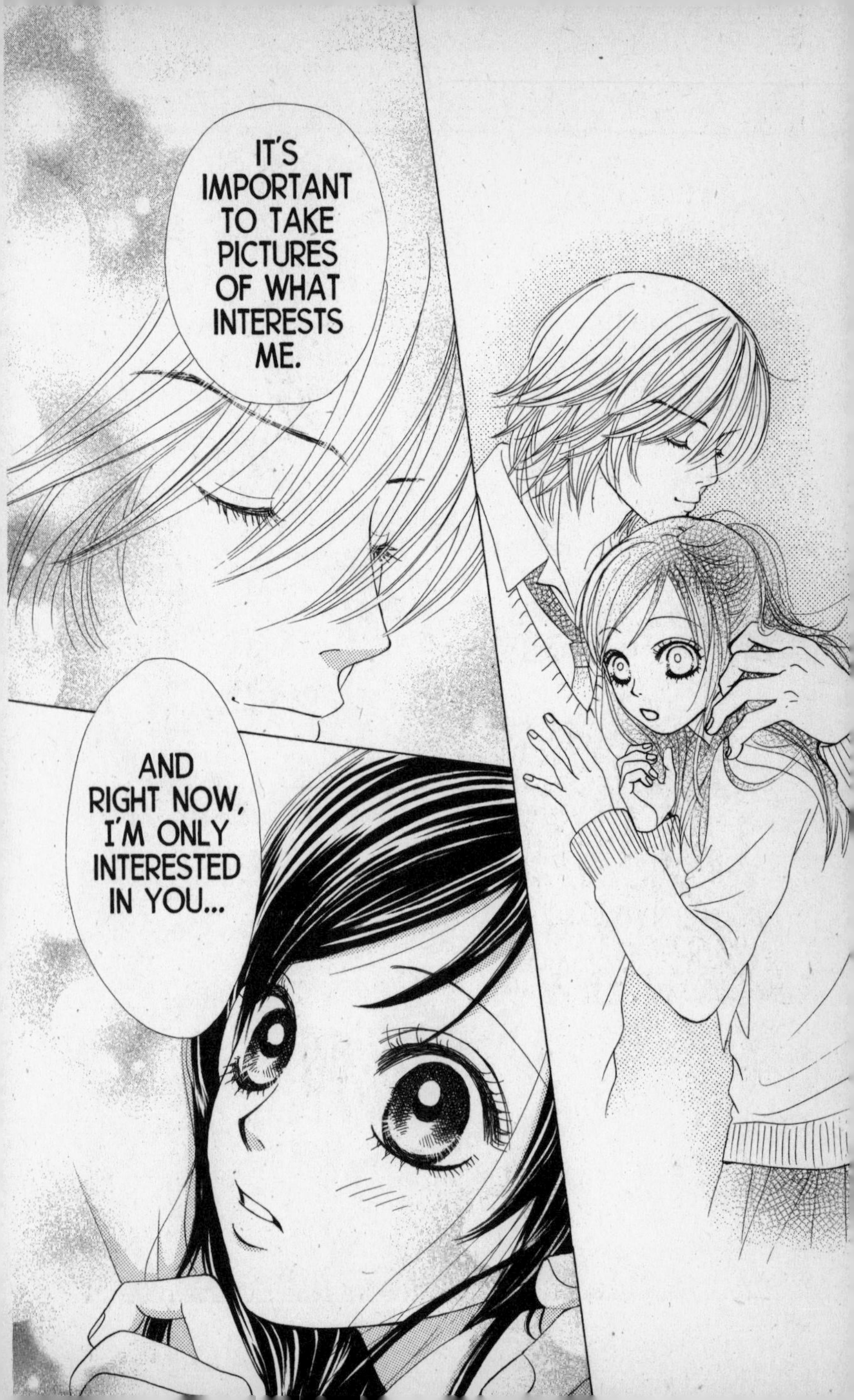
IT'S IMPORTANT TO TAKE PICTURES OF WHAT INTERESTS ME.
AND RIGHT NOW, I'M ONLY INTERESTED IN YOU...

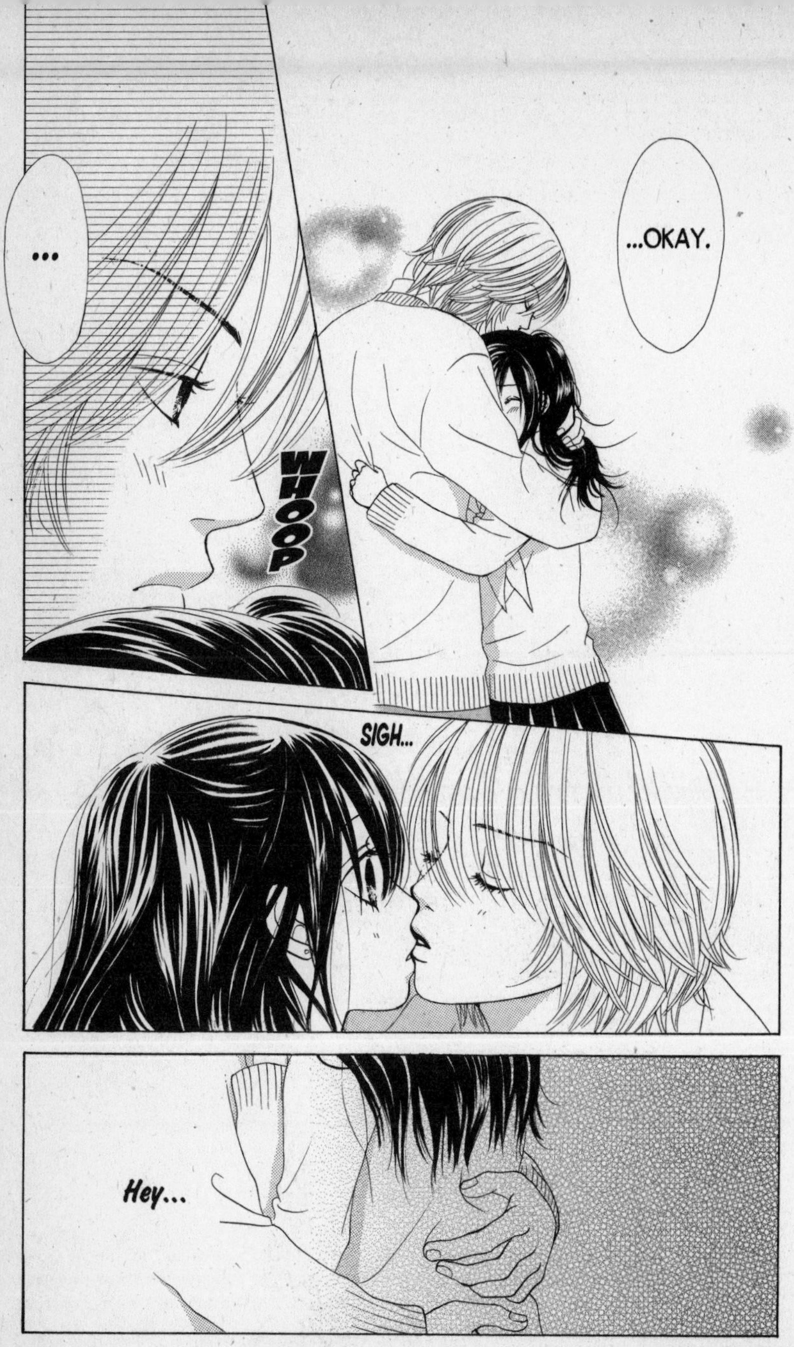
...OKAY.
WHOOP
...
SIGH...
Hey...

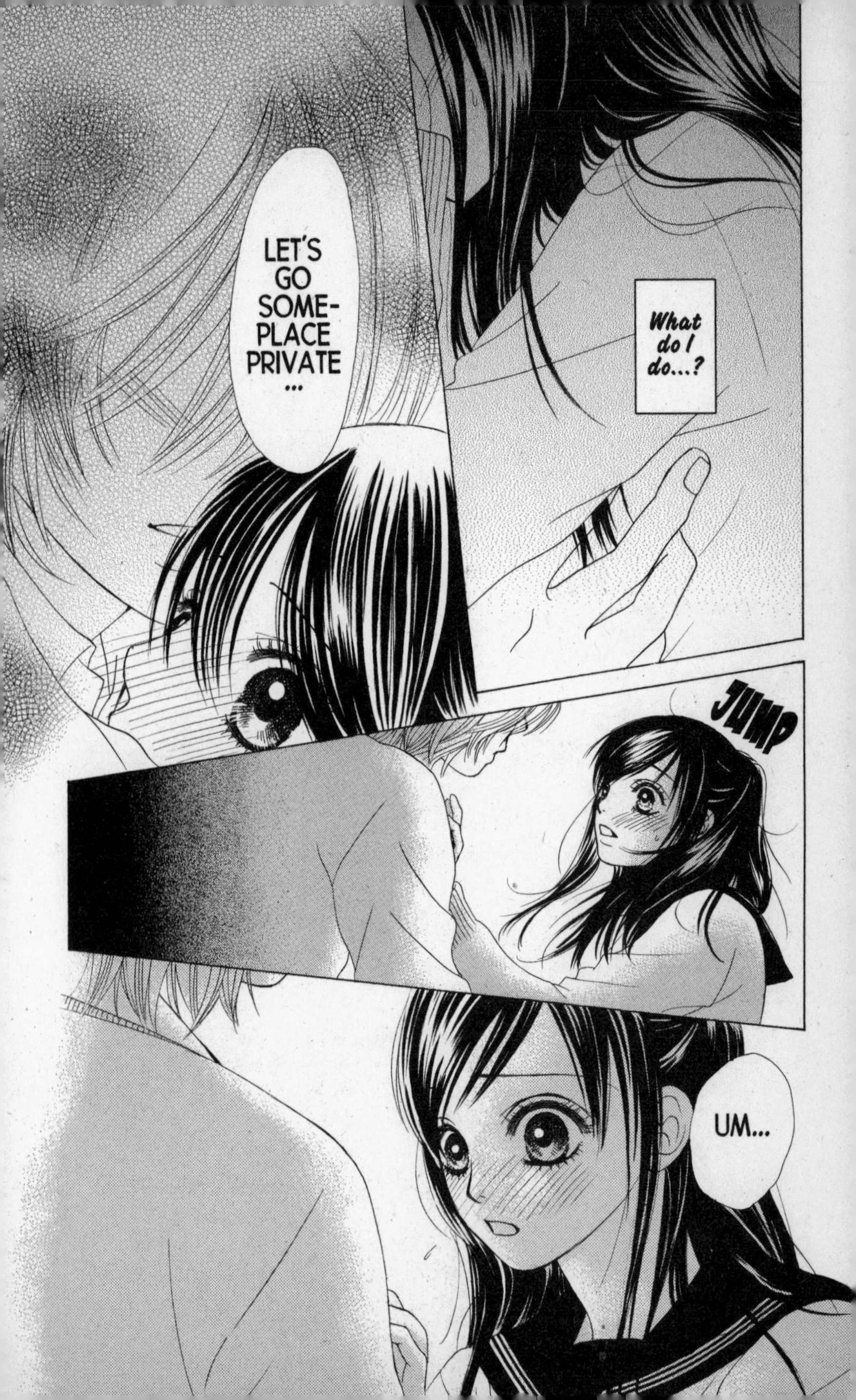
What do I do...?
LET'S GO SOME-PLACE PRIVATE...
JUMP
UM...

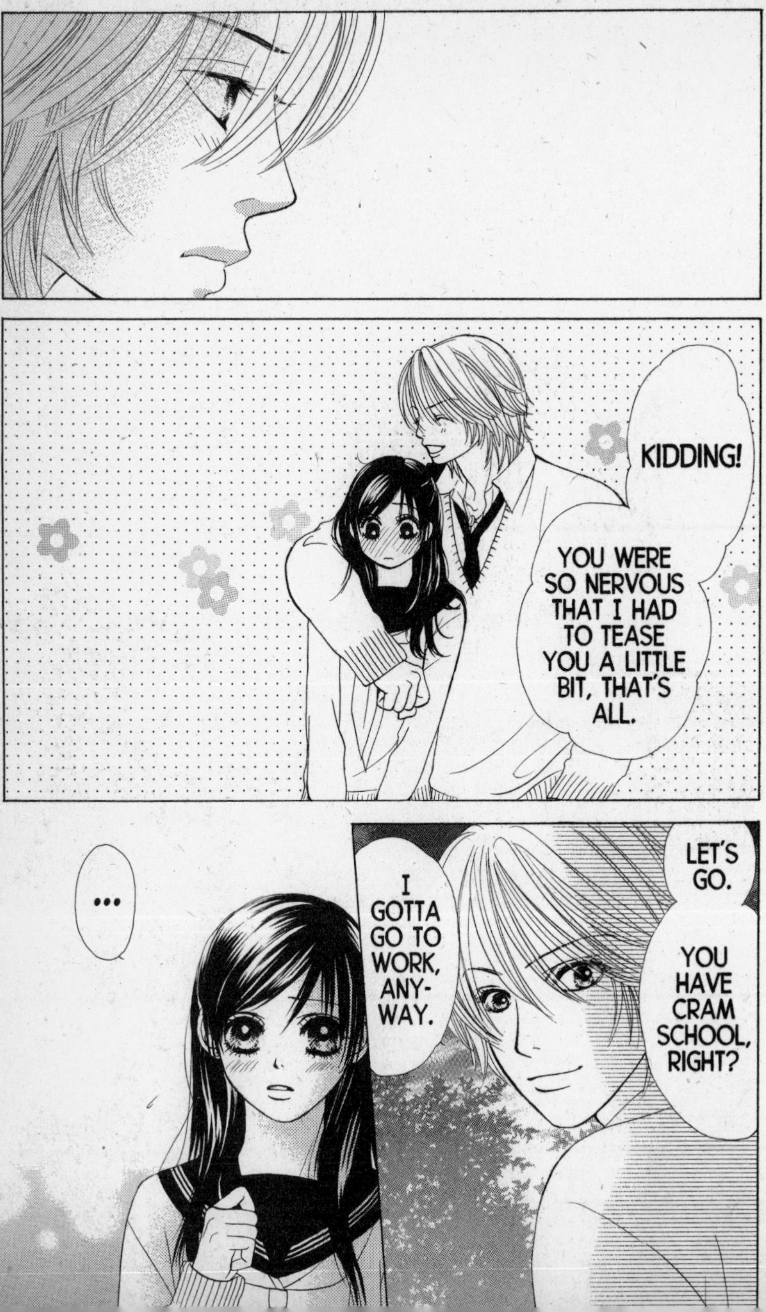
KIDDING!
YOU WERE SO NERVOUS THAT I HAD TO TEASE YOU A LITTLE BIT, THAT'S ALL.
LET'S GO.
YOU HAVE CRAM SCHOOL, RIGHT?
I GOTTA GO TO WORK, ANY-WAY.
...

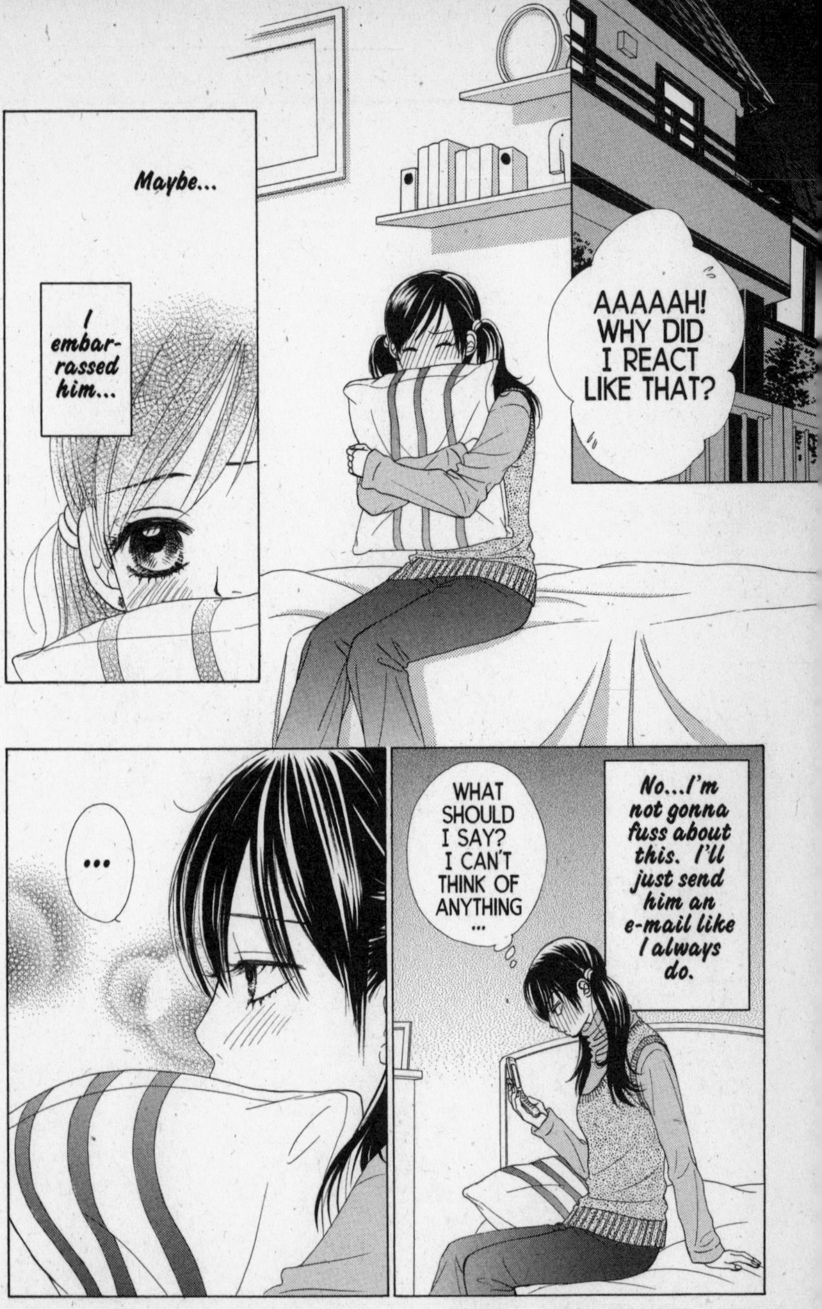
AAAAAH! WHY DID I REACT LIKE THAT?
Maybe...
I embarrassed him...
No...I'm not gonna fuss about this. I'll just send him an e-mail like I always do.
WHAT SHOULD I SAY? I CAN'T THINK OF ANYTHING...
...

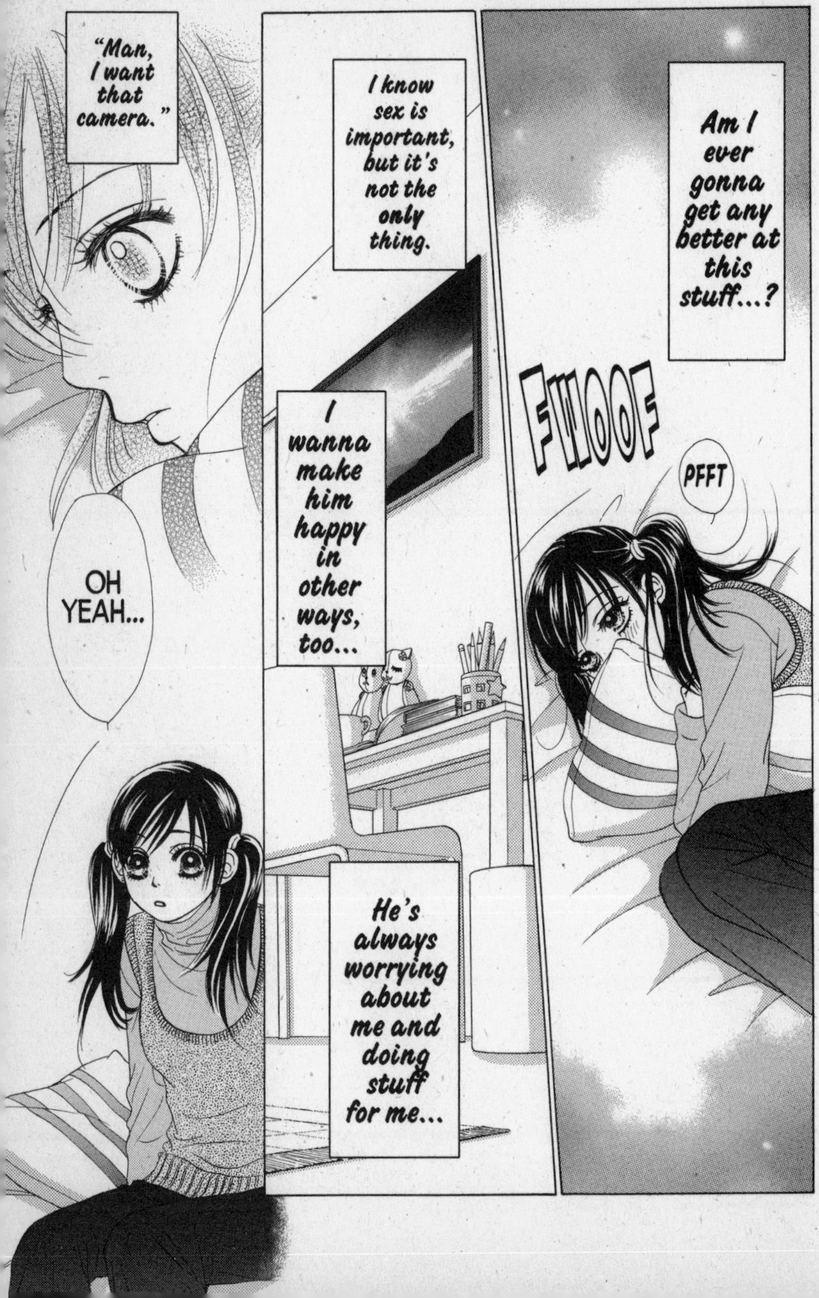
Am I ever gonna get any better at this stuff...?
FWOOF
PFFT
I know sex is important, but it's not the only thing.
I wanna make him happy in other ways, too...
He's always worrying about me and doing stuff for me...
"Man, I want that camera."
OH YEAH...

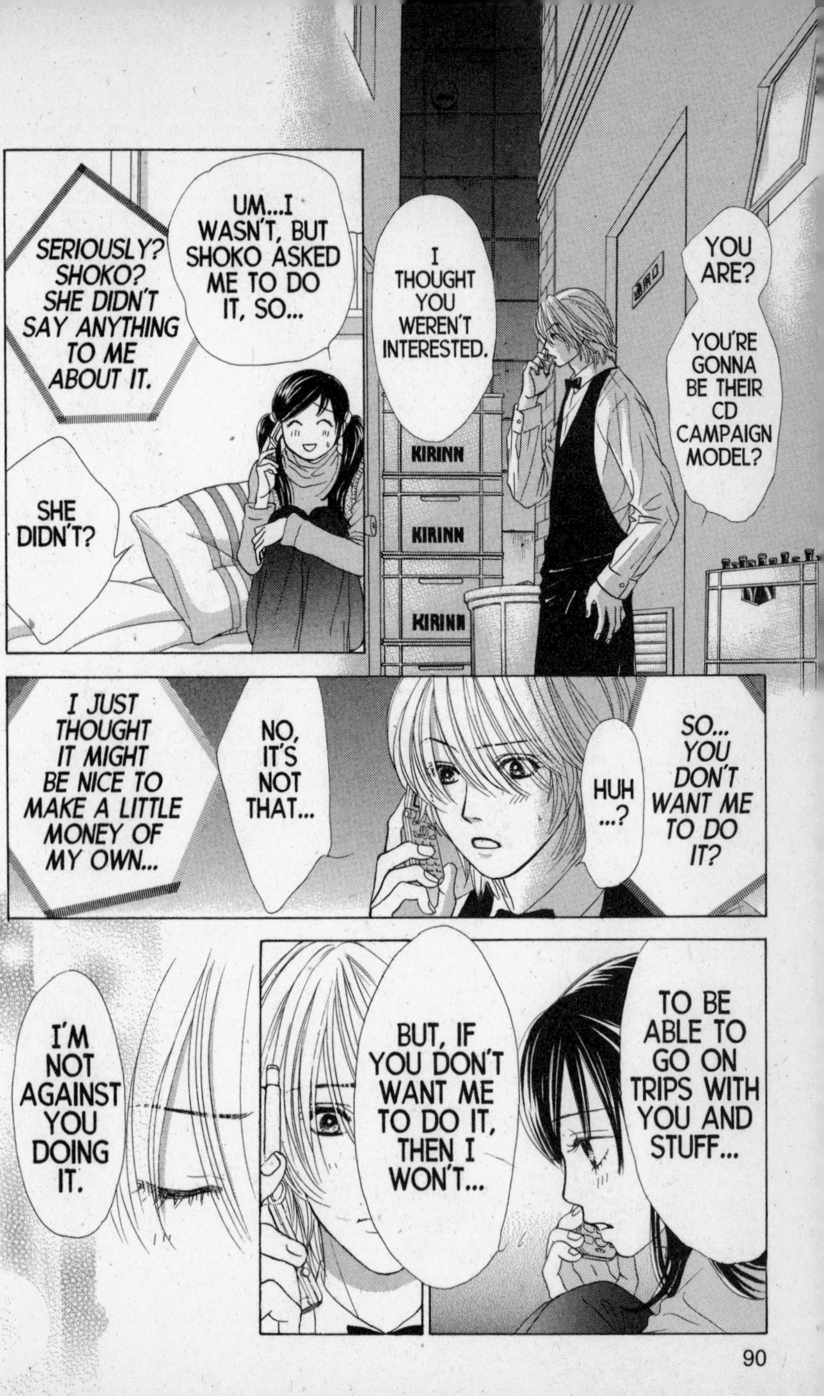
YOU ARE?
YOU'RE GONNA BE THEIR CD CAMPAIGN MODEL?
I THOUGHT YOU WEREN'T INTERESTED.
KIRINN
KIRINN
KIRINN
UM...I WASN'T, BUT SHOKO ASKED ME TO DO IT, SO...
SERIOUSLY? SHOKO? SHE DIDN'T SAY ANYTHING TO ME ABOUT IT.
SHE DIDN'T?
SO... YOU DON'T WANT ME TO DO IT?
HUH ...?
NO, IT'S NOT THAT...
I JUST THOUGHT IT MIGHT BE NICE TO MAKE A LITTLE MONEY OF MY OWN...
TO BE ABLE TO GO ON TRIPS WITH YOU AND STUFF...
BUT, IF YOU DON'T WANT ME TO DO IT, THEN I WON'T...
I'M NOT AGAINST YOU DOING IT.

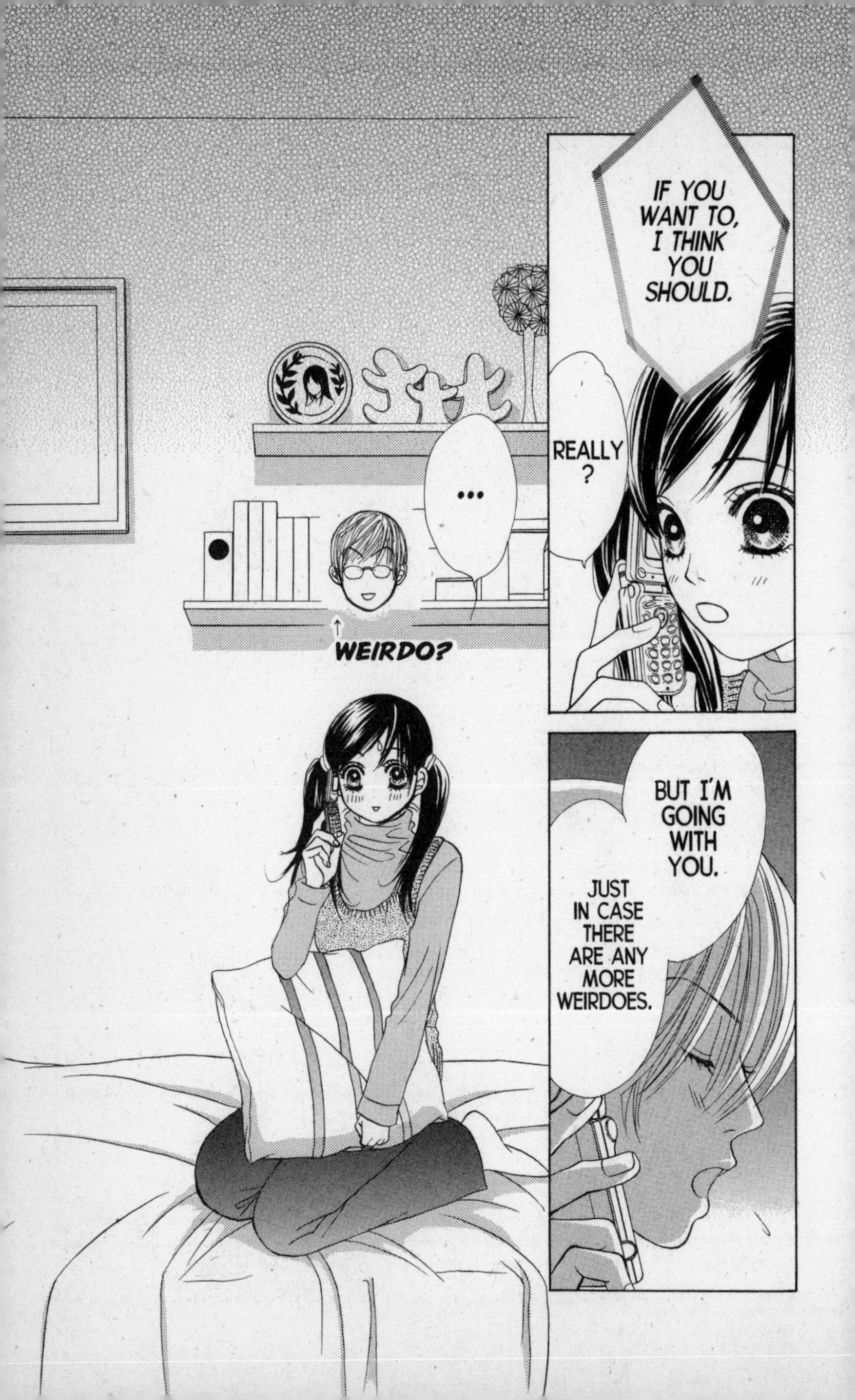
IF YOU WANT TO, I THINK YOU SHOULD.
REALLY?
BUT I'M GOING WITH YOU.
JUST IN CASE THERE ARE ANY MORE WEIRDOES.
...
WEIRDO?

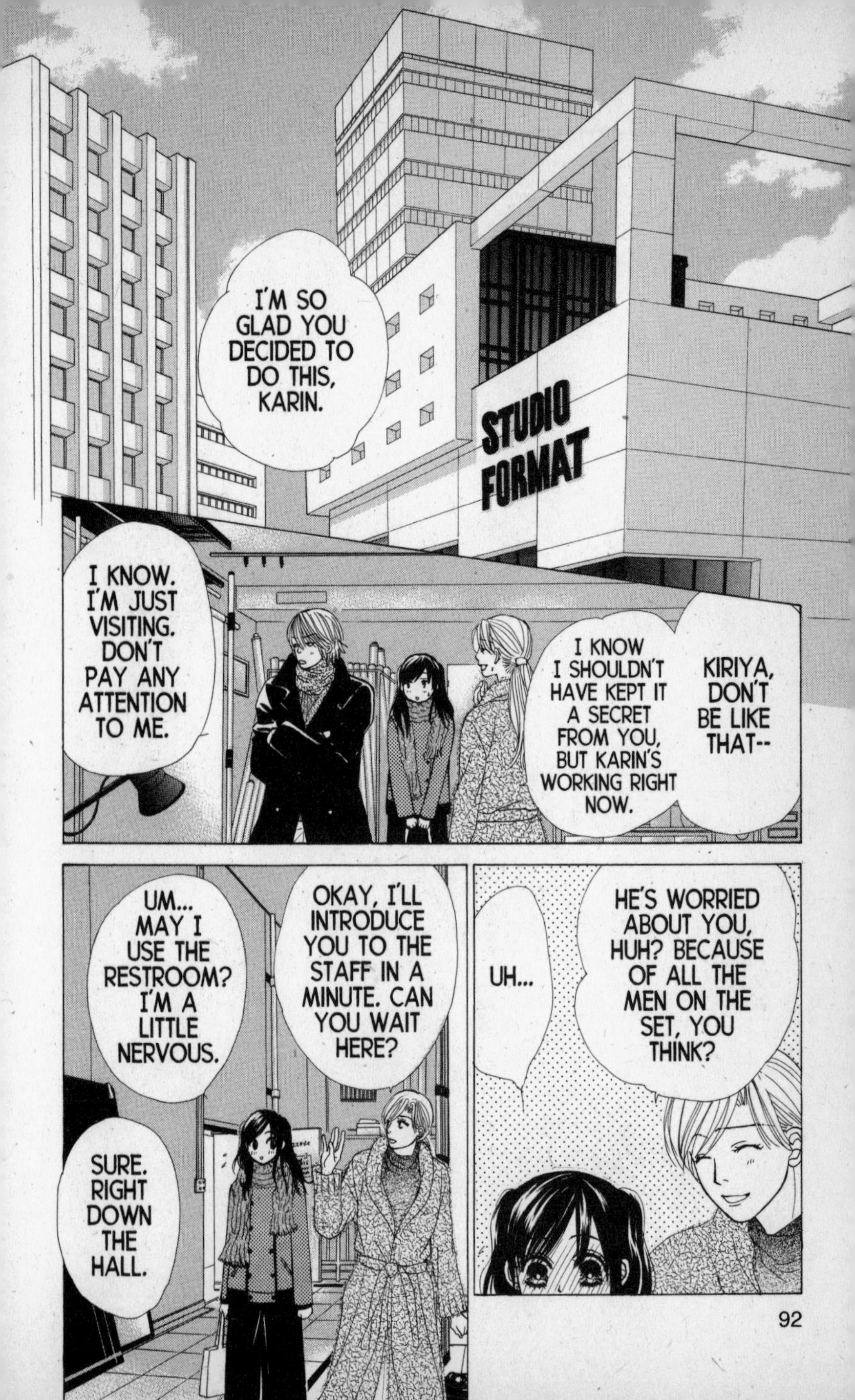
STUDIO FORMAT
I'M SO GLAD YOU DECIDED TO DO THIS, KARIN.
KIRIYA, DON'T BE LIKE THAT--
I KNOW I SHOULDN'T HAVE KEPT IT A SECRET FROM YOU, BUT KARIN'S WORKING RIGHT NOW.
I KNOW. I'M JUST VISITING. DON'T PAY ANY ATTENTION TO ME.
HE'S WORRIED ABOUT YOU, HUH? BECAUSE OF ALL THE MEN ON THE SET, YOU THINK?
UH...
OKAY, I'LL INTRODUCE YOU TO THE STAFF IN A MINUTE. CAN YOU WAIT HERE?
UM... MAY I USE THE RESTROOM? I'M A LITTLE NERVOUS.
SURE. RIGHT DOWN THE HALL.

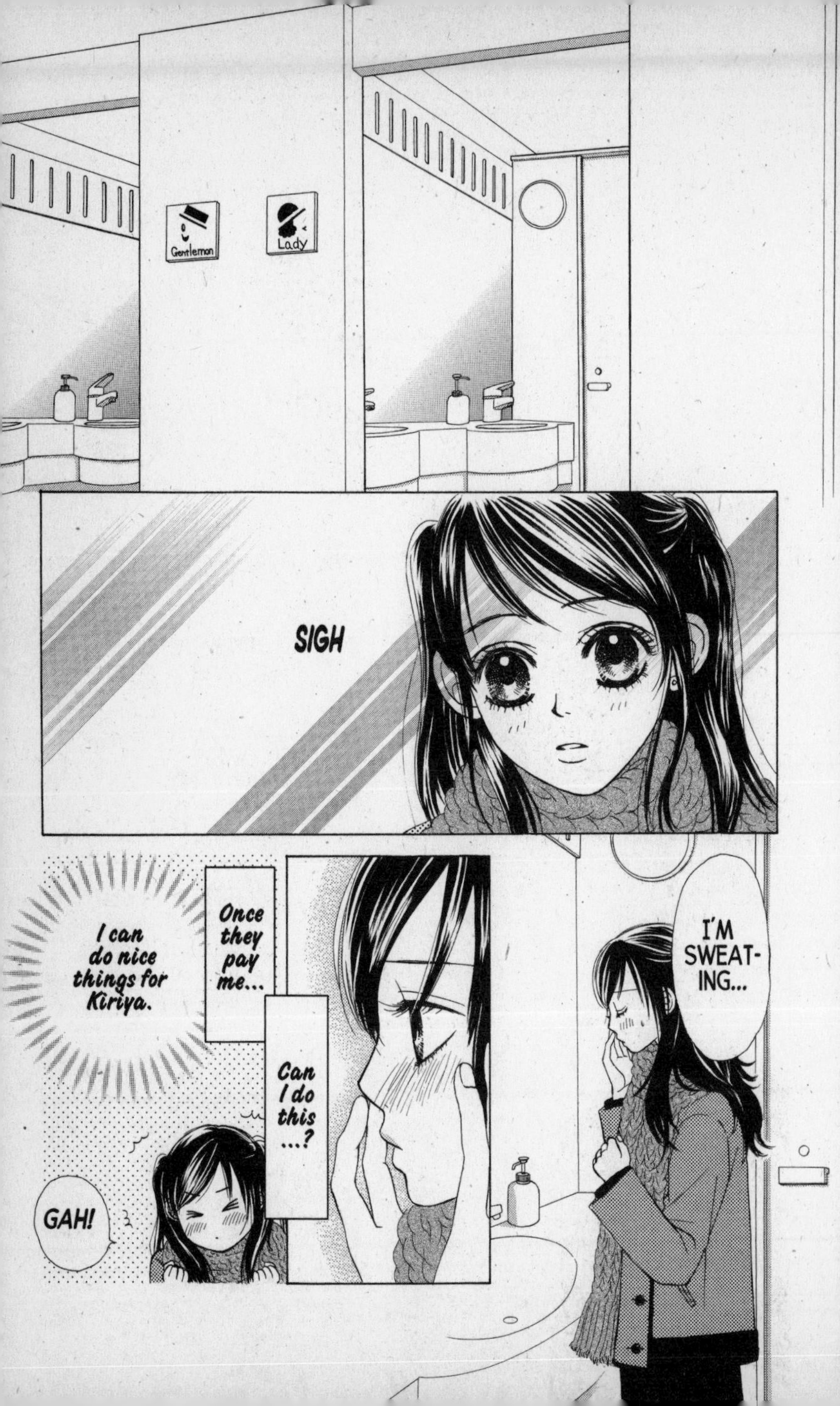
Gentleman
Lady
SIGH
I'M SWEAT-ING...
Once they pay me...
Can I do this ...?
I can do nice things for Kiriya.
GAH!

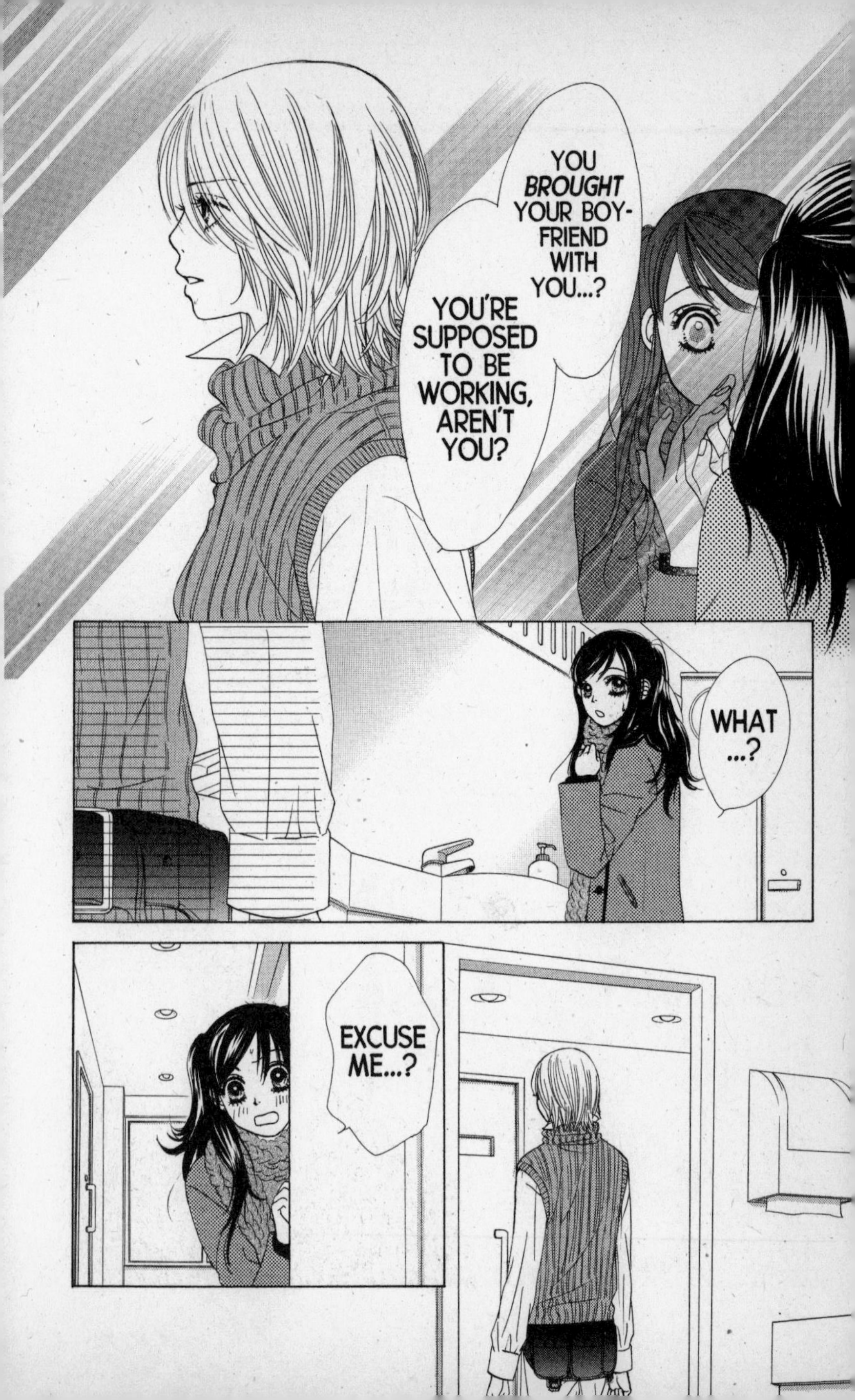
YOU *BROUGHT* YOUR BOY-FRIEND WITH YOU...?
YOU'RE SUPPOSED TO BE WORKING, AREN'T YOU?
WHAT ...?
EXCUSE ME...?

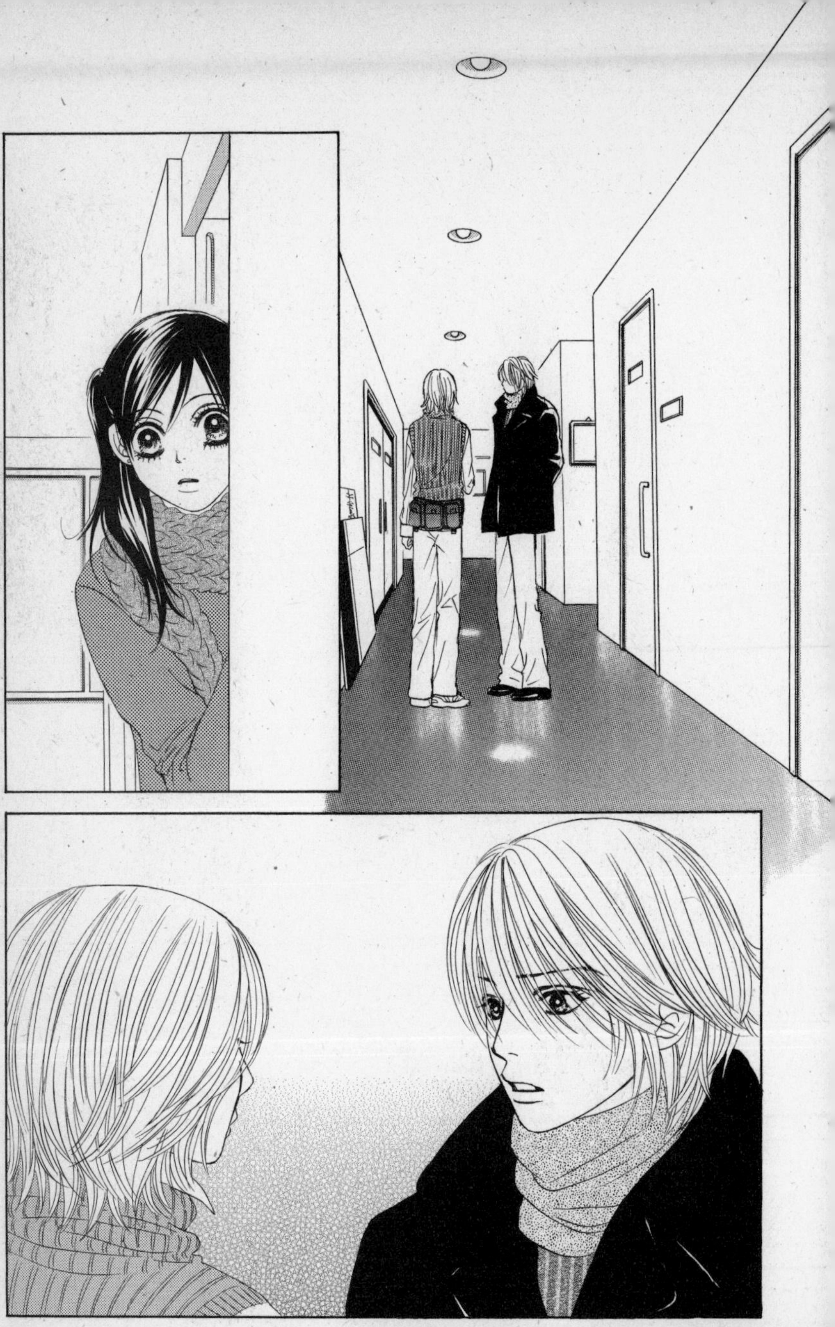

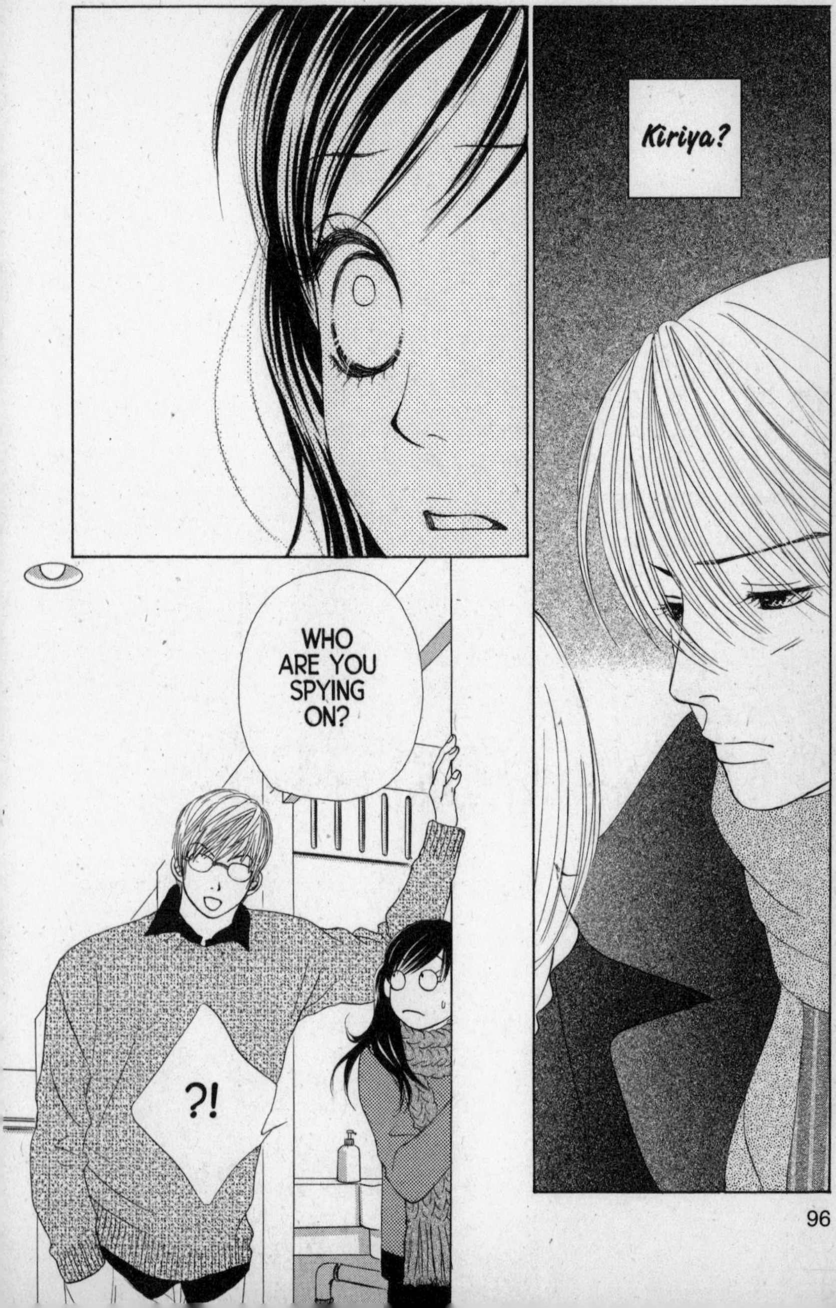
Kiriya?
WHO ARE YOU SPYING ON?
?!

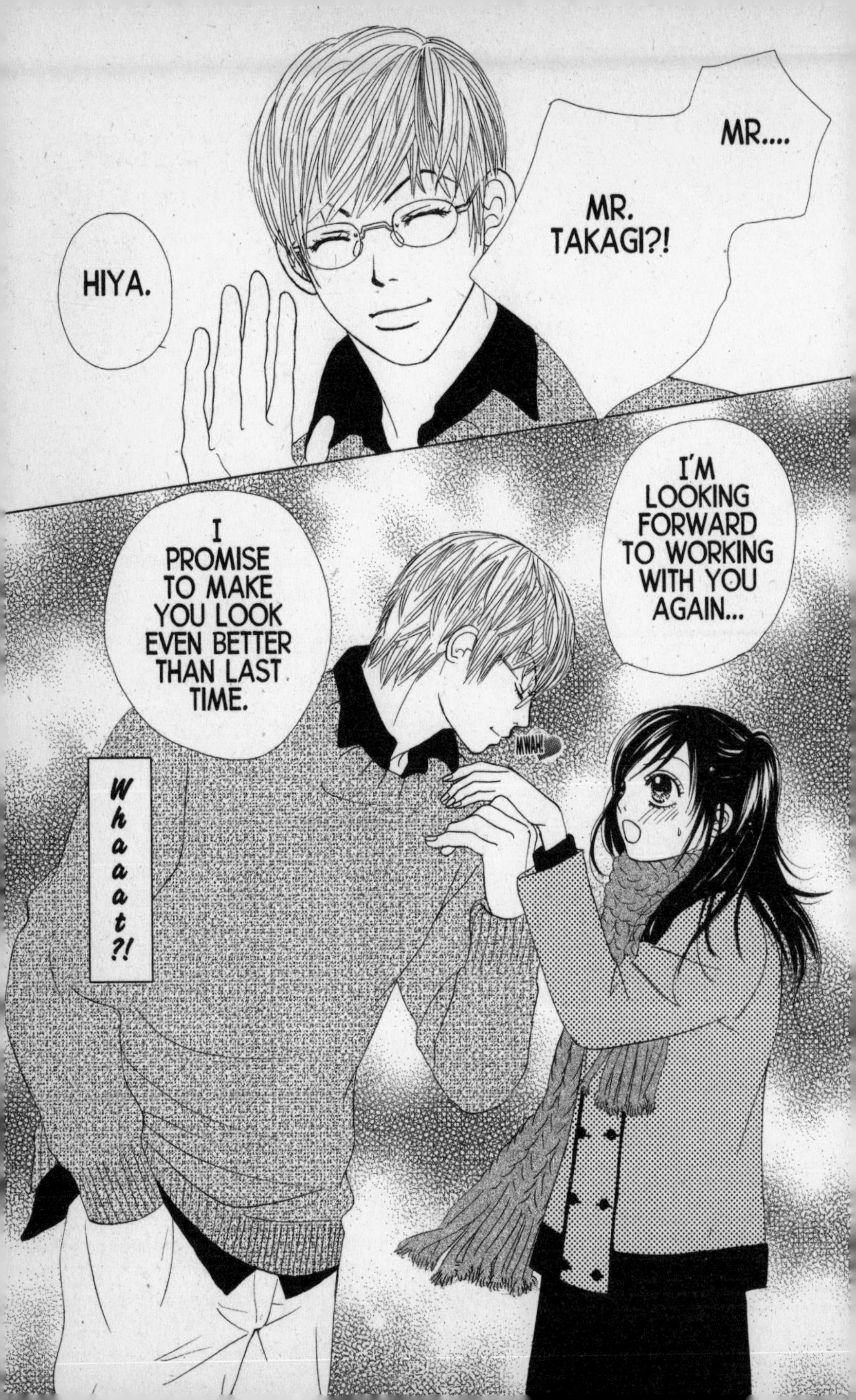
MR....
MR. TAKAGI?!
HIYA.
I'M LOOKING FORWARD TO WORKING WITH YOU AGAIN...
I PROMISE TO MAKE YOU LOOK EVEN BETTER THAN LAST TIME.
MWAH!
Whaaaat?!

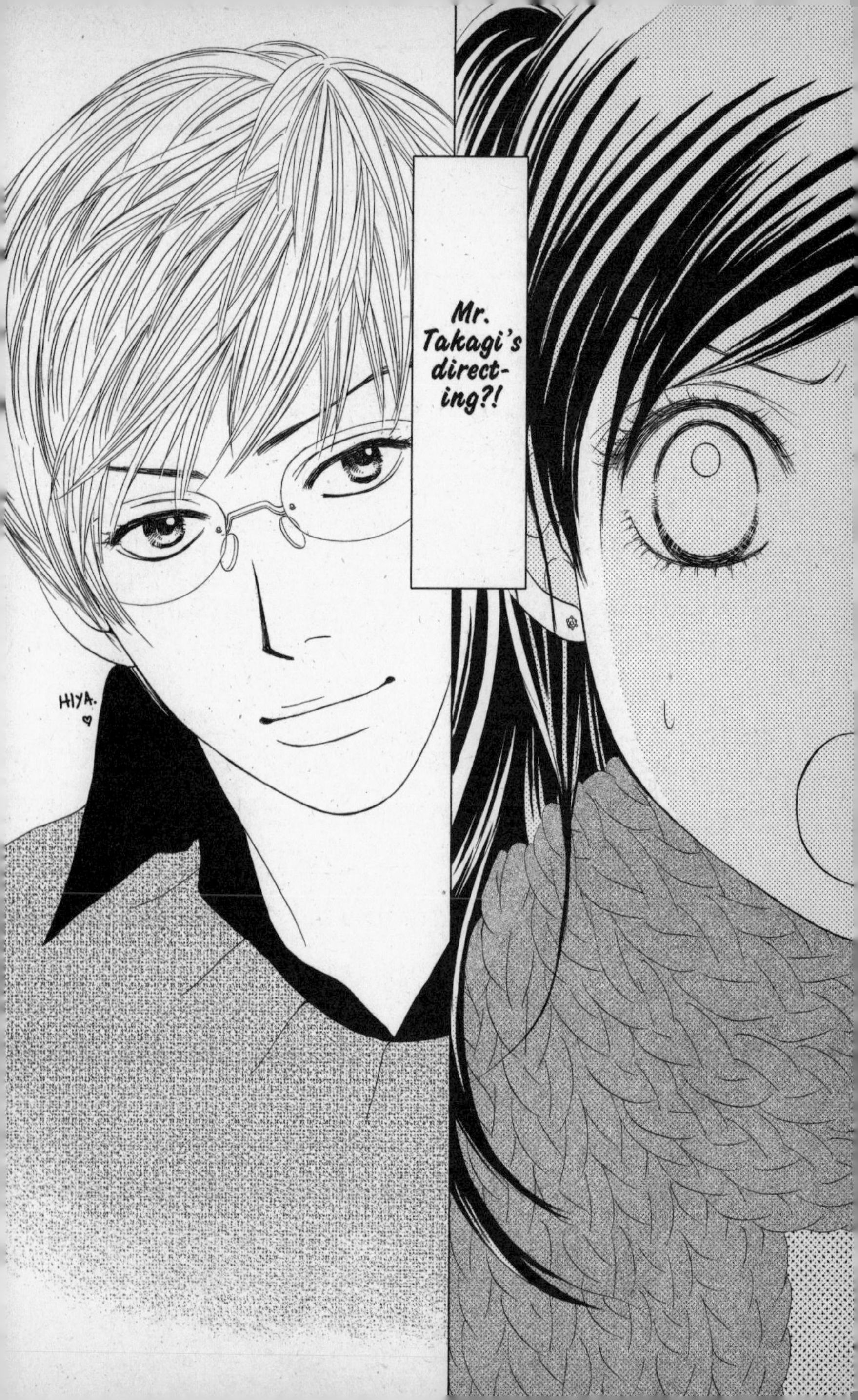
Mr. Takagi's direct-ing?!
HIYA. ♥

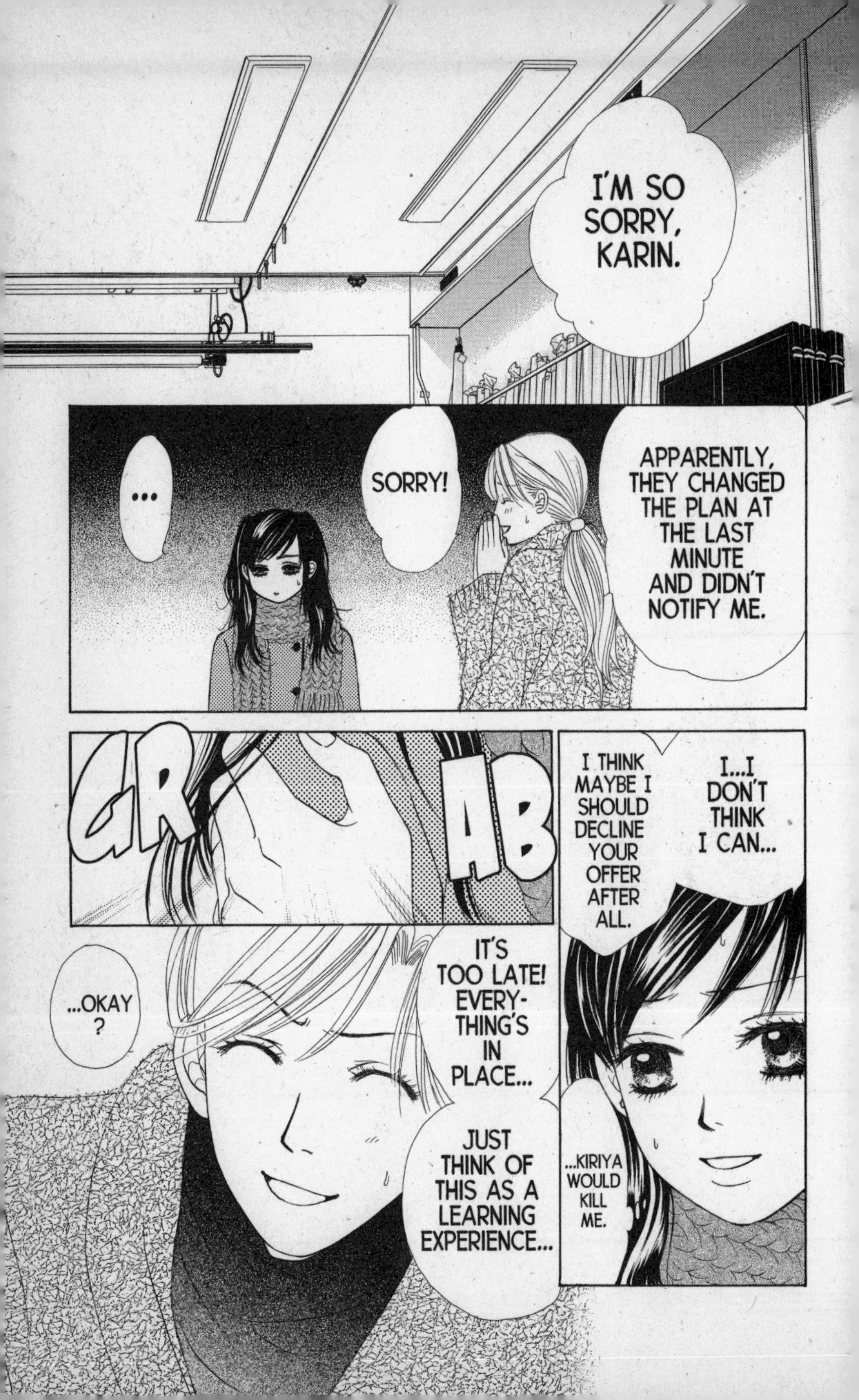
I'M SO SORRY, KARIN.
APPARENTLY, THEY CHANGED THE PLAN AT THE LAST MINUTE AND DIDN'T NOTIFY ME.
SORRY!
...
I...I DON'T THINK I CAN...
I THINK MAYBE I SHOULD DECLINE YOUR OFFER AFTER ALL.
...KIRIYA WOULD KILL ME.
GRAB
IT'S TOO LATE! EVERY-THING'S IN PLACE...
JUST THINK OF THIS AS A LEARNING EXPERIENCE...
...OKAY?

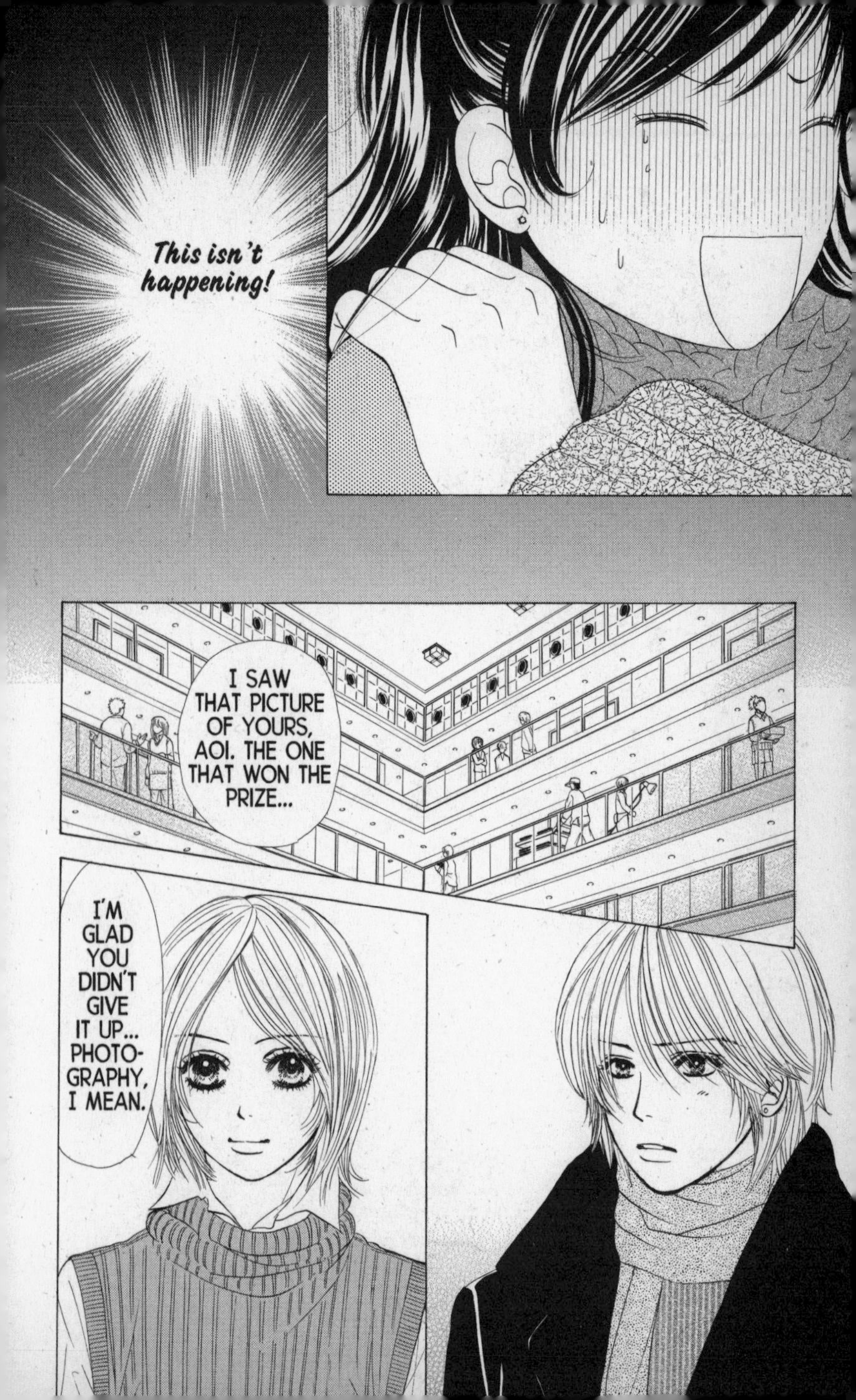
This isn't happening!
I SAW THAT PICTURE OF YOURS, AOI. THE ONE THAT WON THE PRIZE...
I'M GLAD YOU DIDN'T GIVE IT UP... PHOTOGRAPHY, I MEAN.

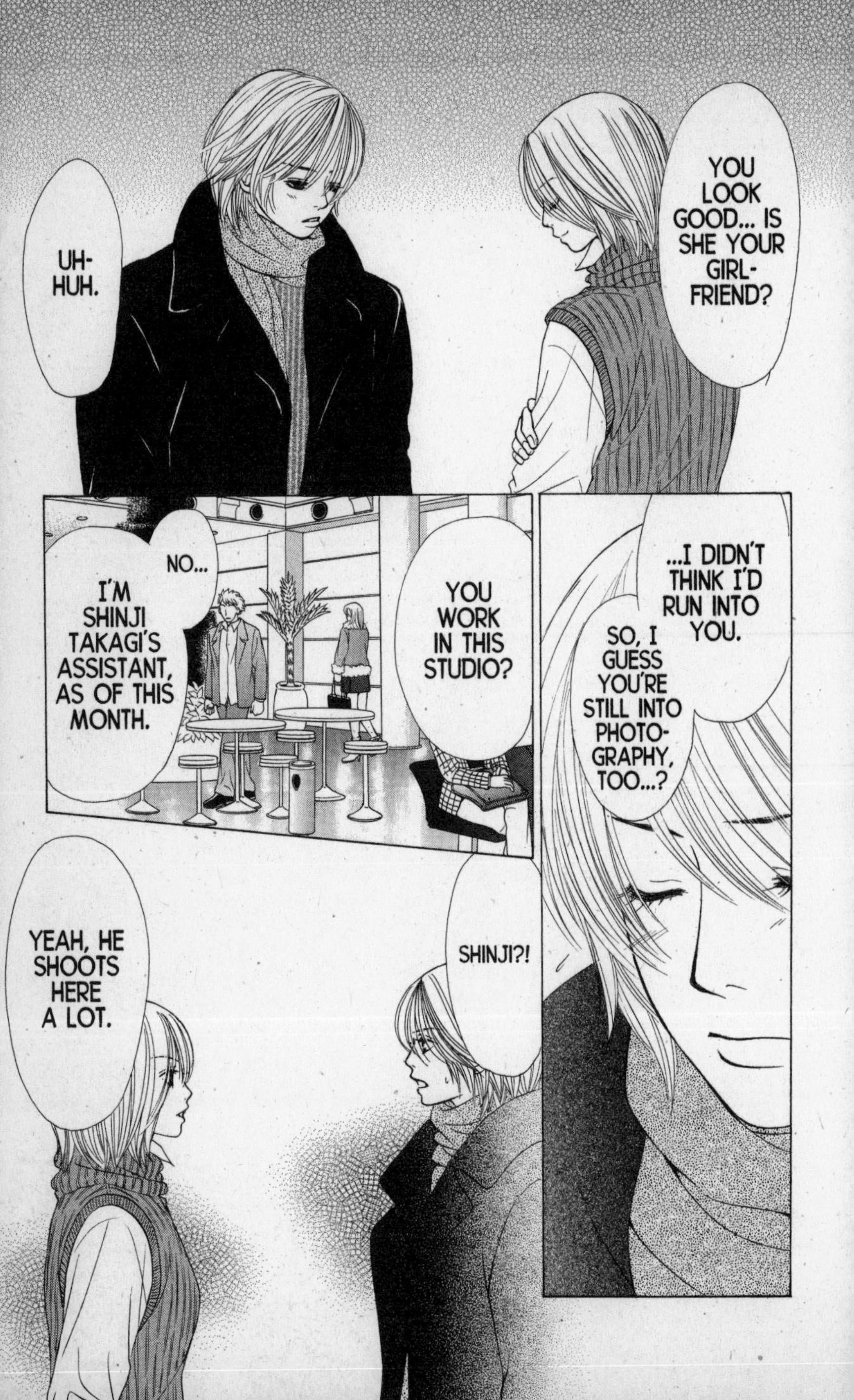
YOU LOOK GOOD... IS SHE YOUR GIRL-FRIEND?
UH-HUH.
...I DIDN'T THINK I'D RUN INTO YOU.
SO, I GUESS YOU'RE STILL INTO PHOTO-GRAPHY, TOO...?
YOU WORK IN THIS STUDIO?
NO...
I'M SHINJI TAKAGI'S ASSISTANT, AS OF THIS MONTH.
SHINJI?!
YEAH, HE SHOOTS HERE A LOT.

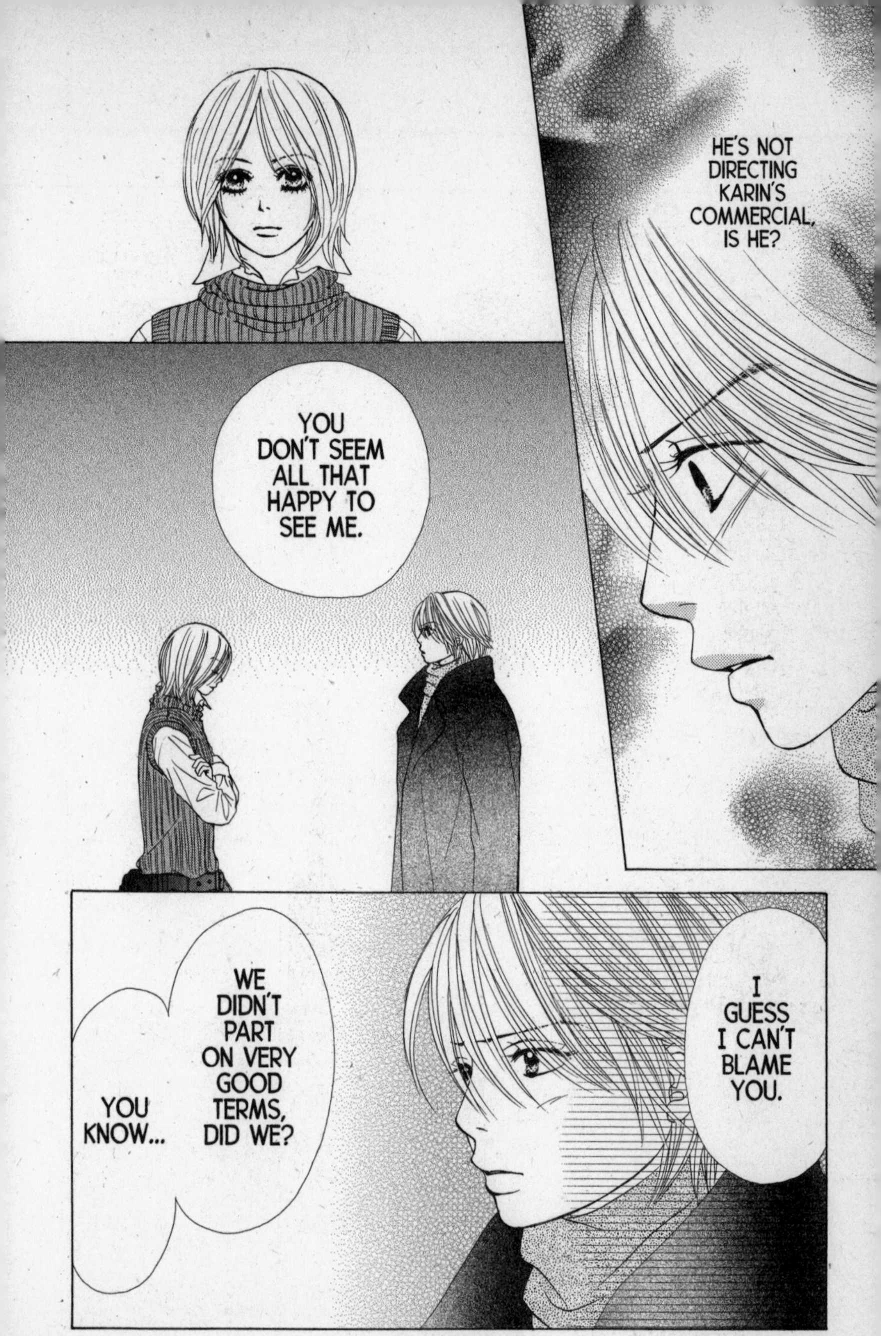
HE'S NOT DIRECTING KARIN'S COMMERCIAL, IS HE?
YOU DON'T SEEM ALL THAT HAPPY TO SEE ME.
I GUESS I CAN'T BLAME YOU.
WE DIDN'T PART ON VERY GOOD TERMS, DID WE?
YOU KNOW...

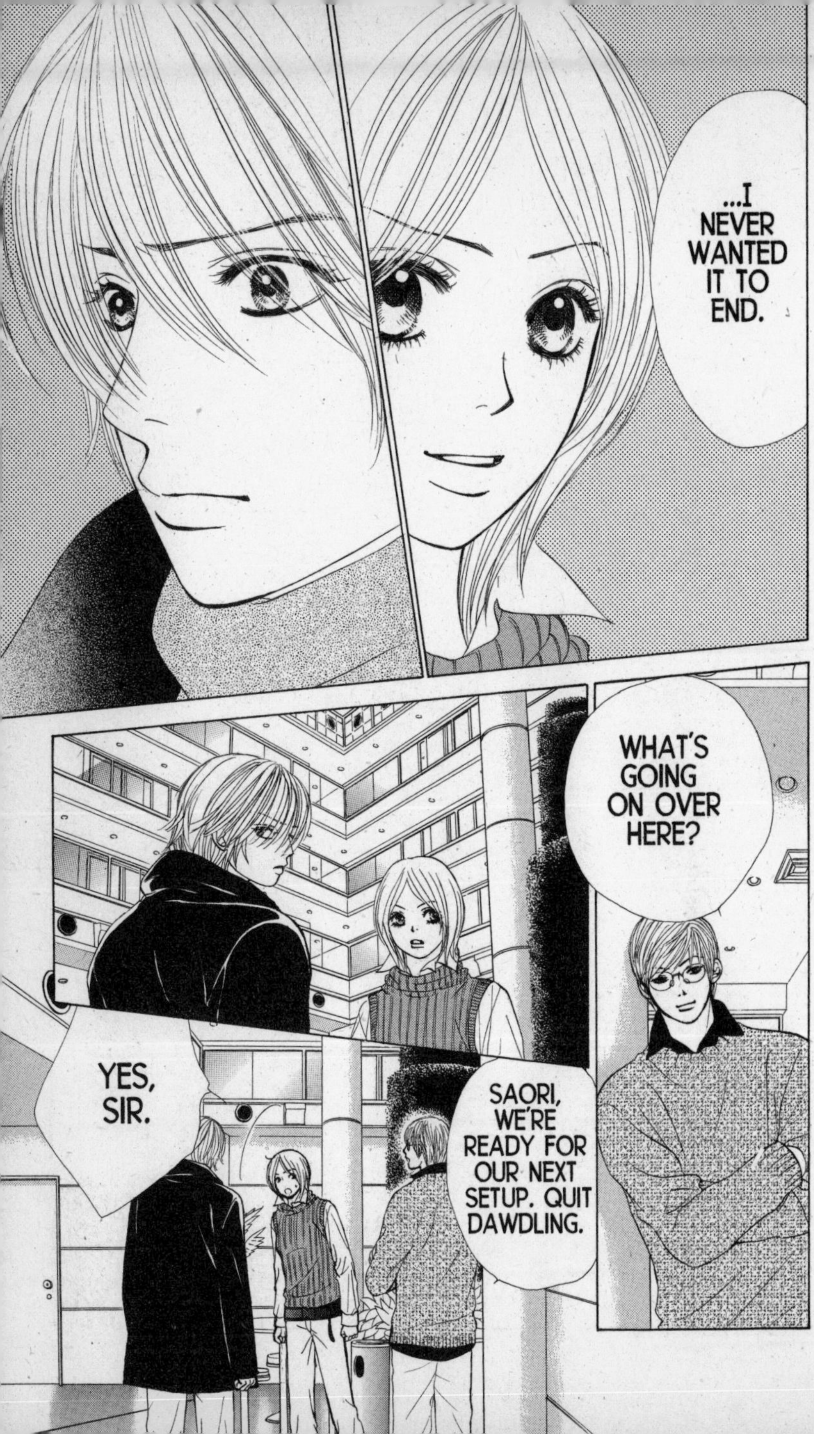
...I NEVER WANTED IT TO END.
WHAT'S GOING ON OVER HERE?
SAORI, WE'RE READY FOR OUR NEXT SETUP. QUIT DAWDLING.
YES, SIR.

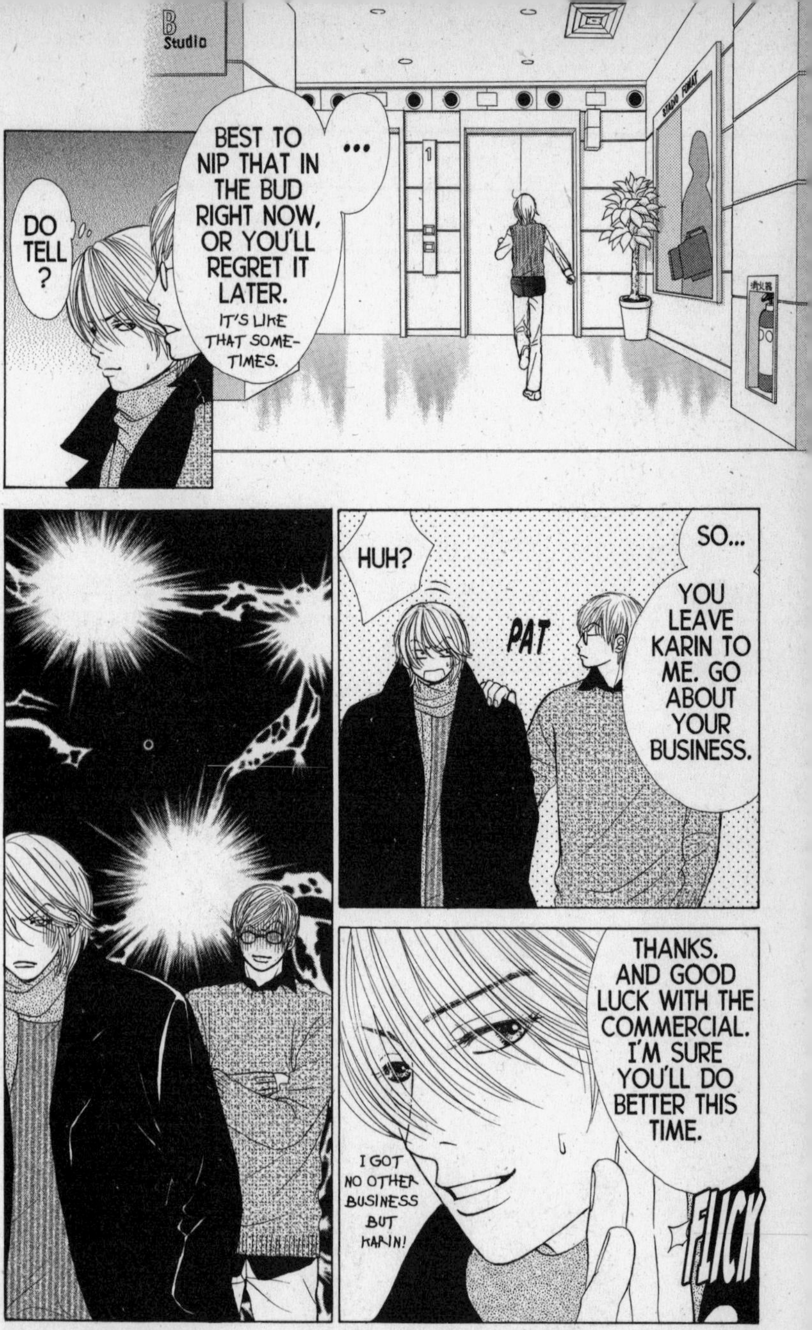
B Studio
...
BEST TO NIP THAT IN THE BUD RIGHT NOW, OR YOU'LL REGRET IT LATER.
IT'S LIKE THAT SOMETIMES.
DO TELL?
SO...
YOU LEAVE KARIN TO ME. GO ABOUT YOUR BUSINESS.
HUH?
PAT
THANKS. AND GOOD LUCK WITH THE COMMERCIAL. I'M SURE YOU'LL DO BETTER THIS TIME.
FLICK
I GOT NO OTHER BUSINESS BUT KARIN!

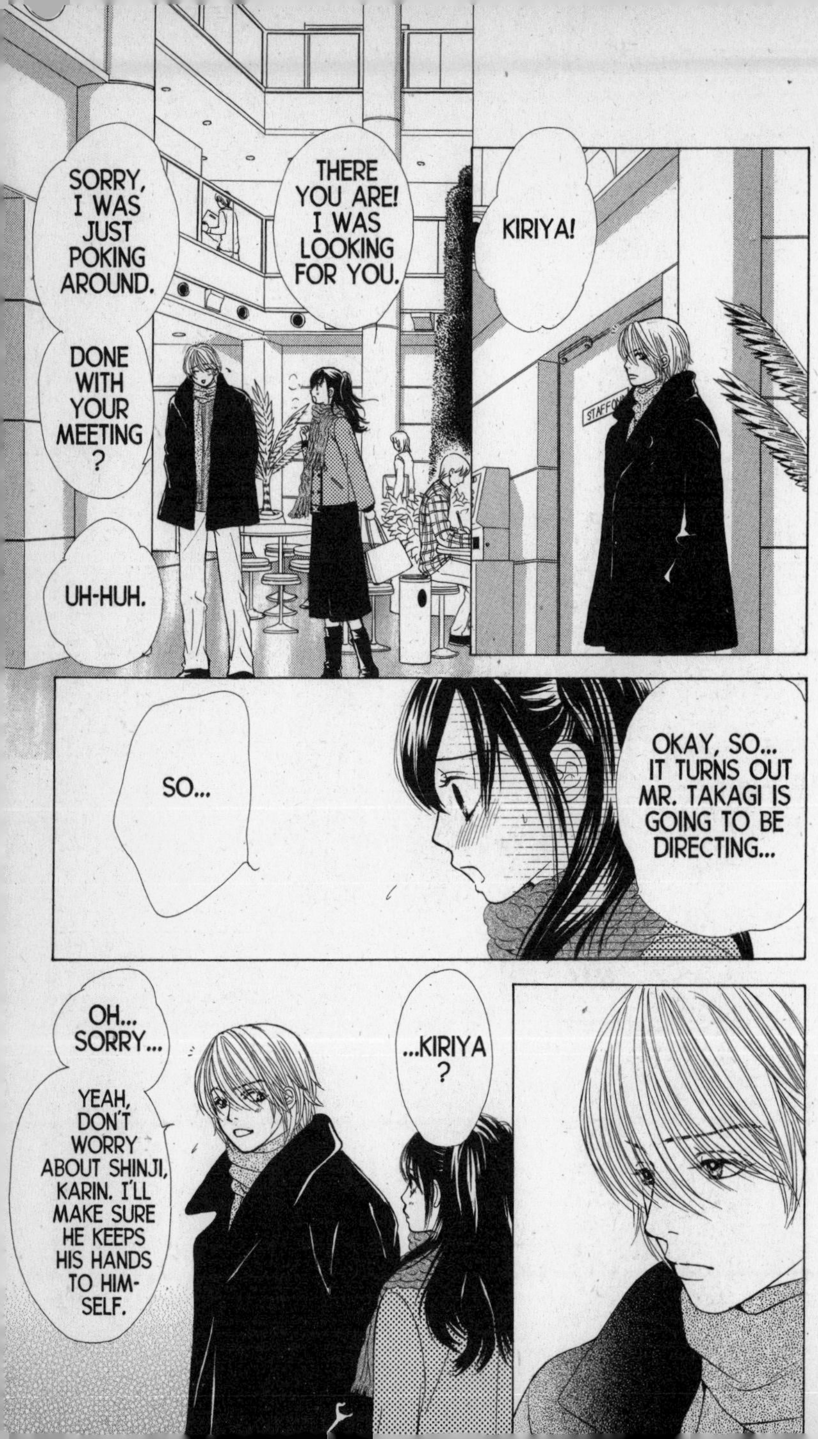
KIRIYA!
THERE YOU ARE! I WAS LOOKING FOR YOU.
SORRY, I WAS JUST POKING AROUND.
DONE WITH YOUR MEETING?
UH-HUH.
OKAY, SO... IT TURNS OUT MR. TAKAGI IS GOING TO BE DIRECTING...
SO...
...KIRIYA?
OH... SORRY...
YEAH, DON'T WORRY ABOUT SHINJI, KARIN. I'LL MAKE SURE HE KEEPS HIS HANDS TO HIM-SELF.

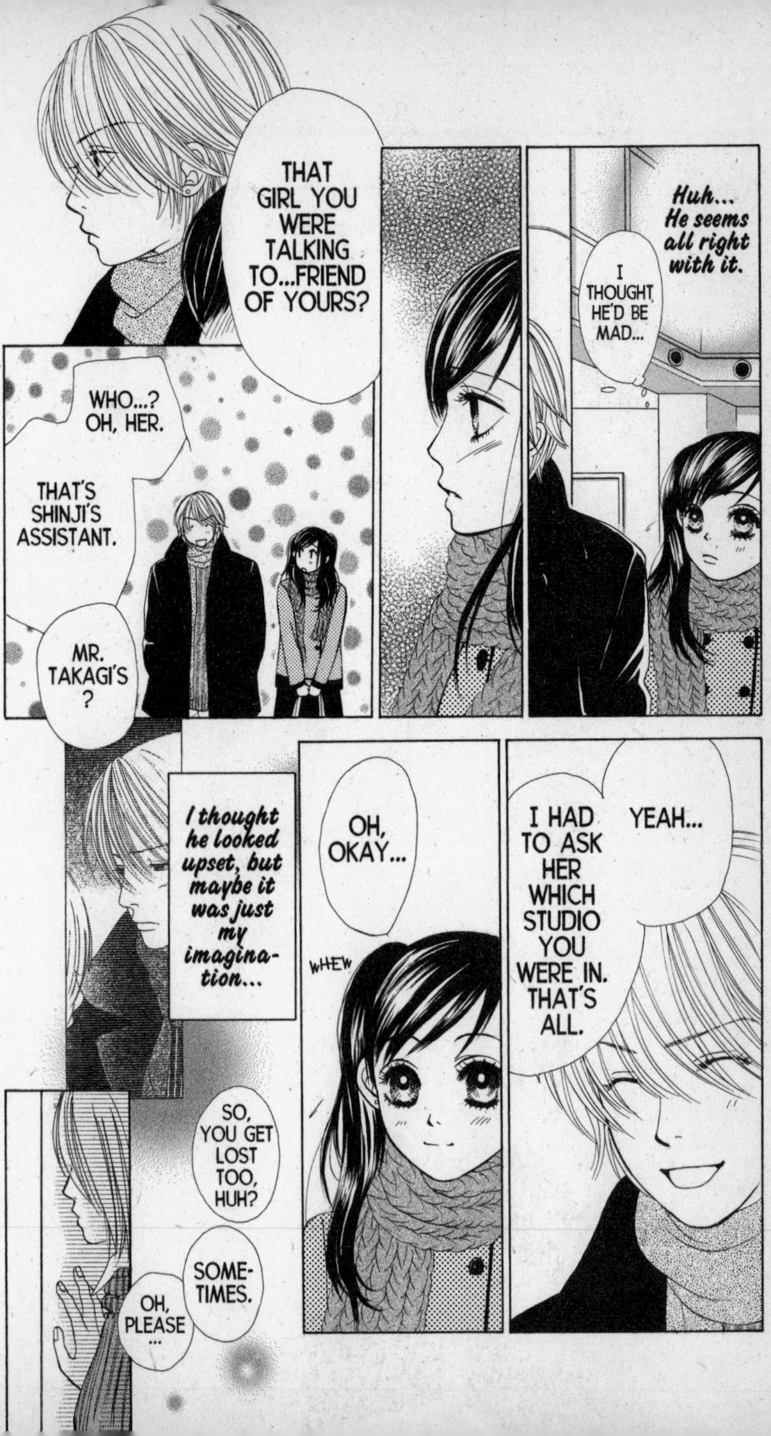
THAT GIRL YOU WERE TALKING TO...FRIEND OF YOURS?
Huh... He seems all right with it.
I THOUGHT HE'D BE MAD...
WHO...? OH, HER.
THAT'S SHINJI'S ASSISTANT.
MR. TAKAGI'S?
YEAH...
I HAD TO ASK HER WHICH STUDIO YOU WERE IN. THAT'S ALL.
OH, OKAY...
WHEW
I thought he looked upset, but maybe it was just my imagination...
SO, YOU GET LOST TOO, HUH?
SOME-TIMES.
OH, PLEASE...

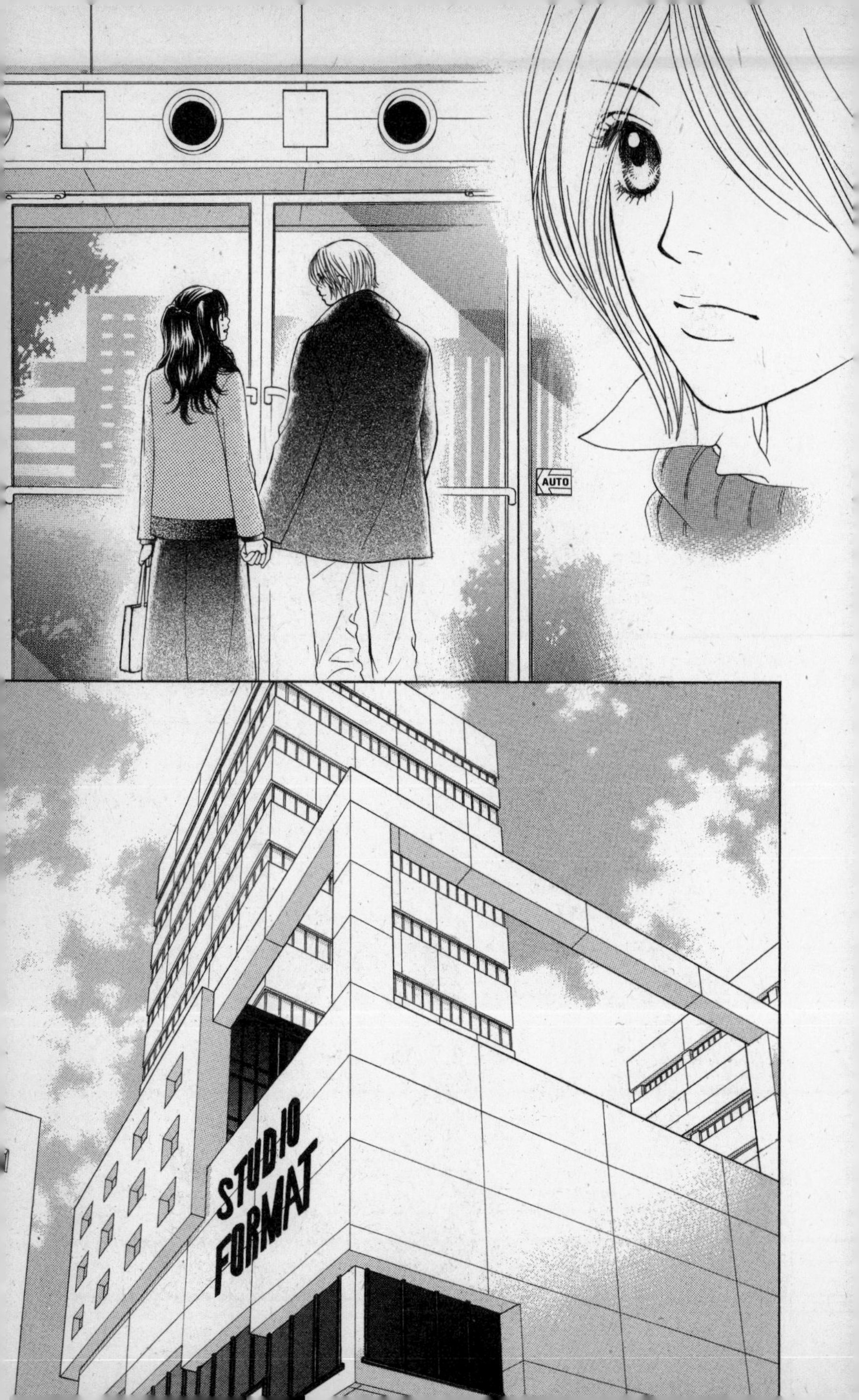
AUTO
STUDIO
FORMAT

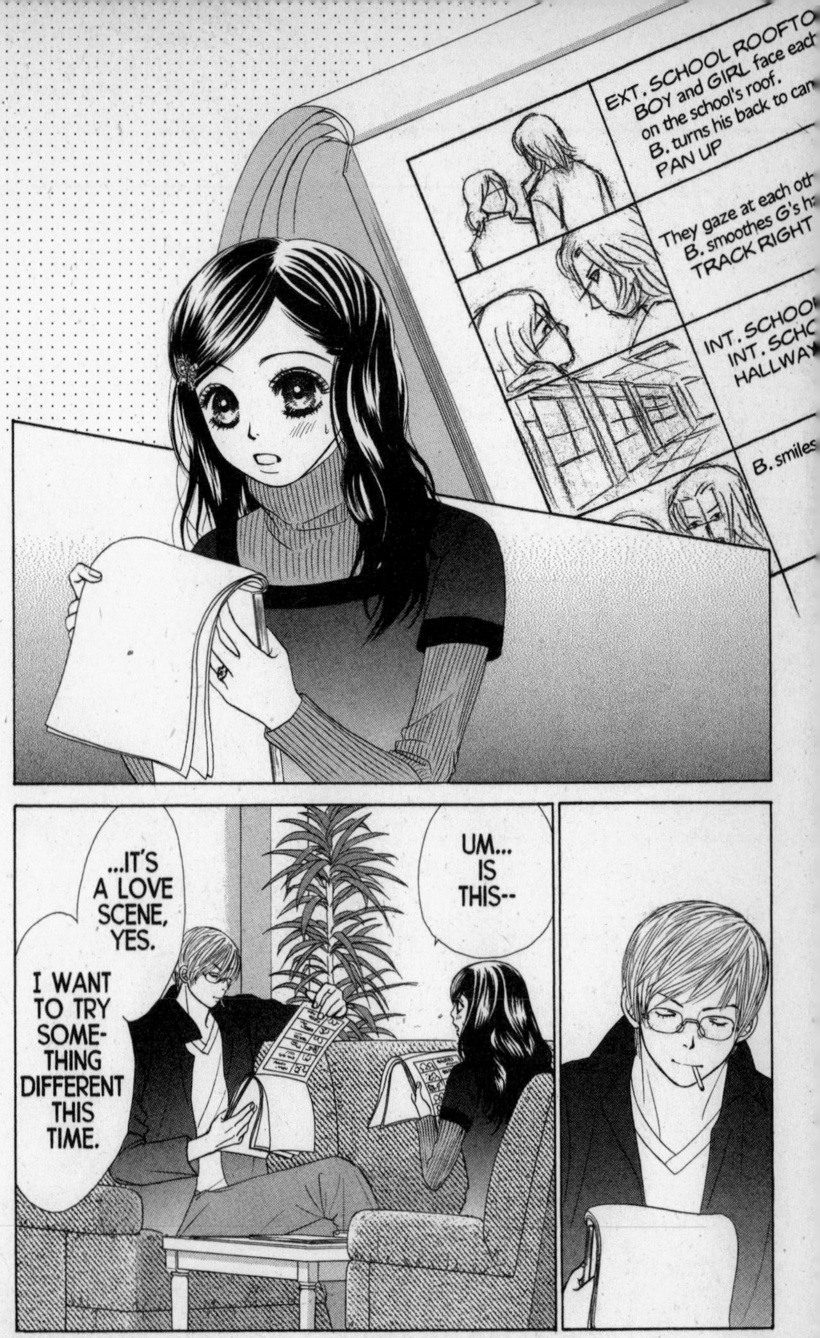
EXT. SCHOOL ROOFTO
BOY and GIRL face each
on the school's roof.
B. turns his back to cam
PAN UP
They gaze at each oth
B. smoothes G's ha
TRACK RIGHT
INT. SCHOO
INT. SCHO
HALLWAY
B. smiles
UM... IS THIS--
...IT'S A LOVE SCENE, YES.
I WANT TO TRY SOME-THING DIFFERENT THIS TIME.

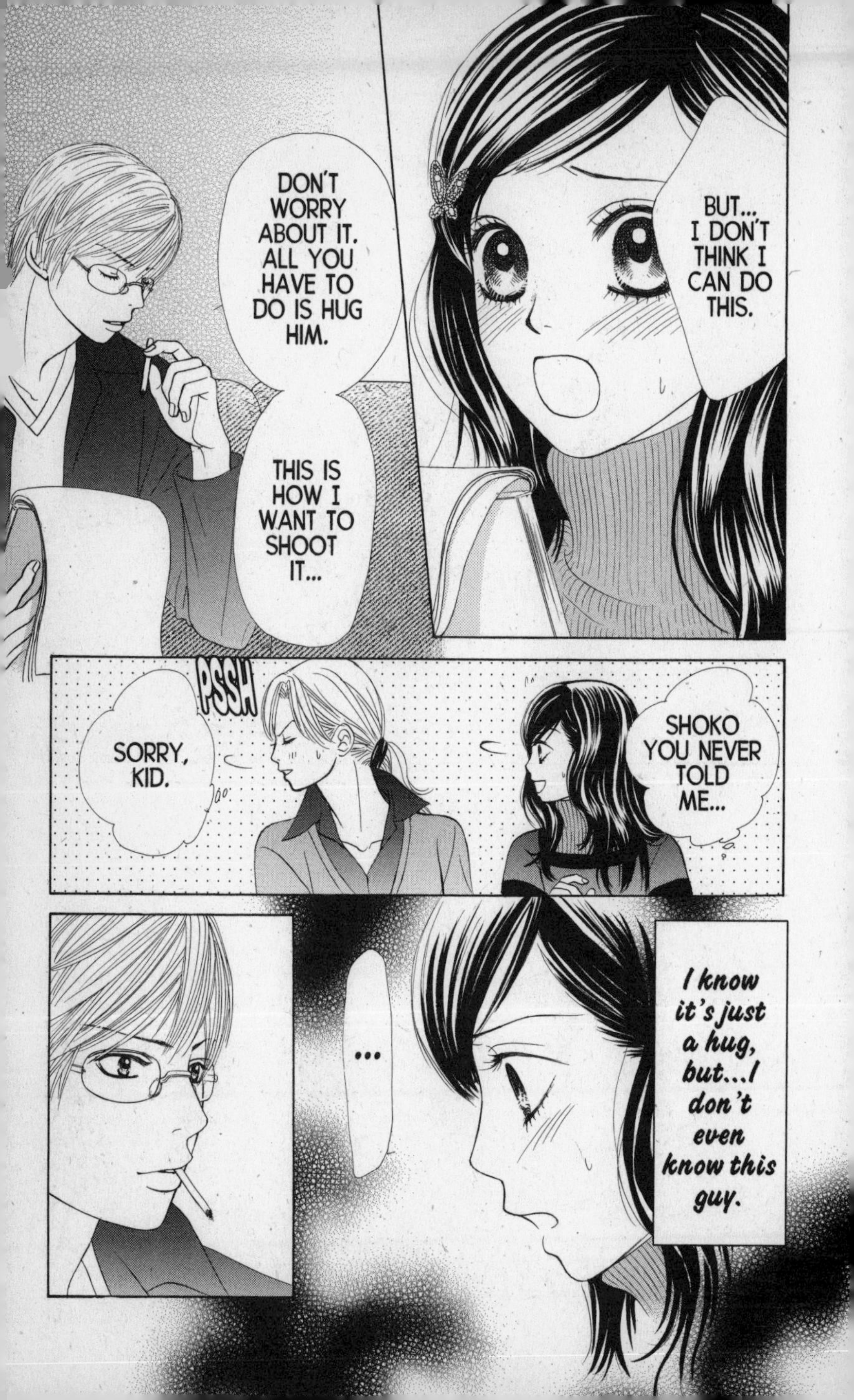
BUT... I DON'T THINK I CAN DO THIS.
DON'T WORRY ABOUT IT. ALL YOU HAVE TO DO IS HUG HIM.
THIS IS HOW I WANT TO SHOOT IT...
SHOKO YOU NEVER TOLD ME...
PSSH
SORRY, KID.
I know it's just a hug, but...I don't even know this guy.
...

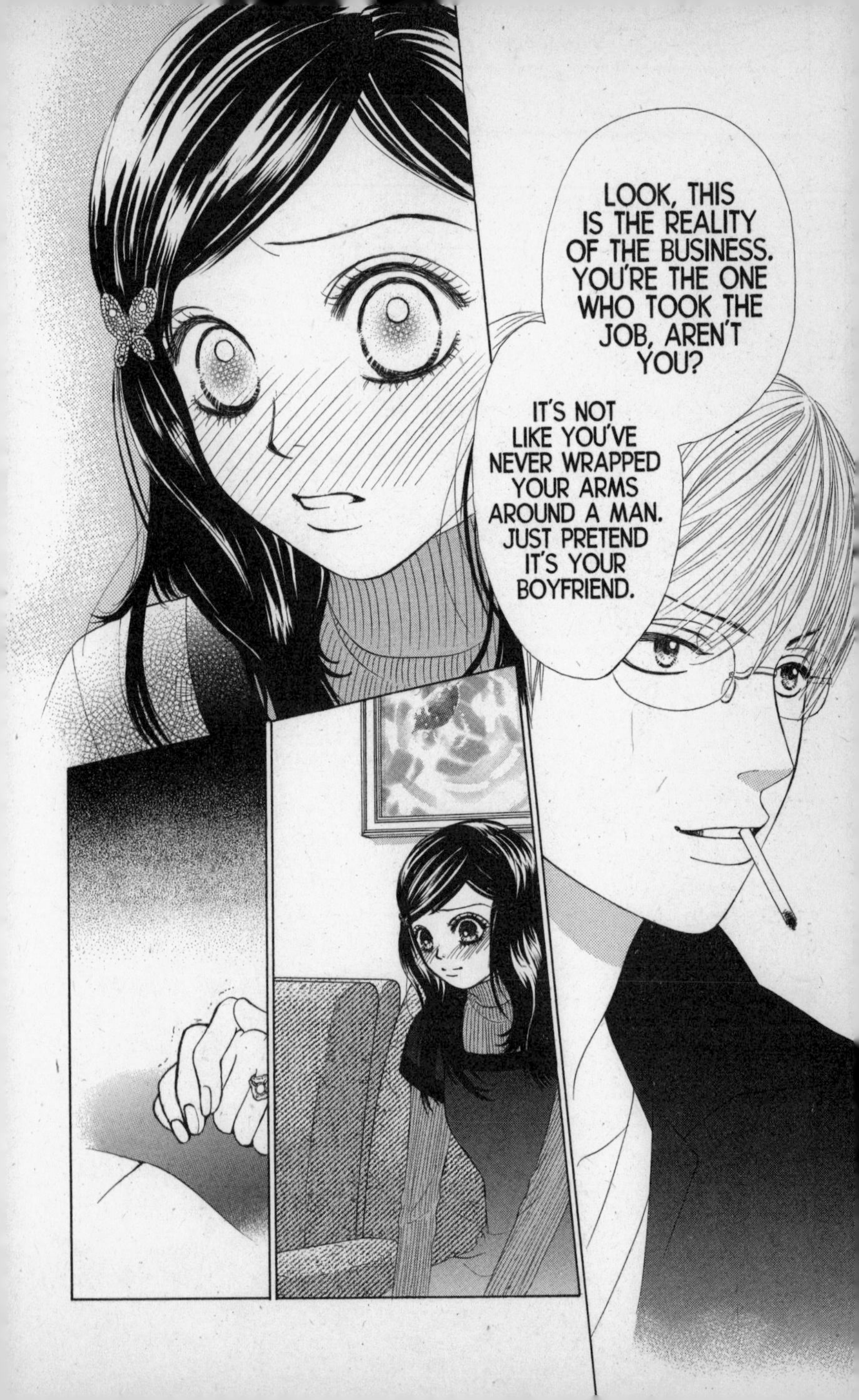
LOOK, THIS IS THE REALITY OF THE BUSINESS. YOU'RE THE ONE WHO TOOK THE JOB, AREN'T YOU?
IT'S NOT LIKE YOU'VE NEVER WRAPPED YOUR ARMS AROUND A MAN. JUST PRETEND IT'S YOUR BOYFRIEND.

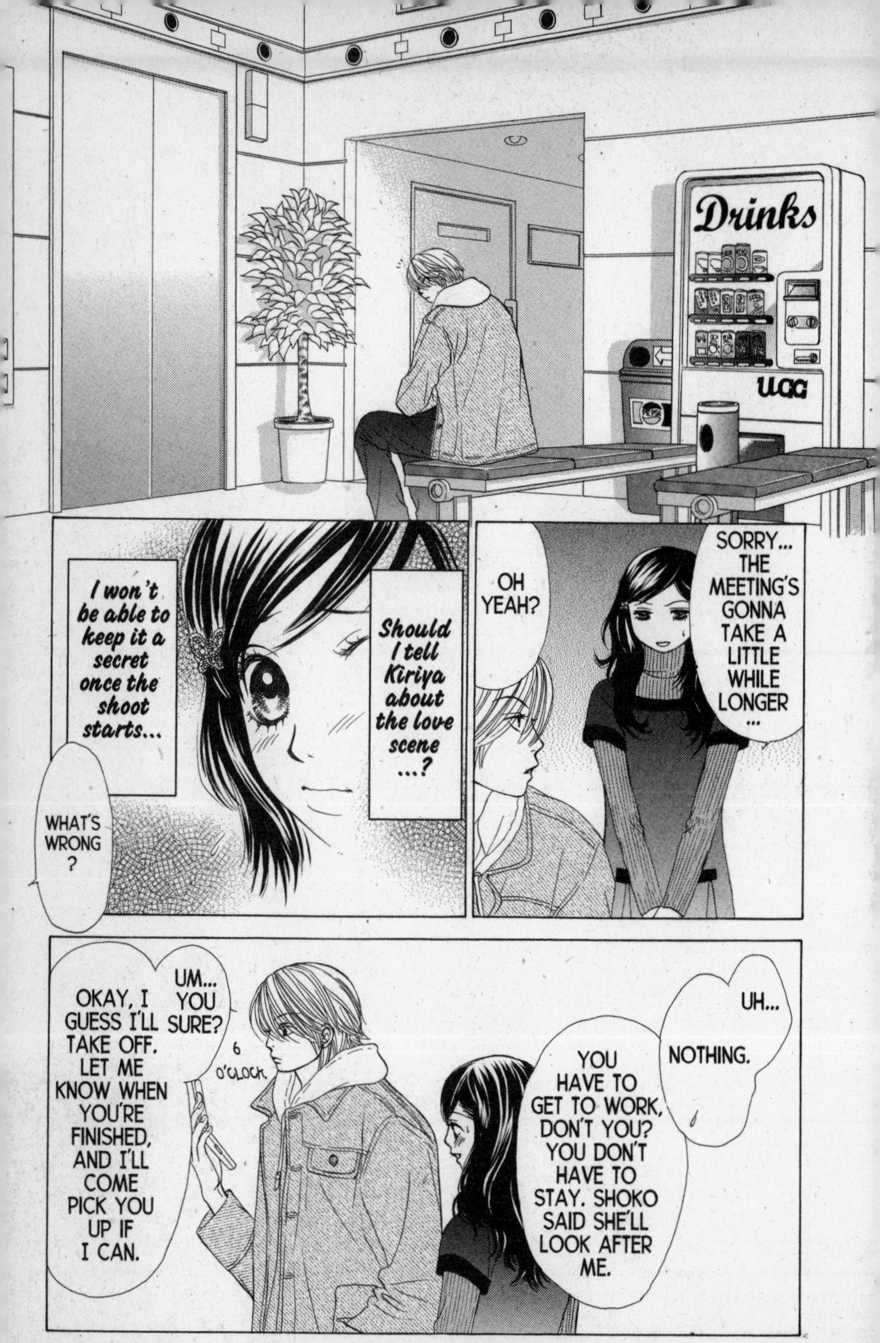
Drinks
UCC
SORRY... THE MEETING'S GONNA TAKE A LITTLE WHILE LONGER...
OH YEAH?
Should I tell Kiriya about the love scene...?
I won't be able to keep it a secret once the shoot starts...
WHAT'S WRONG?
UH...
NOTHING.
YOU HAVE TO GET TO WORK, DON'T YOU? YOU DON'T HAVE TO STAY. SHOKO SAID SHE'LL LOOK AFTER ME.
6 O'CLOCK.
UM... YOU SURE?
OKAY, I GUESS I'LL TAKE OFF. LET ME KNOW WHEN YOU'RE FINISHED, AND I'LL COME PICK YOU UP IF I CAN.

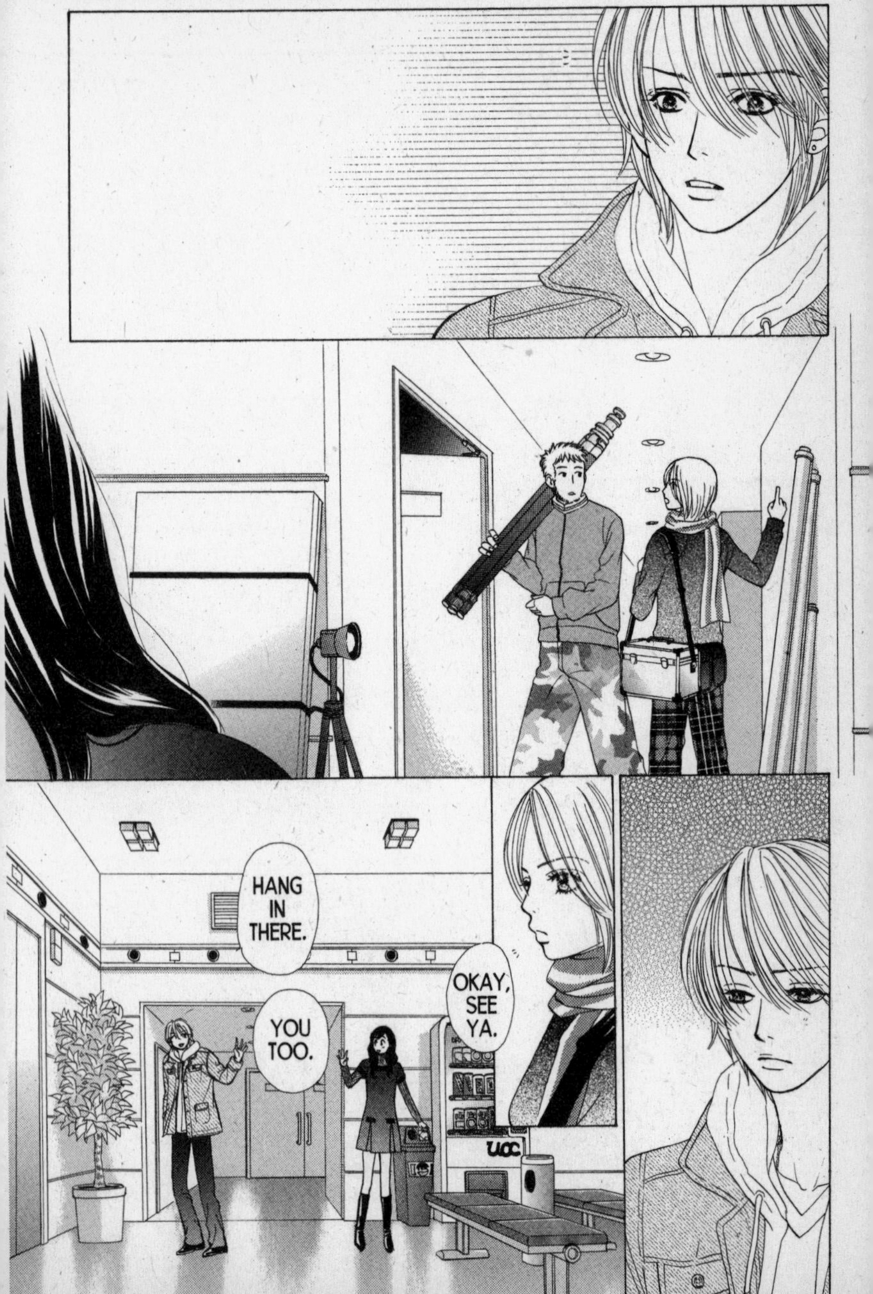
HANG IN THERE.
YOU TOO.
OKAY, SEE YA.

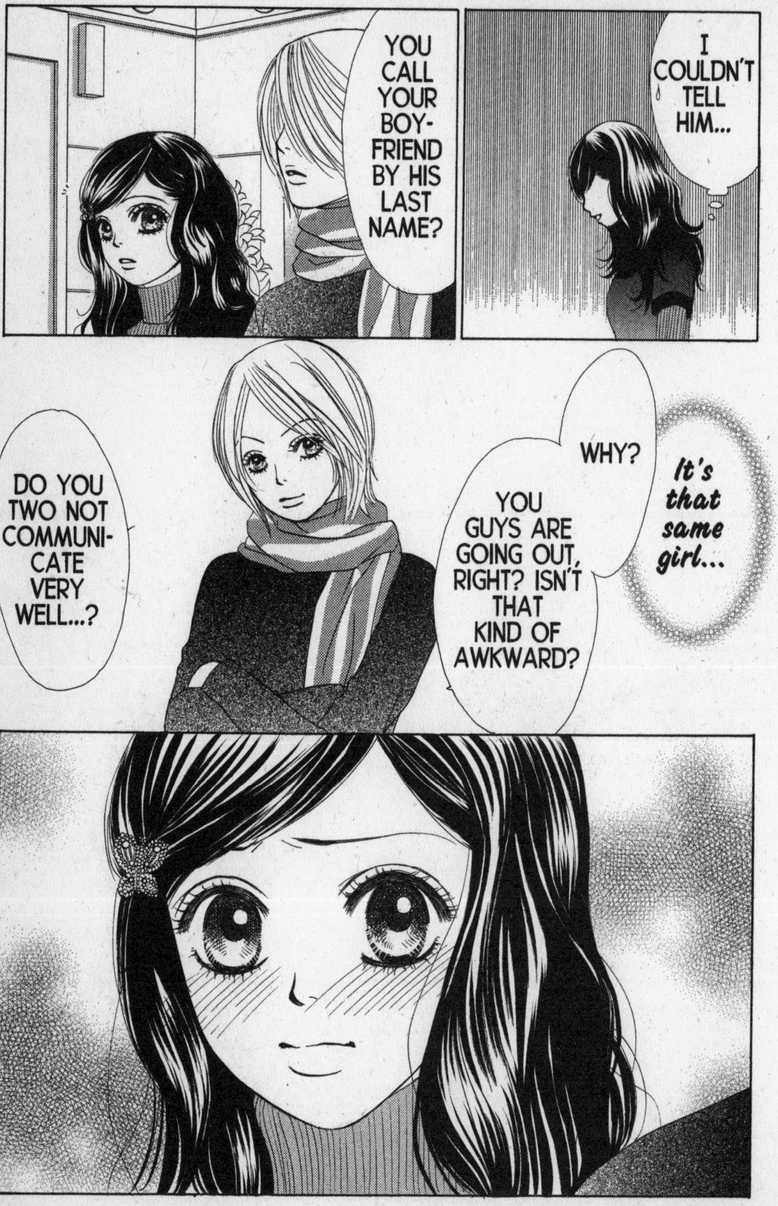
I COULDN'T TELL HIM...
YOU CALL YOUR BOY-FRIEND BY HIS LAST NAME?
It's that same girl...
WHY?
YOU GUYS ARE GOING OUT, RIGHT? ISN'T THAT KIND OF AWKWARD?
DO YOU TWO NOT COMMUNI-CATE VERY WELL...?

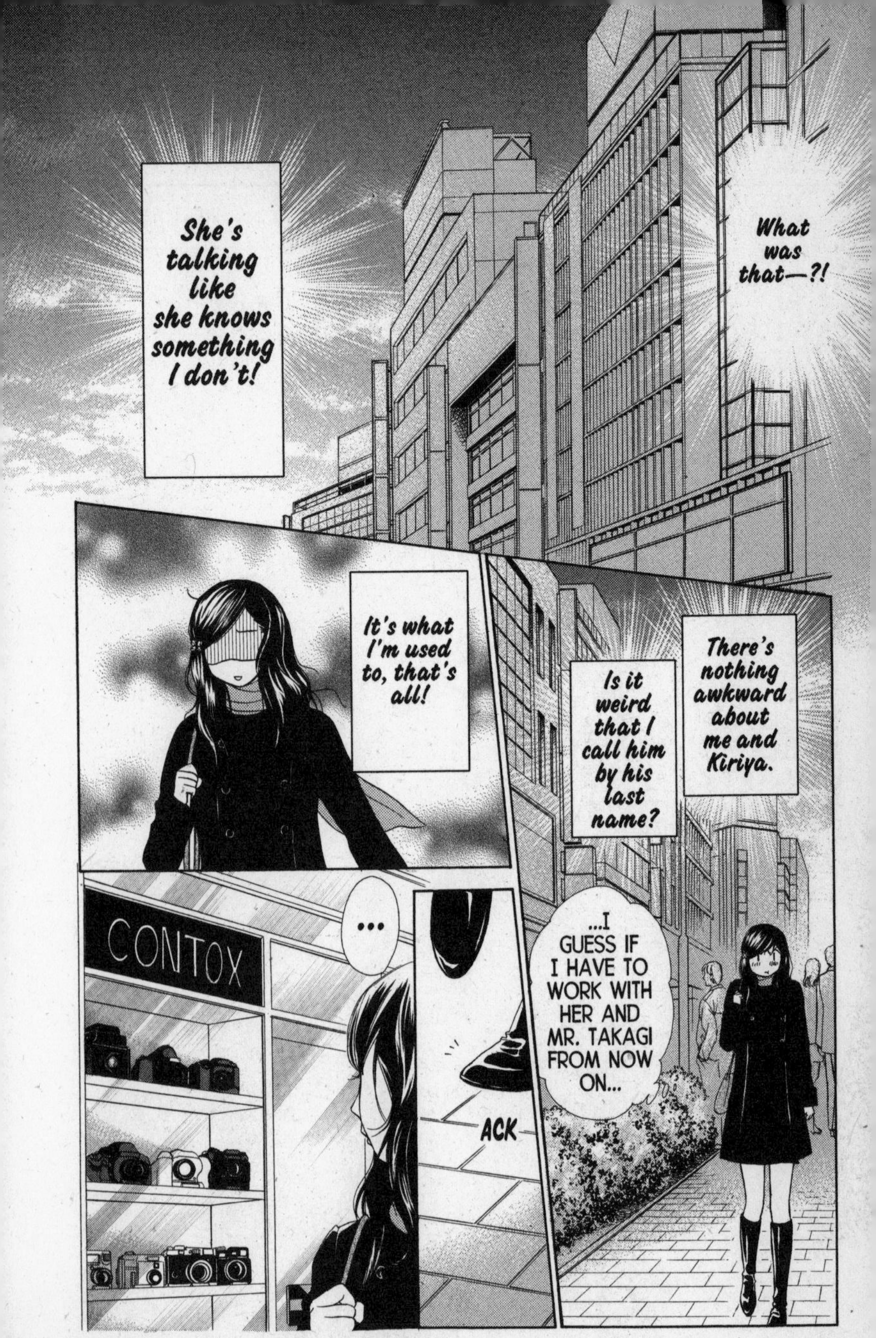
What was that—?!
She's talking like she knows something I don't!
There's nothing awkward about me and Kiriya.
Is it weird that I call him by his last name?
...I GUESS IF I HAVE TO WORK WITH HER AND MR. TAKAGI FROM NOW ON...
It's what I'm used to, that's all!
ACK
...
CONTOX

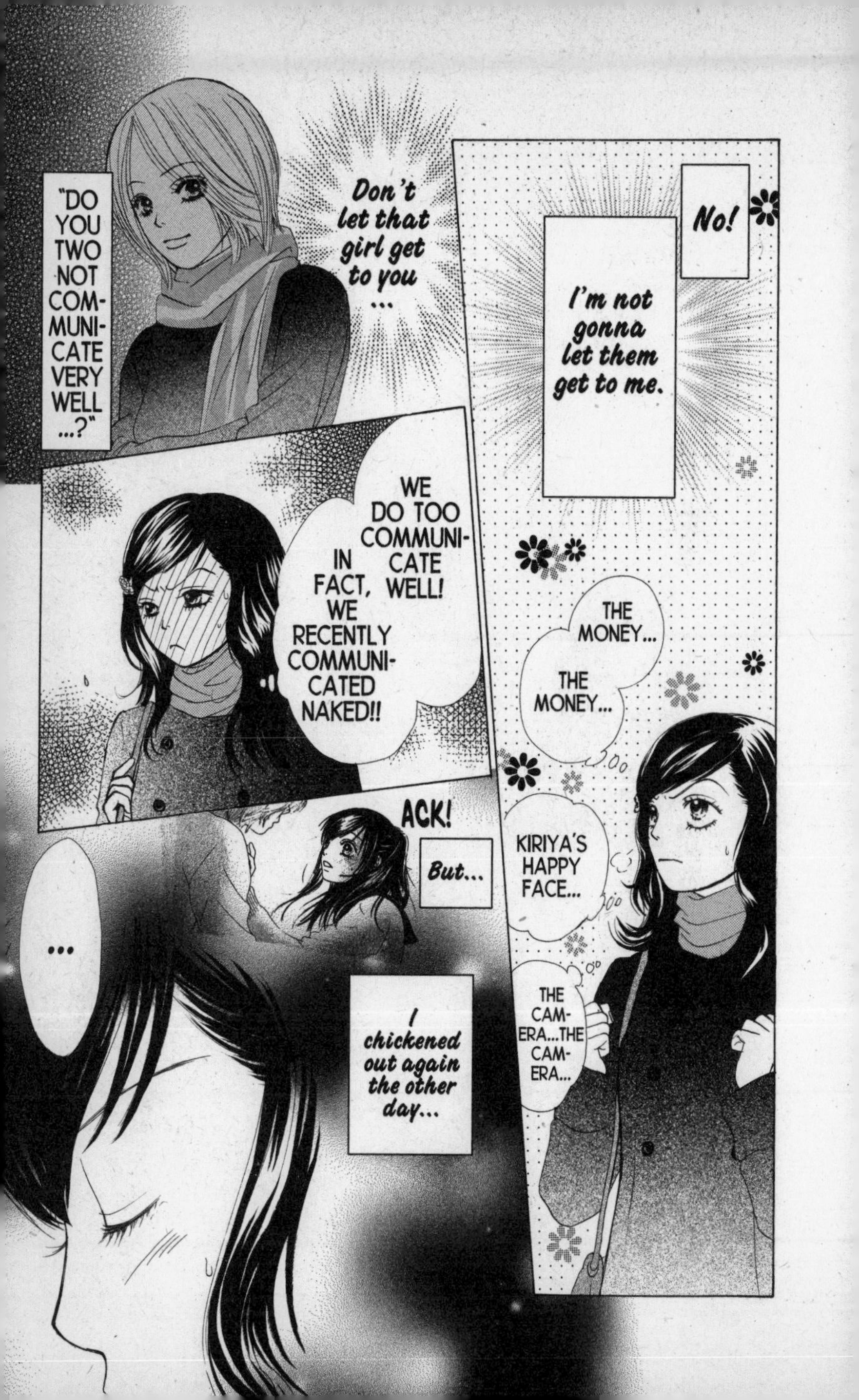
"DO YOU TWO NOT COMMUNICATE VERY WELL ...?"
Don't let that girl get to you ...
WE DO TOO COMMUNICATE WELL!
IN FACT, WE RECENTLY COMMUNICATED NAKED!!
No!
I'm not gonna let them get to me.
THE MONEY...
THE MONEY...
KIRIYA'S HAPPY FACE...
THE CAMERA...THE CAMERA...
But...
ACK!
I chickened out again the other day...
...

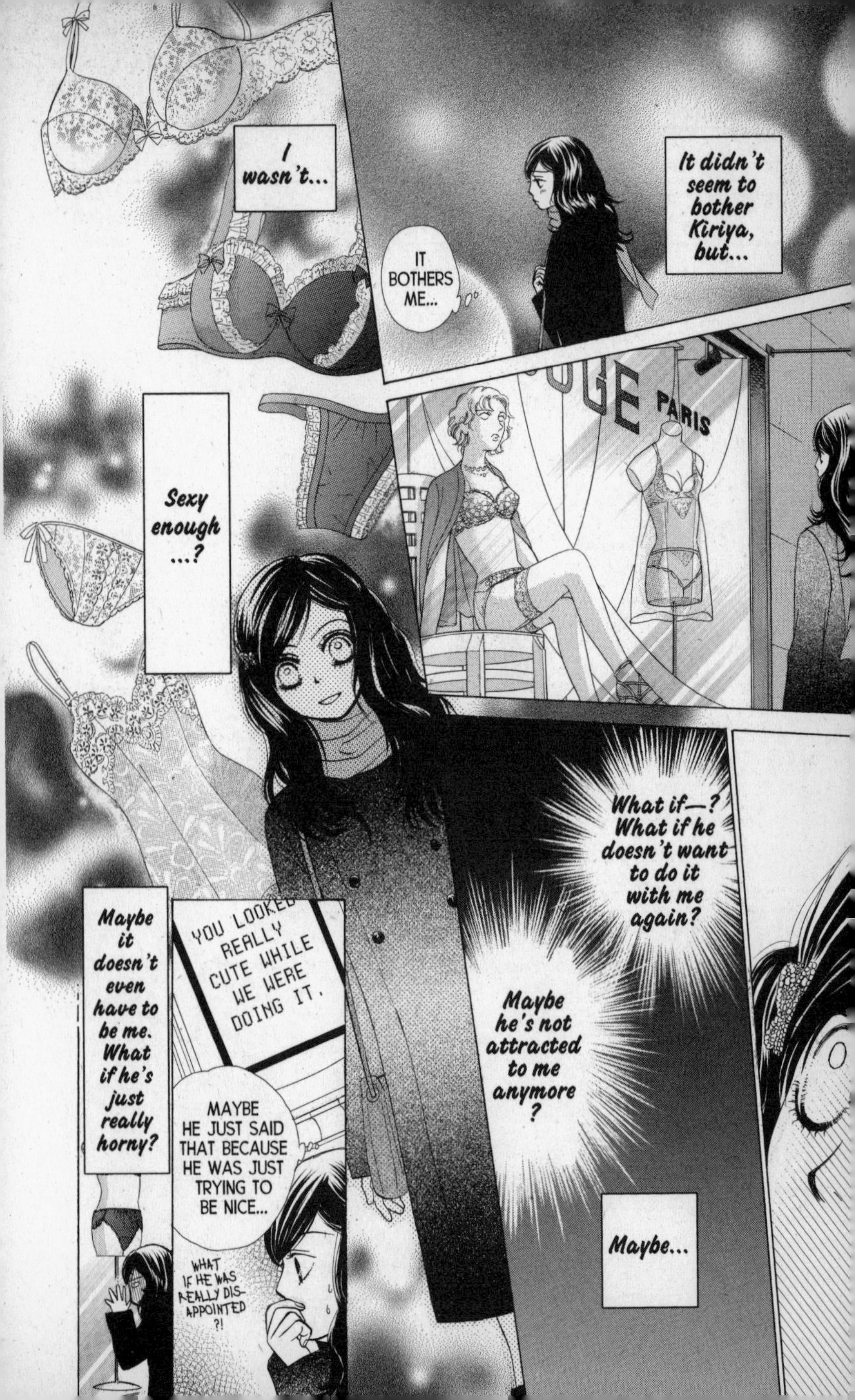

It didn't seem to bother Kiriya, but...
IT BOTHERS ME...
I wasn't...
PARIS
Sexy enough ...?
What if—? What if he doesn't want to do it with me again?
Maybe he's not attracted to me anymore ?
Maybe...
YOU LOOKED REALLY CUTE WHILE WE WERE DOING IT.
MAYBE HE JUST SAID THAT BECAUSE HE WAS JUST TRYING TO BE NICE...
WHAT IF HE WAS REALLY DIS-APPOINTED ?!
Maybe it doesn't even have to be me. What if he's just really horny?

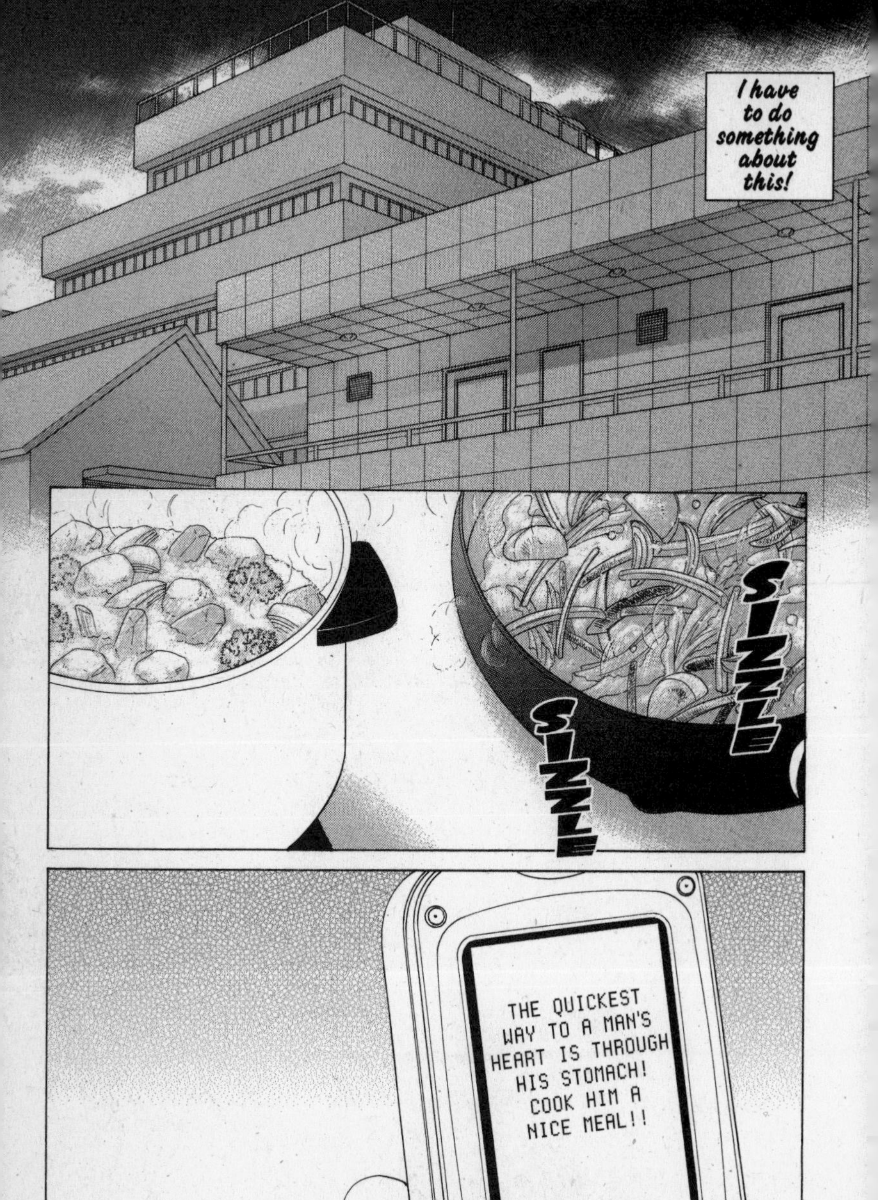
I have to do something about this!
SIZZLE
SIZZLE
THE QUICKEST WAY TO A MAN'S HEART IS THROUGH HIS STOMACH! COOK HIM A NICE MEAL!!
MENU

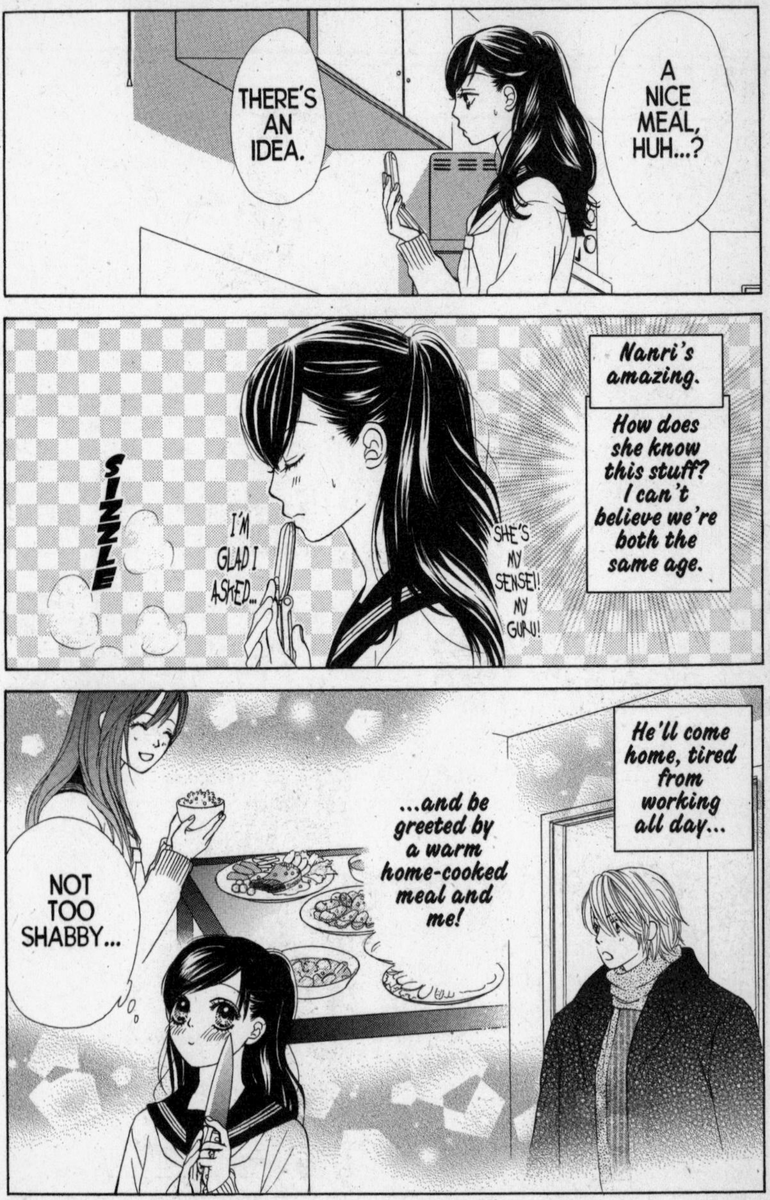
A NICE MEAL, HUH...?
THERE'S AN IDEA.
Nanri's amazing.
How does she know this stuff? I can't believe we're both the same age.
SHE'S MY SENSEI! MY GURU!
I'M GLAD I ASKED...
SIZZLE
He'll come home, tired from working all day...
...and be greeted by a warm home-cooked meal and me!
NOT TOO SHABBY...

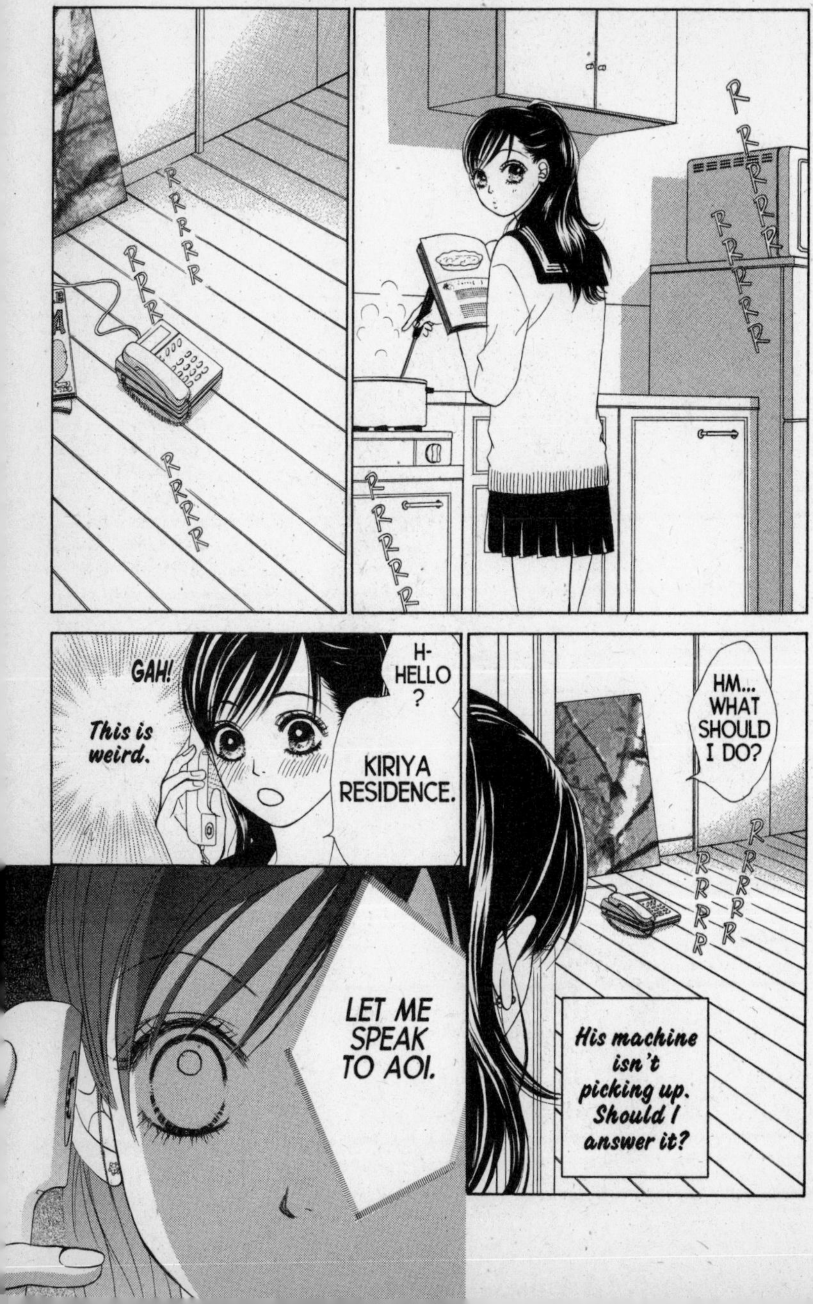
RRRRRR
RRRRRRR
RRRRRR
RRRRR
RRRR
RRRR
HM... WHAT SHOULD I DO?
RRRRRR
RRRRR
His machine isn't picking up. Should I answer it?
H-HELLO?
KIRIYA RESIDENCE.
GAH!
This is weird.
LET ME SPEAK TO AOI.

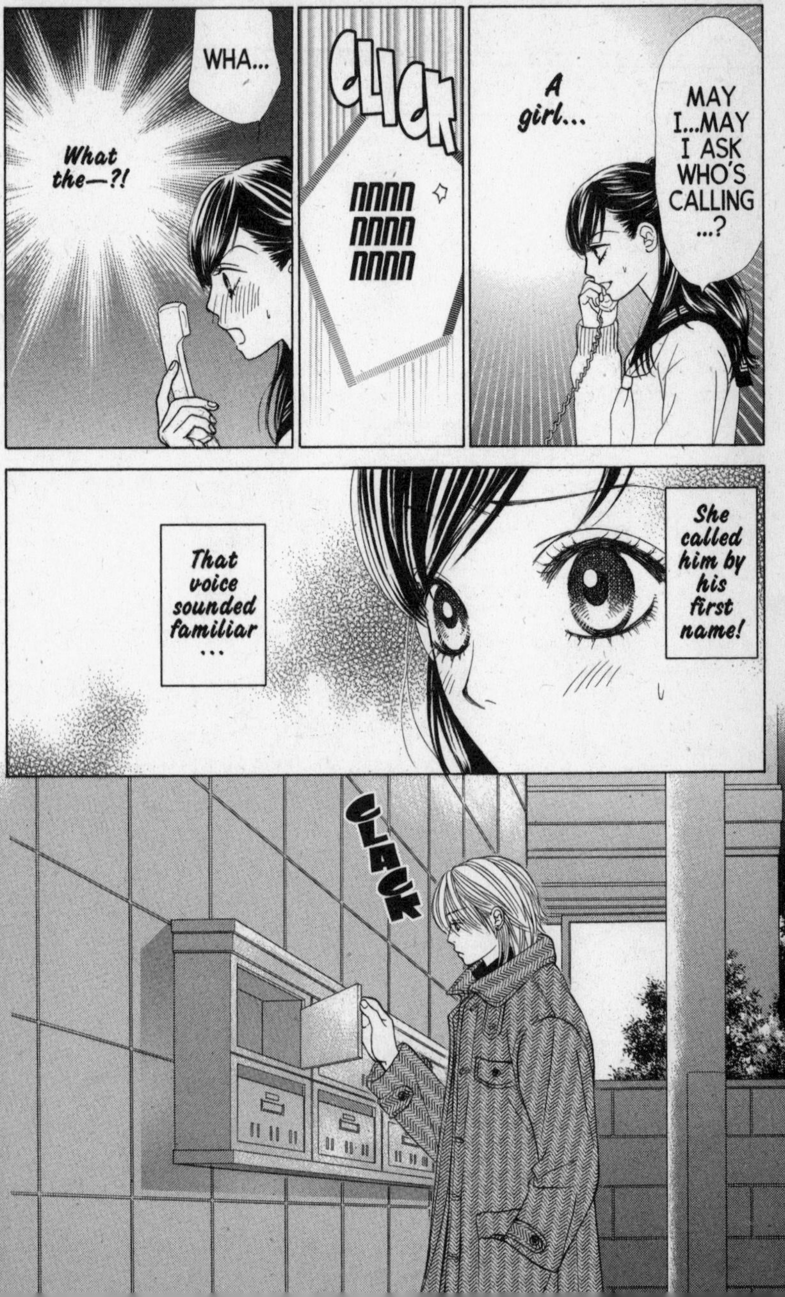
MAY I...MAY I ASK WHO'S CALLING ...?
A girl...
CLICK
nnnn nnnn nnnn
WHA...
What the—?!
She called him by his first name!
That voice sounded familiar ...
CLACK

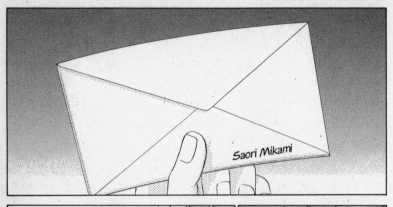

Saori Mikami

RATTLE
RATTLE

···

WELCOME HOME!

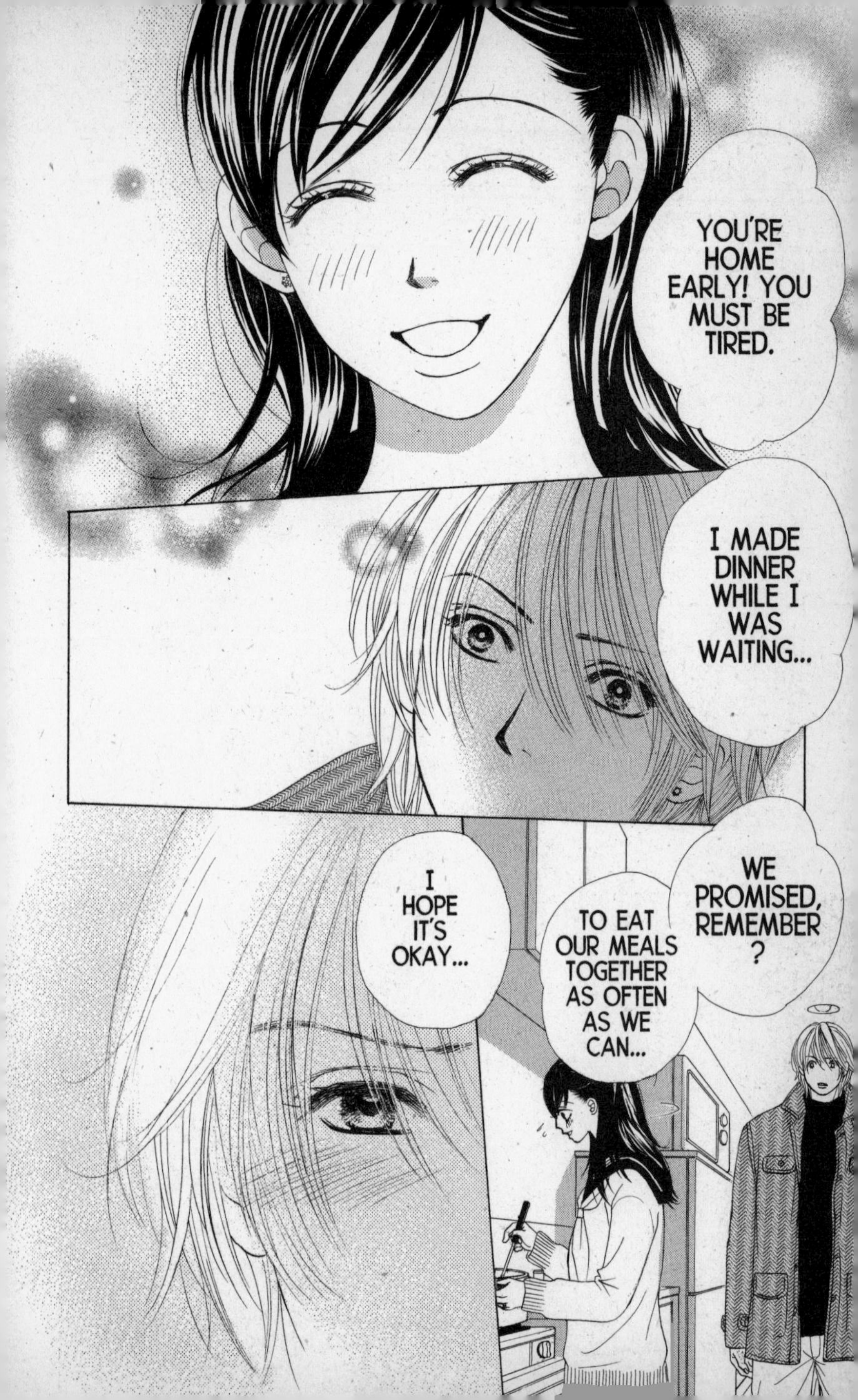
YOU'RE HOME EARLY! YOU MUST BE TIRED.
I MADE DINNER WHILE I WAS WAITING...
WE PROMISED, REMEMBER?
TO EAT OUR MEALS TOGETHER AS OFTEN AS WE CAN...
I HOPE IT'S OKAY...

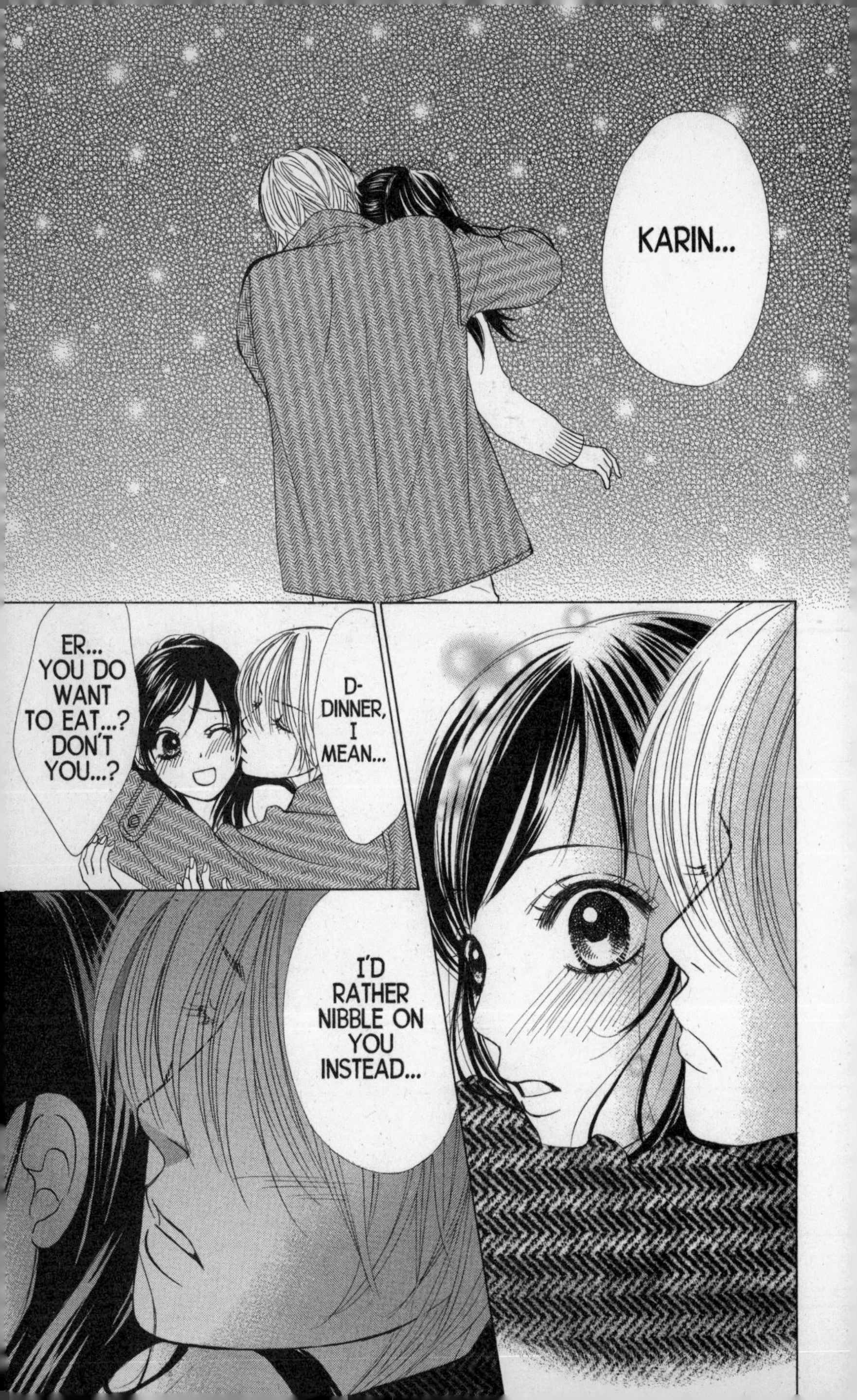
KARIN...
ER... YOU DO WANT TO EAT...? DON'T YOU...?
D-DINNER, I MEAN...
I'D RATHER NIBBLE ON YOU INSTEAD...

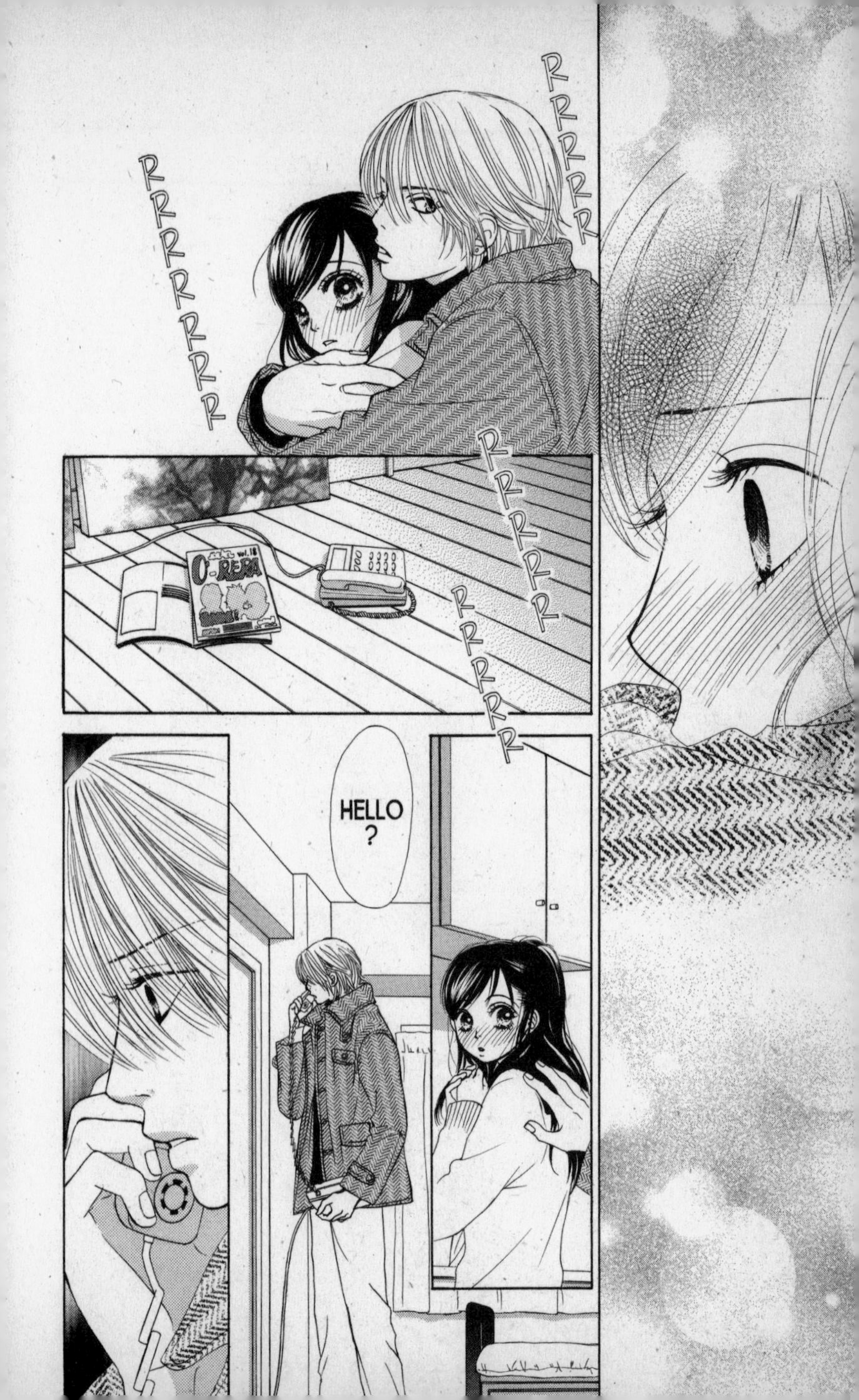
RRRRRRR
RRRRRRRR
RRRRRRR
RRRRR
HELLO ?

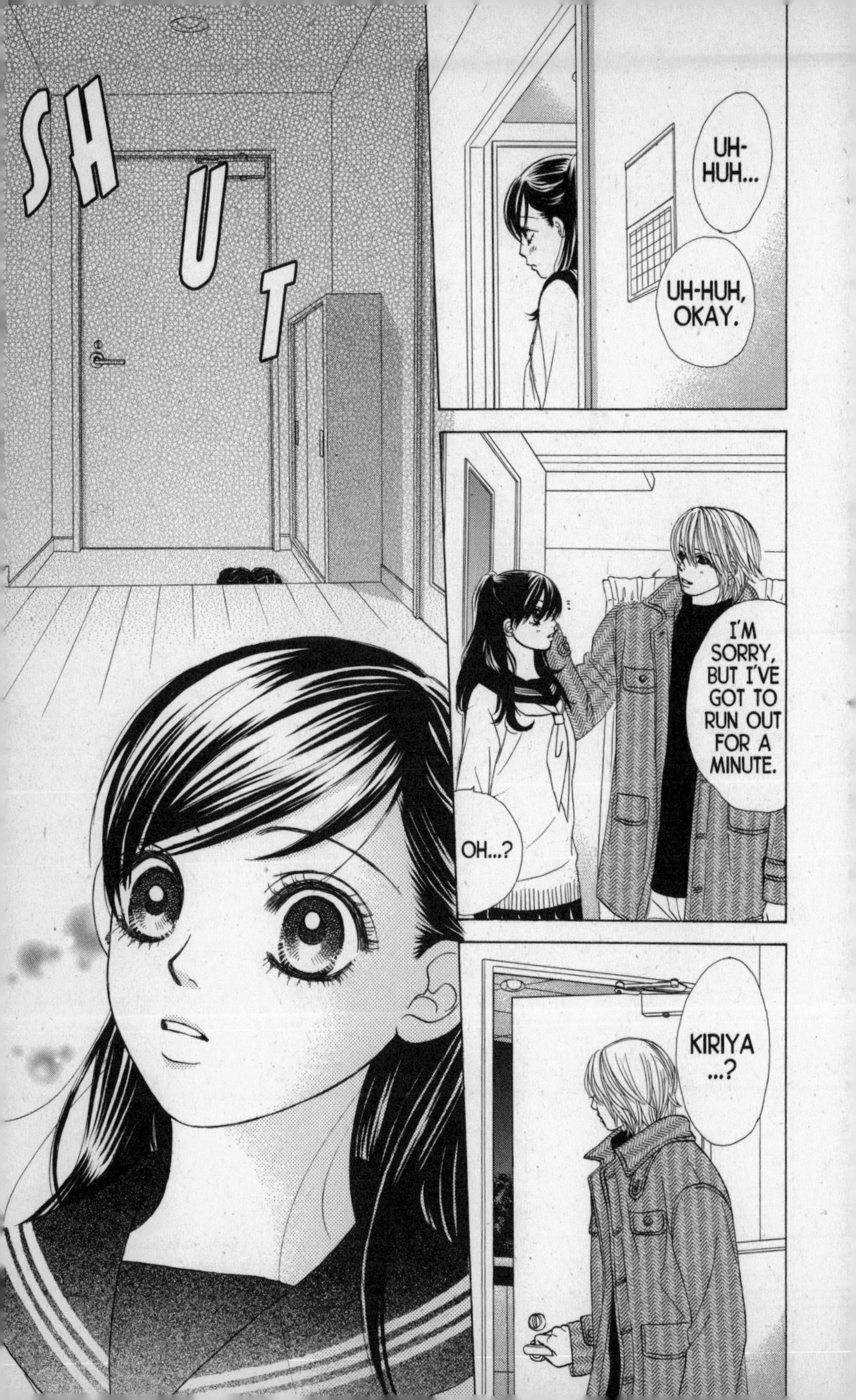
UH-HUH...
UH-HUH, OKAY.
I'M SORRY, BUT I'VE GOT TO RUN OUT FOR A MINUTE.
OH...?
KIRIYA ...?
SHUT

「彼」 KARE First Love

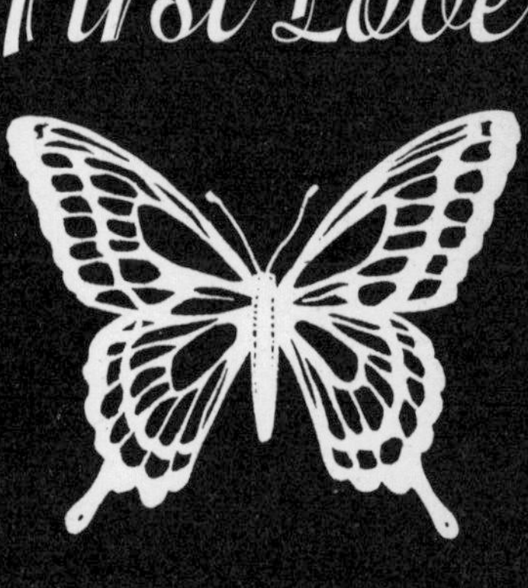

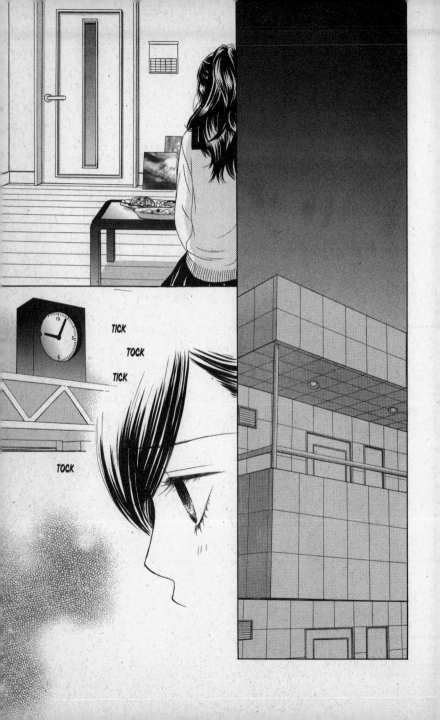

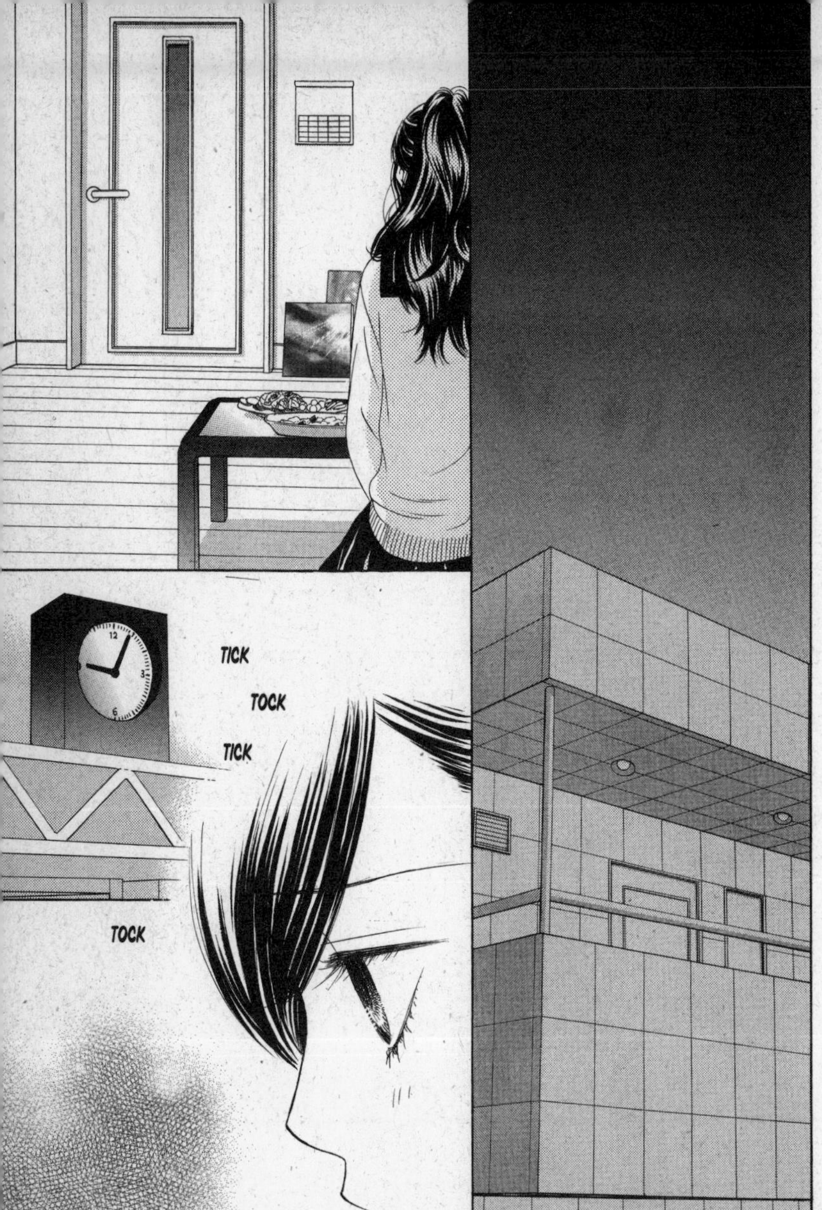
TICK
TOCK
TICK
TOCK

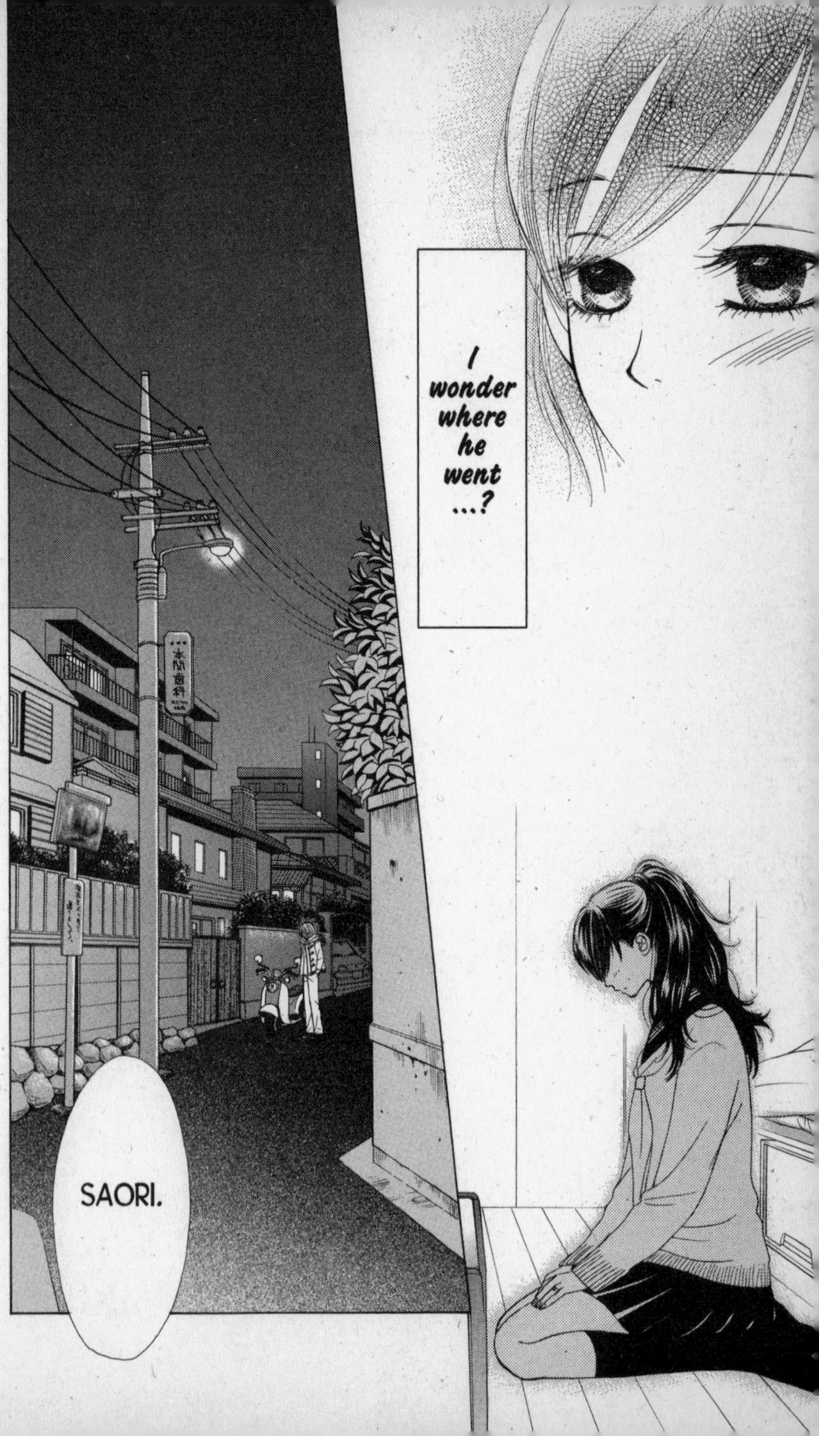
I wonder where he went ...?
SAORI.

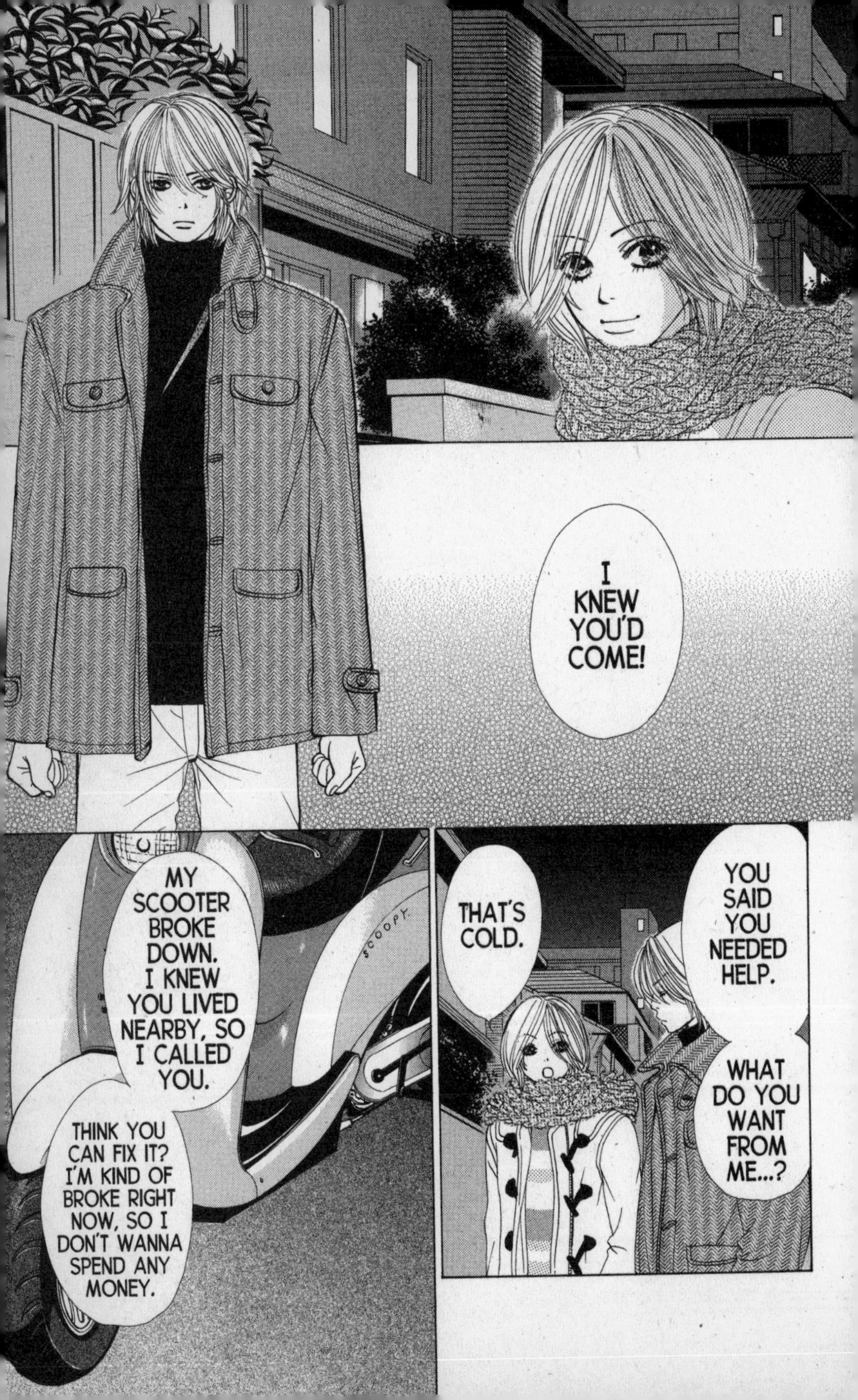
I KNEW YOU'D COME!
YOU SAID YOU NEEDED HELP.
WHAT DO YOU WANT FROM ME...?
THAT'S COLD.
MY SCOOTER BROKE DOWN. I KNEW YOU LIVED NEARBY, SO I CALLED YOU.
SCOOPY
THINK YOU CAN FIX IT? I'M KIND OF BROKE RIGHT NOW, SO I DON'T WANNA SPEND ANY MONEY.

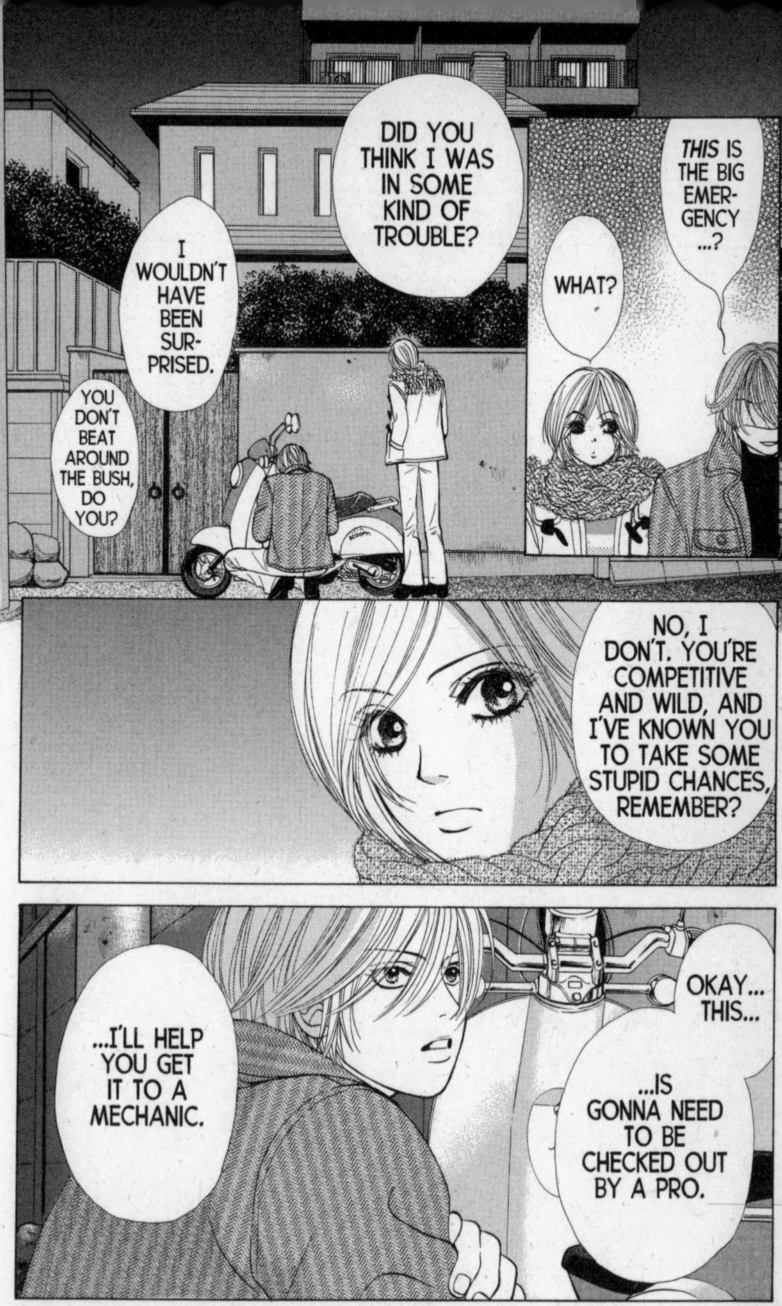
THIS IS THE BIG EMER-GENCY ...?
WHAT?
DID YOU THINK I WAS IN SOME KIND OF TROUBLE?
I WOULDN'T HAVE BEEN SUR-PRISED.
YOU DON'T BEAT AROUND THE BUSH, DO YOU?
NO, I DON'T. YOU'RE COMPETITIVE AND WILD, AND I'VE KNOWN YOU TO TAKE SOME STUPID CHANCES, REMEMBER?
OKAY... THIS...
...IS GONNA NEED TO BE CHECKED OUT BY A PRO.
...I'LL HELP YOU GET IT TO A MECHANIC.

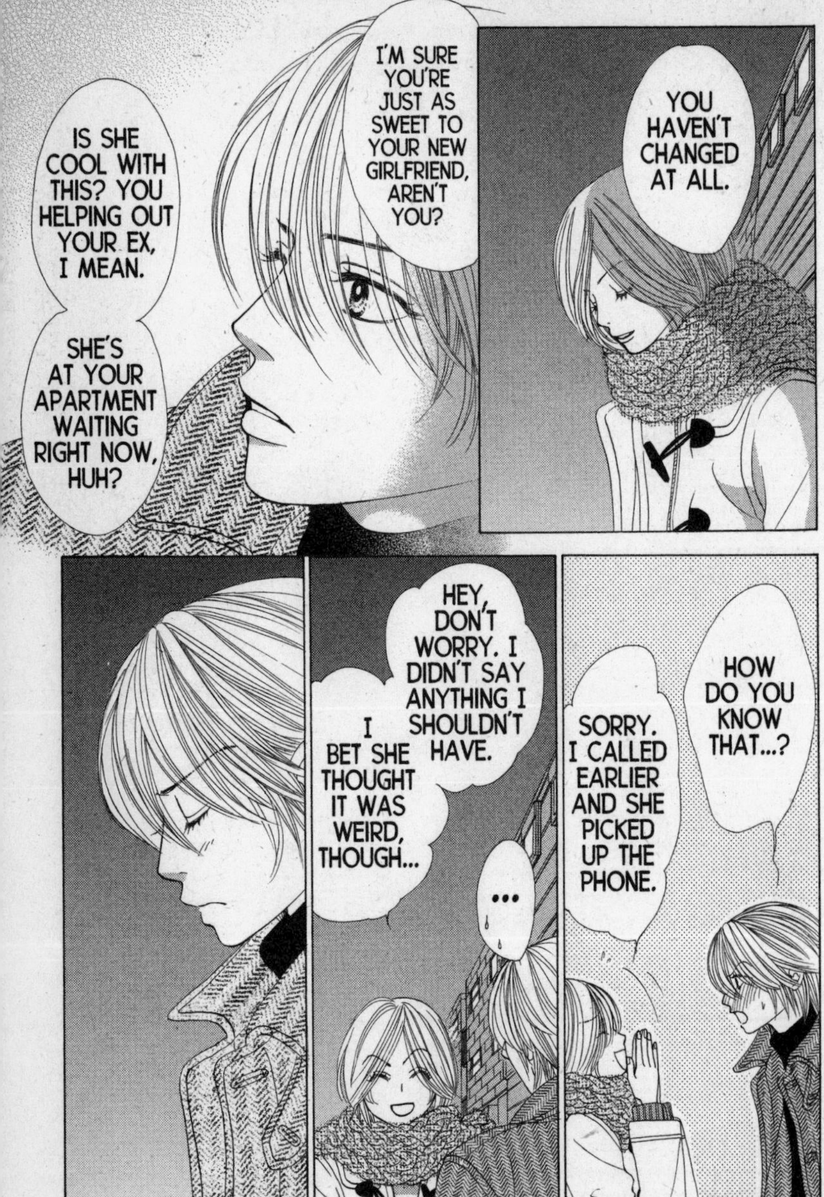
YOU HAVEN'T CHANGED AT ALL.
I'M SURE YOU'RE JUST AS SWEET TO YOUR NEW GIRLFRIEND, AREN'T YOU?
IS SHE COOL WITH THIS? YOU HELPING OUT YOUR EX, I MEAN.
SHE'S AT YOUR APARTMENT WAITING RIGHT NOW, HUH?
HOW DO YOU KNOW THAT...?
SORRY. I CALLED EARLIER AND SHE PICKED UP THE PHONE.
HEY, DON'T WORRY. I DIDN'T SAY ANYTHING I SHOULDN'T HAVE.
I BET SHE THOUGHT IT WAS WEIRD, THOUGH...
...

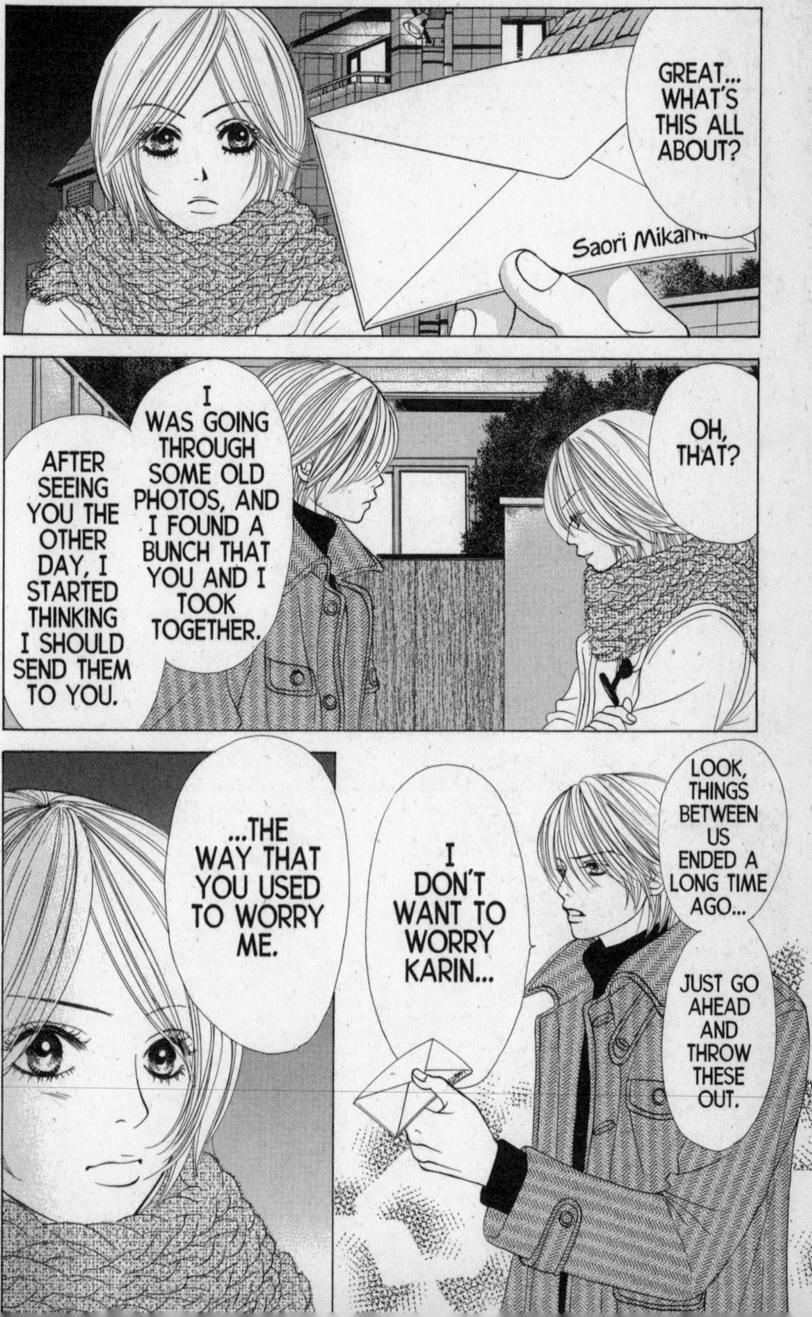
GREAT... WHAT'S THIS ALL ABOUT?
Saori Mikam
OH, THAT?
I WAS GOING THROUGH SOME OLD PHOTOS, AND I FOUND A BUNCH THAT YOU AND I TOOK TOGETHER.
AFTER SEEING YOU THE OTHER DAY, I STARTED THINKING I SHOULD SEND THEM TO YOU.
LOOK, THINGS BETWEEN US ENDED A LONG TIME AGO...
JUST GO AHEAD AND THROW THESE OUT.
I DON'T WANT TO WORRY KARIN...
...THE WAY THAT YOU USED TO WORRY ME.

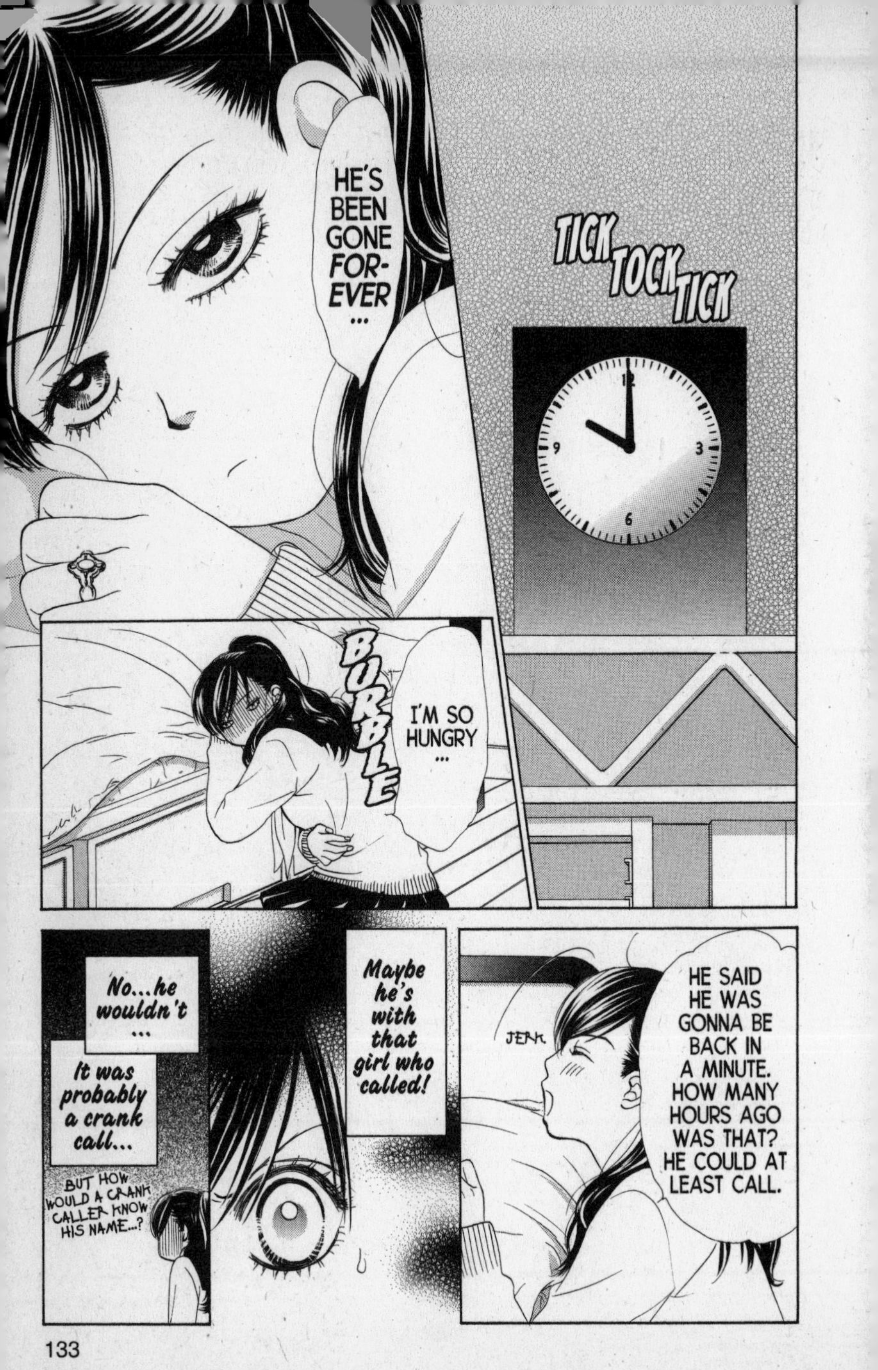
TICK TOCK TICK
HE'S BEEN GONE FOR-EVER ...
BURBLE
I'M SO HUNGRY ...
JERK
HE SAID HE WAS GONNA BE BACK IN A MINUTE. HOW MANY HOURS AGO WAS THAT? HE COULD AT LEAST CALL.
Maybe he's with that girl who called!
No...he wouldn't ...
It was probably a crank call...
BUT HOW WOULD A CRANK CALLER KNOW HIS NAME...?

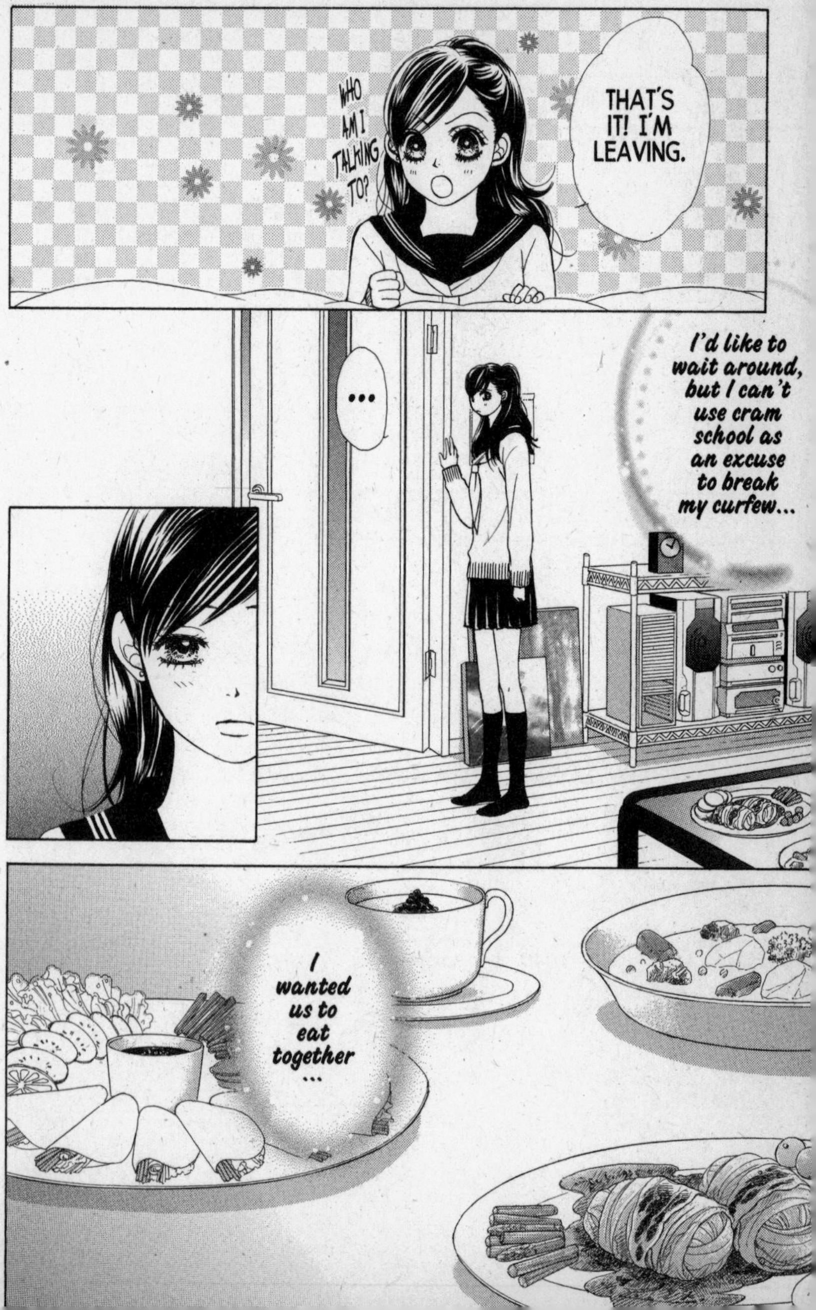
THAT'S IT! I'M LEAVING.
WHO AM I TALKING TO?
I'd like to wait around, but I can't use cram school as an excuse to break my curfew...
...
I wanted us to eat together...

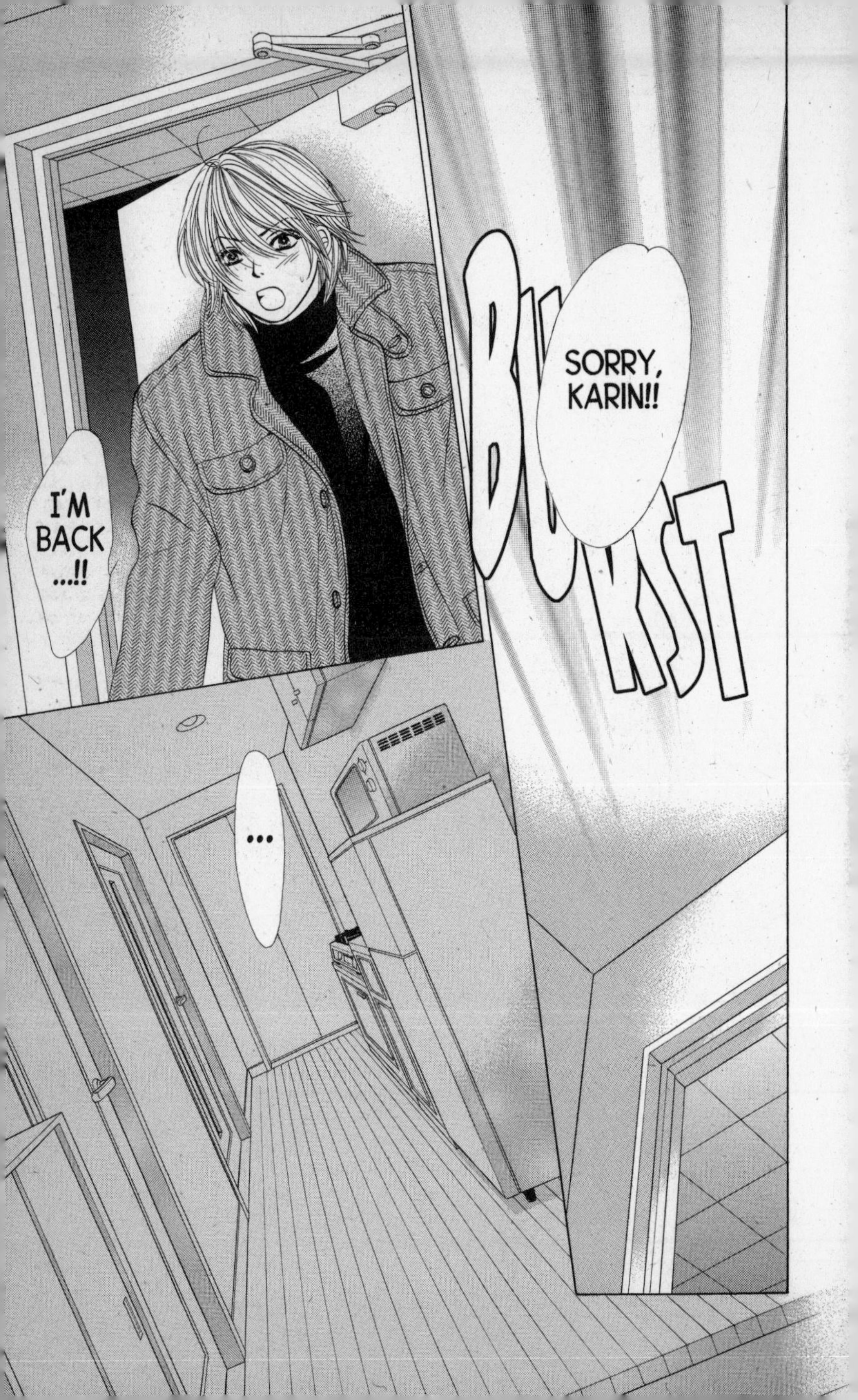
BURST
SORRY, KARIN!!
I'M BACK ...!!
...

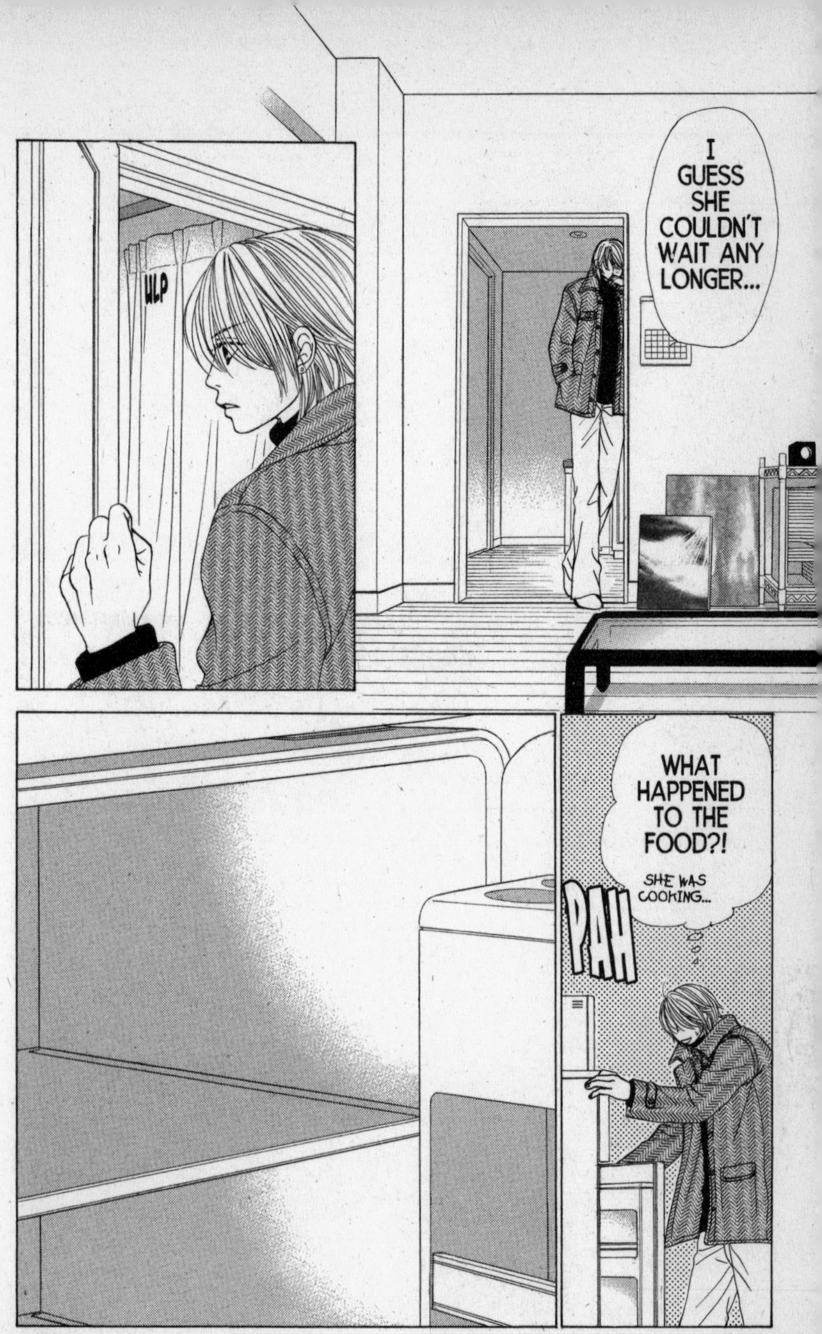
I GUESS SHE COULDN'T WAIT ANY LONGER...
HLP
WHAT HAPPENED TO THE FOOD?!
SHE WAS COOKING...
PAH

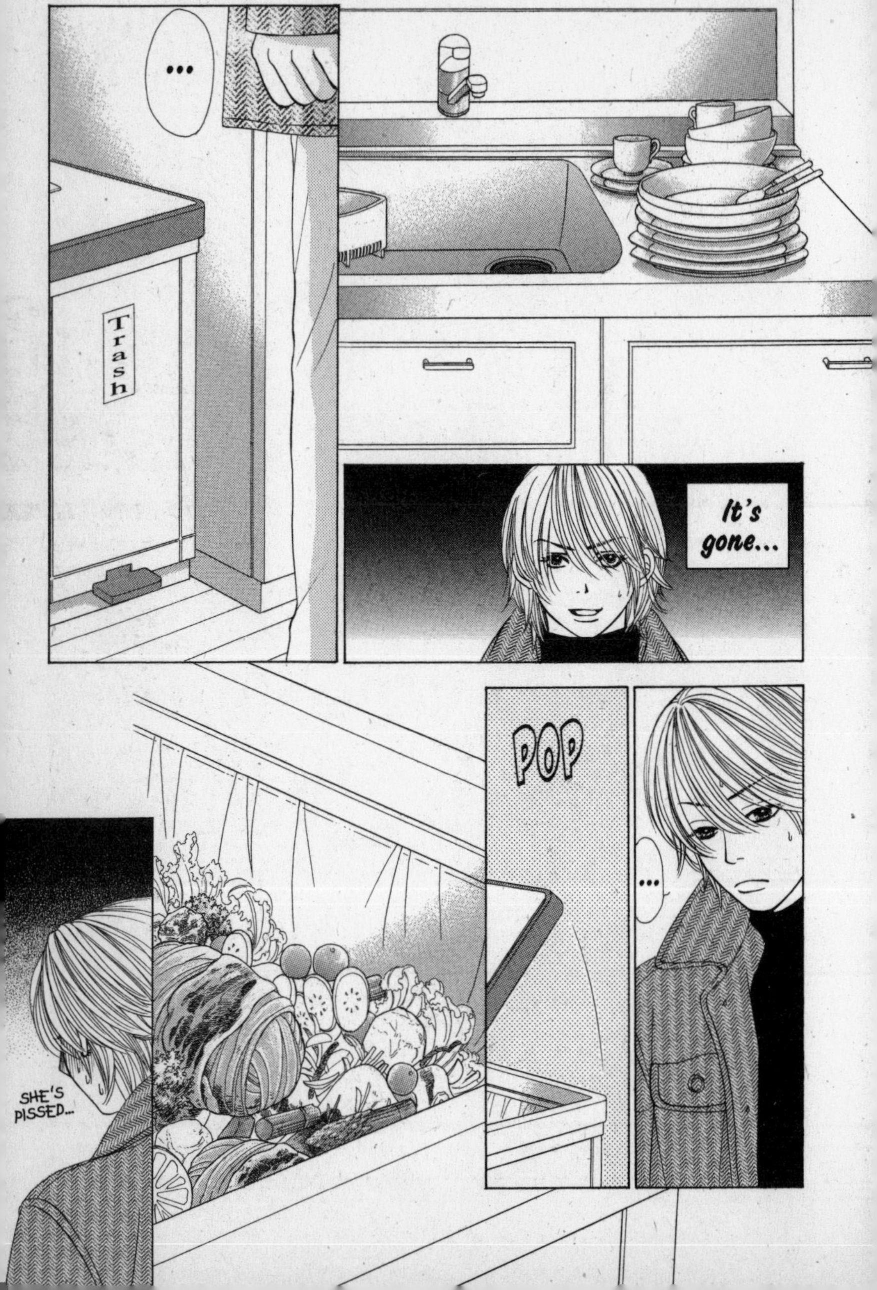
It's gone...
Trash
...
...
POP
SHE'S PISSED...

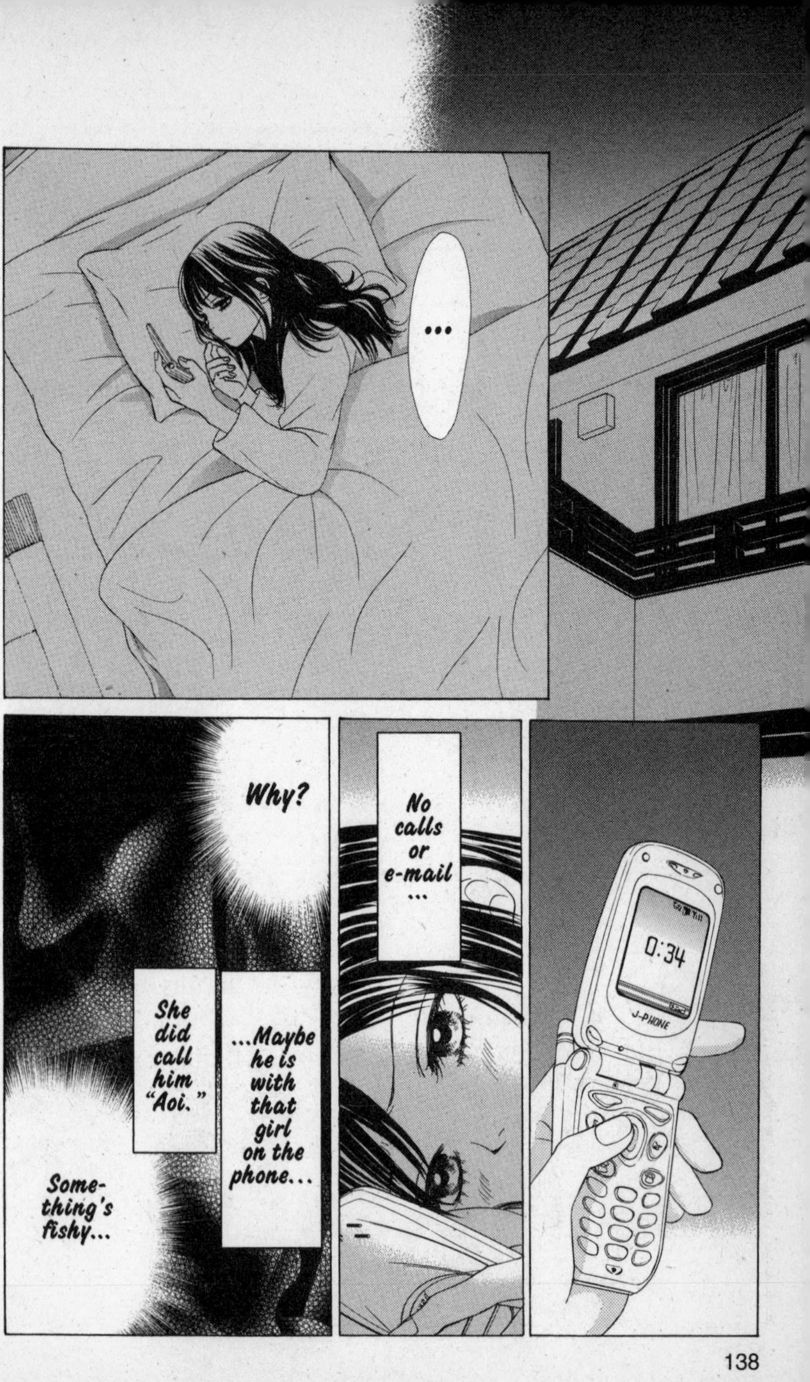
...
No calls or e-mail...
Why?
...Maybe he is with that girl on the phone...
She did call him "Aoi."
Some-thing's fishy...

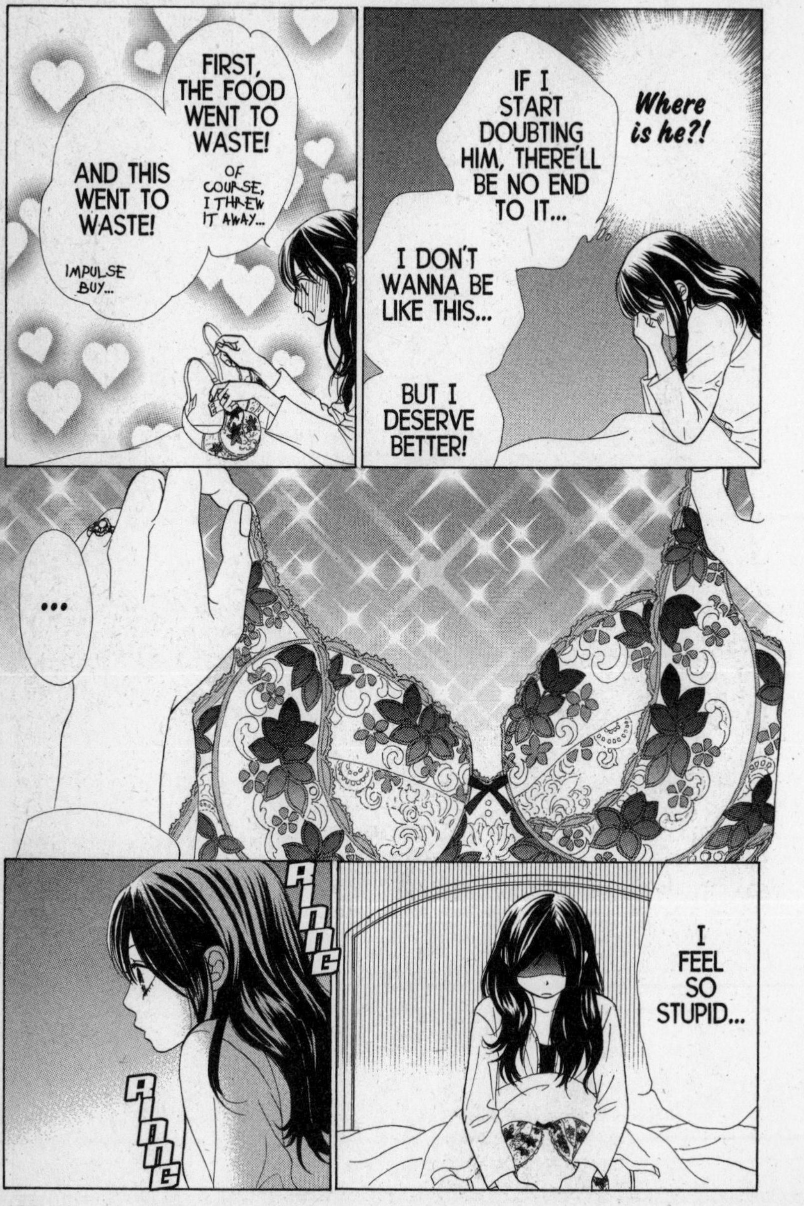
Where is he?!
IF I START DOUBTING HIM, THERE'LL BE NO END TO IT...
I DON'T WANNA BE LIKE THIS...
BUT I DESERVE BETTER!
FIRST, THE FOOD WENT TO WASTE!
OF COURSE, I THREW IT AWAY...
AND THIS WENT TO WASTE!
IMPULSE BUY...
...
I FEEL SO STUPID...
RINNG
RINNG

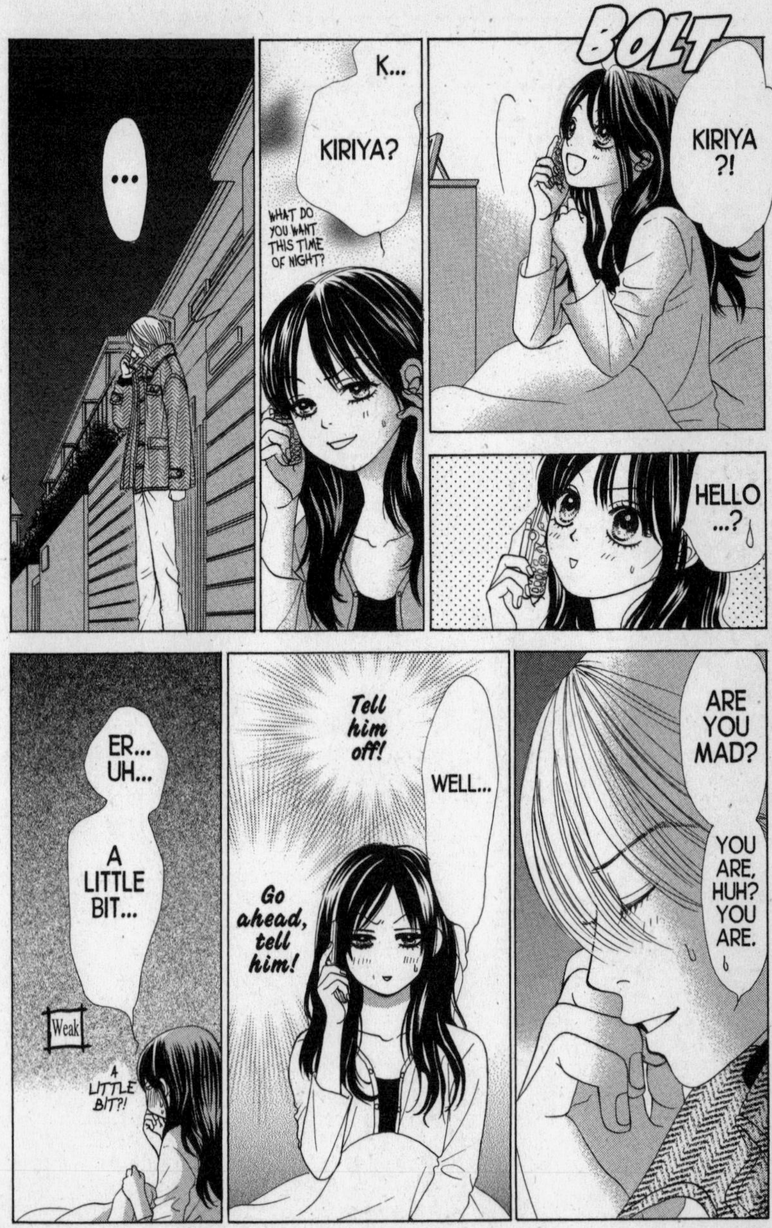
BOLT
KIRIYA ?!
HELLO ...?
K...
KIRIYA?
WHAT DO YOU WANT THIS TIME OF NIGHT?
...
ARE YOU MAD?
YOU ARE, HUH? YOU ARE.
WELL...
Tell him off!
Go ahead, tell him!
ER... UH...
A LITTLE BIT...
Weak
A LITTLE BIT?!

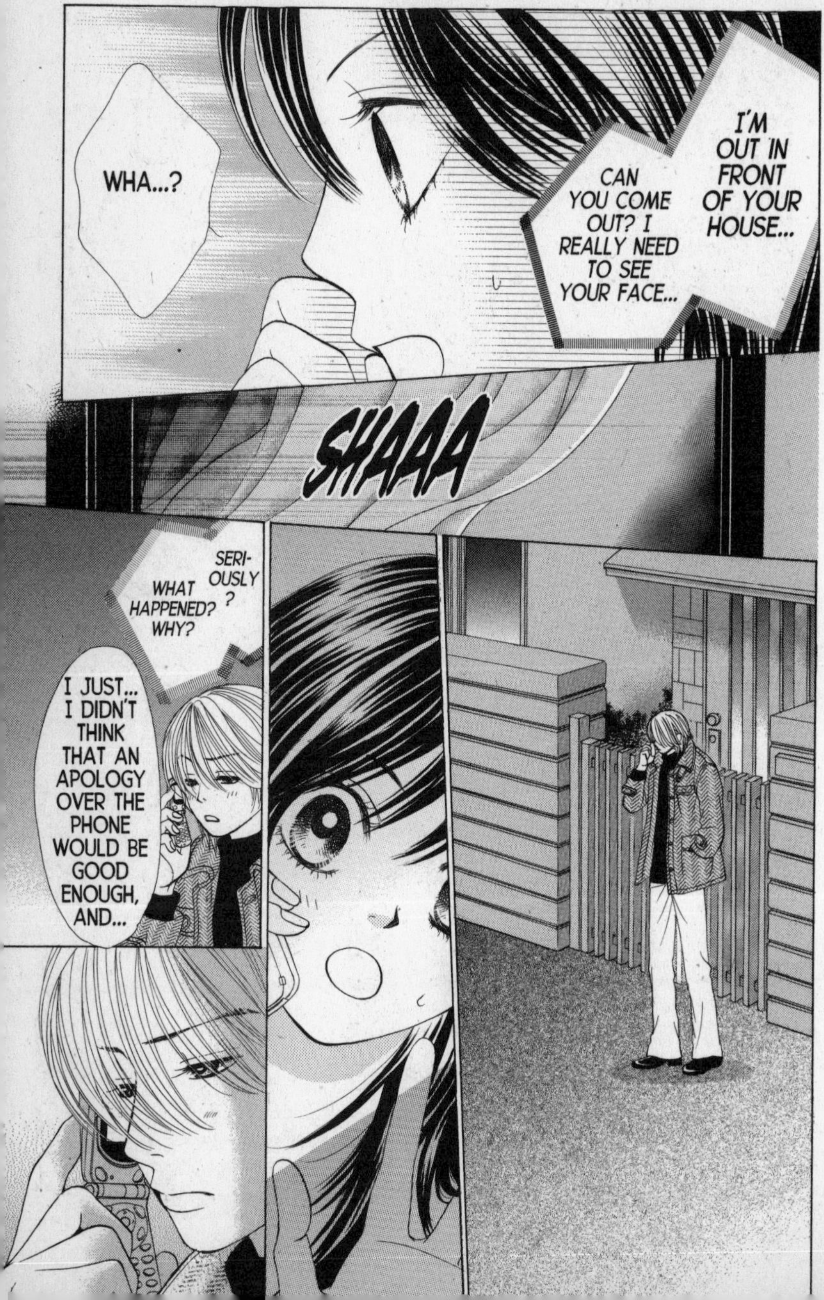
I'M OUT IN FRONT OF YOUR HOUSE...
CAN YOU COME OUT? I REALLY NEED TO SEE YOUR FACE...
WHA...?
SHAAA
SERIOUSLY?
WHAT HAPPENED? WHY?
I JUST... I DIDN'T THINK THAT AN APOLOGY OVER THE PHONE WOULD BE GOOD ENOUGH, AND...

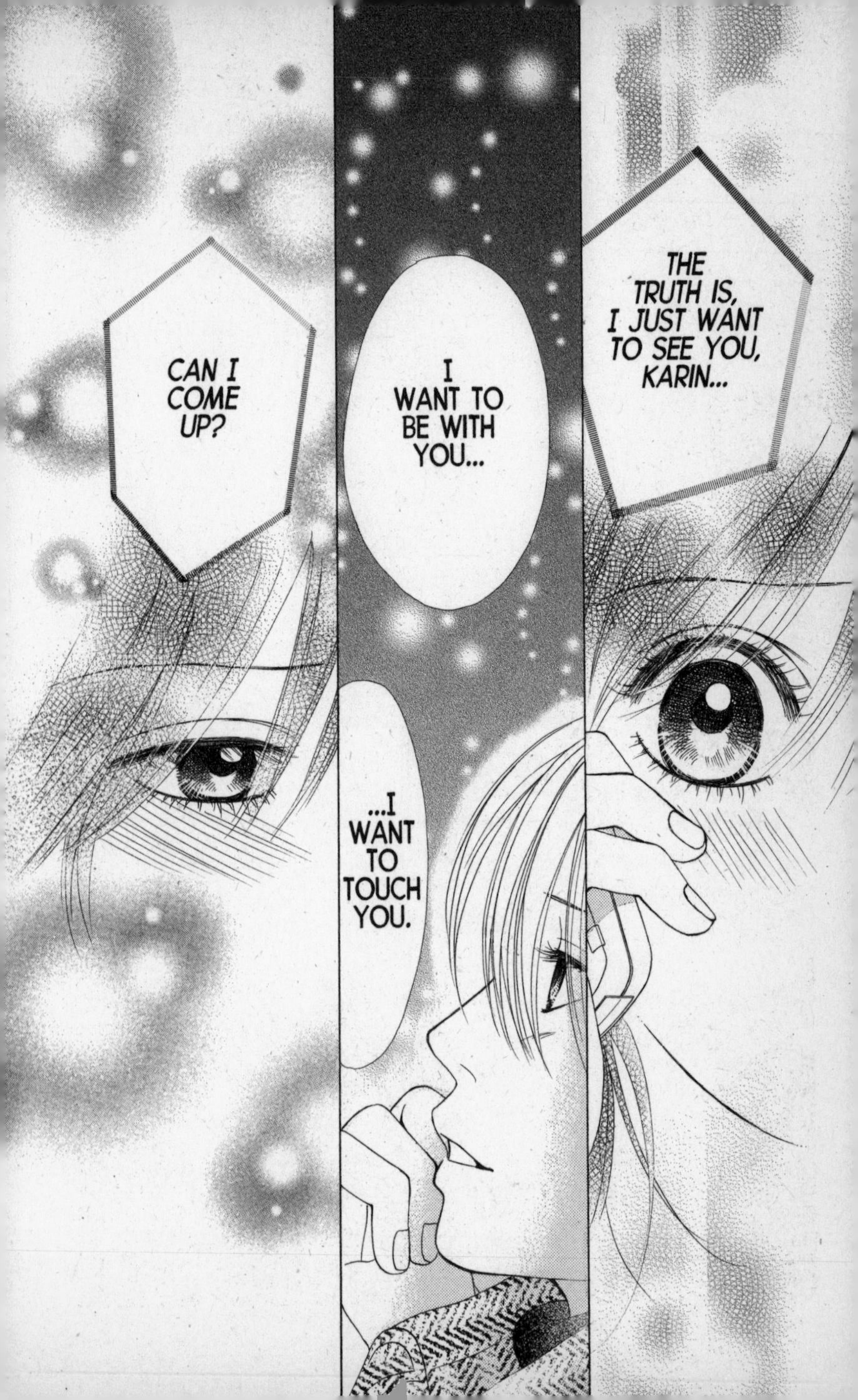
THE TRUTH IS, I JUST WANT TO SEE YOU, KARIN...
I WANT TO BE WITH YOU...
...I WANT TO TOUCH YOU.
CAN I COME UP?

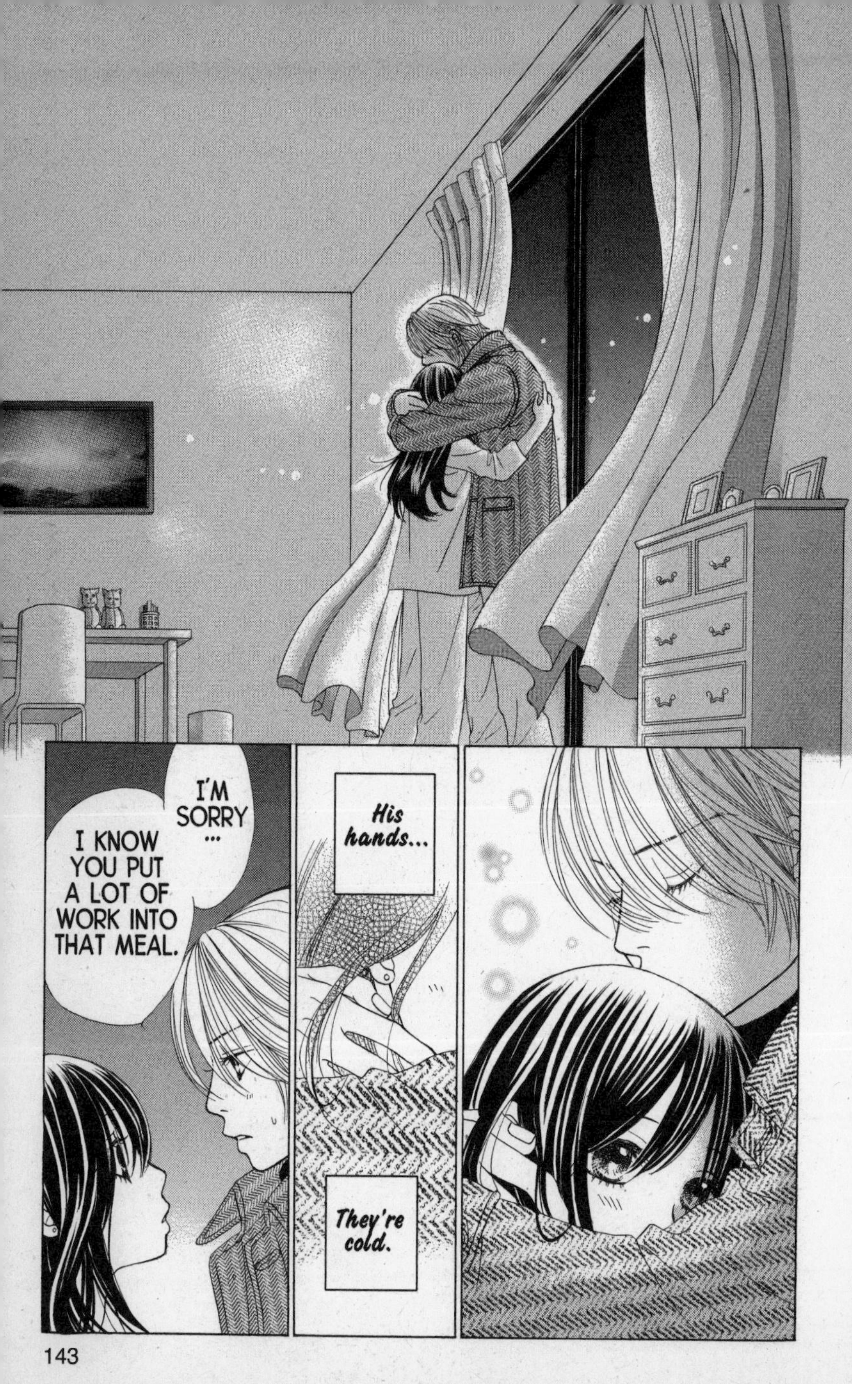
His hands...
They're cold.
I'M SORRY ...
I KNOW YOU PUT A LOT OF WORK INTO THAT MEAL.

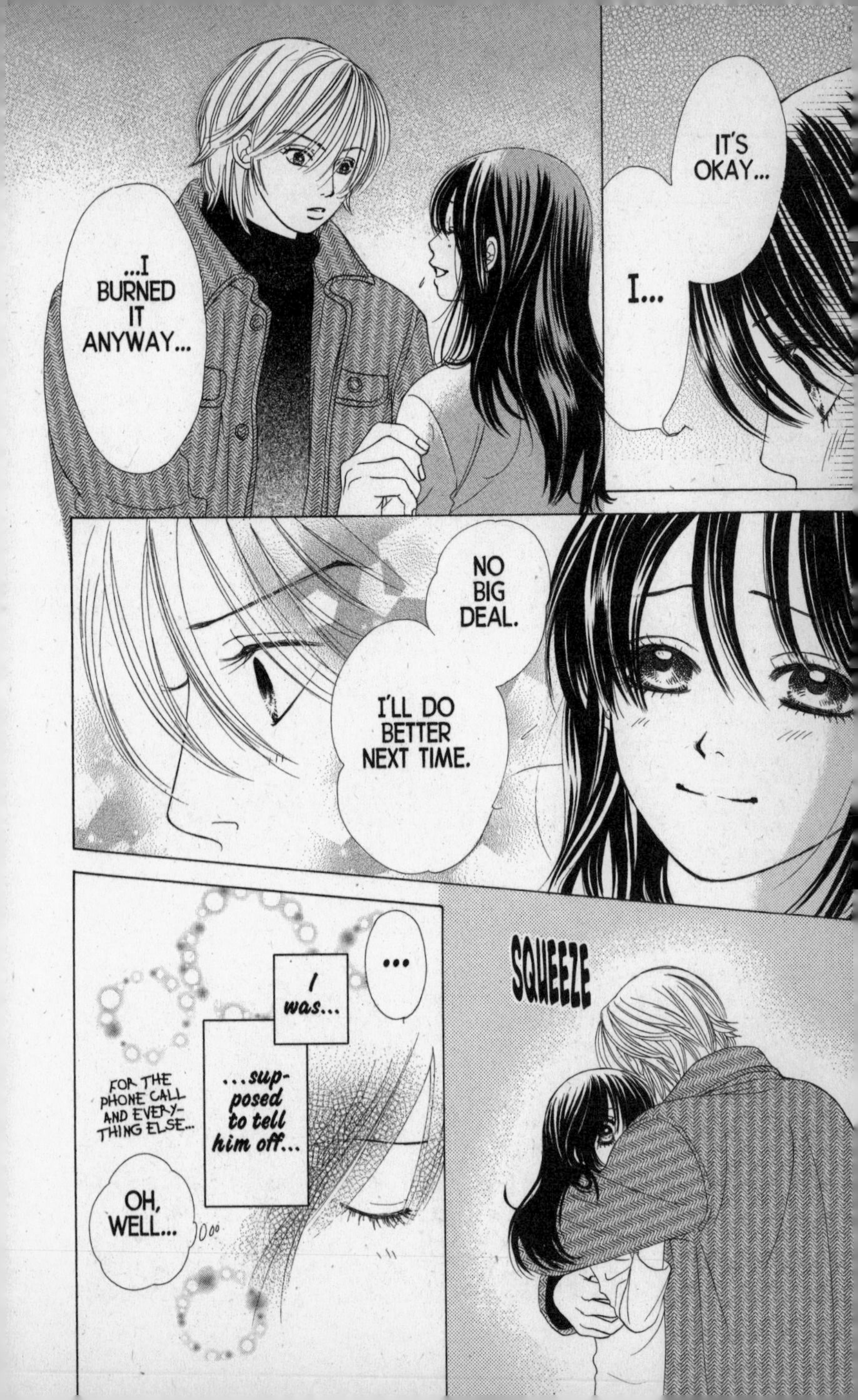
IT'S OKAY...
I...
...I BURNED IT ANYWAY...
NO BIG DEAL.
I'LL DO BETTER NEXT TIME.
SQUEEZE
...
I was...
...sup-posed to tell him off...
FOR THE PHONE CALL AND EVERY-THING ELSE...
OH, WELL...

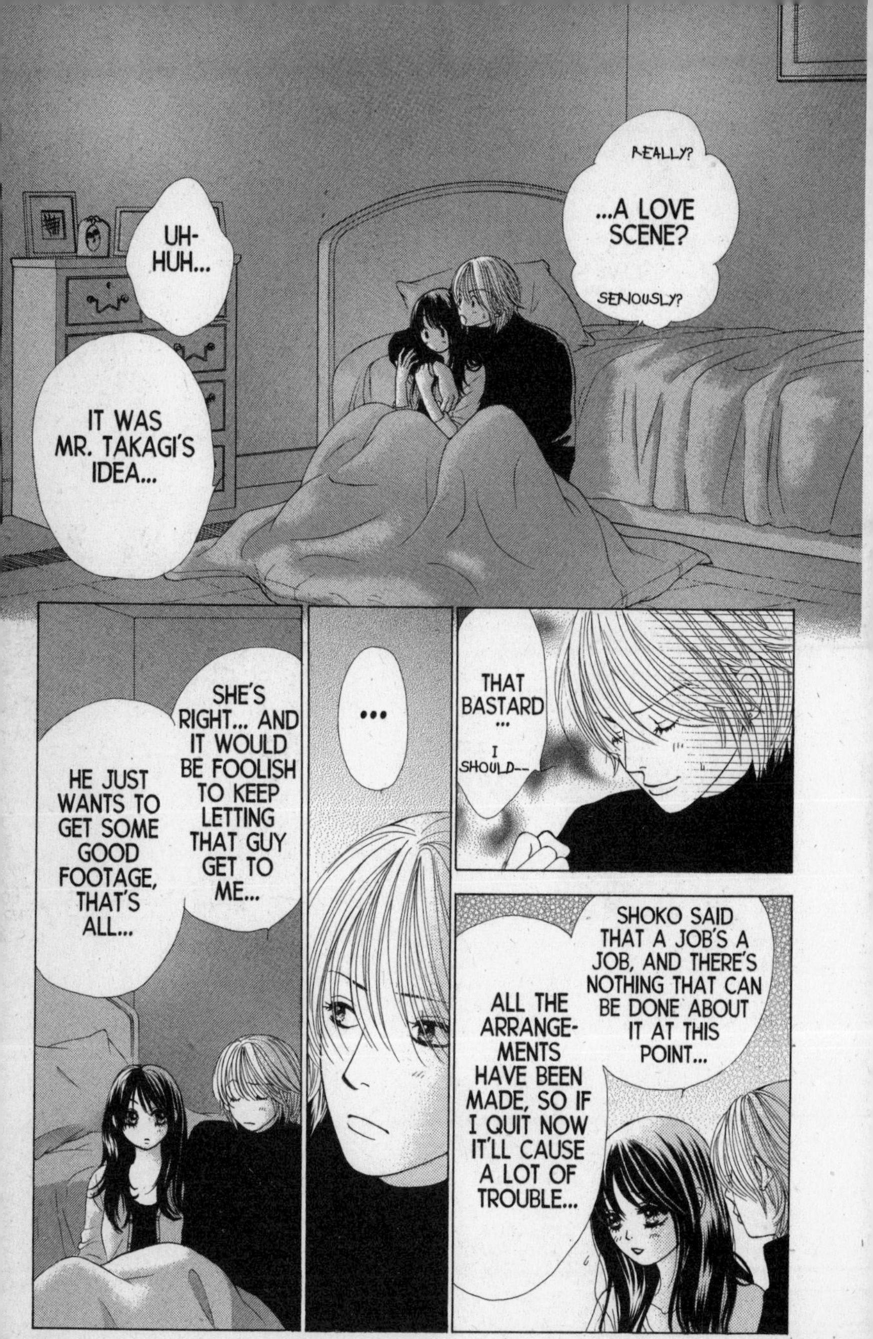
REALLY?
...A LOVE SCENE?
SERIOUSLY?
UH-HUH...
IT WAS MR. TAKAGI'S IDEA...
THAT BASTARD...
I SHOULD--
SHOKO SAID THAT A JOB'S A JOB, AND THERE'S NOTHING THAT CAN BE DONE ABOUT IT AT THIS POINT...
ALL THE ARRANGE-MENTS HAVE BEEN MADE, SO IF I QUIT NOW IT'LL CAUSE A LOT OF TROUBLE...
...
SHE'S RIGHT... AND IT WOULD BE FOOLISH TO KEEP LETTING THAT GUY GET TO ME...
HE JUST WANTS TO GET SOME GOOD FOOTAGE, THAT'S ALL...

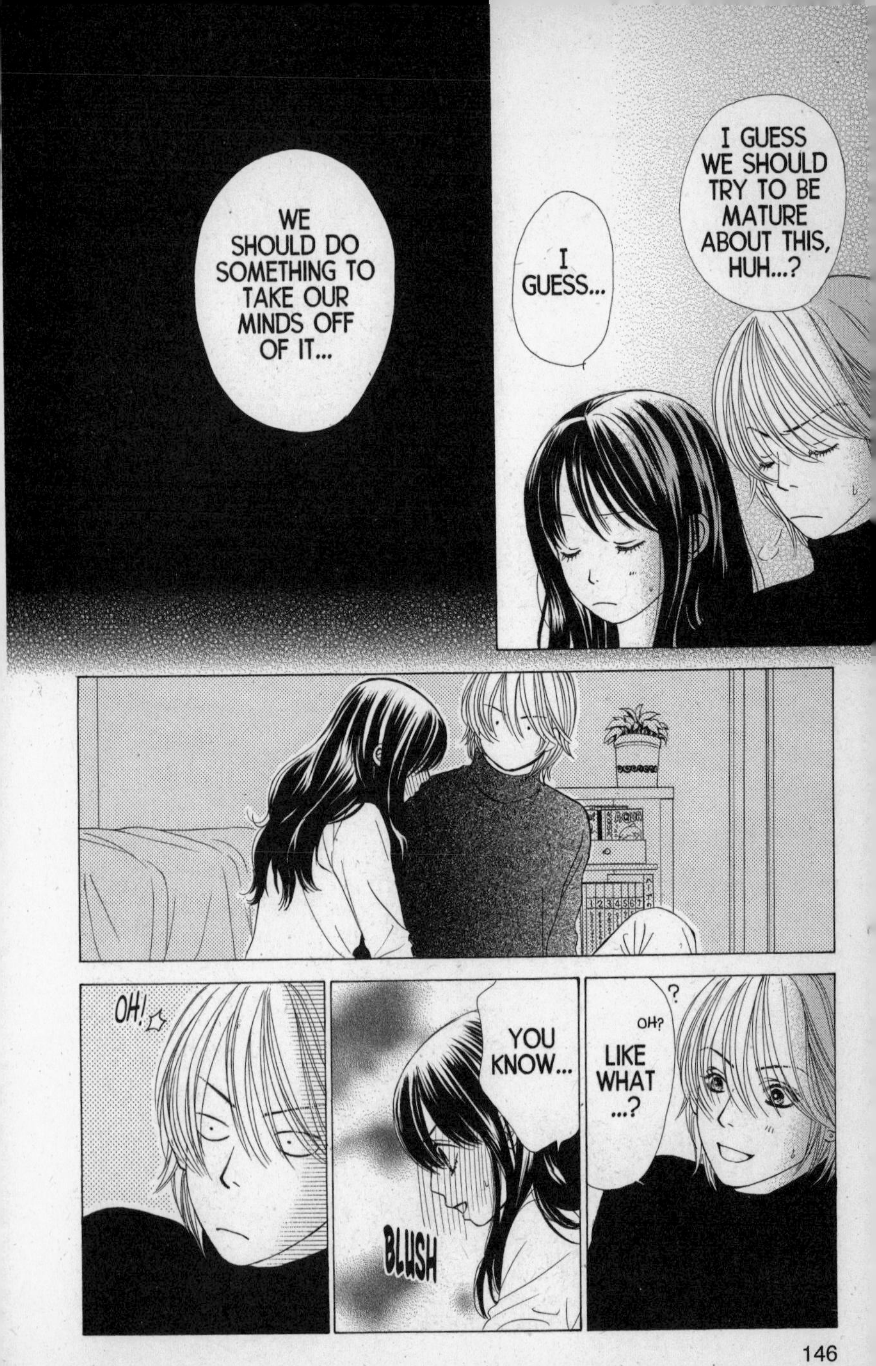
I GUESS WE SHOULD TRY TO BE MATURE ABOUT THIS, HUH...?
I GUESS...
WE SHOULD DO SOMETHING TO TAKE OUR MINDS OFF OF IT...
?
OH?
LIKE WHAT ...?
YOU KNOW...
BLUSH
OH!

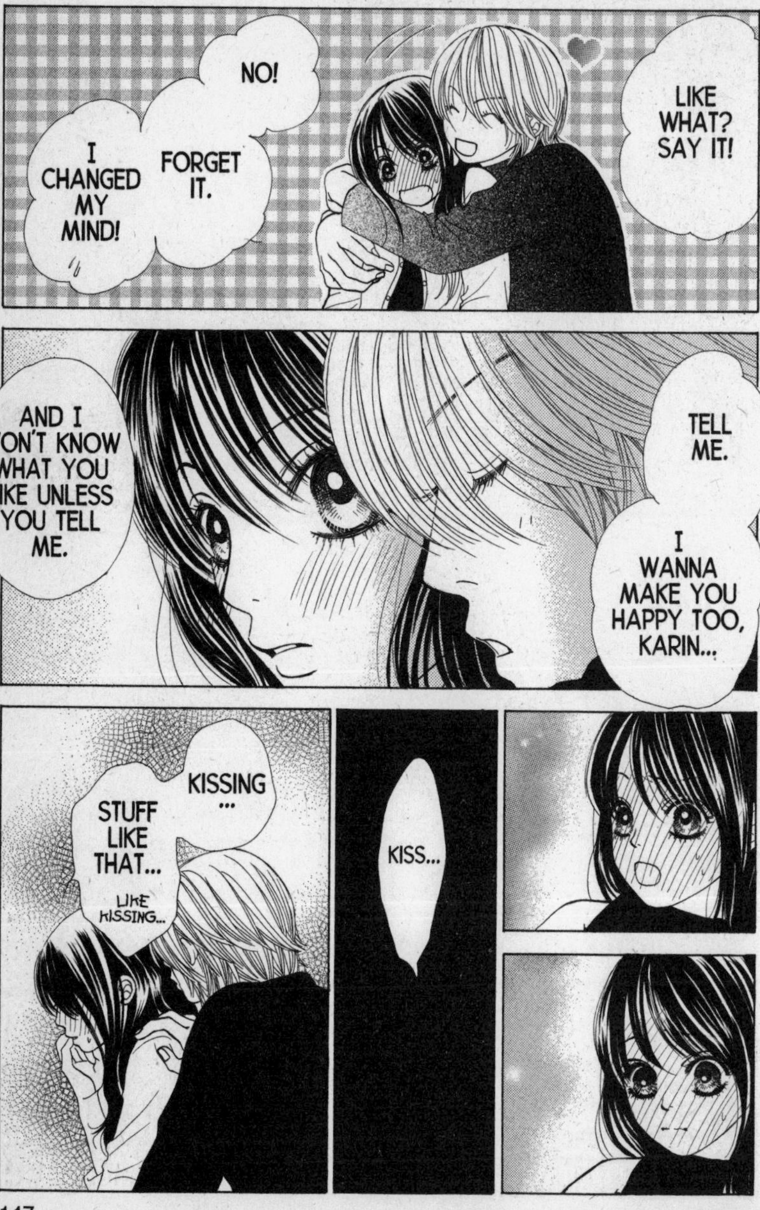
LIKE WHAT? SAY IT!
NO!
FORGET IT.
I CHANGED MY MIND!
TELL ME.
I WANNA MAKE YOU HAPPY TOO, KARIN...
AND I WON'T KNOW WHAT YOU LIKE UNLESS YOU TELL ME.
KISS...
KISSING...
STUFF LIKE THAT...
LIKE KISSING...

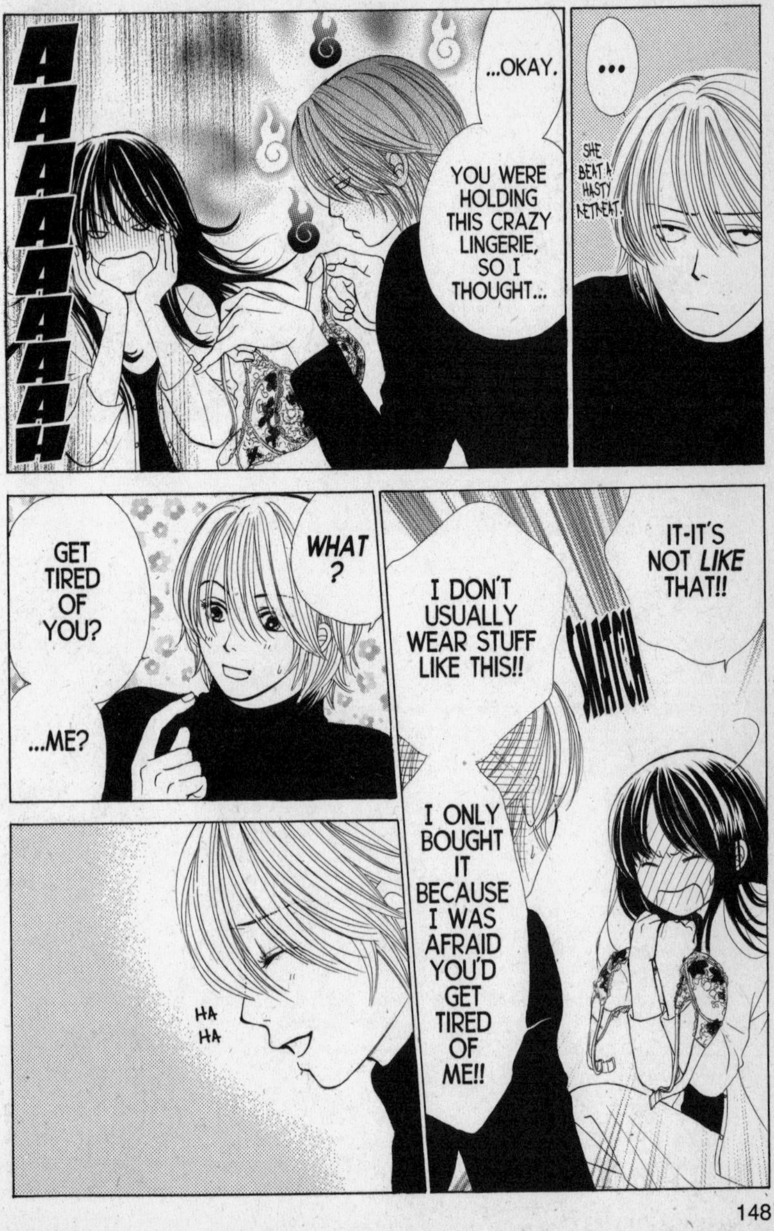
...
SHE BEAT A HASTY RETREAT.
...OKAY.
YOU WERE HOLDING THIS CRAZY LINGERIE, SO I THOUGHT...
AAAAAAAAH
IT-IT'S NOT *LIKE* THAT!!
SNATCH
I DON'T USUALLY WEAR STUFF LIKE THIS!!
I ONLY BOUGHT IT BECAUSE I WAS AFRAID YOU'D GET TIRED OF ME!!
WHAT?
GET TIRED OF YOU?
...ME?
HA HA

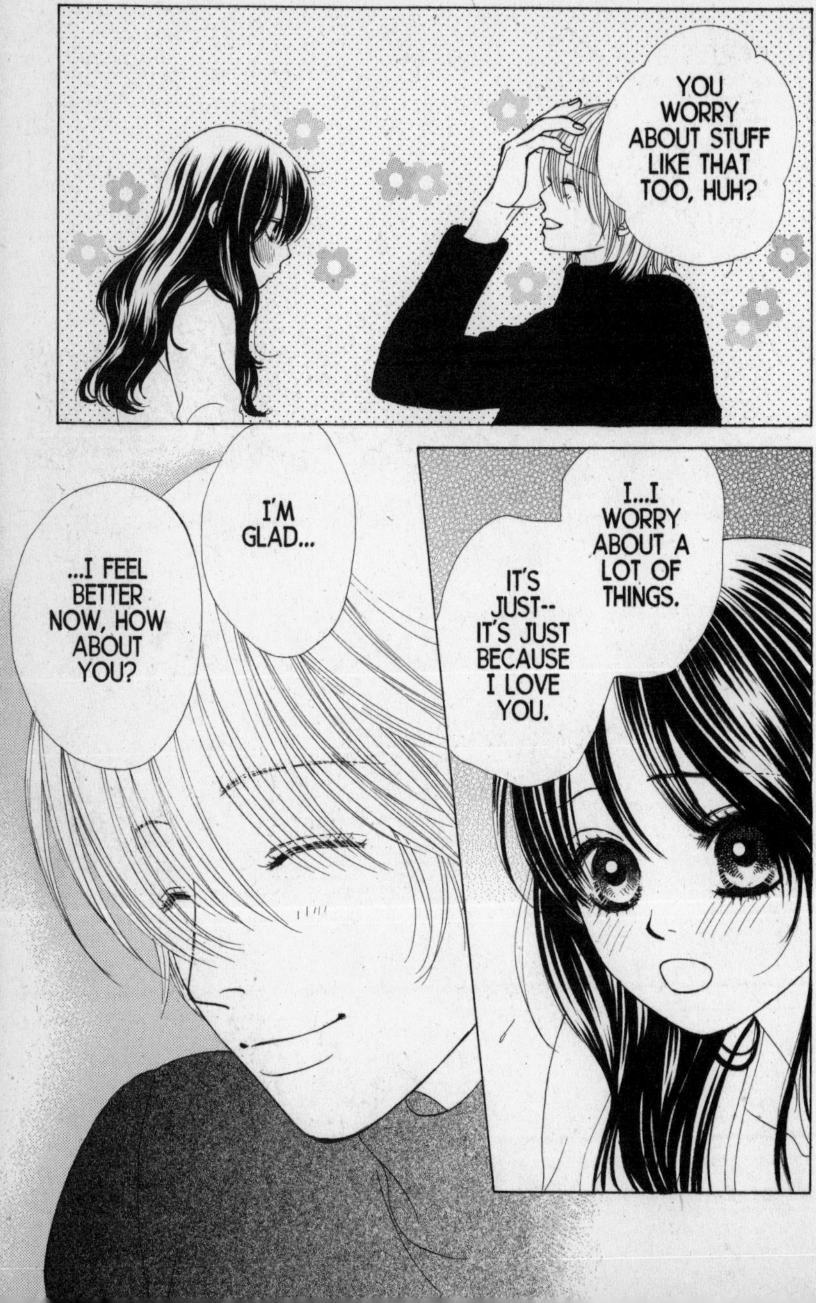
YOU WORRY ABOUT STUFF LIKE THAT TOO, HUH?
I...I WORRY ABOUT A LOT OF THINGS.
IT'S JUST-- IT'S JUST BECAUSE I LOVE YOU.
I'M GLAD...
...I FEEL BETTER NOW, HOW ABOUT YOU?

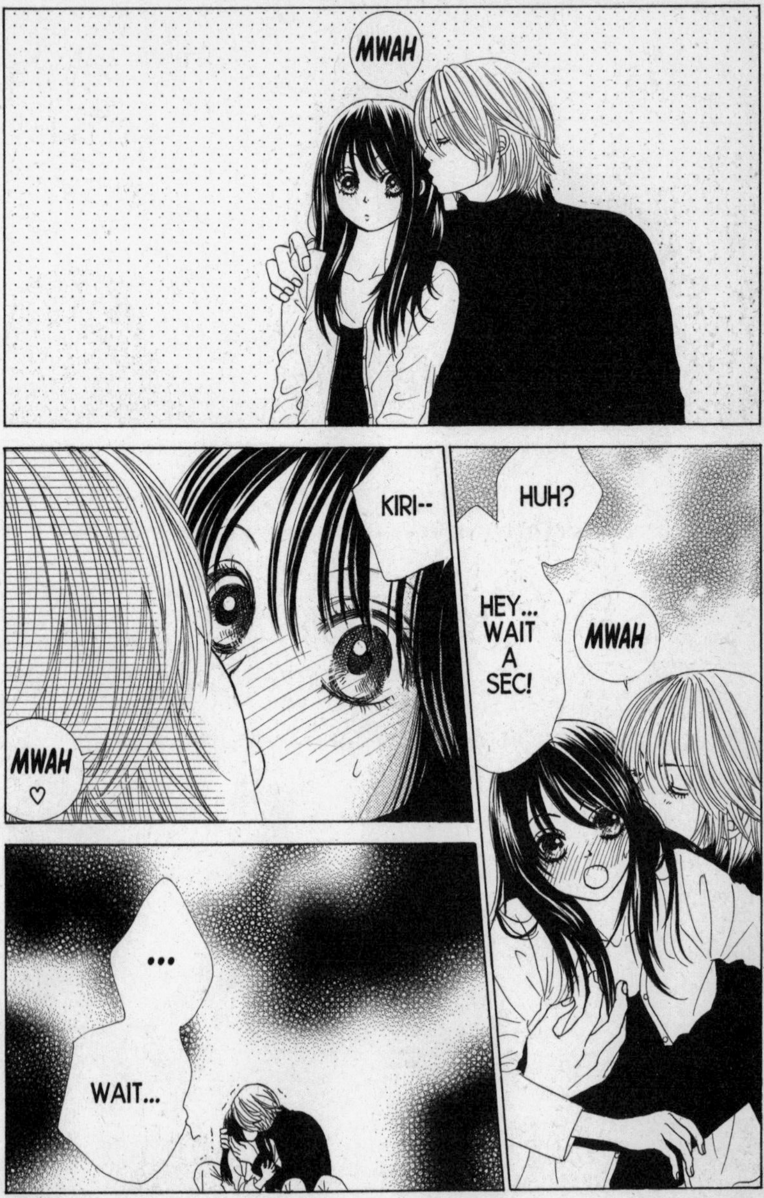
MWAH
HUH?
MWAH
HEY... WAIT A SEC!
KIRI--
MWAH ♡
...
WAIT...

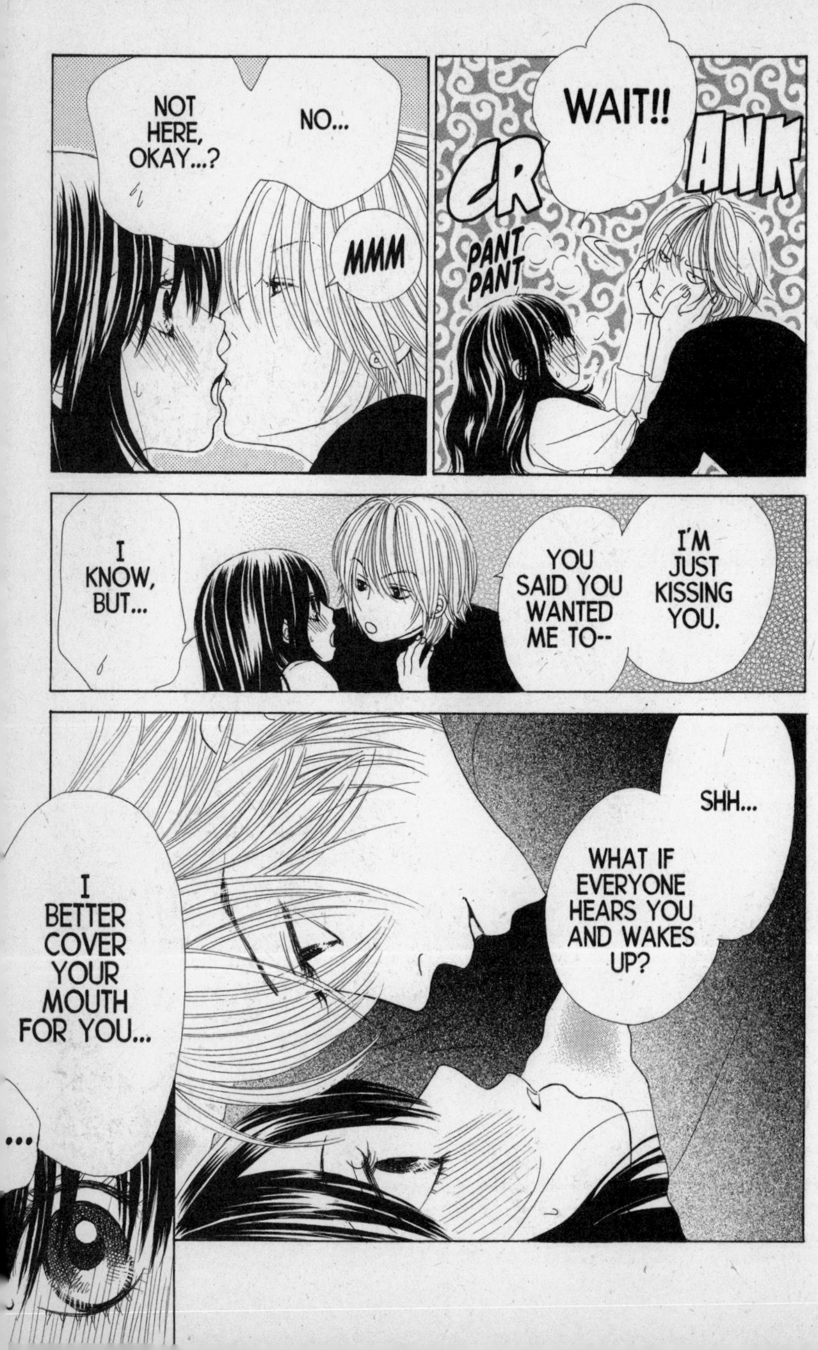
WAIT!!
CRANK
PANT PANT
NO...
NOT HERE, OKAY...?
MMM
I'M JUST KISSING YOU.
YOU SAID YOU WANTED ME TO--
I KNOW, BUT...
SHH...
WHAT IF EVERYONE HEARS YOU AND WAKES UP?
I BETTER COVER YOUR MOUTH FOR YOU...
...

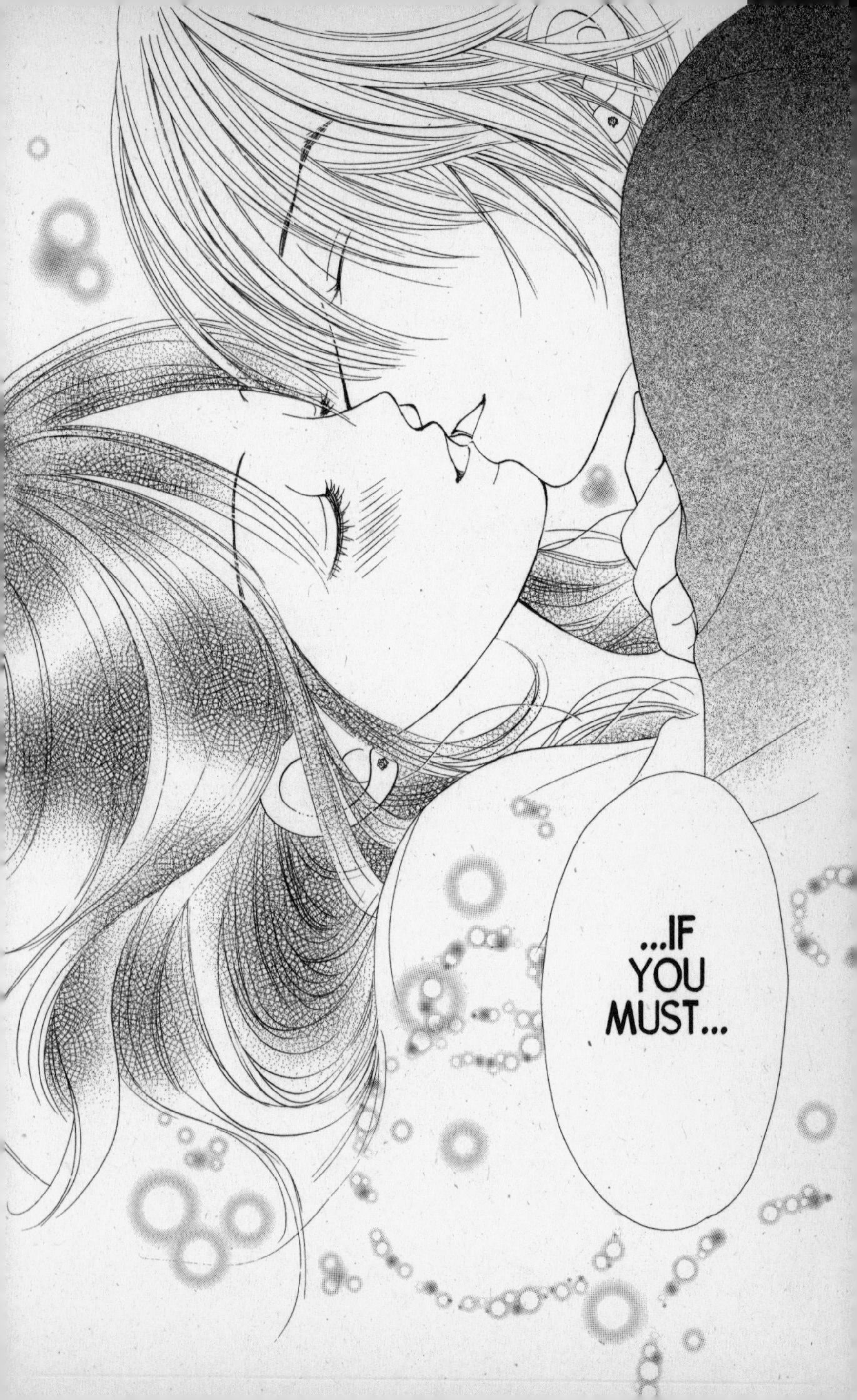
...IF YOU MUST...

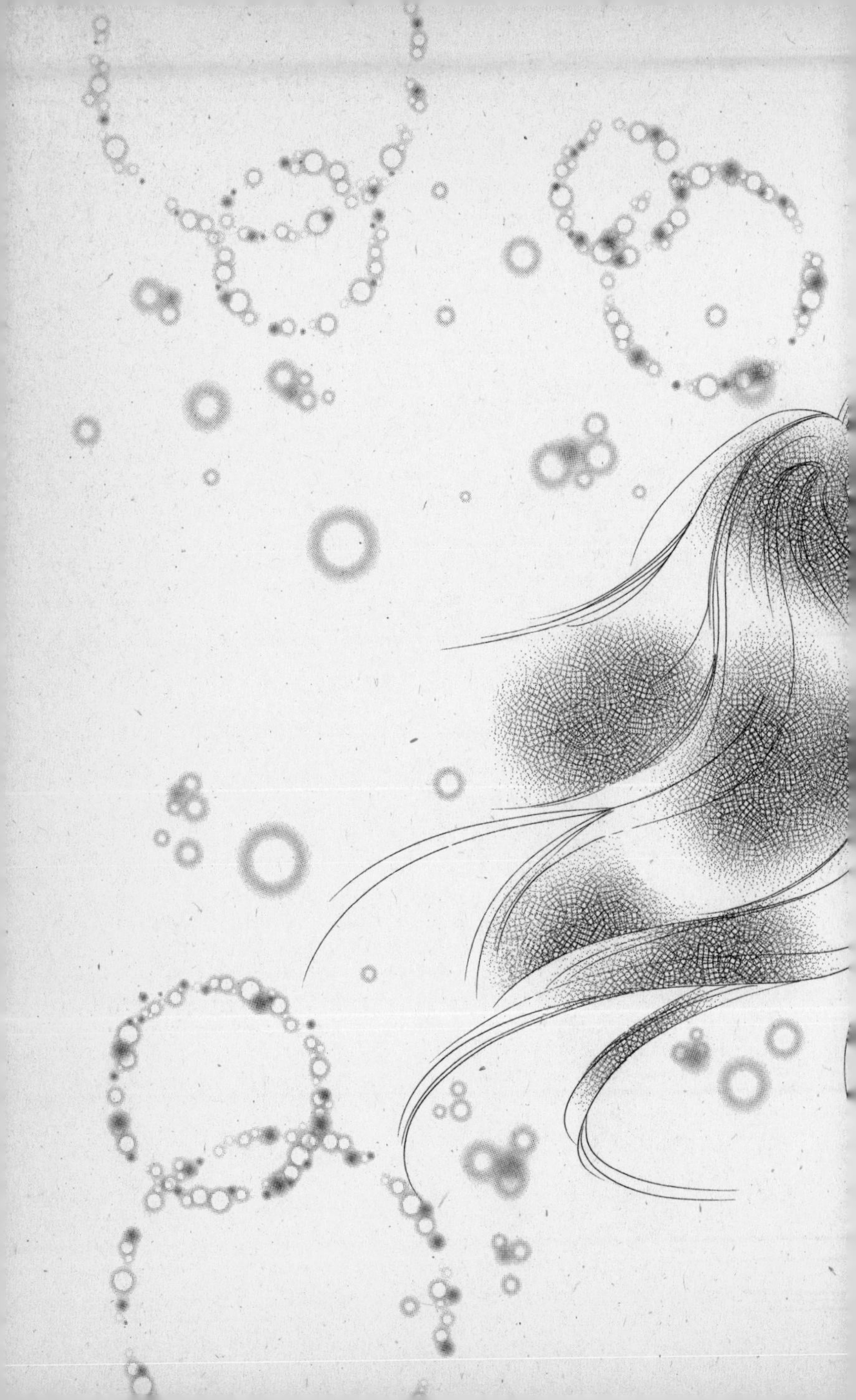

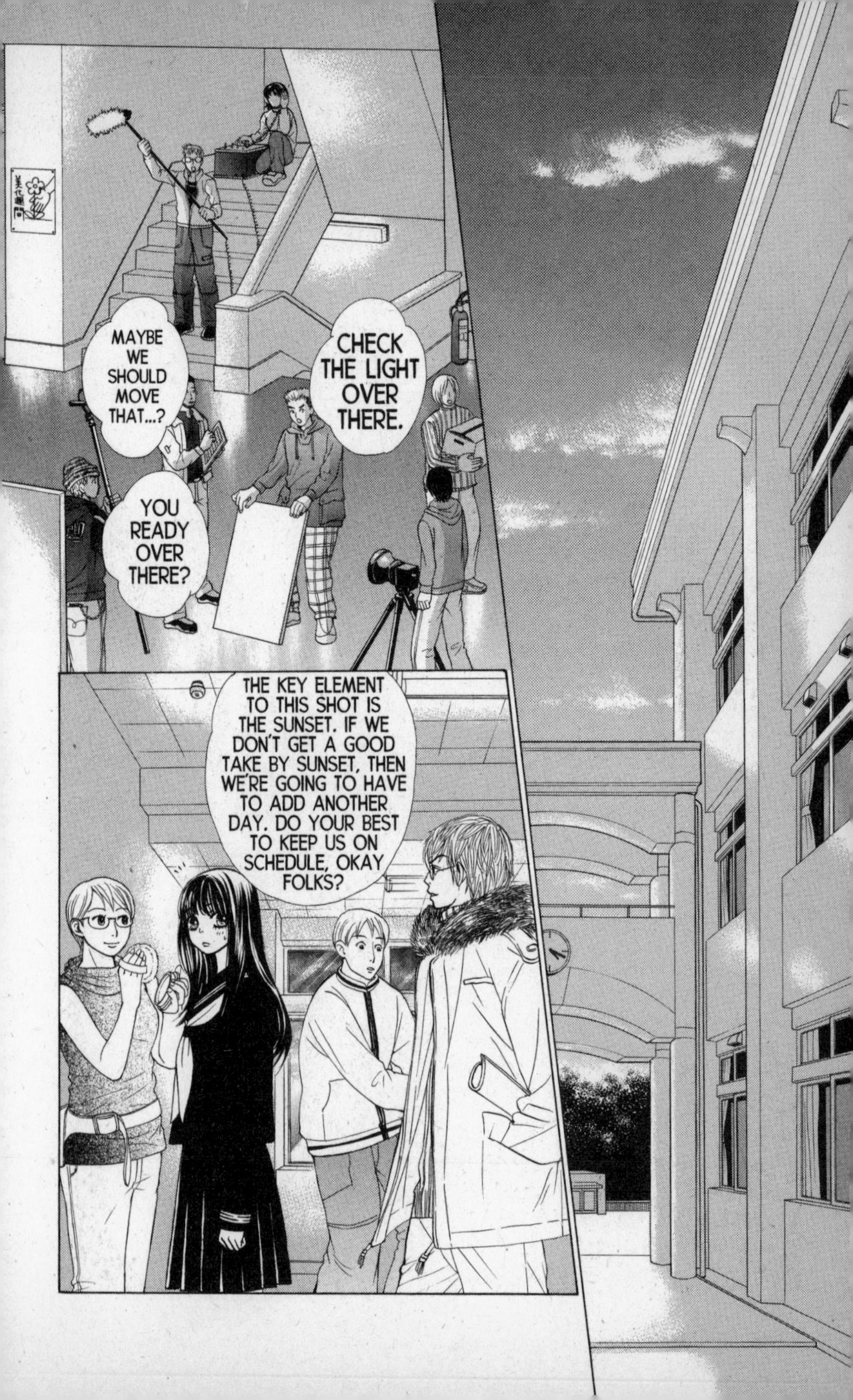
CHECK THE LIGHT OVER THERE.
MAYBE WE SHOULD MOVE THAT...?
YOU READY OVER THERE?
THE KEY ELEMENT TO THIS SHOT IS THE SUNSET. IF WE DON'T GET A GOOD TAKE BY SUNSET, THEN WE'RE GOING TO HAVE TO ADD ANOTHER DAY. DO YOUR BEST TO KEEP US ON SCHEDULE, OKAY FOLKS?

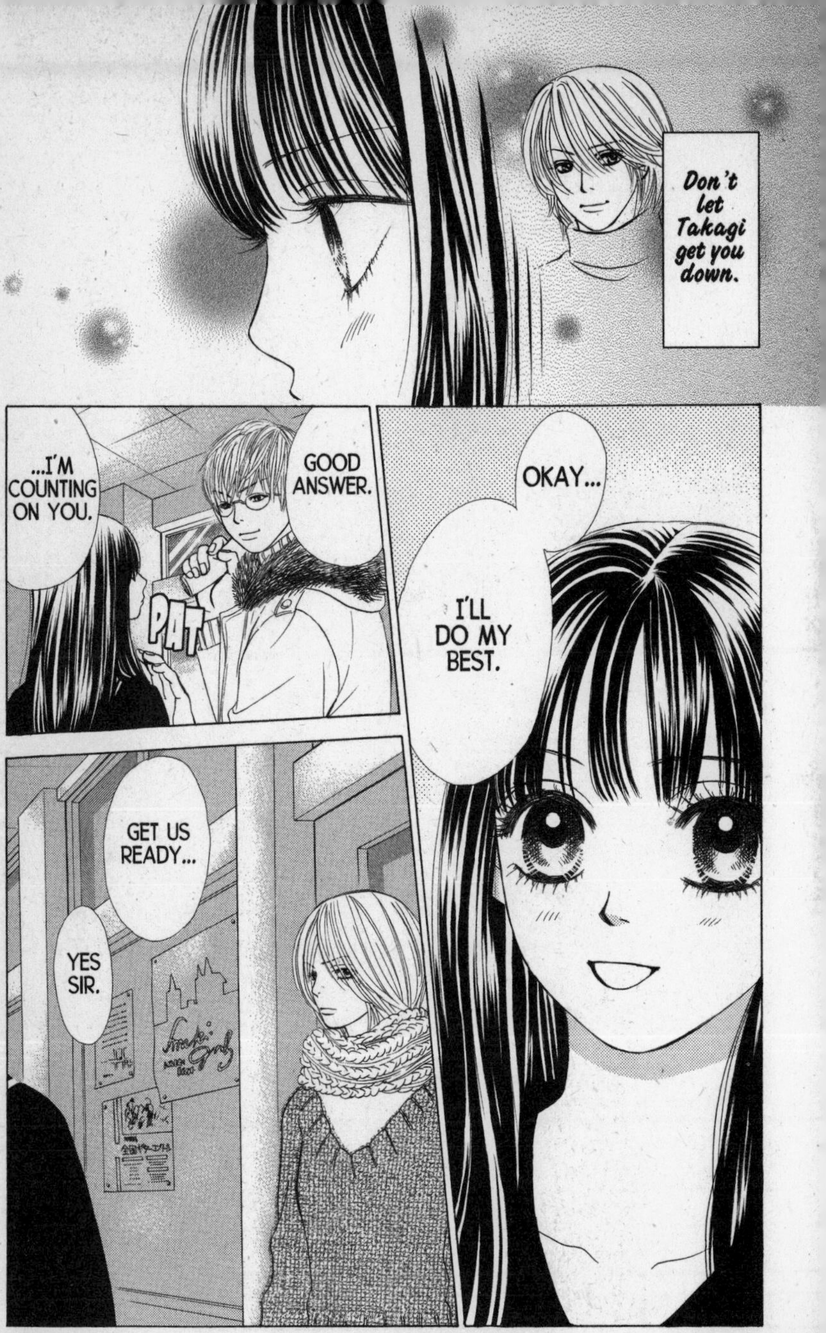
Don't let Takagi get you down.
OKAY...
I'LL DO MY BEST.
GOOD ANSWER.
PAT
...I'M COUNTING ON YOU.
GET US READY...
YES SIR.

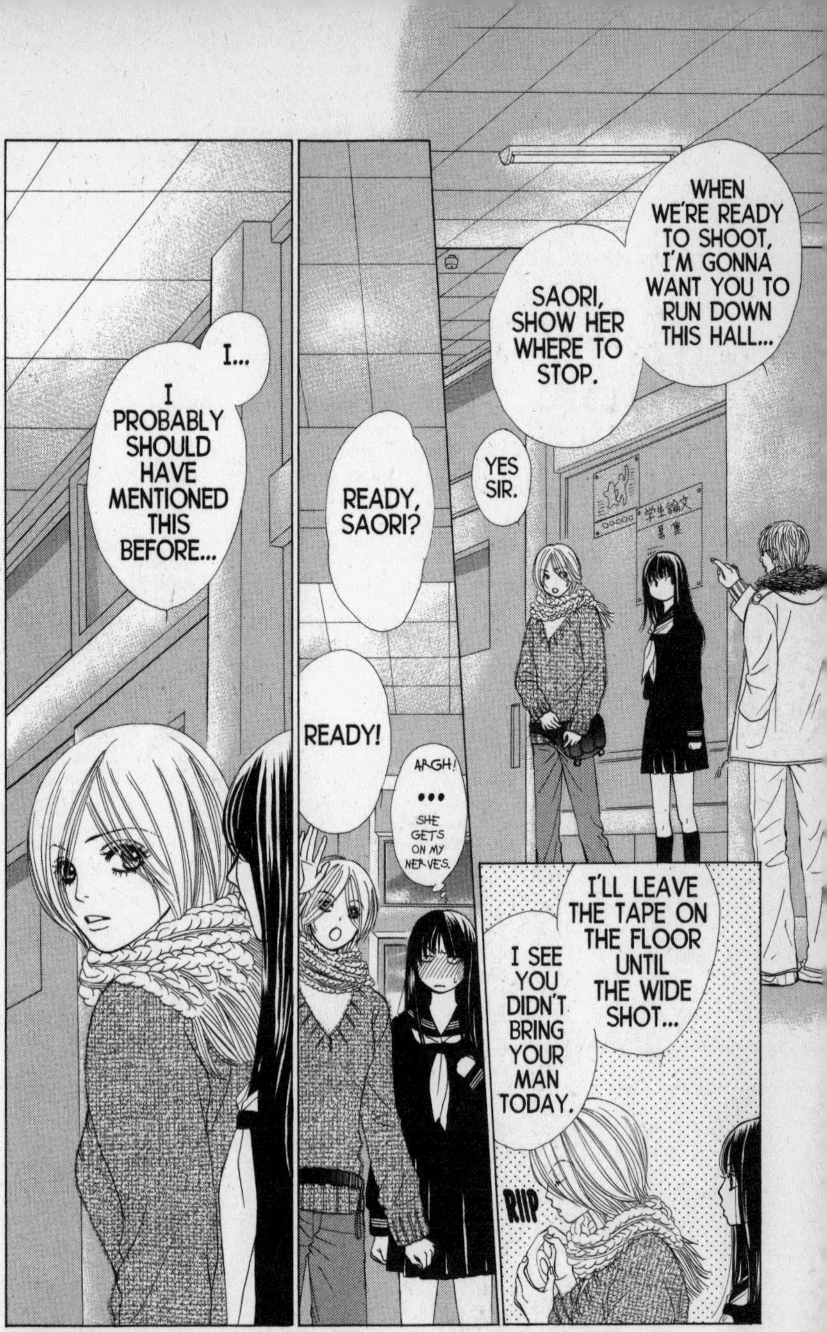
WHEN WE'RE READY TO SHOOT, I'M GONNA WANT YOU TO RUN DOWN THIS HALL...
SAORI, SHOW HER WHERE TO STOP.
YES SIR.
学生論文
募集
I'LL LEAVE THE TAPE ON THE FLOOR UNTIL THE WIDE SHOT...
I SEE YOU DIDN'T BRING YOUR MAN TODAY.
RIIP
READY, SAORI?
READY!
ARGH! ... SHE GETS ON MY NERVES.
I...
I PROBABLY SHOULD HAVE MENTIONED THIS BEFORE...

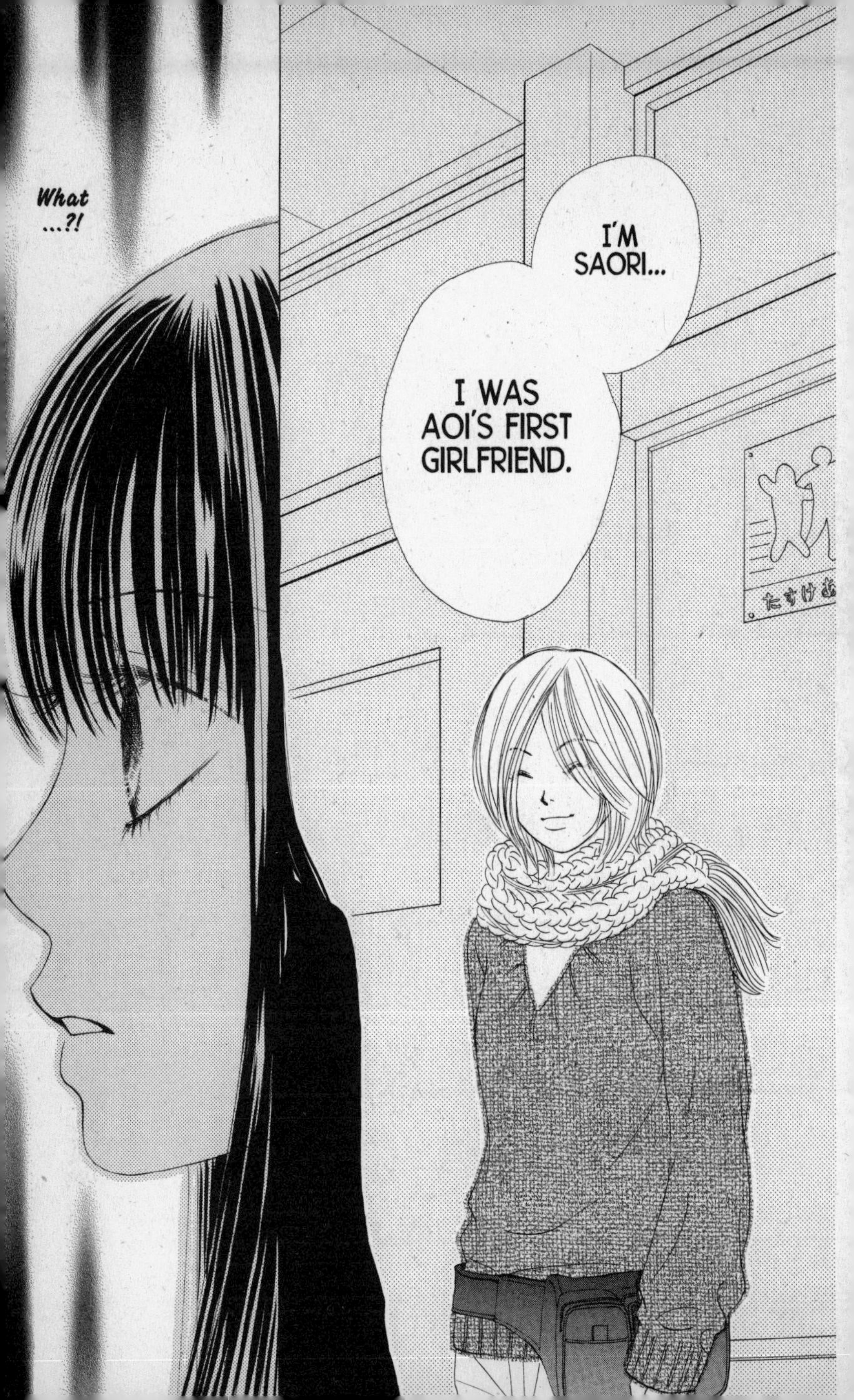
I'M SAORI...
I WAS AOI'S FIRST GIRLFRIEND.
What ...?!

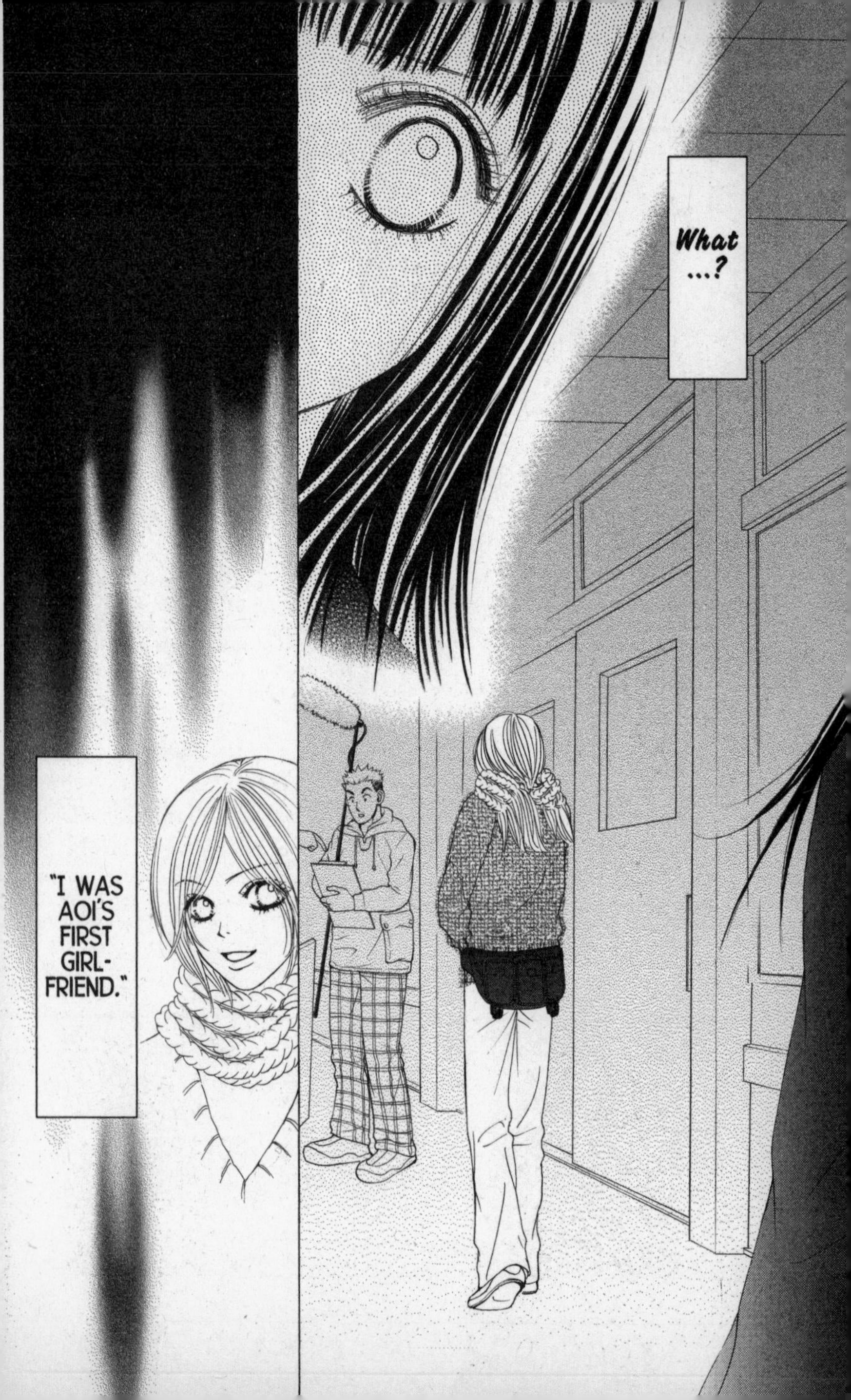
What ...?
"I WAS AOI'S FIRST GIRL-FRIEND."

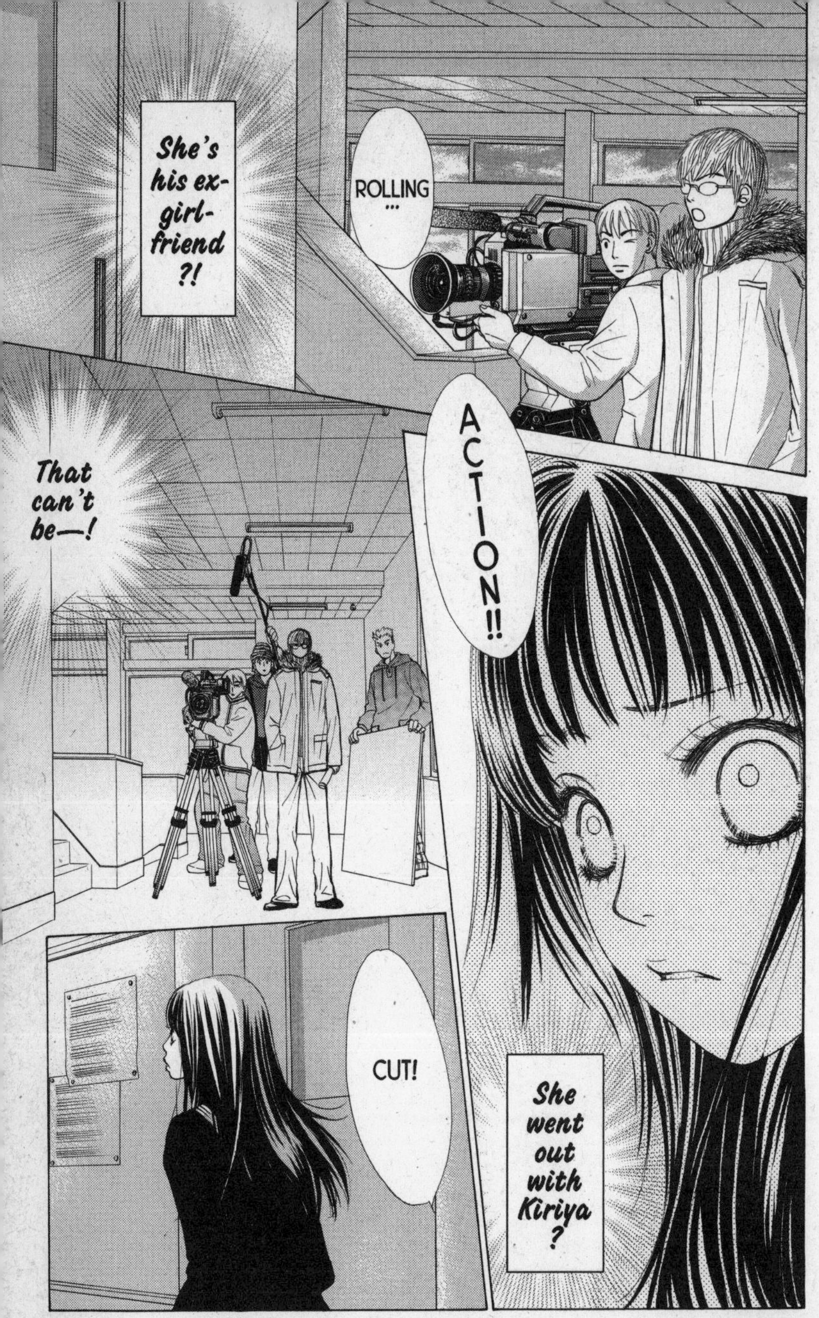
ROLLING...
She's his ex-girlfriend ?!
ACTION!!
She went out with Kiriya ?
That can't be—!
CUT!

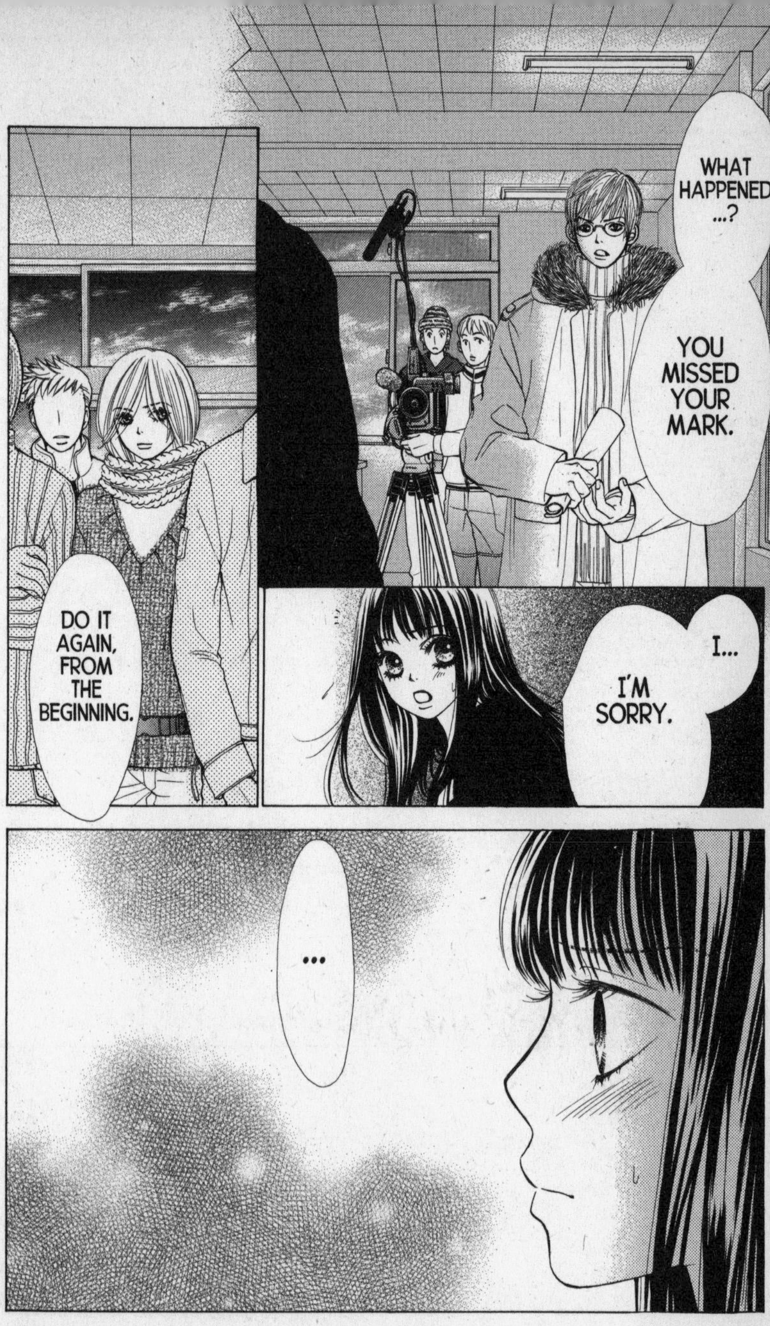
WHAT HAPPENED ...?
YOU MISSED YOUR MARK.
I...
I'M SORRY.
DO IT AGAIN, FROM THE BEGINNING.
...

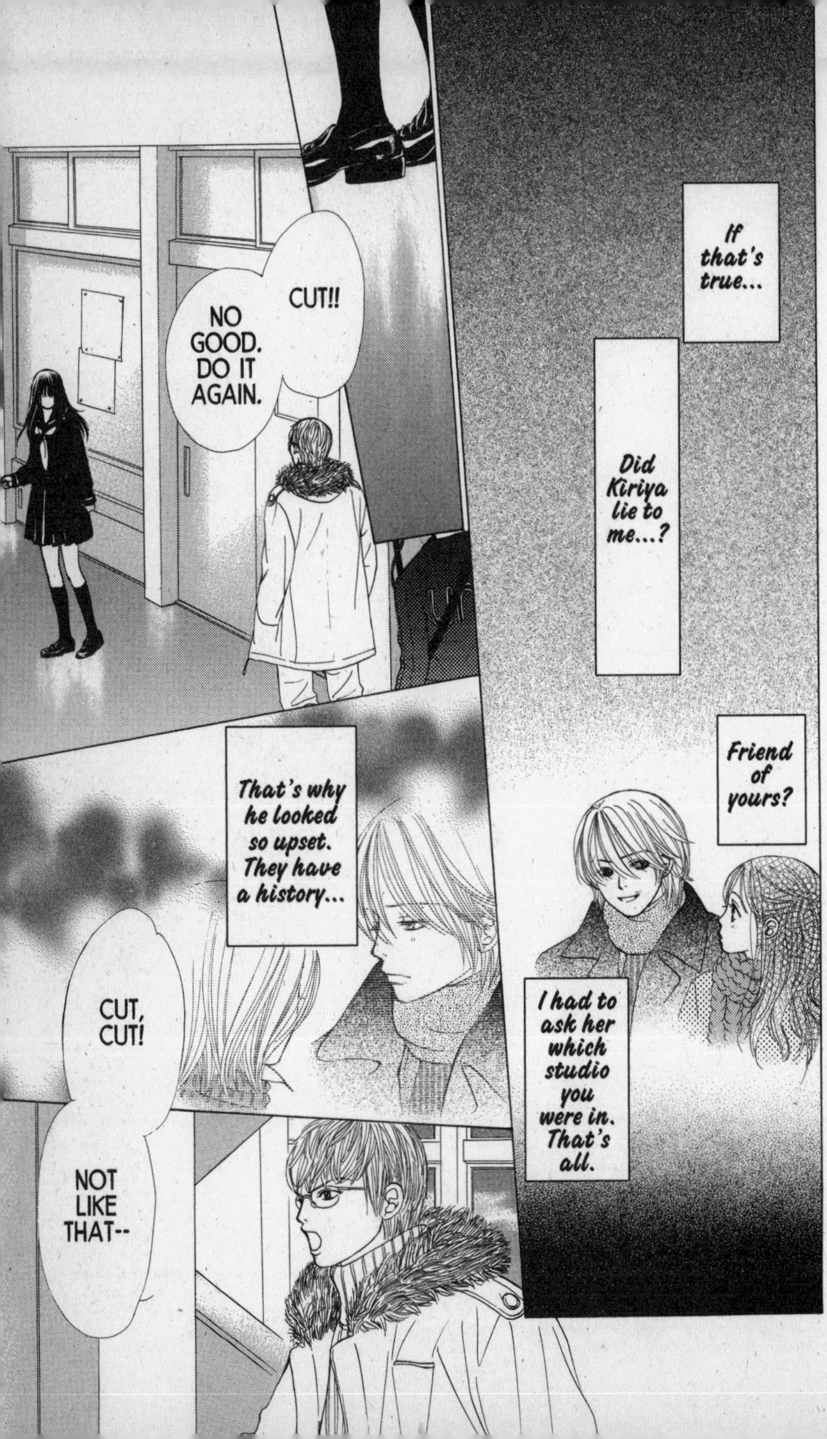
If that's true...
Did Kiriya lie to me...?
Friend of yours?
I had to ask her which studio you were in. That's all.
CUT!!
NO GOOD. DO IT AGAIN.
That's why he looked so upset. They have a history...
CUT, CUT!
NOT LIKE THAT--

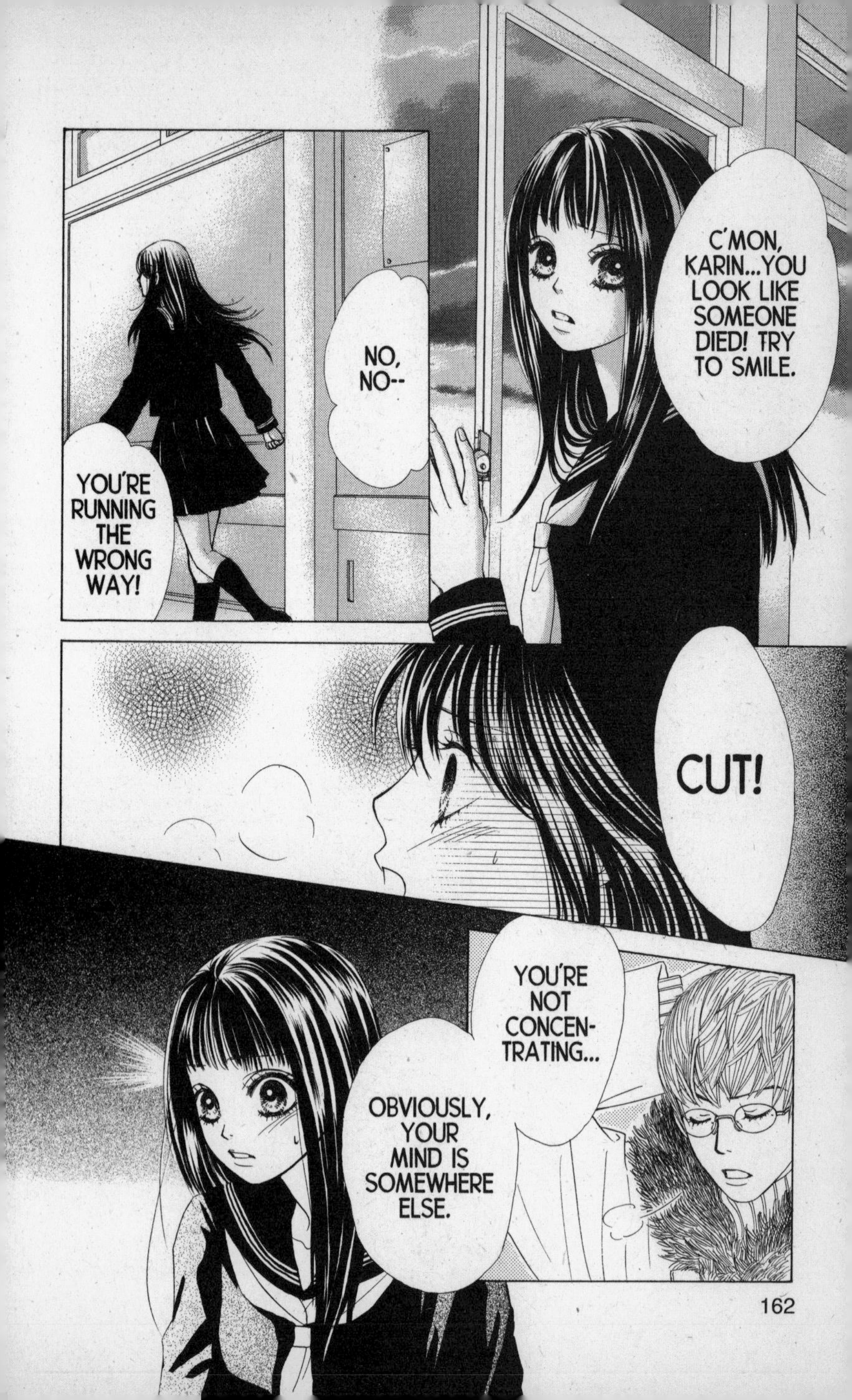
C'MON, KARIN...YOU LOOK LIKE SOMEONE DIED! TRY TO SMILE.
NO, NO--
YOU'RE RUNNING THE WRONG WAY!
CUT!
YOU'RE NOT CONCEN-TRATING...
OBVIOUSLY, YOUR MIND IS SOMEWHERE ELSE.

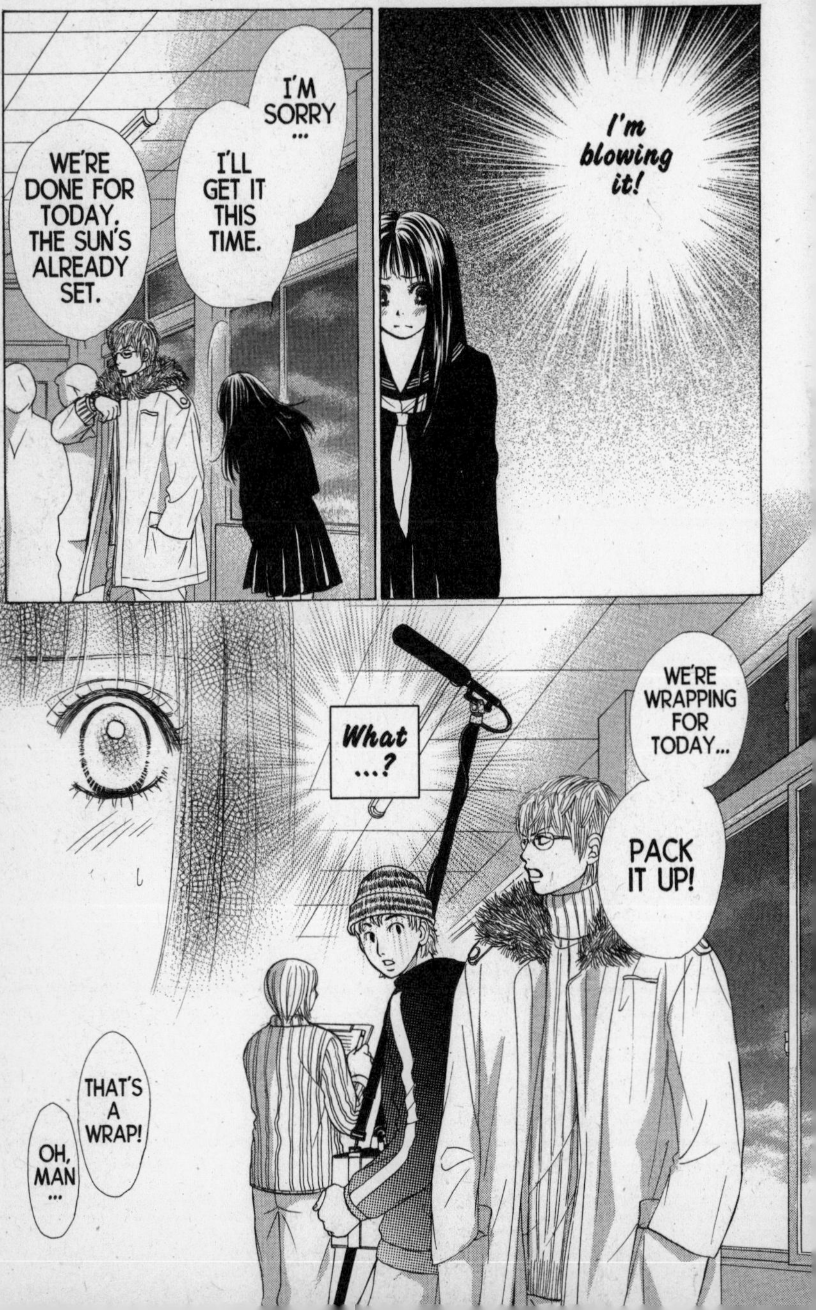
I'm blowing it!
I'M SORRY...
I'LL GET IT THIS TIME.
WE'RE DONE FOR TODAY. THE SUN'S ALREADY SET.
WE'RE WRAPPING FOR TODAY...
PACK IT UP!
What...?
THAT'S A WRAP!
OH, MAN...

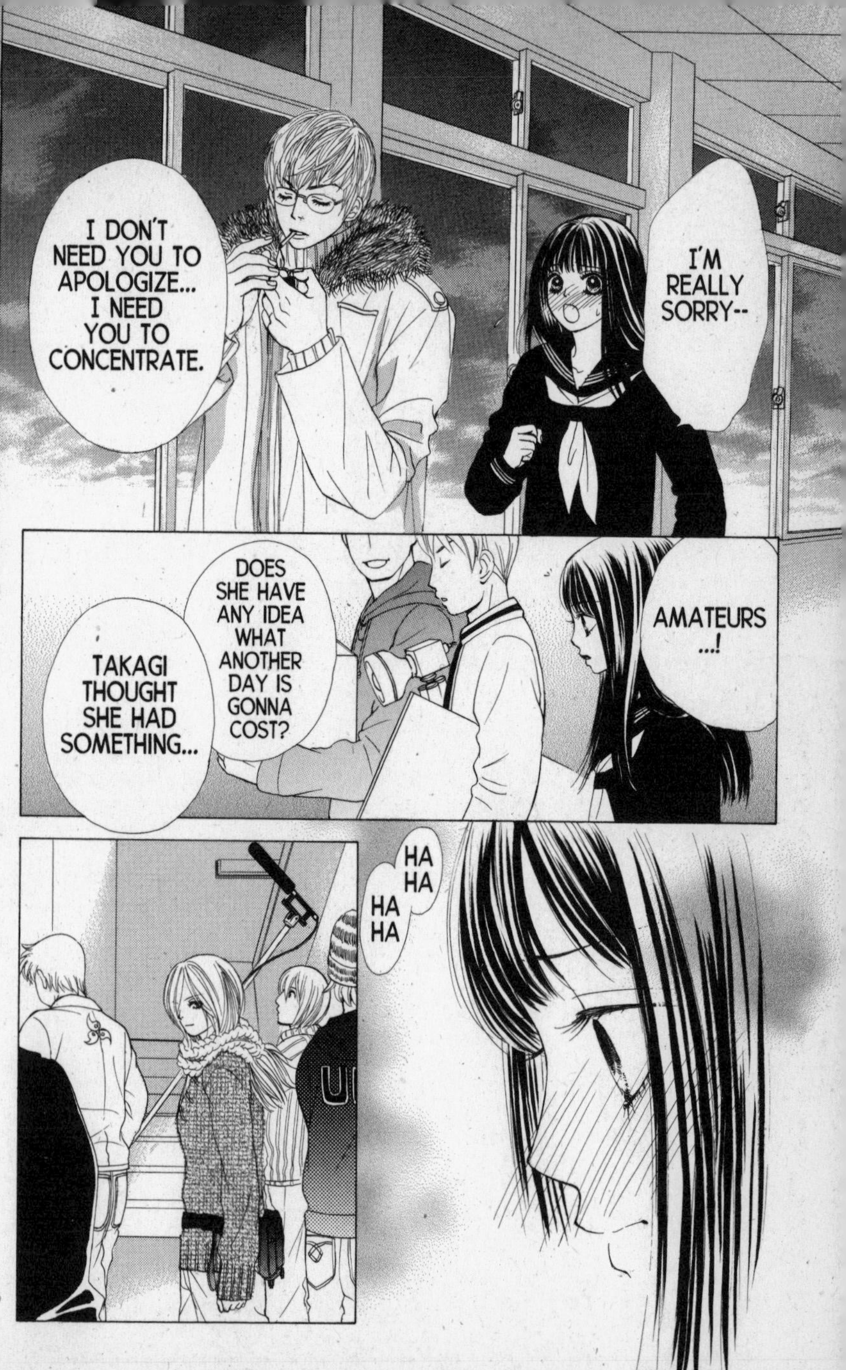
I'M REALLY SORRY--
I DON'T NEED YOU TO APOLOGIZE... I NEED YOU TO CONCENTRATE.
AMATEURS ...!
DOES SHE HAVE ANY IDEA WHAT ANOTHER DAY IS GONNA COST?
TAKAGI THOUGHT SHE HAD SOMETHING...
HA HA HA HA

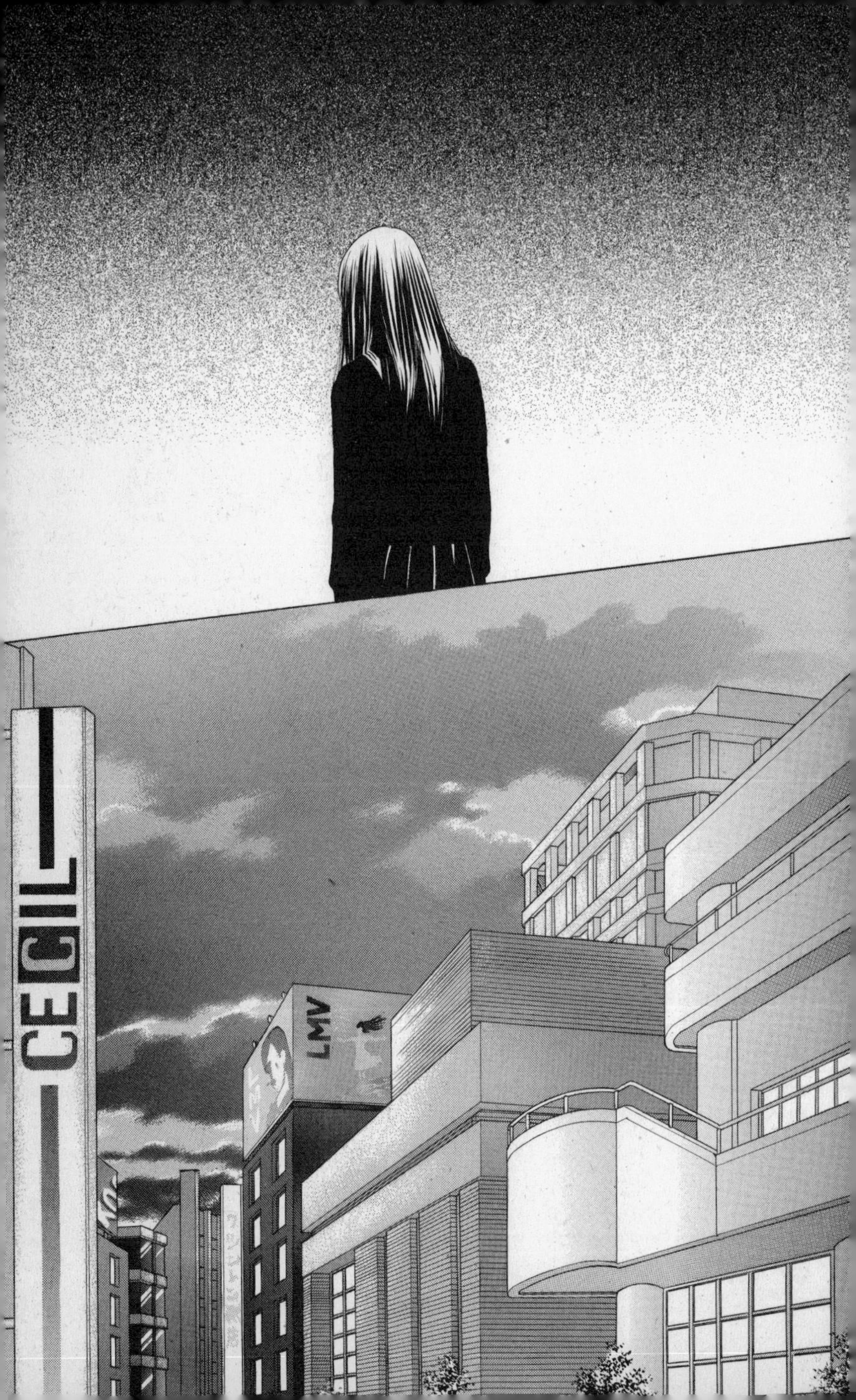
CECIL
LMV

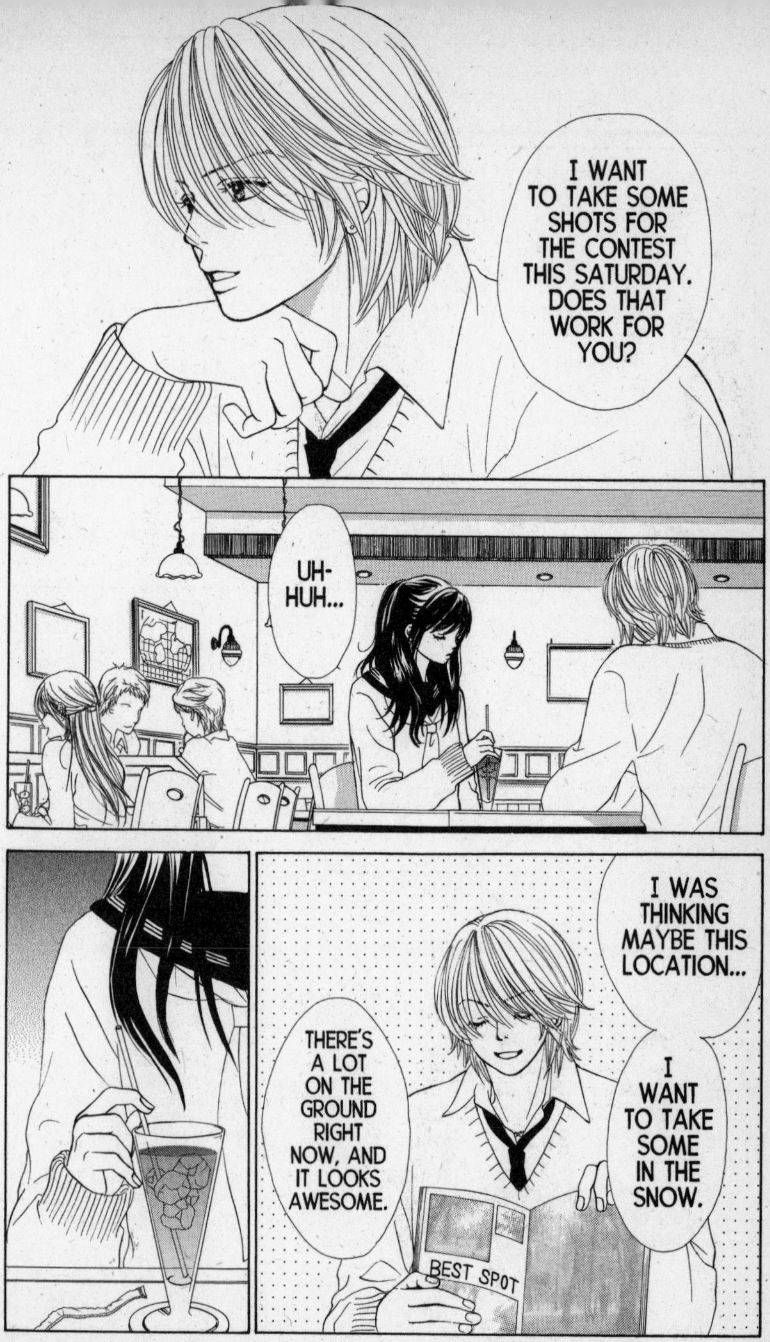
I WANT TO TAKE SOME SHOTS FOR THE CONTEST THIS SATURDAY. DOES THAT WORK FOR YOU?
UH-HUH...
I WAS THINKING MAYBE THIS LOCATION...
I WANT TO TAKE SOME IN THE SNOW.
THERE'S A LOT ON THE GROUND RIGHT NOW, AND IT LOOKS AWESOME.
BEST SPOT

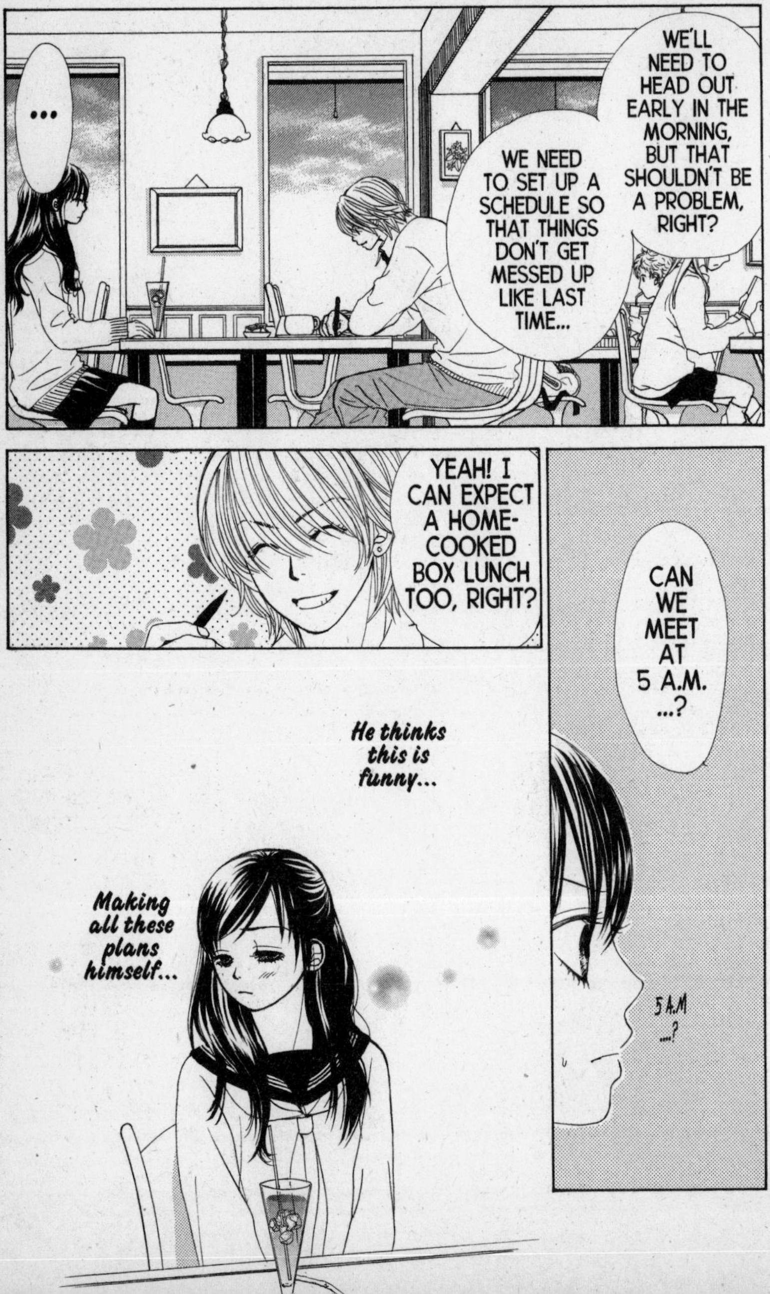
WE'LL NEED TO HEAD OUT EARLY IN THE MORNING, BUT THAT SHOULDN'T BE A PROBLEM, RIGHT?
WE NEED TO SET UP A SCHEDULE SO THAT THINGS DON'T GET MESSED UP LIKE LAST TIME...
...
CAN WE MEET AT 5 A.M. ...?
5 A.M ...?
YEAH! I CAN EXPECT A HOME-COOKED BOX LUNCH TOO, RIGHT?
He thinks this is funny...
Making all these plans himself...

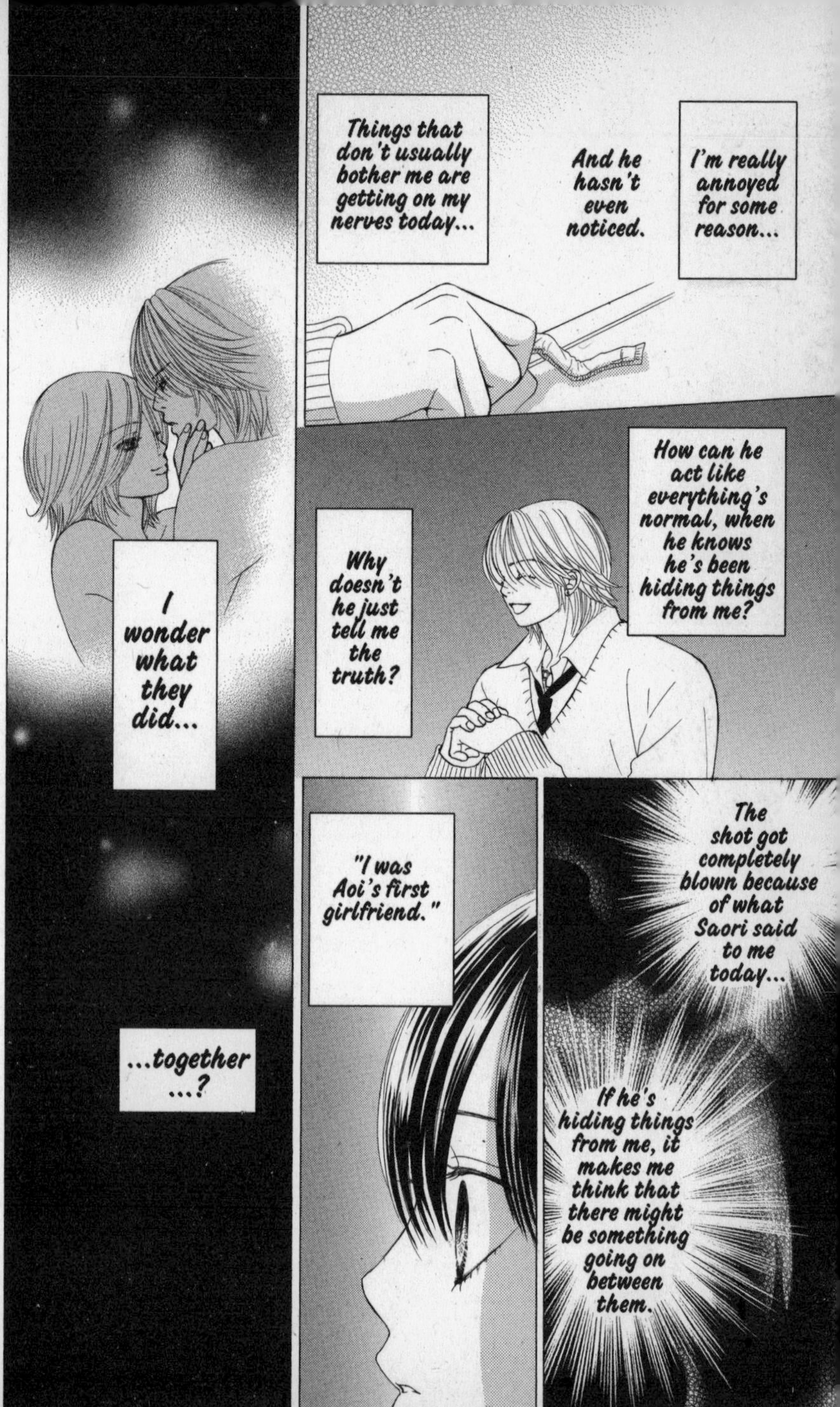
I'm really annoyed for some reason...
And he hasn't even noticed.
Things that don't usually bother me are getting on my nerves today...
How can he act like everything's normal, when he knows he's been hiding things from me?
Why doesn't he just tell me the truth?
The shot got completely blown because of what Saori said to me today...
If he's hiding things from me, it makes me think that there might be something going on between them.
"I was Aoi's first girlfriend."
I wonder what they did...
...together...?

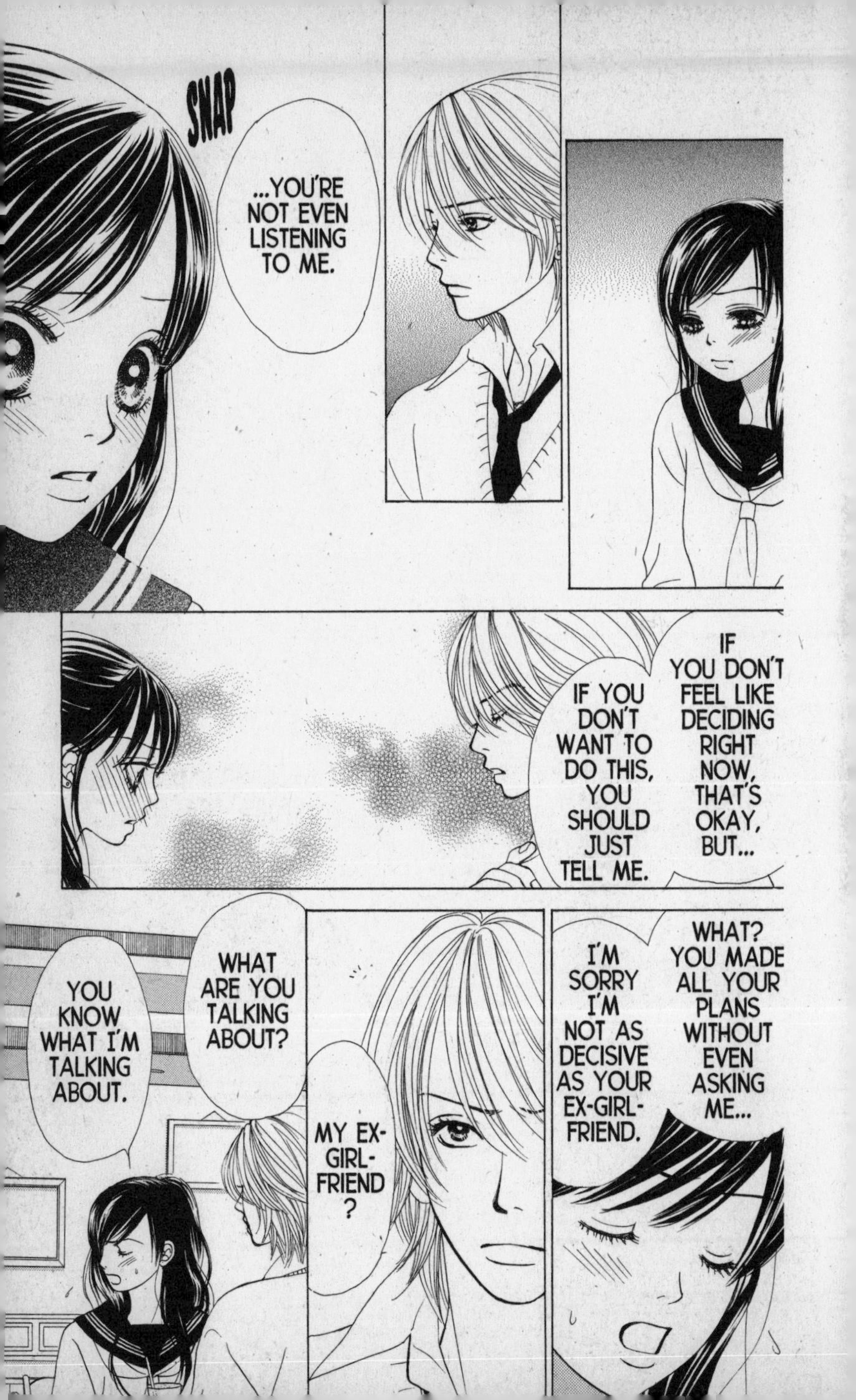
SNAP
...YOU'RE NOT EVEN LISTENING TO ME.
IF YOU DON'T FEEL LIKE DECIDING RIGHT NOW, THAT'S OKAY, BUT...
IF YOU DON'T WANT TO DO THIS, YOU SHOULD JUST TELL ME.
WHAT? YOU MADE ALL YOUR PLANS WITHOUT EVEN ASKING ME...
I'M SORRY I'M NOT AS DECISIVE AS YOUR EX-GIRL-FRIEND.
MY EX-GIRL-FRIEND?
WHAT ARE YOU TALKING ABOUT?
YOU KNOW WHAT I'M TALKING ABOUT.

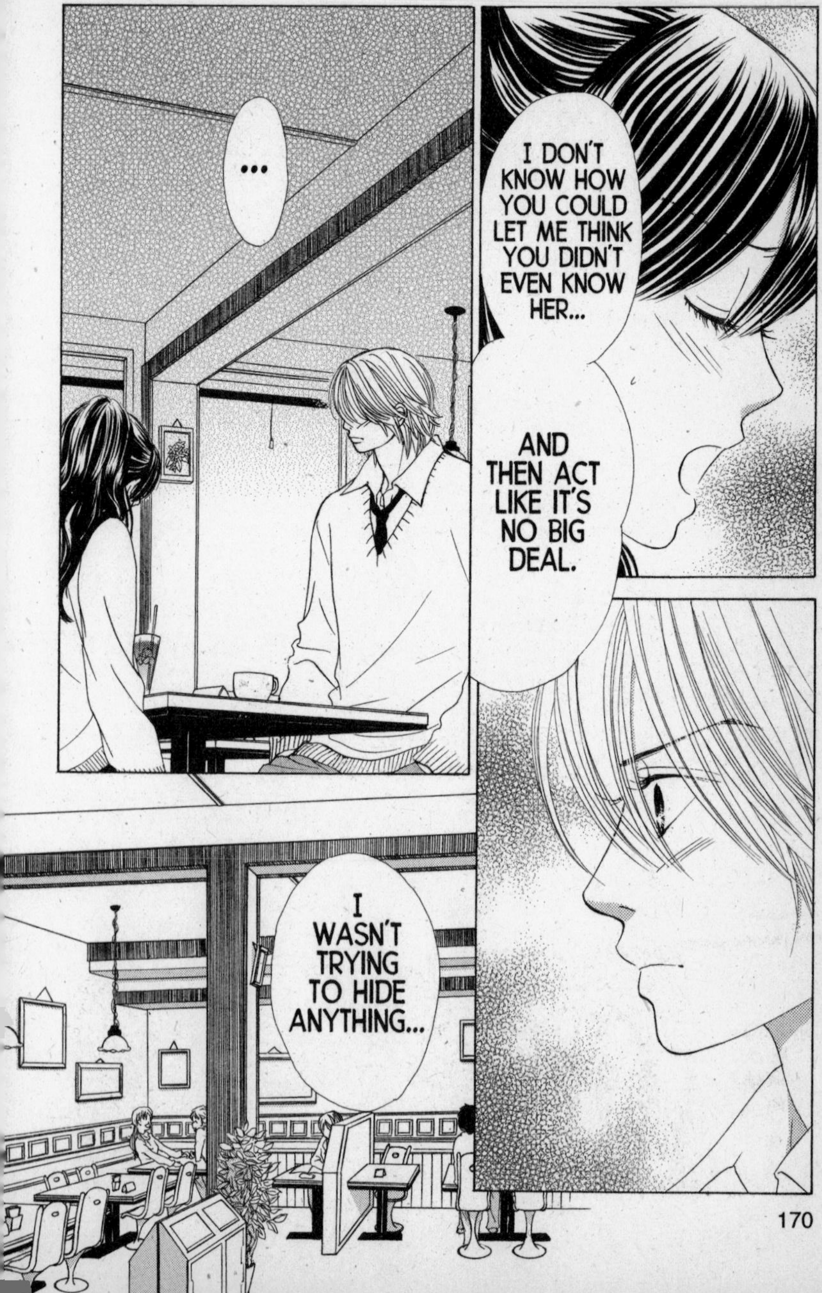

I DON'T KNOW HOW YOU COULD LET ME THINK YOU DIDN'T EVEN KNOW HER...
AND THEN ACT LIKE IT'S NO BIG DEAL.
...
I WASN'T TRYING TO HIDE ANYTHING...

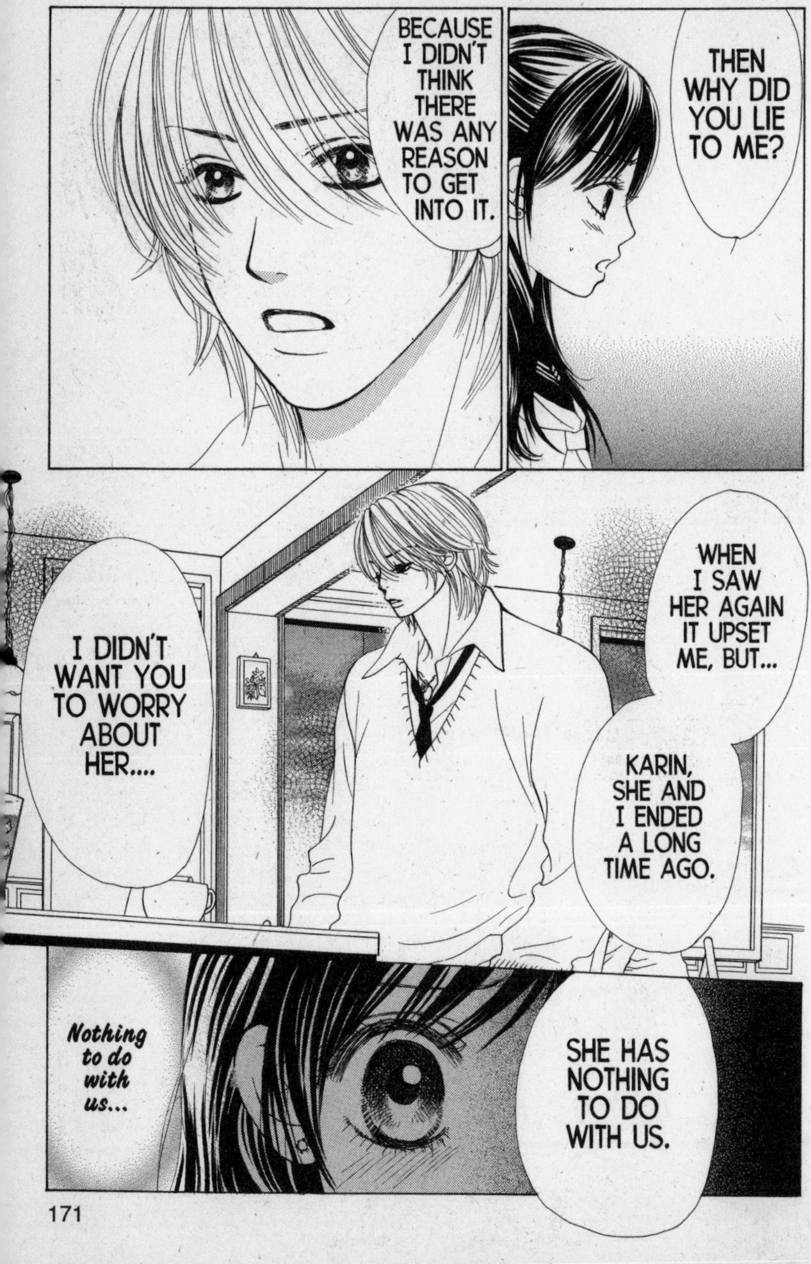
THEN WHY DID YOU LIE TO ME?
BECAUSE I DIDN'T THINK THERE WAS ANY REASON TO GET INTO IT.
WHEN I SAW HER AGAIN IT UPSET ME, BUT...
KARIN, SHE AND I ENDED A LONG TIME AGO.
I DIDN'T WANT YOU TO WORRY ABOUT HER....
SHE HAS NOTHING TO DO WITH US.
Nothing to do with us...

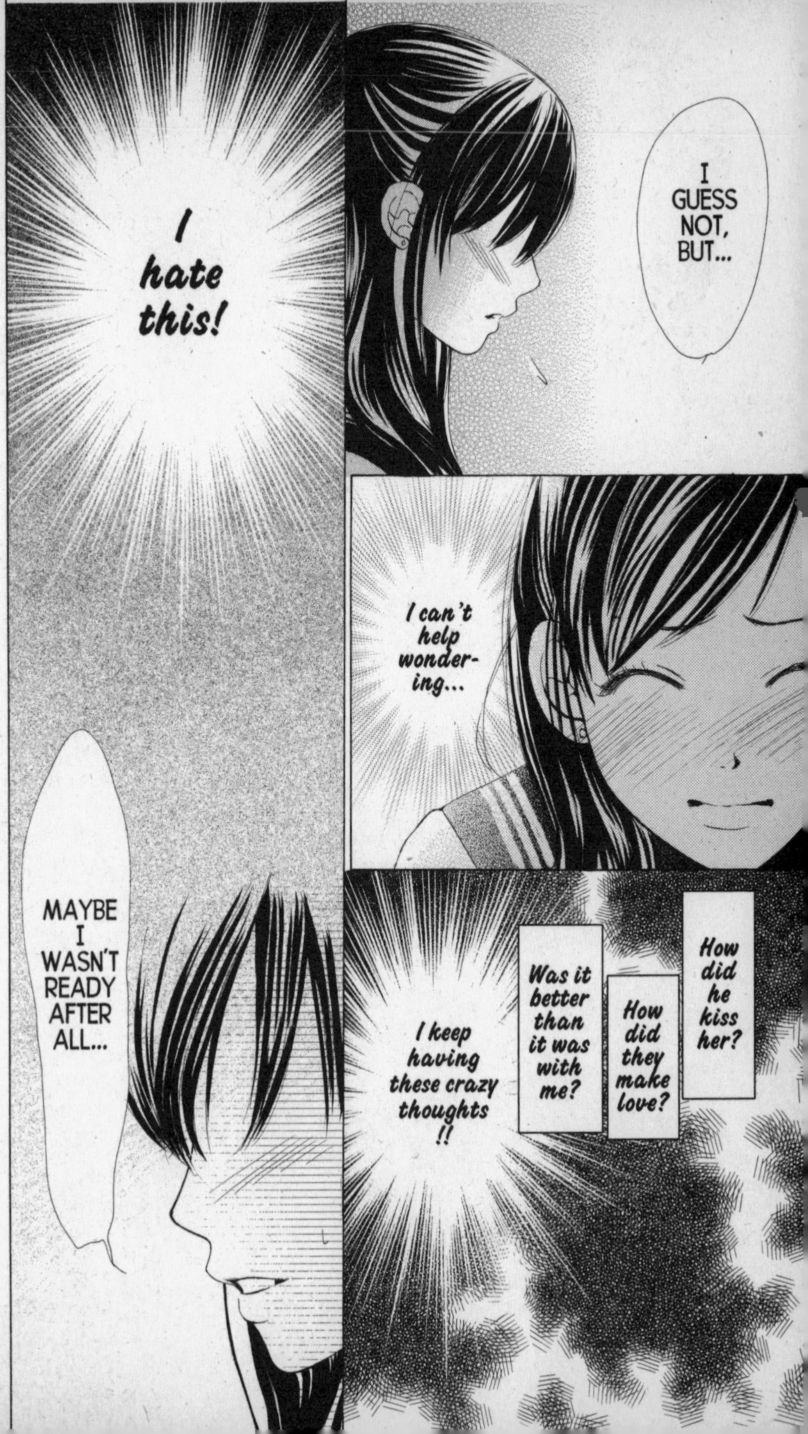
I GUESS NOT, BUT...
I can't help wondering...
How did he kiss her?
How did they make love?
Was it better than it was with me?
I keep having these crazy thoughts!!
I hate this!
MAYBE I WASN'T READY AFTER ALL...

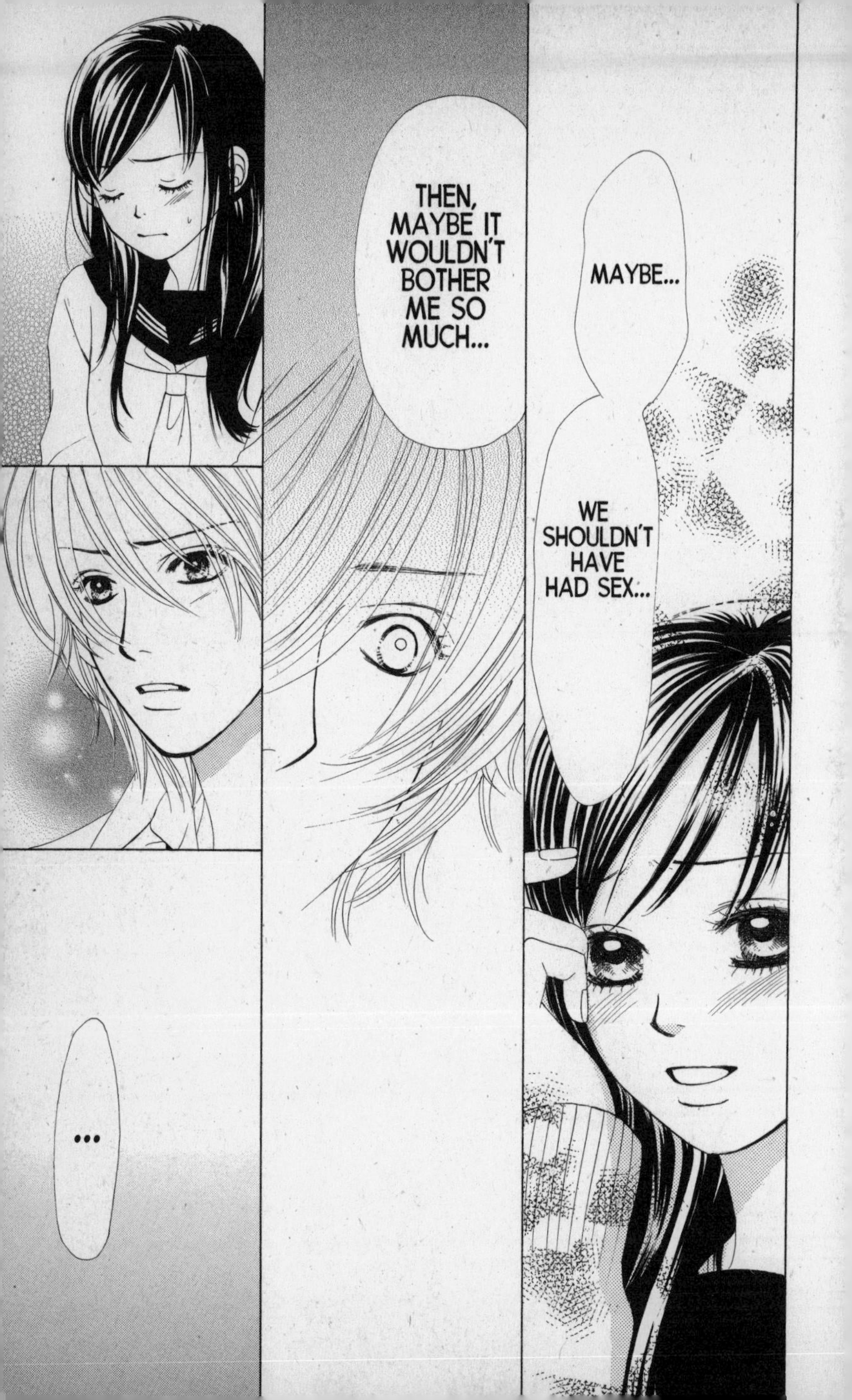
MAYBE...
WE SHOULDN'T HAVE HAD SEX...
THEN, MAYBE IT WOULDN'T BOTHER ME SO MUCH...
...

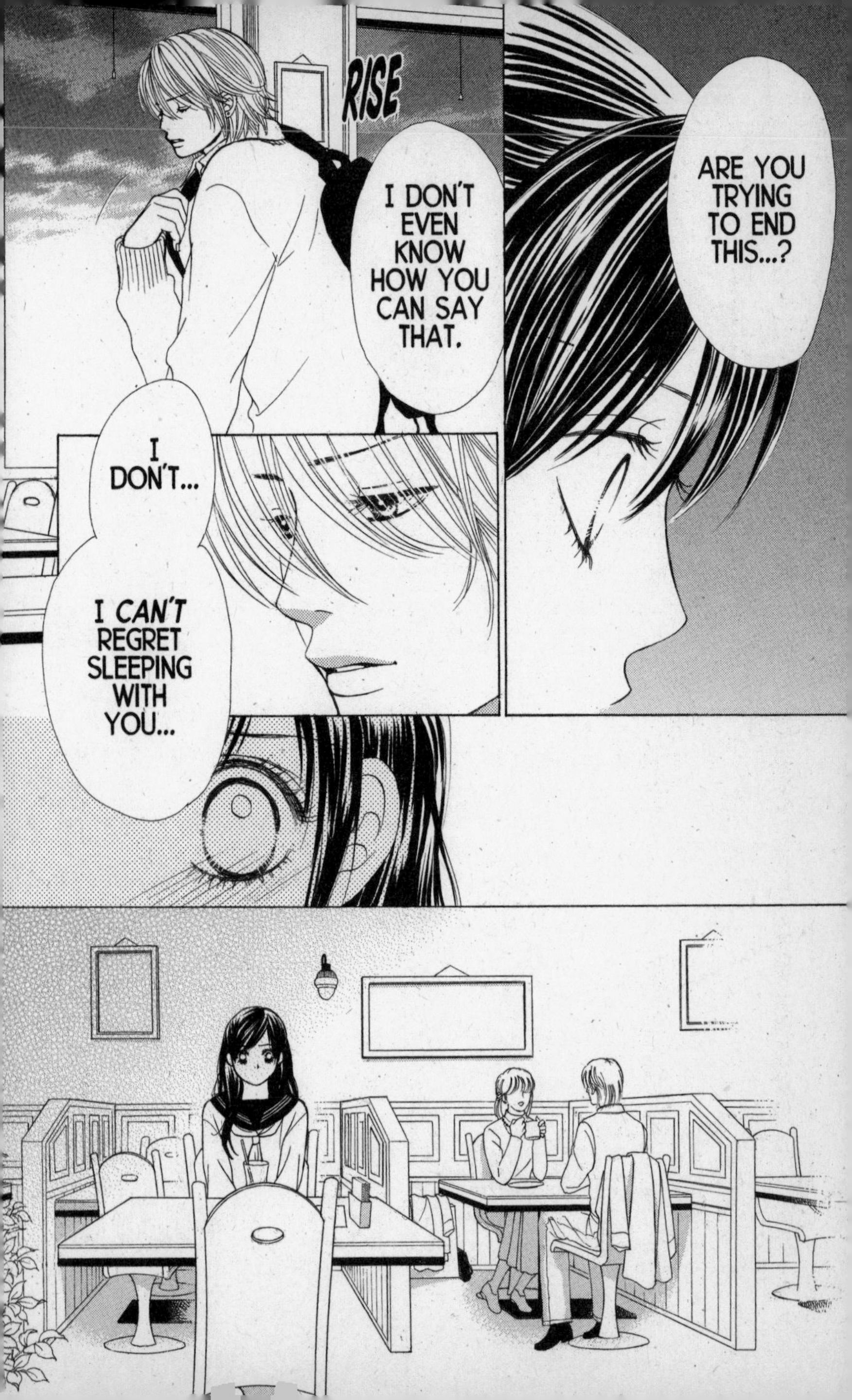
ARE YOU TRYING TO END THIS...?
RISE
I DON'T EVEN KNOW HOW YOU CAN SAY THAT.
I DON'T...
I *CAN'T* REGRET SLEEPING WITH YOU...

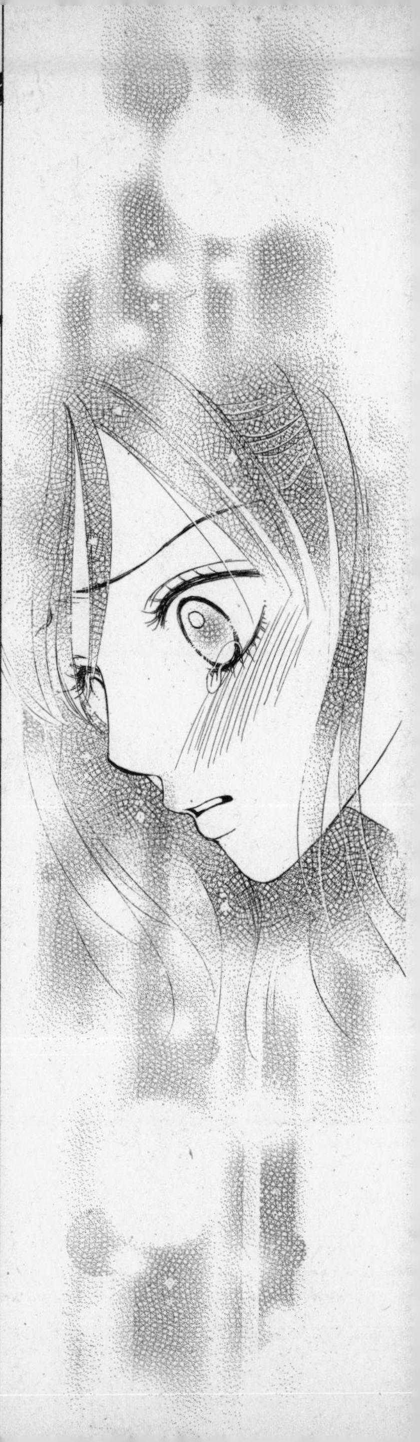

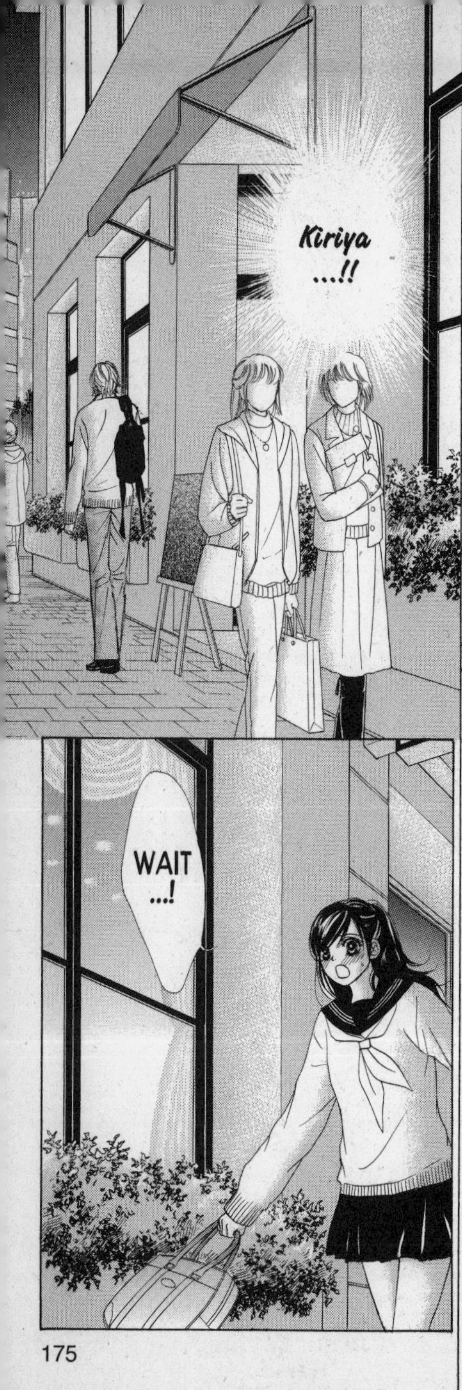
Kiriya ...!!
WAIT ...!

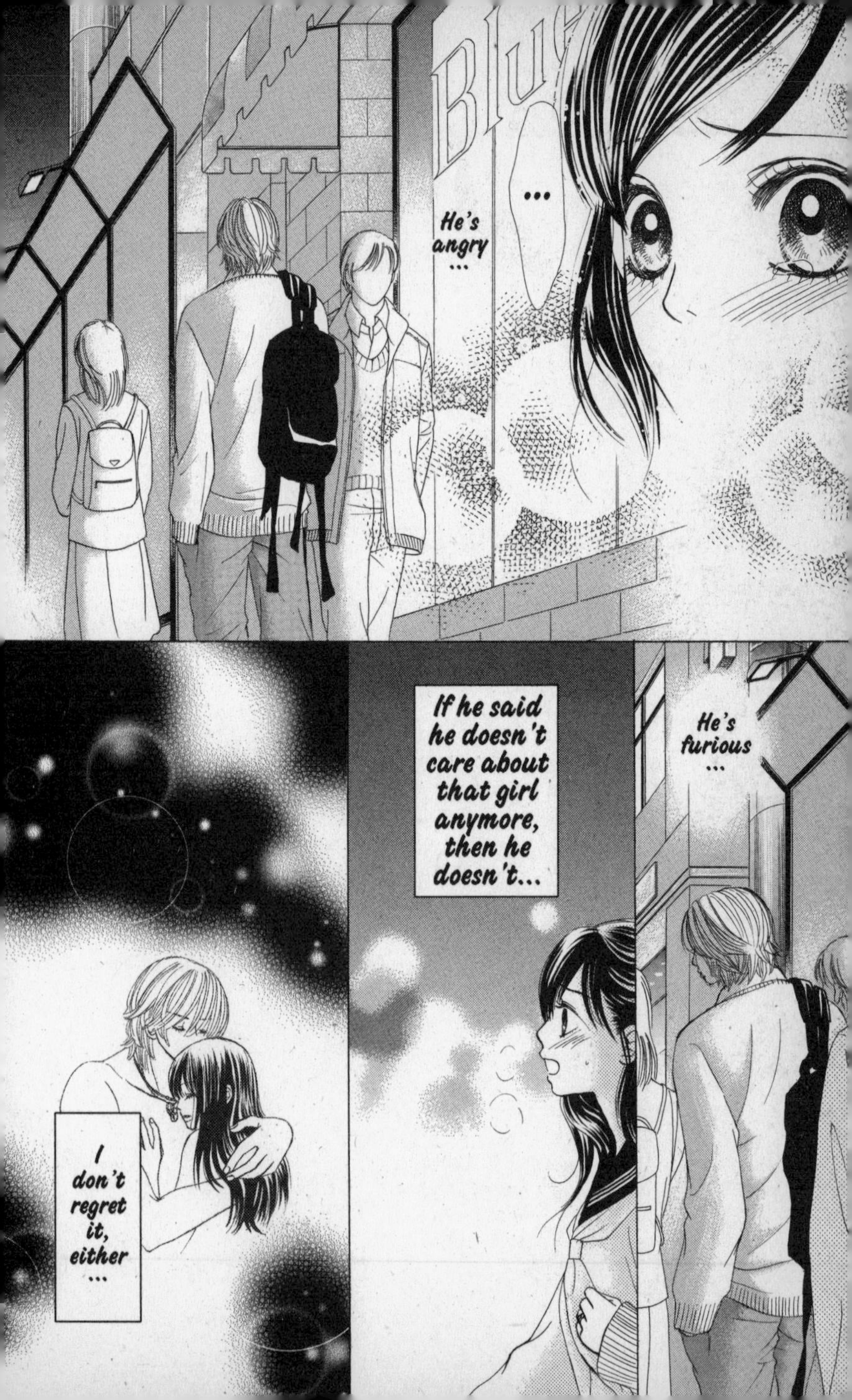
...
He's angry ...
He's furious ...
If he said he doesn't care about that girl anymore, then he doesn't...
I don't regret it, either ...

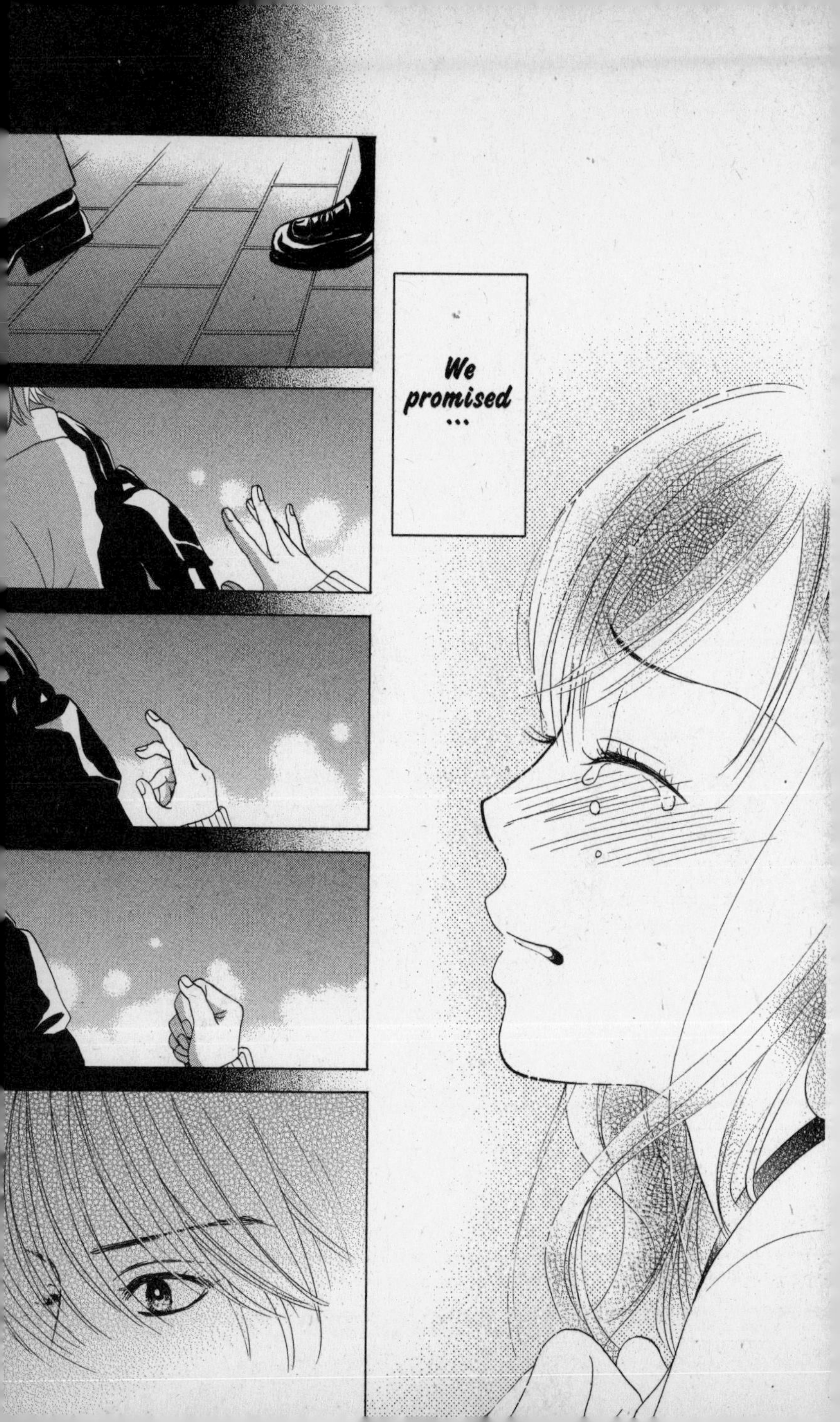
We promised ...

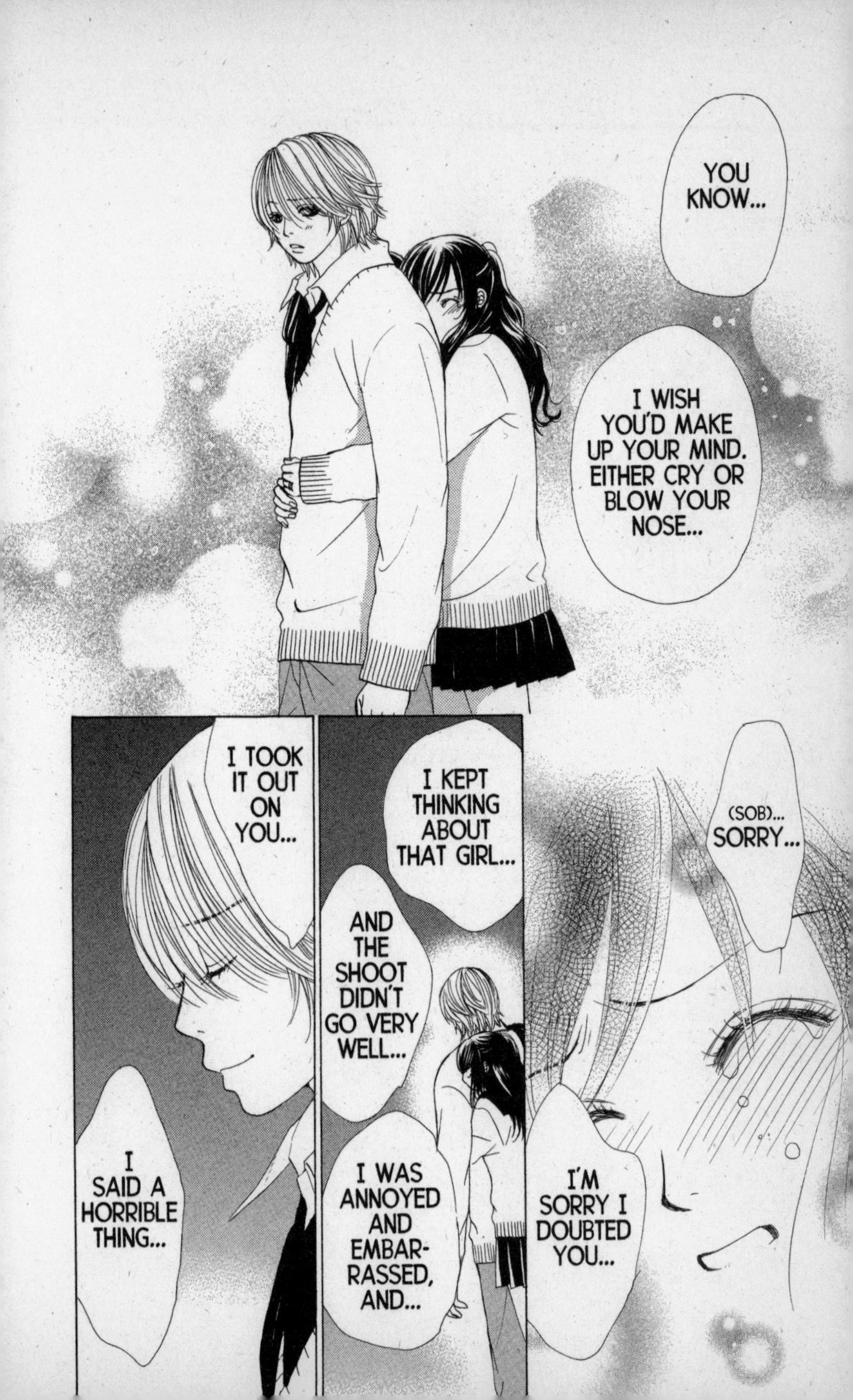
YOU KNOW...
I WISH YOU'D MAKE UP YOUR MIND. EITHER CRY OR BLOW YOUR NOSE...
(SOB)... SORRY...
I'M SORRY I DOUBTED YOU...
I KEPT THINKING ABOUT THAT GIRL...
AND THE SHOOT DIDN'T GO VERY WELL...
I WAS ANNOYED AND EMBAR-RASSED, AND...
I TOOK IT OUT ON YOU...
I SAID A HORRIBLE THING...

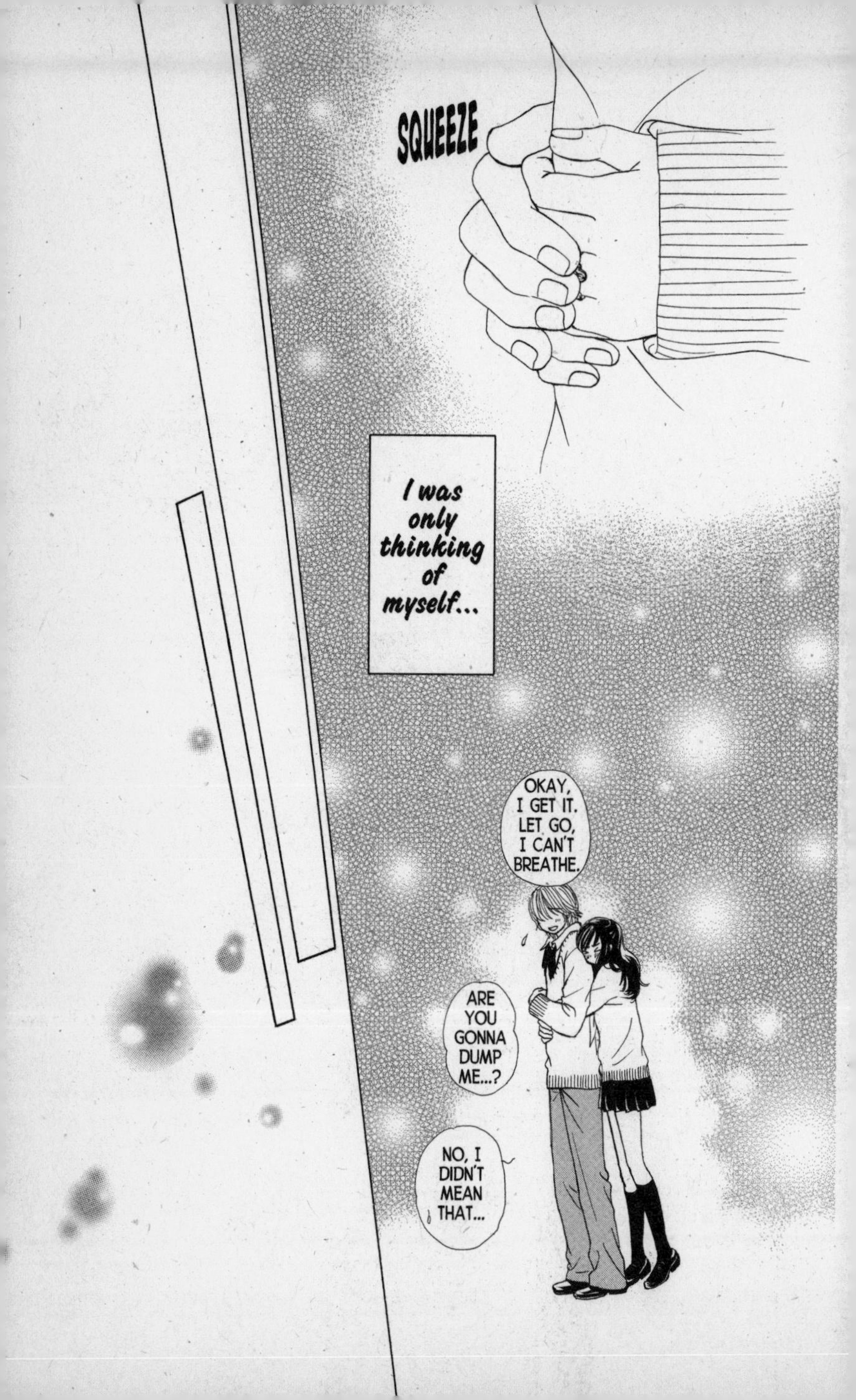
SQUEEZE
I was only thinking of myself...
OKAY, I GET IT. LET GO, I CAN'T BREATHE.
ARE YOU GONNA DUMP ME...?
NO, I DIDN'T MEAN THAT...

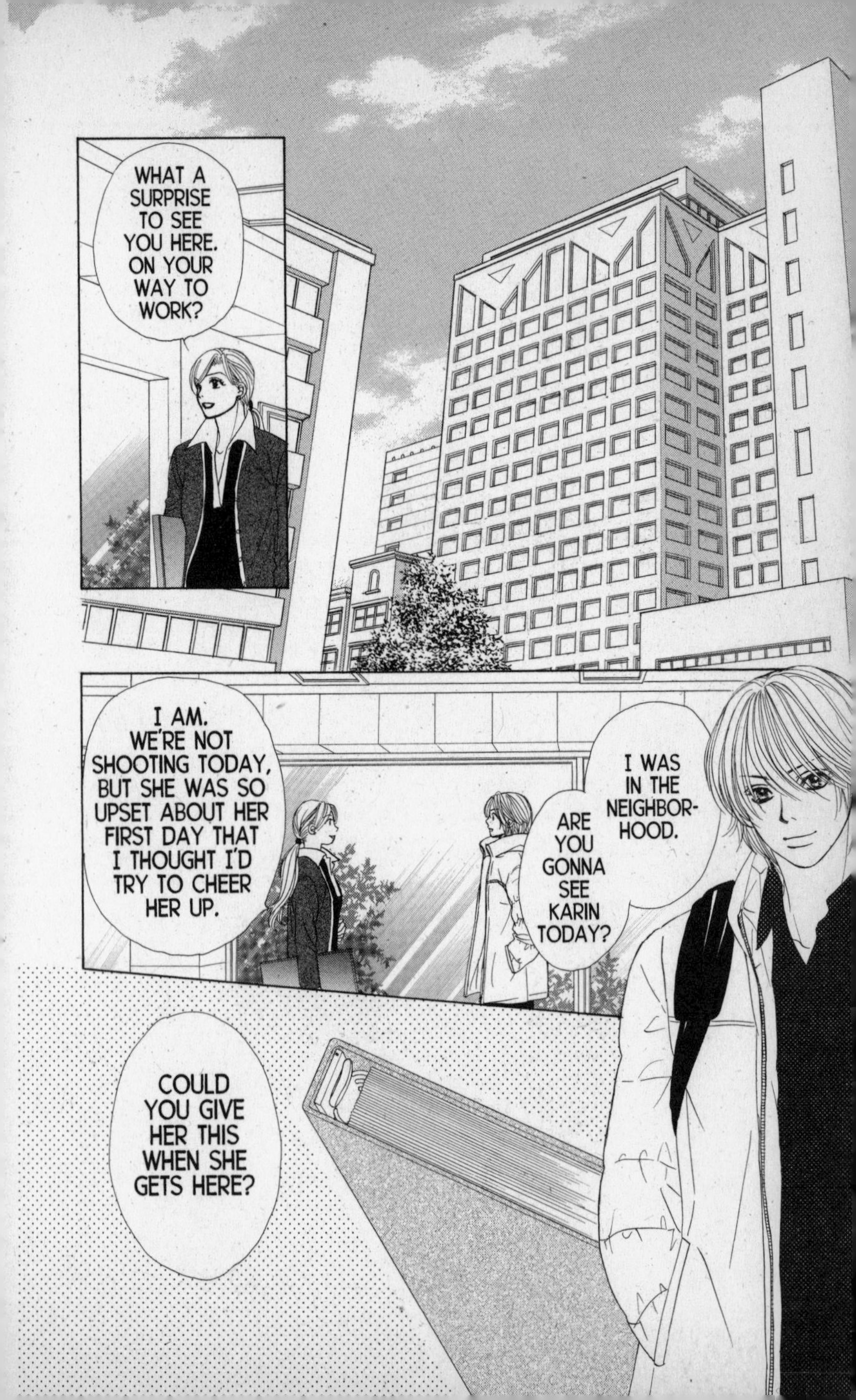
WHAT A SURPRISE TO SEE YOU HERE. ON YOUR WAY TO WORK?
I WAS IN THE NEIGHBOR-HOOD.
ARE YOU GONNA SEE KARIN TODAY?
I AM. WE'RE NOT SHOOTING TODAY, BUT SHE WAS SO UPSET ABOUT HER FIRST DAY THAT I THOUGHT I'D TRY TO CHEER HER UP.
COULD YOU GIVE HER THIS WHEN SHE GETS HERE?

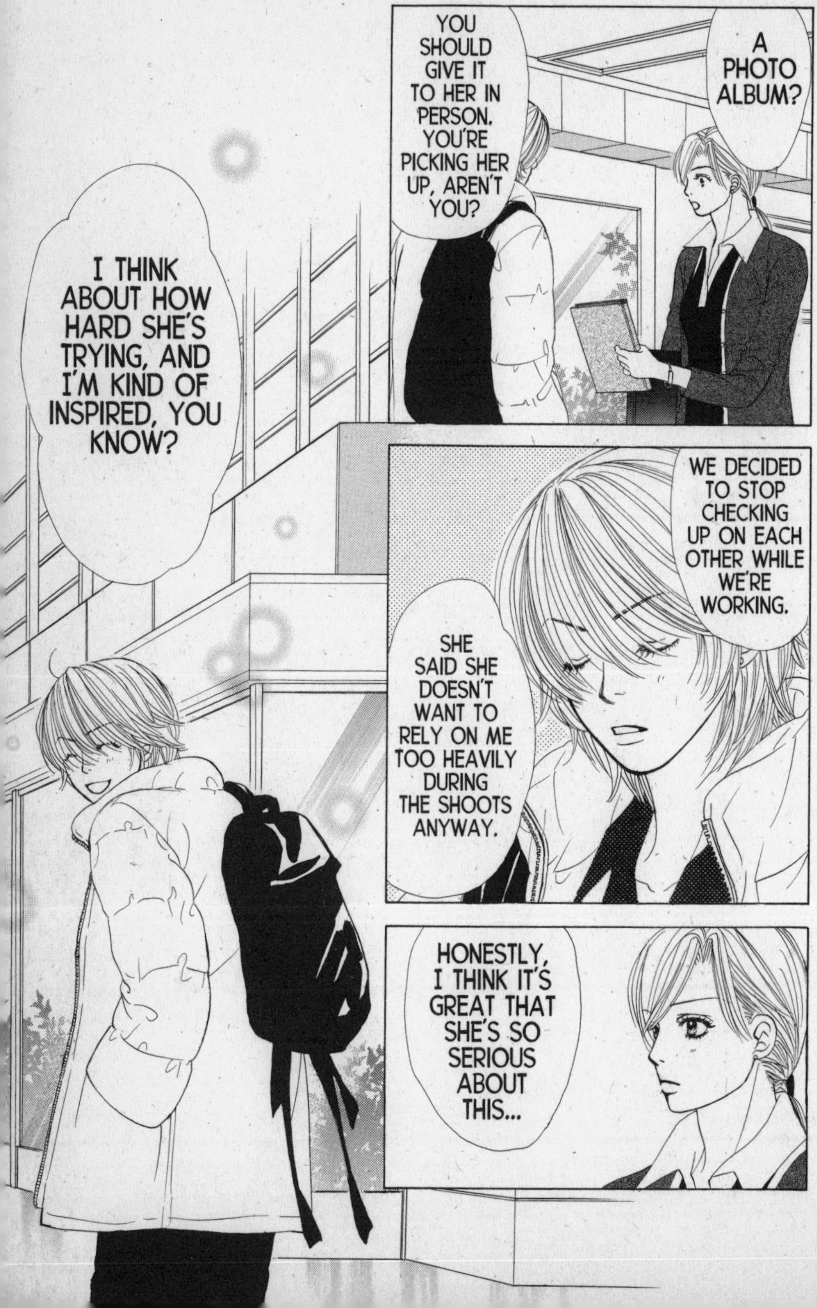
A PHOTO ALBUM?
YOU SHOULD GIVE IT TO HER IN PERSON. YOU'RE PICKING HER UP, AREN'T YOU?
WE DECIDED TO STOP CHECKING UP ON EACH OTHER WHILE WE'RE WORKING.
SHE SAID SHE DOESN'T WANT TO RELY ON ME TOO HEAVILY DURING THE SHOOTS ANYWAY.
HONESTLY, I THINK IT'S GREAT THAT SHE'S SO SERIOUS ABOUT THIS...
I THINK ABOUT HOW HARD SHE'S TRYING, AND I'M KIND OF INSPIRED, YOU KNOW?

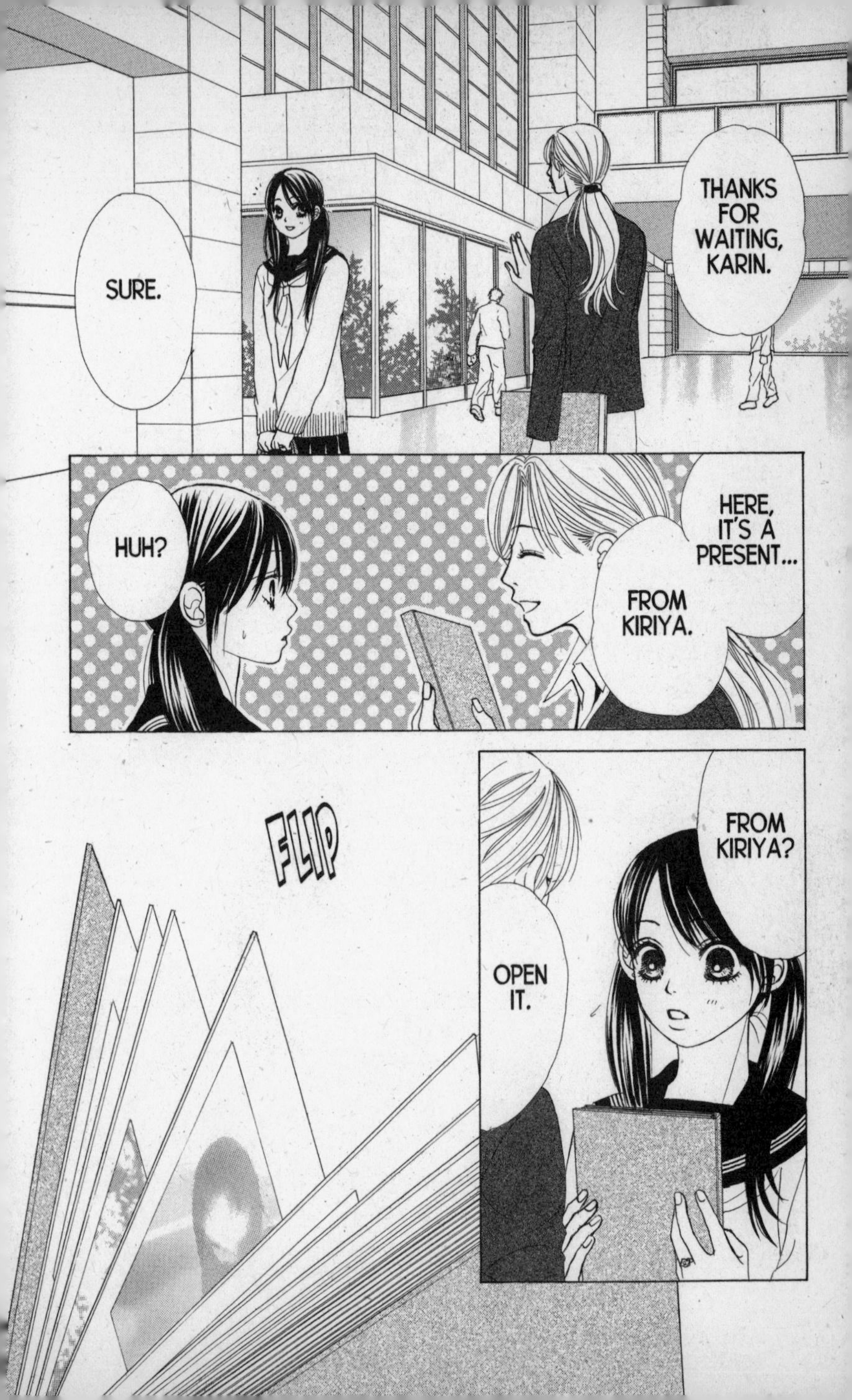
THANKS FOR WAITING, KARIN.
SURE.
HERE, IT'S A PRESENT...
FROM KIRIYA.
HUH?
FROM KIRIYA?
OPEN IT.
FLIP

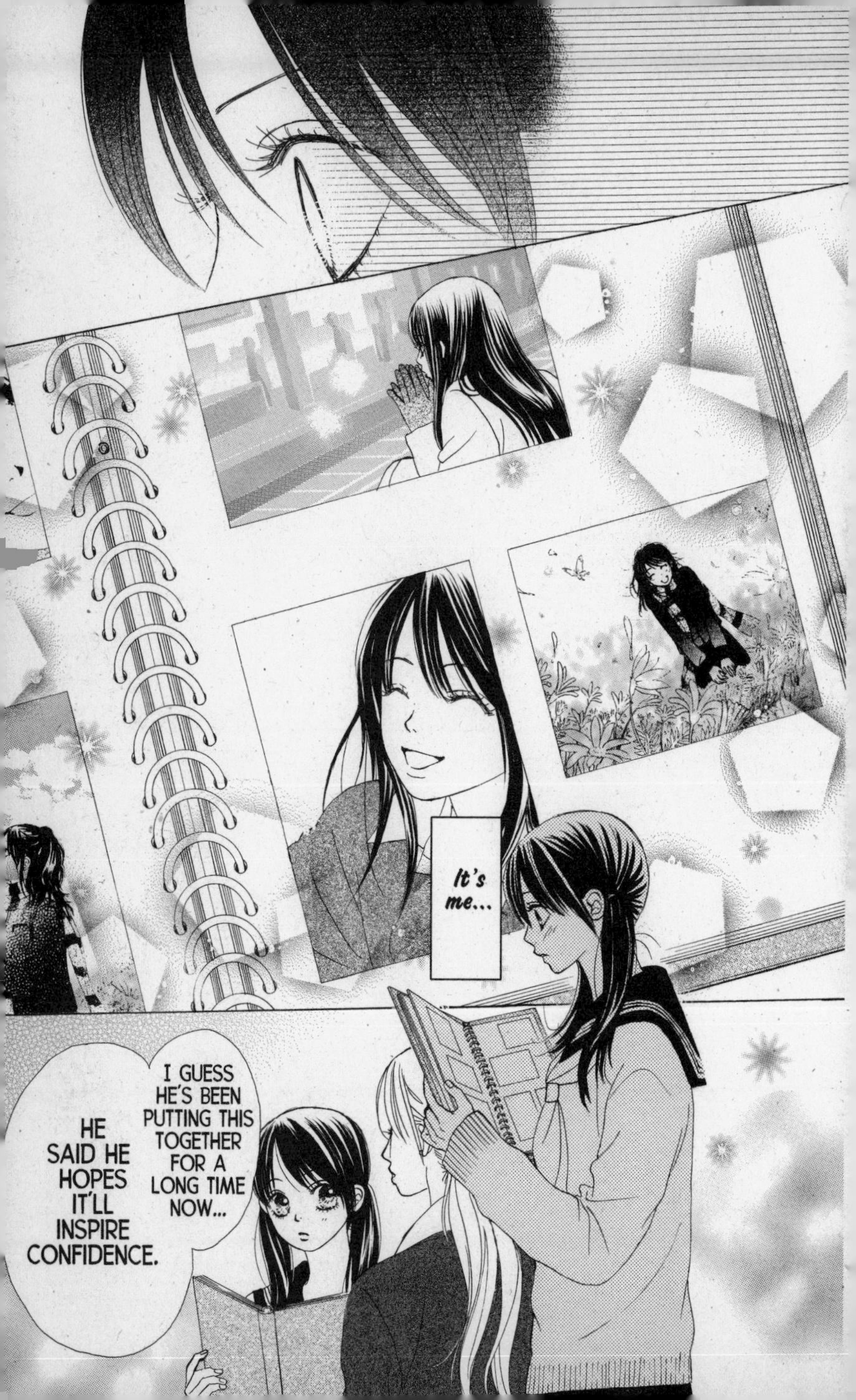
It's me...
I GUESS HE'S BEEN PUTTING THIS TOGETHER FOR A LONG TIME NOW...
HE SAID HE HOPES IT'LL INSPIRE CONFIDENCE.

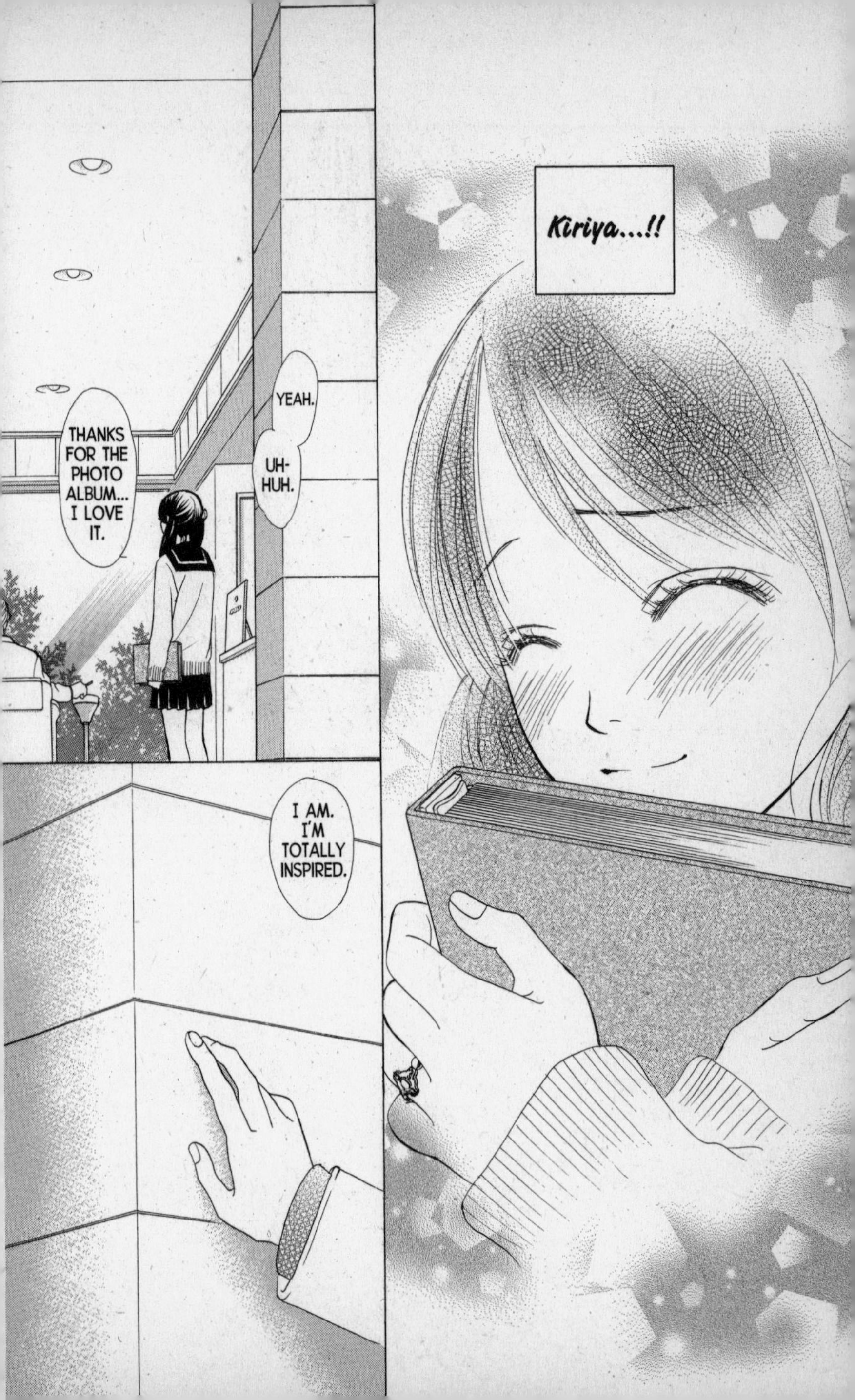
Kiriya...!!
YEAH.
UH-HUH.
THANKS FOR THE PHOTO ALBUM... I LOVE IT.
I AM. I'M TOTALLY INSPIRED.

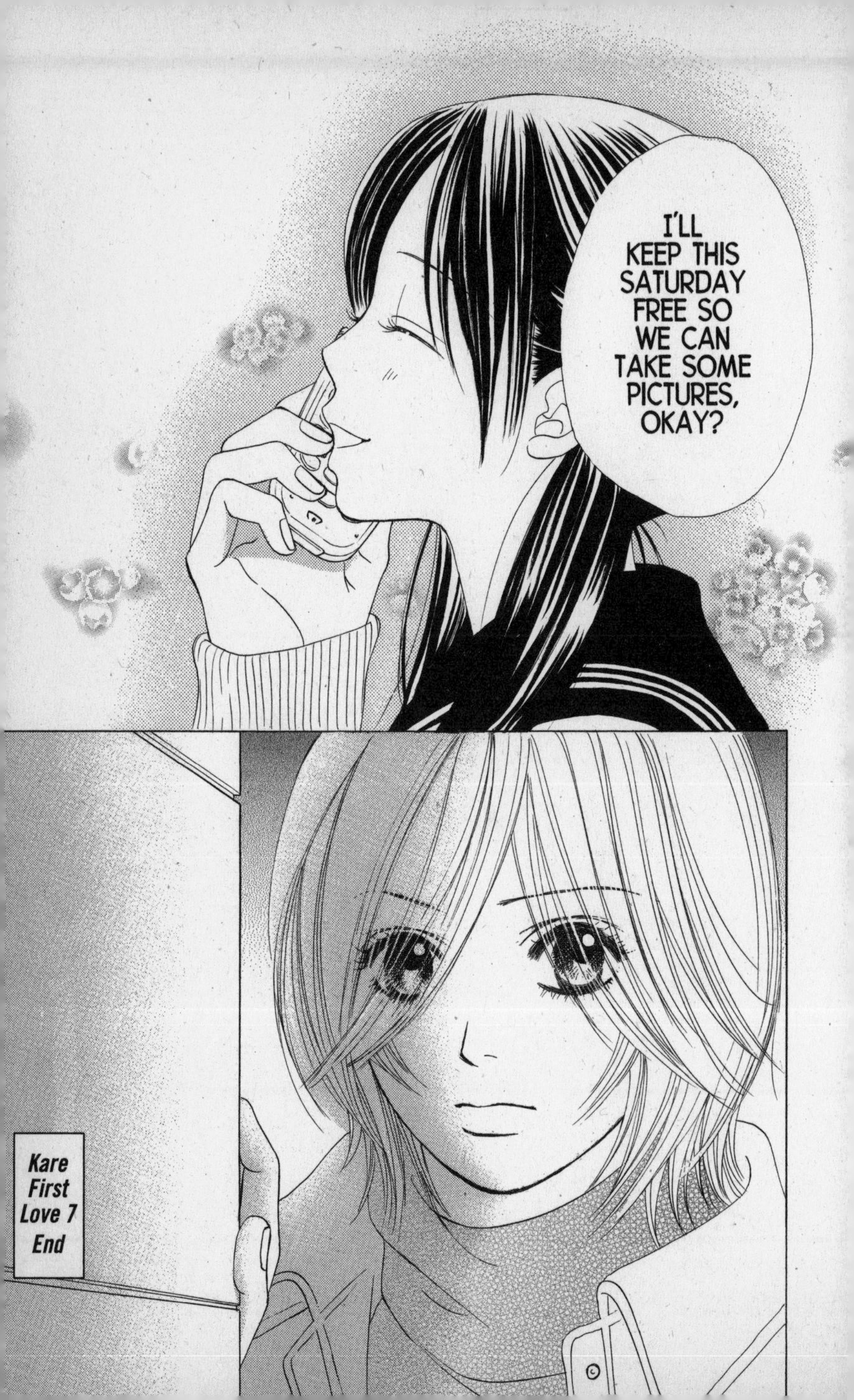
I'LL KEEP THIS SATURDAY FREE SO WE CAN TAKE SOME PICTURES, OKAY?
Kare First Love 7 End

Message From the Author

I'm not very good at writing commentary, so I have a hard time writing one for each volume. I always forget what I planned to write once I actually get ready to write it. I knew that I had to do something about this, so I began to occasionally jot down some notes, but now I have too many ideas and can't decide what to write. Maybe it won't be interesting unless I write some "behind the scenes" stuff. These are the kinds of neurotic thoughts that I am plagued with. Actually, there are many readers who have no idea that there is any kind of commentary included in the book. That's the reality of it (crying). I don't know how many days I've spent writing these few words...I get the feeling that my manager's going to tell me that if I have that much spare time on my hands, I ought to spend it working on the manga instead. (Is that another neurotic thought...?)

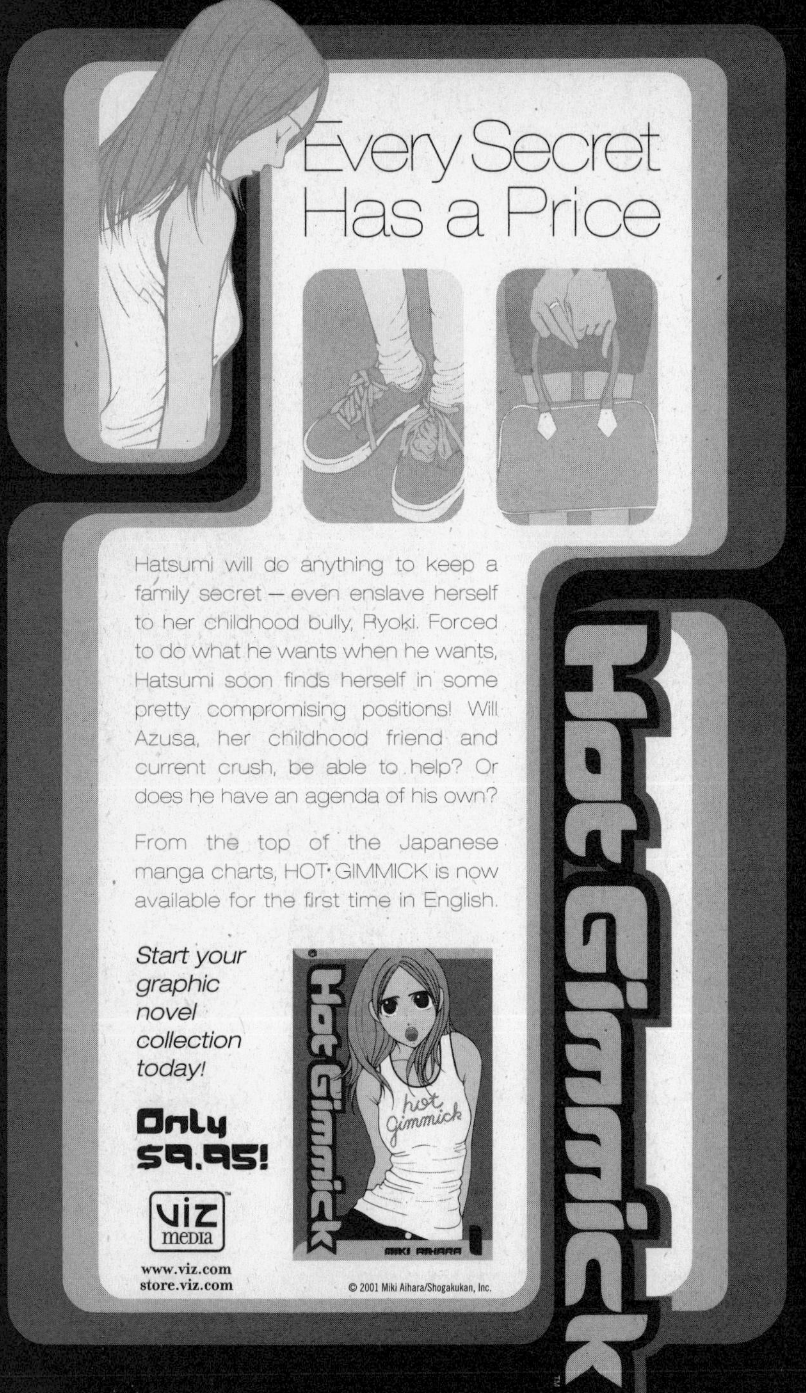
Every Secret
Has a Price
Hatsumi will do anything to keep a family secret — even enslave herself to her childhood bully, Ryoki. Forced to do what he wants when he wants, Hatsumi soon finds herself in some pretty compromising positions! Will Azusa, her childhood friend and current crush, be able to help? Or does he have an agenda of his own?
From the top of the Japanese manga charts, HOT·GIMMICK is now available for the first time in English.
Start your graphic novel collection today!
Only $9.95!
VIZ MEDIA
www.viz.com
store.viz.com
Hot Gimmick
hot gimmick
MIKI AIHARA
1
© 2001 Miki Aihara/Shogakukan, Inc.
Hot Gimmick
TM